D1370369

T IT IN
ITING

Get It In Writing

by

Brian McPherson, Esq.

First Edition

HAL•LEONARD®

7777 W. BLUEMOUND RD. P.O. BOX 13819
MILWAUKEE, WISCONSIN 53213

Visit Hal Leonard Online at
www.halleonard.com

REFERENCE

© 1999 Rockpress Publishing Company
Exclusively distributed by Hal Leonard Corporation
All rights reserved

First printing

ISBN 0-7935-6699-1

This publication is designed to provide accurate and authoritative information in
regard to the subject matter covered. It is sold with the understanding that the
publisher is not engaged in rendering legal, accounting, or other professional
service. If legal advice or other expert assistance is required, the services of a
competent professional person should be sought.

Every effort has been made to provide correct information, however, the publisher does not guarantee the accuracy of the listings and does not assume
responsibility for listings included in or omitted from this publication. Listings in
this publication do not constitute an endorsement or recommendation from
the publisher, except where noted.

Cover and book design by Gary Hustwit.
Cover illustration by Danny Hellman

Printed in the USA.

contents

Acknowledgements

The following people/things made this book possible in one way or another (in no particular order):

Michael Rosenfeld, Esq.
Michael Leventhal, Esq.
Bill Berrol, Esq.
Beck Hansen
Bill Skrzyniarz, Esq.
Mark Nishita
Lenny Waronker
Peter Taylor
Jack at Rimrock Ranch
Bill Gates
Starbucks Coffee
Carlos
Hewlett Packard
Susan Deneau
Mitch Schneider
Lorrie Boula
William Grantham, Esq.
Peter Koepke
Max Burgos

Rosemary Carroll, Esq.
Lon Sobel, Esq.
David Lowery
Mac McCaughan
Jad Fair
Larry Einbund
Chuck Arnold
Russ Bach
Johan Kugelberg
Elvis Costello
Balance Bars
Bumpy
Bob Biggs
Jay Boberg
Rick Riccobono
Maalox
Lisa Jacobsen, Esq.
Roger Ames
Osman Eralp
Steve Fayne, Esq.

David Codikow, Esq.
Larry Kartiganer, Esq.
Jackson Haring
Laura Ballance
Rick Rubin
Mike Stoller
Dianne Bissell
Jodi Sax, Esq.
Alan Susman, Esq.
Marvin Meyer, Esq.
Tom Triggs, Esq.
Jerry Nagin, Esq.
Fred 62
Dennis Herring
Ron Sobel
Stan Ridgway
David Ulich, Esq.
Don Robertson
Nick Gatfield

Thanks to Mom, Aunt Moni, my sisters Barbara, Jane, Mary, Jacque and Laura, and to my brother Charlie. Now that this book is done, I hope to see more of y'all.

Extra special thanks to Gary Hustwit at Rockpress and Brad Smith at Hal Leonard.

Finally, thanks to Lisa Mary Moreno for her love (not to mention her expert editing, transcribing and proofreading skills).

This book is dedicated to my parents,
Dr. Alan McPherson (1927-1991) and Lilas McPherson.

Foreword

Gotta do it. Gotta play music. And thank god you picked up a copy of this book early on in your career in rock. Brian was, like myself, born in the mid-'60s — we are of the age where the initial energies towards life-long music fandom came from the punk rock movement. A movement driven by being a fan, and a movement like the hippie movement where the dollars and cents aspect of it all was (and still is) taboo. This is a false taboo. Records are sold. Bands and record companies are commercial ventures. People get paid. Or don't.

And the buck does de facto go somewhere, and where that buck goes should be fair and just. Over the years, I've heard a plethora of horror stories about childhood pals suing each other's asses off after having spent 20 years in a band together, and these people weren't greedy people — they were punk rockers! But punkers grow old too and worry about car payments and mortgages and health care, and many other things that are next to impossible to think about when you are 19 years old and kicking out your heaviest jams in garages and basements all across the USA. I am not saying that you need to be a financial and legal expert to be in a band, but I am saying that you need to have access to this kind of expertise. It took me years to realize that music can be a business as well as a passion without these seeming contradictions confronting each other more than once in a while. That there are elements of business being in a band is one of those facts of life that one has to discover, not unlike those other facts of life (which come to think of it are the greatest motivator for actually being in a band, no?). You have made a great first step by buying this book. Now get yourself a good lawyer.

Brian has accomplished something rare here: a stellar shoot-from-the-hip distribution of insider knowledge written in an everyman language that is almost identical to the way Brian talks to his friends and clients. Me being both, I got a great sense of Brian pontificating the entire thing to me over a couple of pints of Guinness. The narrative has that kind of intimacy which makes it so much easier to absorb all the finesses. I read the book in one sitting, stopping once in a while to reflect upon how clear and useful it is. Useful, being the ultimate operative. The business of music is not always smooth sailing, but how rough it gets has more to do with knowledge about how the whole rigamarole works than anything else. Notwithstanding who you are, there are people who are going to shove pieces of paper into your hand to sign, and those pieces of paper will affect your life for a whole bunch of years to come. Sometimes leading to great things indeed, but sometimes fucking you up in a way so serious that it can affect how you make music for years, or in horror-scenarios preventing you from making music at all. The best way to prevent bad things from happening to you in the music business is to be informed. And to have a good lawyer.

Use this book as food for thought. The interviews with a variety of certified smart people are not only informative, but they reminded me that the lion's share of the people in this business are in it for their love of music as much as for making a living. Reading the interview with Lenny Waronker is evidence of how a record executive at the very top can maintain passion, enthusiasm and drive in this business for many decades. This is an inspiration for all of us.

A book like this would have saved me a whole lot of time, anguish and money back in the day. I would have kept it next to my Stooges records and copies of *Kicks* magazine. And after having read *Get It In Writing*, gotten myself a good lawyer.

Johan Kugelberg
Brooklyn, NY
January, 1999

Johan Kugelberg is a veteran A&R executive and producer who has worked with Matador Records and American Recordings. He lives and cooks in Brooklyn with a shelf full of records and reissues he has produced.

Preface

When I was approached by Gary Hustwit to write a book on the legal and business aspects of the music business, I thought to myself, "Does the world really need another book on the music business?" Then he handed me a check. So here's the book.

The information in this book is not meant to take the place of a competent lawyer, manager, accountant, publisher, booking agent, priest or rabbi. If you are getting into any deal where the rights to your services and intellectual properties are changing hands, please do yourself a favor and hire a good attorney who specializes in music (I happen to know a very good one in Los Angeles). That being said, it is my hope that this book will give you a good introduction to the business and a very basic understanding of the kinds of deals you will encounter in the music business.

After you get through the ten chapters, take some time to check out the Appendices. Appendix A is comprised of interviews I conducted with various music industry professionals over the past few years. Appendix B is a collection of sample agreements. Warning: DO NOT use these sample agreements to start your own record company or to sign your neighbor to a publishing deal. Every deal is different, and if you attempt to use these sample agreements as templates, you will likely end up in serious trouble. Appendix C is a list of addresses, websites and phone numbers that may come in handy.

Thanks for buying the book, and remember that it's all about the music.

Brian McPherson
Silverlake, California
January 1999

CHAPTER ONE

Attorneys, Managers, Agents & Accountants

So you're in a band. You've been playing local bars and colleges, you are starting to draw decent-size crowds and you just put out your first seven inch single. Pretty soon, A&R scouts from labels start coming around to your shows, taking you to dinner and telling you how great you are. Before you get sucked into the great gaping maw of the music business, you should start thinking about attorneys, managers, agents and accountants. If you are like most bands, your first step is to hire an attorney or manager to shepherd you through the process of getting your act together and getting signed, so let's start there.

I. ATTORNEYS

First off, I prefer the term *attorney* to *lawyer*, because *lawyer* sounds too much like *liar*. At the earliest stages of your career, it is important for you to procure the services of an experienced attorney or a manager. We'll start with attorneys, primarily because it will be much easier to attract the attention of an experienced music attorney than a competent manager at this point in your career. Additionally, an experienced attorney can make sure that you do not end up in crippling record or publishing deals before you really have a chance to make a go of it in the music business.

WHAT (GOOD) MUSIC ATTORNEYS DO:

* They help you find a record or publishing deal if you are unsigned by shopping your tape to labels and publishers and getting A&R people down to your shows. Note that most record companies only accept unsolicited material from established attorneys and managers.

* They help you find a personal manager, booking agent and business manager if you do not already have one.

* They negotiate every deal for your services as a recording artist, songwriter or producer. Note that they do not negotiate agreements for live shows. This is generally left to the booking agent, although attorneys are often involved in negotiations for large scale tours (such as Lollapalooza and H.O.R.D.E) because these deals often involve large sums of money and merchandising tie-ins and recording agreements.

* They negotiate merchandising deals if you decide to hire an outside party to manufacture and sell your tour and retail "merch" (T-shirts, hats, etc.).

★ They negotiate your agreements with managers, agents and the producers and engineers who help you make your records.

★ They help set up band agreements so that everyone is clear on who gets what and who owns the band name if the shit hits the fan.

★ They help you get out of bad deals, if possible.

★ They attempt to help you understand all of the complex deals they negotiate for you.

HIRING AN ATTORNEY

Attorneys are not supposed to contact you unless you have contacted them first (this activity runs afoul of the ethical rules established for attorneys — does the term "ambulance chaser" mean anything to you?). Nevertheless, some attorneys do contact potential clients directly, and you should be wary of "cold calls" from such attorneys, especially if they haven't heard a note of your music. These guys probably just read about you in *HITS* (an industry magazine) or heard from an A&R guy that you are going to get signed, and they are usually only interested in making a quick deal for you and ignoring you thereafter. In most cases, however, you will be referred to a couple of attorneys by your manager, other bands, a publisher or a record company A&R person. You are most likely to reach qualified music attorneys through a solid, informed referral. The person making the referral is usually very familiar with the attorney's style, ability, work habits and clout. I would, however, caution you to make sure that you meet with a few attorneys who do not appear on a record company's or manager's referral list. I say this not because I don't appreciate the occasional referral from these sources (I do), but because managers and record companies typically recommend the same two or three attorneys who they always deal with. These may be perfectly capable attorneys, but you want to have a little distance between yourself and the people you are going to be working with for the next several years of your life, if only to avoid the specter of conflict. More on this later.

OK, let's assume you have your short list, you have made the calls, and a few of these guys actually called you back. I suggest that you meet the potential attorneys at their office so that you can see what kind of operation they are running (and to make sure their "office" is more than a corner booth at Denny's). Once you've handed him a tape and taken your first drink of bad office coffee, ask him the following questions:

IS YOUR PRACTICE LIMITED TO MUSIC?

I am a big believer in specialization. If your interviewee tells you that he specializes in litigation, motion picture work, corporate law, interactive, family law and tax law, be a little wary. Being a music attorney is a full-time job, and if this guy is boasting that he is a jack of all trades, it is very likely that he is a master of none. Granted, a little background in litigation or copyright can be helpful, but you should make sure that the attorney spends most of his time practicing music law. If he does focus exclusively on music, you should ask if there are other departments or attorneys at his firm that specialize in the other areas of practice I mentioned, because they will come in handy later.

HOW MUCH EXPERIENCE DO YOU HAVE?

Let's face it, experience is important, but do not base your decision solely on how many years this attorney has been practicing. There are so-called "music attorneys" that have been practicing for many years that have not even negotiated a major label recording agreement. Conversely, there are attorneys who have been practicing for only a few years that have vast experience with all kinds of deals, from the simple 7-inch single agreements to complex worldwide recording and publishing agreements. Of course, most attorneys do get better with age (provided they don't get completely burned out, as some do — you should be able to spot these guys pretty easily) but you would rather have an attorney who has been negotiating complex and competitive deals with major companies for five years than one whose experience is limited to filing copyright registration forms on behalf of shitty bar bands for twenty years.

Also, active and "hot" attorneys have their fingers on the pulse of the industry. They know what kinds of deals are being made for their clients and for other artists and songwriters. This is very important, because the music business in 1999 is a very different animal from the music business in 1979 or even 1989. The deals are much more complex, and artists (especially new artists in "bidding war" situations) are getting much better deals than even "Superstar" artists were getting ten years ago. If an attorney is not aware of the current trends in deal making, he won't ask for certain things in a deal. Here's a little rule of thumb for you: If you don't ask, you don't get. The other side doesn't care if your attorney is a little rusty, and they will always try to take advantage of your attorney's lack of knowledge.

WHO DO YOU REPRESENT?

This is pretty simple. If an attorney represents platinum artists and successful companies and has for a number of years, this is a pretty good sign. After all, when artists become successful, the work gets very heavy and very complex. An attorney who has renegotiated recording, publishing and merchandising agreements for successful artists usually has a higher level of skill and clout than an attorney who represents less successful or underground artists. But there is another reason you need to ask this question, and it concerns conflicts of interest. Many attorneys represent managers, publishers and record labels as well as artists and songwriters. Attorneys are generally prohibited from representing a client in a transaction with another client, for obvious reasons. However, you might be surprised to learn that many attorneys and law firms see conflicts as beneficial to both sides in a negotiation, because they feel they can "cut to the chase" and make a mutually beneficial deal very quickly.

Let's look at an example. You get offered a contract from Misanthrope Records and you go to meet an attorney recommended by a friend in another band. It turns out that this attorney represents Misanthrope Records. In this situation, the attorney is obligated to inform you of this potential conflict. If you decide to hire him despite the conflict, he is required to inform Misanthrope that he represents you. If you and the label have been fully informed of the conflict and still want to go ahead with negotiations, the attorney will ask each of you to sign a waiver which protects his ass down the road in case either side ever feels that it got burned as a result of the conflict. You sign the waiver and the attorney makes the deal with Misanthrope, but five years later you discover that the deal was extremely unfair and one-sided in favor of Misanthrope. While you can still sue the attorney for malpractice, the fact that you signed a conflict waiver makes it unlikely that a court will find in your favor. The moral of this story: Take conflicts very seriously. You are likely to run into a conflict or two at some point in your career, inasmuch as most law firms tend to represent both talent (that's you) and the companies that sign talent. Some conflicts are more problematic than others, but if you are faced with a conflict and feel at all uncomfortable about it, choose another company or look for another attorney.

HOW MUCH DO YOU CHARGE?

A crucial question, and one that an attorney should address directly. I have observed five different fee arrangements:

HOURLY

Under this arrangement, the attorney keeps track of the time he spends working on your behalf and you are billed monthly. Most major music attorneys in New York, Los Angeles and Nashville (the three centers of the music business in the United States) charge at least $150 per hour for their services, and many charge as much as $400 per hour. Most firms charge time in minimum increments of 1/4 of an hour. This means that every time the attorney picks up the phone on your behalf, you get charged. For instance, a five minute phone call with a $200 an hour attorney can cost you $50. In addition to time, attorneys bill for expenses incurred on your behalf. Expenses include faxes (incoming *and* outgoing), long distance phone calls, postage (including FedEx or express mail costs), messenger fees, photocopies, computerized legal research, online fees and word processing.

The **pros** of the hourly billing arrangement are as follows: you can keep track of your fees from month to month; if an attorney can get your deals done without too much hassle, the fee may be relatively low compared to other fee arrangements. The **cons**? Even if an attorney has a relatively low hourly rate, it goes up every year. Secondly, you may be reluctant to call your attorney when you realize that you are charged for every business-related conversation. Third, if a negotiation becomes protracted and difficult, hourly fees can spiral upward very quickly. Finally, attorneys expect hourly clients to pay their bills on a monthly basis, and this could present a problem for you if the deal has not yet been completed (because you haven't received your advance yet and you probably don't have thousands of dollars at your disposal).

FIXED FLAT FEE

Under this fee arrangement, the attorney will propose a flat fee (which may or may not be inclusive of expenses) as payment for negotiating a particular deal. For instance, if your band has been offered a recording agreement by a major label, your attorney might suggest a flat fee of $10,000. This number is negotiable, and factors to consider in arriving at this figure include how much time the attorney anticipates it will take to negotiate the deal, whether or not the attorney was instrumental in securing the deal and how good the deal is (money, deal points, creative control, etc.) I have heard of attorneys charging as little as $5,000 and as much as $100,000 to negotiate a recording or publishing agreement. **Pros:** You know what you are going to pay and you can use as much of the attorney's time as you need. **Cons:** if you are extremely cost conscious, you may pay less by going with an hourly or percentage arrangement.

REASONABLE FEE

This fee arrangement is very similar to the flat fee arrangement. The factors which determine the fee are the same as those which are considered in arriving at the fixed flat fee, but the "reasonable" fee amount is not arrived at until after the deal is completed. At this point, the attorney and client sit down and arrive at a figure which is (theoretically) supposed to reflect the value the attorney added to the deal. **Pros:** If the attorney is unable to get you all the bells and whistles (read: money and favorable royalty rates) he promised, or if his clout had little to do with orchestrating the deal, you can make a good case for a lower fee. **Cons:** The fee suggested by the attorney can be relatively large compared to what the fee might have been under the other four fee arrangements. If you feel that the suggested fee is unreasonable, the attorney will either cave and feel cheated or you will grudgingly pay the fee and feel cheated (and perhaps fire the attorney). This is a potentially messy arrangement, but it has been my experience that most clients are able to recognize when they have received service which warrants a higher fee.

PERCENTAGE

This fee arrangement is also gaining popularity among attorneys, especially among attorneys who are in high demand. In a nutshell, you pay the attorney a percentage (typically 5%) of monies generated from any deals the attorney negotiates. For example, if your attorney negotiates a recording agreement which provides for a signing advance of $50,000, you are obligated to pay the attorney $2,500. The attorney is also entitled to receive 5% of whatever monies are left over after recording costs for the first album are paid, and 5% of any future royalties and advances. **Pros:** There are several. First, the client is (theoretically) entitled to an unlimited amount of the attorney's time. This can be valuable when you ask your attorney to spend several hours going over your deals with you or hustling new business for you. Second, you only have to pay if you make money. If you flop and make zero, you pay only expenses. Finally, an attorney representing you on a percentage basis is much more motivated to get you the best deal possible, since he knows that he will be a direct beneficiary of that deal. **Cons:** None unless you hit it really big and start to balk at the fees. For example, if you get to the point where you are bringing in $3,000,000 a year, the attorney's take is $150,000. This may be much more than the hourly value of the attorney's time. However, attorneys working under a percentage arrangement are typically "upside down" (that is, the 5% of monies coming in is less than the hourly value of the time he has spent working on your behalf) for many years. If this is the case, it is unfair to ask the attorney to change the fee arrangement once you have hit it big.

RETAINER

There are two kinds of retainers. In most cases, a retainer is simply an advance payment of fees. Some attorneys will require you to pay a retainer before the attorney commences representation. The retainer may be a few hundred dollars, or (in the case of top-notch litigators) a five-figure sum. As each monthly bill is issued, the appropriate fees and expenses are deducted from the retainer. A second kind of retainer is nothing more than a flat fee. For example, clients with a steady flow of work (such as record companies or publishers) often pay their attorneys a flat fee every month, quarter or year.

All of these fee arrangements have their pros and cons for the client and attorney. Some attorneys are flexible and will represent you on the basis of any fee arrangement you are comfortable with, as long as it is relatively fair. However, it is my experience that more and more firms (especially small "boutique" firms) are working strictly on a percentage basis — take it or leave it. In any case, it is important to establish the fee arrangement before any work is commenced.

HOW STRONG ARE YOUR RELATIONSHIPS WITH LABELS AND PUBLISHERS?

Aside from good work habits and strong legal skills, ACCESS is the most important thing a music attorney can offer you. Look, nearly any experienced attorney knows what to ask for in a deal, but relationships with key players are hard to develop and are almost as important as the attorney's legal skills. If a particular record company is after your band, ask the attorney if he knows the interested A&R person. Better yet, ask him if he can get the company president on the phone. Of course, nearly all attorneys will answer in the affirmative, but not all of them can follow through. These relationships come in very handy early on when negotiations hit a snag, but they are truly valuable when the inevitable problems arise.

For example, let us assume that your band is having problems extracting contractually guaranteed tour support funds from your record company. An attorney with clout and access can make a few phone calls and (sometimes) make things better. Is this because the company loves and respects the attorney? HELL NO!! More likely, the attorney has a platinum artist on the same label or maybe he represents a hot artist that the company covets. In any event, the company knows that attorneys are a primary A&R source and that alienating the attorney is a sure way to be knocked back to the bottom of the list (or knocked off the list completely) when the Next Big Thing comes along. Remember, ACCESS is key.

HOW HEAVY IS YOUR WORKLOAD?

A very good question. Every successful music attorney is extremely busy, but this should not preclude the attorney from being able to pick up the phone or return your call within a reasonable period of time. What is reasonable? 24 hours if it is not urgent, and within an hour if it is. If your attorney has many clients, make sure that he has gifted associates, partners or paralegals who can assist you when he cannot.

Of course, you should feel free to ask any other questions that come to mind. At this point, I should point out a few red flags to look for in a meeting that might not seem so bad at face value:

★ If an attorney starts discussing the deal points of one of his client's deals in great detail, run away. Do you want him discussing your deals with other people? I didn't think so.

★ If the attorney starts ranting about how he is going to get you the biggest deal in history and make you a star, he's full of shit. Sometimes it is possible to accurately estimate what you might be able to command on the open market (especially if you are the subject of a huge bidding war or you are already successful and your deal is ripe for renegotiation), but even the most heavily connected attorney can only get you so far. The kind of deal you get depends on how many companies want to sign you and how good your attorney is. The level of success you achieve is a function of: your deal; the ability of the record company to sell your records; and the quality of your records. If you suck, the best attorney in the world and the best record deal in the history of recorded music will not help you sell more records (Then again, take a look at some of the crappy bands in the Top 200). Anyway, you know what I'm getting at.

Beyond grilling the attorney and discussing fee agreements, all you can really go on is references and vibe. Some attorneys are very businesslike and humorless. Others (like myself) tend to dress casually and get more excited about their clients' work. Both kinds of attorneys will serve you well as long as the work gets done correctly in a timely fashion and the attorney keeps in touch with you. But do make sure to interview several attorneys from different referral sources and check references. You should also be aware that most successful attorneys have their own set of criteria when it comes to taking on new clients.

For instance, when I get a call from a potential client, I always ask what kind of band they are, whether or not they currently have legal representation (out of respect for my colleagues, I will not take on a new client until they have terminated or decide to terminate their current attorney) and whether there is any current interest from a label or a publisher. (Note: When I say "interest", I do not mean that a guy from the mail room at Warner Bros. came to one of your shows — "interest" means that a real A&R person has attended many of your shows, knows your material, and has more or less said "We want to sign you — you'd better get an attorney.") That being said, "interest" is not always the most important factor I use in determining whether or not to pursue a potential client. You may in fact have ZERO interest, but if you have great songs and can really play, it's not hard to get people interested in a hurry. At this point, I will ask you to send in a demo tape or a copy of your most recent record. If the tunes are promising, I will come out to see you play, and we'll sit down and have a nice chat. Then you get to ask me all the questions I just laid out for you.

Note that not all attorneys operate in this fashion, and that's just fine too. Some will only take you on if a deal is already on the table or seems imminent. Some don't like music and don't want to hear yours. This does not mean that they won't do a good job for you, it just means that they are a lot more sensible than I am when it comes to making money.

2. MANAGERS

"Do we need a manager?" This is a question I am asked time and time again. Despite the great emphasis I placed on the importance of the attorney, I am here to tell you that a personal manager is ultimately the most important advisor you will have. Accordingly, a better question is *"When* do we need a manager?" The simple answer is that you should hire a manager whenever you find someone who is capable, enthusiastic and bright enough to further your career in a meaningful way. You may find this person (if at all) at the very beginning of your career or several years after your first rehearsal. In any case, I tend to think that a manager is absolutely necessary when you get signed and the relationship with the record company (and the real work) begins.

Some artists are inclined to wait until after their record or publishing deal is done to hire a manager in order to avoid paying a management commission on the signing advance. Hey, it's your money, but keep in mind that any manager worth a damn will (rightfully) demand a piece of the action even if he comes in after these deals are struck, so try to think about the big picture and use common sense. But enough of my lecturing — let's get into what it is a manager is supposed to do for you.

WHAT MANAGERS DO:

* ★ He advises you with respect to every aspect of your career, from what you wear on stage to choosing a producer and selecting agents, attorneys and business managers.

* ★ He helps you secure and negotiate recording, publishing and merchandising agreements (although the fine points of these agreements are usually hammered out by the attorney).

* ★ He tries to make your records sell. Your manager is your sole ambassador to the record company once you get signed. He attends marketing meetings and leans on key players at the company to make sure they don't drop the ball. In some cases, he calls radio stations to make sure your records have a shot at getting played.

* ★ He deals with your booking agent to set up your tours.

* ★ He deals with your attorney to make sure the deals are done.

* ★ He deals with the business manager to make sure the bills are paid and the van is insured.

* ★ In the early days, he may even drive the van and make sure you get to your gigs on time.

* ★ In some cases, he loans you money to keep you alive or get you to a showcase.

★ He deals with your fragile ego and attempts to assure you that everything is going to be OK.

HIRING A MANAGER

There are many different types of managers. I will oversimplify by placing them into three classes: The heavyweight, the middleweight and the lightweight. Let us take a look at the characteristics of each.

THE HEAVYWEIGHT

Generally represents "Superstar" acts with multi-platinum record sales and millions of faithful fans. The Heavyweight is typically a shareholder of or a partner in a large management company with two or three other managers of similar stature. He typically operates out of Los Angeles, Nashville or New York and may in fact have offices in all three cities. The heavyweight has a great deal of clout with the record companies, publishers and promoters by virtue of his experience and the talent he represents.

THE MIDDLEWEIGHT

Doesn't have a stable of superstars, but looks after the careers of gold and near platinum acts. The Middleweight has some clout with the labels but doesn't wield the same power as the Heavyweight. Nevertheless, the Middleweight commands respect, because there is always the possibility that one or all of his acts will break into the superstar category.

THE LIGHTWEIGHT

This is your friend Gus who comes to all of your shows, helps you load your gear, purports to love your music and "really wants to break into the music industry." Gus would like to further this goal by becoming your manager. Gus has no experience, no clout, no office, no assistants and represents no other artists. Should you keep Gus at bay until a Heavyweight shows up? Not necessarily. Nearly every Heavyweight in the business started as a Lightweight. If Gus has passion, dedication and street smarts, he may be perfect for you.

These are the contenders, so how do you find them? Your best shot at getting access to the Heavyweights and Middleweights is through your attorney, agent, publisher or label. Sometimes they will come to you if you are uncommonly talented or are the subject of a massive bidding war. During one such bidding war I was involved in a few years back, I was contacted by no less than fifteen managers seeking to manage my client. The Lightweight will be apparent, inasmuch as he usually starts out as a fan or a friend. Once you have lined up the prospects, here are some good questions to ask:

ARE YOU INTO THE MUSIC?

You might be saying to yourself, "Who cares as long as he gets the job done?" Not so fast, Sparky. If your manager loves you and your music, he is more likely to do whatever it takes to get the job done. Additionally, it doesn't hurt to have an advisor who can give you an informed opinion about a mix or the bridge to a new song you have written. I am constantly surprised by the number of young managers I meet who don't know squat about their band's music (or music in general). Finally, a manager in love with the music is much more likely to stick with you during the lean years. Avoid any manager who asks for a large advance against future commissions, because his heart is in the wrong place.

HOW MANY ARTISTS DO YOU MANAGE?

An attorney is able to represent hundreds of clients because his role is limited to specific transactions, and not all of his clients are negotiating deals at the same time. Conversely, management is an incredibly time-intensive job. Most managers speak to their clients every day to discuss a wide variety of matters. Accordingly, if a manager already has five or six artists, it is unlikely that you will get the attention you need. This can be mitigated somewhat if the manager has a staff of "day-to-day" managers or assistants who deal with the details and have time to talk to you. This allows the primary manager to concentrate on the more important areas where influence and relationships are essential. Make sure you meet any assistants or day-to-day managers employed by the primary manager, because it is likely that these are the people you will be dealing with on a day-to-day basis.

HOW MUCH DO YOU CHARGE?

Managers generally charge between fifteen and twenty percent of your gross income (with a few deductions, but we will get into that later). The Lightweight may even agree to less than fifteen percent. What the Heavyweight and Middleweight will ask for depends on a number of factors. If you are the hottest band in the world, even a Heavyweight may agree to less than twenty percent. If you are not in a position to be choosy, you should gladly pay twenty percent if a quality manager agrees to take you on.

HOW STRONG ARE YOUR RELATIONSHIPS WITHIN THE INDUSTRY?

This is self explanatory. If a manager represents a platinum act who records for the company you just signed with, there is an implied level of clout, and this can be very helpful if you are a baby band. Of course, many managers will lie about this in order to induce you to sign on with them, so check them out before you commit.

Ultimately, you will have to take what you can get. Although there are a few bands who do quite well without management (Superchunk and Fugazi come to mind), these bands don't have to deal with major labels and are perfectly happy with their place in the universe. If you want to sell millions, a manager is essential. Don't be discouraged if you cannot attract the attention of a Heavyweight manager right away. Remember, every Heavyweight started out as a Lightweight. Of course, if a Heavyweight or Middleweight is genuinely interested, you owe it to yourself to explore these options.

Once your search for the perfect manager has concluded, you need to get into the specifics of your relationship. These specifics are usually spelled out in the form of a written management agreement. Some managers don't like to have written agreements and prefer to operate on a handshake. Others would like to have a written agreement but are unable to obtain one due to the relative bargaining power of the artist. When I was a young law clerk, I handled the bulk of the drafting duties for a very large and successful management company. I drafted a management agreement for a new band from the Northwest United States and proceeded to the third or fourth draft when it became apparent that the band's sudden unexpected massive worldwide success made them extremely uninterested in signing any kind of long term deal. At this point, the manager had no choice but to back off — better to manage a superstar act without a contract than to lose them because they wouldn't sign. After all, if you are already selling millions of records and playing stadiums, why the hell would you sign a contract when you can enjoy the luxury of firing your manager any time you want? But you're not there yet, so let's assume that you will have to sign on the dotted line.

THE MANAGEMENT AGREEMENT

Before we get into the gory details, I must state what should be obvious to you: NEVER, EVER SIGN ANY KIND OF AGREEMENT BEFORE CONSULTING WITH AN EXPERIENCED MUSIC ATTORNEY. While this may seem obvious, I mention it here because although management agreements can appear to be incredibly simple and brief (most are less than 10 pages long) they are actually very complex. A management agreement is the first kind of contract most of you will see, and if you don't go into negotiations with your eyes wide open you may ruin any chances for meaningful success, especially if the manager is a lying scumbag. In light of the foregoing, let's take a close look at the major provisions of a typical management agreement.

SCOPE OF EMPLOYMENT AND EXCLUSIVITY

Nearly every management agreement starts out with a proclamation that the manager will be the artist's "sole and exclusive personal manager, representative and advisor, throughout the world, in all of Artist's affairs in the entertainment industry." This simply means that you cannot hire anyone else to be your manager during the life of this agreement and that if any entertainment-related work comes up, the manager is entitled to be your sole advisor. This is completely customary and reasonable language, but let's assume for the sake of argument that you are very serious about painting and film directing in addition to music. If you feel that you may be doing work in this area in the future, ask yourself whether your manager is equipped to properly advise you in these areas. If not, you had better speak now, because all standard first draft management agreements define "entertainment industry" to mean much more than recording, performing and writing music. For example, the manager's attorney will likely include your acting, screenwriting, painting and literary endeavors in his definition of "entertainment industry." Therefore, unless you carve out exceptions to these areas at the outset, you may be surprised when your manager asks for twenty percent of the profits you just received from the sale of your finger painting collection.

Of course, if you feel you are in fact well served by your manager in every possible facet of the "entertainment industry," you need not worry. Just keep in mind that if you become a film or stage actor, you will probably need an agent specializing in this area, and if you add his commission on top of your manager's cut, your take will be less than you might expect. Be prepared for the manager's counter argument, which will go something like "I made you a famous rock star, and you wouldn't have any acting gigs if I hadn't been here to help you get there." Not a bad argument, come to think of it.

TERM

The term is the pre-specified length of time during which the manager is entitled to be your exclusive manager. For most new artists, managers will require a term of three to five years. As long as things are going well and you are happy with your manager, the term is fairly unimportant. Of course, all human relationships have a way of deteriorating over time, so let's take a look at a hypothetical which illustrates how the term can be a crucial component of your management agreement. Let's say the attorneys have done their thing and you end up signing with our old friend Gus, who has now moved up into the Middleweight division. The term of the agreement is five years and the commission rate is fifteen percent. Things are going great for the first few years, but you wake up one day and decide that you have outgrown Gus and that you want to hire Cliff, a Heavyweight, to take your career to the next level. So you call your attorney and break the news to him. Then he breaks the bad news to you. He tells you that simply wanting a different or "better" manager is not sufficient legal cause to terminate your contract with Gus. "I don't care" you tell your attorney "I'm going with Cliff." So you hire Cliff, and Gus promptly sues you. Probable outcome? You pay Gus his commissions for the remainder of the term (*and* after the term, for the duration of deals struck during the term — more on this later). The problem is that Cliff will not work for free. In fact, he charges twenty percent and he doesn't love you enough to reduce his commission rate. Now you are paying a total of thirty-five percent to two managers.

How could this have been avoided? A short term always works, but there are a few other loopholes your attorney could have probably built into the deal which might have helped you out, so let's take a look at a common one — performance plateaus.

PERFORMANCE PLATEAUS

This is a simple provision in an agreement which allows you to terminate the term of your agreement in the event that your total "gross income" during the first year or two has not equaled or exceeded a pre-negotiated amount. Take a look at the following sample provision:

> Manager will have the option to extend the Term for the First Option Period only in the event that (i) Artist's Gross Income for the Initial Period is equal to or greater than Two Hundred Thousand Dollars ($200,000.00) or (ii) an LP by Artist released prior to termination of the Initial Period has achieved sales in excess of one hundred thousand (100,000) units as certified by SoundScan®.

The reasoning behind this provision is that if your manager has not helped you make X amount of dollars or sell Y amount of records in the first few years, he must not be doing a good job. This isn't always the case, of course, and your manager will argue that it may be three or four years before you can expect to earn significant gross income. This is a compelling argument in the case of new artists, but I still think you should try to get performance plateaus in your deal. After all, you don't have to utilize this escape hatch if you don't want to. If your manager agrees to such a provision, the only other question concerns the dollar amount of gross income or number of records sold that must be exceeded before the manager can veto your right to trigger the termination right. The higher the number, the better. If you are an unsigned artist, you may want to try for a similar provision which allows you to terminate if you have not signed a legitimate recording or publishing agreement within a certain time frame.

POWER OF ATTORNEY

This has nothing to do with how much weight your attorney can bench press or whether or not he can get a choice table at Morton's on short notice. If you give someone power of attorney, that person has the legal right to take actions and enter into binding agreements on your behalf. For instance, a client of mine was once in the middle of buying a house, but he had to leave on tour. Rather than FedExing documents all around the globe, he gave me power of attorney to execute certain documents on his behalf. Let's look at a typical power of attorney provision in a management agreement:

> Artist hereby irrevocably authorizes and appoints Manager as Artist's true and lawful agent and attorneyinfact to execute for Artist in Artist's name and on Artist's behalf, any and all agreements, documents, and contracts for Artist's services. Artist hereby ratifies and affirms all acts performed by Manager pursuant to this power of attorney and confirms that this power is coupled with an interest.

This brief paragraph gives the manager the power to enter into any kind of music business-related agreement on your behalf without your consent. How would you like to come back from a shitty US van tour only to find out that you (courtesy of your manager) just sold your publishing for $100? You wouldn't? OK, so let's say your attorney is able to get rid of this clause. Now let's turn back the clock and put you in the middle of that shitty US van tour for a moment. You are in the deep south in the midst of a thirty hour drive to Tallahassee. Meanwhile, your manager in LA gets a call from a big promoter who tells him that the Smashing Pumpkins can't make their final H.O.R.D.E. date next week. He wants to know if you can fill in, but he needs to know by the end of the day. Unfortunately, a freak bongwater accident shorted out both your cell phone *and* your SkyPager, and you are unreachable as you rumble down the highway in your '69 Econoline. Your manager tears his hair out as the day ends, unable to enter into any commitments on your behalf, and the promoter gives the gig to the newly re-united Poison instead. Get the picture? The reality is that managers do need *some* authority to sign agreements on your behalf. The solution? Try adding the following language to the end of the "power of attorney" clause:

> Notwithstanding the foregoing, Manager shall not execute for Artist in Artist's name and on Artist's behalf any major agreement committing Artist's time, services and/or artistic and musical materials, the terms of which Agreement shall not have been previously approved by Artist.

That's better. Now your manager can book so called "one nighters" (as long as the money is in the ballpark) without running afoul of the management agreement. The limited power of attorney clause also allows the manager to approve photos, biographies and advertisement when you are busy touring or recording, which is something you probably don't want to bother with anyway.

COMMISSION

This is the most important and most heavily negotiated part of a management agreement. You already know that managers work on a commission basis (versus an hourly fee or a fixed fee). The typical arrangement is fifteen to twenty percent of your gross income. The actual number you arrive at depends on the stature of the manager and whether or not you are a baby band, a superstar or something in between. Let's use the deal you struck with Gus to illustrate the complexity of this area. You agreed to pay Gus fifteen percent of your gross income for the next five years. The agreement defines gross income as follows:

> For the purposes of this Agreement, "Gross Income" shall include, without limitation, all forms of income, consideration and compensation relating to Artist's endeavors in the entertainment industry, including, salaries, advances, earnings, fees, royalties, partnership interests, shares of stock, bonuses, shares of profits, shares of receipts, music publishing income, recording funds, tour support received from record companies, gifts, income in kind, and other considerations of any kind or nature whatsoever earned or received directly or indirectly by Artist, individually or as a member of a group or by any party or entity on Artist's behalf or by any party or entity which has furnished Artist's services in the entertainment industry, regardless of by whom procured.

This is potentially very bad for you. As we discussed earlier, unless you specifically provide to the contrary, "your endeavors in the entertainment industry" can be interpreted to mean not only your career as a musician, but your work in any other field of the arts that generates money. There are other problems with Gus' definition of "gross income." Under your deal, Gus is entitled to his fifteen percent commission on every penny you bring in, whether or not that money is spent on legitimate band expenses or not. This isn't really fair to you, because a great deal of the money you receive from your record company is used to pay expenses. Accordingly, you need to define "gross income" in such a way that monies expended for the following purposes are not deemed gross income and thus are not commissionable by the manager:

RECORDING COSTS

Recording costs include recoupable monies expended by you or the record company to pay for studio time, tape, mastering costs, producer advances and producer royalties. Video production costs (which are sometimes enormous) also fall into this category. Let's assume that you have secured a recording agreement and that your total all-in advance for the first record is $200,000. Gus and your A&R person have prepared a recording budget that earmarks $100,000 for recording costs. This leaves

$100,000 for you to put in your pocket. Under your agreement with Gus, he is entitled to receive fifteen percent of the entire $200,000, leaving you and the rest of your band with only $70,000 to split among yourselves. This is bad for you, and your attorney should have had no trouble deleting recording costs from commissionable gross income. The rationale for excising recording costs from the definition of gross income is that it would be unfair for the manager to take a commission on these monies since you don't really even get to spend it.

TOUR SUPPORT

The term tour support refers to monies advanced to you by the record company to cover the high costs of touring. Once again, these monies are usually one hundred percent recoupable from your future royalty earnings *and* are not available for you to spend however you please. Let's take a look at the numbers: Suppose your total expenses for a tour equal $100,000 while gross income from the tour is $60,000. After subtracting twenty-five percent of your gross income to pay your manager and agent, you are left with $45,000 in gross income. The record company has agreed to pay the $55,000 deficit as a tour support advance so that you can break even. Under your agreement with Gus, you owe him fifteen percent of the $55,000 tour support payment (in addition to his commission on the gross income), even though you don't see a penny of it. Unless you feel like accruing large debts to your manager early on, your only option is to exclude tour support from the definition of gross income. Most managers won't put up too much of a fight on this exclusion.

TOURING PRODUCTION COSTS

Staging a tour is very expensive, even at the club level. Touring costs include per diems (daily salaries) for the band and crew, tour manager salary, "side musician" salaries, sound person salaries, fees paid to opening acts (if you are a more successful artist) and equipment costs. Equipment costs include transportation (the van or bus, fuel and driver) and sound and lighting equipment. You are likely to face stiff resistance from your manager when you attempt to exclude all of these expenses from gross income. My experience is that most managers will allow sound and lighting expenses and opening act fees to be deleted, but little else. The manager's reasoning behind this is that live shows are the only ongoing source of commission during the lean years, and that without this commission, he cannot afford to "carry" a new artist until the records start to sell.

AGENCY FEES

Ask your manager to deduct all or part of the agent's fee from gross tour income before he takes his cut. This is not standard, but I really think it should be. After all, the manager benefits from the agent's services as much as you do, so he should shoulder his share of agency fees.

There are other exclusions from gross income, but these are the biggies. Most respectable managers will include some of these (in one form or another) in the first draft of the management agreement they submit to you. The fact that Gus did not do so should tell you something.

POST-TERM COMMISSIONS

Assuming you have agreed on the term, commission rate and definition of gross income, the only other major deal point to be determined is how long *after* the term your manager is entitled to receive his commission. This is yet another extremely important and highly negotiated part of a management agreement. To illustrate, let's take another look at the relevant paragraph of your agreement with Gus:

(c) Manager's Commission shall be payable upon all Gross Income as and when such Gross Income is paid to Artist or to any third party on Artist's behalf, during the Term or after the Term, as a result of and/or pursuant to:

(i) any and all engagements, contracts, commitments and agreements now in existence or entered into or negotiated during the Term;

(ii) any and all judgments, awards, settlements, payments, damages and proceeds relating to any suits, claims, actions or proceedings arising out of alleged breach, non-performance or infringement by others of any of the contracts, engagements, etc. referred to in (i), above.

What does this brief provision mean to you? Let's take another trip down hypothetical lane. Your deal with Gus just expired after five fruitful years. Despite your success, you have decided that five years with one manager is quite enough, and you decide to find a new manager. This is fine, since you are no longer bound to Gus. You head for the attorney's office, where he explains a few things to you. It seems that while the term of your agreement with Gus has indeed expired, the recording and publishing agreements you negotiated during the term are still in effect. In fact, you could owe as much as three more records worth of recordings (to the record company) and songs (to the publisher) under these deals. Your attorney points to the provisions I just quoted and breaks the news to you that Gus is still entitled to his full 15% commission on all gross income generated from these deals as long as the deals are in effect. Accordingly, while you are now free to hire whomever you choose, you still have to pay Gus. "But wait" you say, "How can I pay Gus and a new manager?" Your attorney answers that you can, provided you are willing to make fifteen or twenty percent less on your records and publishing for the foreseeable future. At this point, you should fire your attorney and hire one that has the smarts to come up with the following language:

(d) Manager's Commission shall be payable upon all Gross Income as and when such income is paid to Artist or to any third party on Artist's behalf during the Term hereof and for a period of five (5) years ("Post-Term Period") after expiration of the term as follows:

(i) with respect to such Gross Income earned during the two (2) year period following the expiration of the Term, Manager's commission shall be ten percent (10%) with respect to such Gross Income;

(ii) with respect to such Gross Compensation earned after the two (2) year period following the expiration of the Term, but prior to five (5) years following the expiration of the Term, Manager's commission shall be seven and one half percent (7.5%) with respect to such Gross Income.

(iii) with respect to such Gross Compensation earned after the five (5) year period following the expiration of the Term, Manager shall not be entitled to receive any commission with respect to such Gross Income.

This is what we attorneys refer to as a "sunset clause" because the manager's commission reduces as time fades away. However, you are still not completely out of the woods. While you won't have to pay Gus his full commission for the records and songs created under the old recording and publishing agreements, you still have to pay him something. Unless you can get the new manager to subtract commissions payable to Gus from the commissions owed to him, you might be better off staying with Gus. That's why I like to add the following additional language:

(e) Notwithstanding anything to the contrary contained herein, Manager shall be entitled to receive Gross Income generated by records recorded and released during the Term. Manager shall only be entitled to receive Gross Income generated by musical compositions created and initially commercially exploited during the Term.

Problem solved. This simple provision cuts Gus off with the last record (and last batch of songs) that he worked with you on and allows you to pay commissions on future records and songs only to your new manager. It also cuts off Gus' commissions on records and songs that pre-date your agreement with him.

These little provisions sound pretty simple, but they are intensely negotiated points and not always easy to get. Managers tend to feel that if they are instrumental in securing and negotiating a deal and developing a career that they should enjoy the benefits of that career and those deals as long as the deals are in effect, even if the manager is out of the picture. This is not an entirely unreasonable argument. In any case, this is a very important part of your management agreement, so make sure that your attorney clearly explains to you not just *how much* commission the manager is entitled to receive, but *what* he is entitled to commission and for *how long*.

WRITING THE CHECK

Once you and your manager determine how much he is entitled to receive for his efforts, how does he actually get paid? Some managers will suggest that all of your money should be remitted to their office, whereupon they will take out the money they are owed and forward the remainder to you. THIS IS A REALLY BAD IDEA. Others will only ask that their commission be paid directly to them. Look for this neat little clause which attempts to effectuate this concept:

Artist shall notify and irrevocably direct and cause any and all third parties for whom Artist renders services in connection with the entertainment industry to pay directly to Manager the Commission due to Manager hereunder, and such Commission shall be payable to Manager immediately upon payment or credit to Artist or to any person on Artist's behalf of the Gross Income upon which such Commission is based. The aforesaid direction to any such third party shall be included in any and all agreements of every kind and nature in respect of Artist's activities in and throughout the entertainment industry, including, without limitation, recording agreements, publishing agreements and agency agreements and shall be substantially as follows:

"Artist hereby irrevocably authorizes and directs you to pay [name of manager] or its assignee, a sum equal to fifteen percent (15%) of all sums due to, or paid on behalf of, the undersigned hereunder. Such payment shall be made at the same time that payments are due to the undersigned hereunder. Each payment shall be accompanied by a duplicate of the statement rendered to the undersigned."

This provision makes me a little itchy. It also makes me think about the crap I am going to get from all the different companies I am negotiating contracts with on your behalf, because they generally like to write one check and prepare one statement for you. A better solution is to replace the foregoing language with the following:

Artist and Manager shall select an accountant or business manager ("Accountant") who shall have the right collect and receive, on Artist's behalf, all of Artist's Gross Income hereunder and deposit such Gross Income in one or more segregated bank accounts. Manager shall have the right to approve Artist's selection of an Accountant. Artist shall notify and direct any and all third parties to pay all Gross Income directly to Accountant and shall authorize, direct and cause Accountant to pay Manager all Commission due hereunder as well as any reimbursement or payment for expenses, from the first monies received within each month during the Term and thereafter as long as Manager is entitled to receive Commissions hereunder. Such payments shall be made within fourteen (14) days of Artist's receipt of such monies and shall be accompanied by a written accounting statement setting forth all Gross Income received by the Accountant on Artist's behalf during the preceding month and specifying the source thereof.

Frankly, I think this arrangement is best for both parties in that it puts the cash in the hands of a mutually selected accountant. This allows you to have a bit more control over your money in the event of a dispute with your manager.

EXPENSES

In addition to the commissions you pay to your manager, he will ask to be reimbursed for his expenses. Expenses include postage, express mail and messenger costs, long distance phone costs and travel expenses. Here is an example of how your agreement might address expenses:

> Artist shall reimburse Manager for any and all reasonable bona fide expenditures incurred by Manager on Artist's behalf or in connection with Artist's career or in the performance of Manager's services hereunder within thirty (30) days of such expenses being incurred. It is agreed and understood that Artist will be responsible for all booking agency fees and commissions, union dues, publicity and promotion costs, legal fees and accounting fees and any and all taxes due with respect to Gross Income. In the event Manager advances any of the foregoing fees, costs or expenses on Artist's behalf, Artist shall reimburse Manager for such advances within thirty (30) days of Manager's payment.

This is a reasonable and customary arrangement, but your attorney should make sure that something resembling the following language is added to the foregoing paragraph:

> Notwithstanding the foregoing, it is agreed and understood that Manager shall not incur any single item of expense in excess of Three Hundred and Fifty Dollars ($350.00) nor aggregate monthly expenses in excess of one thousand dollars ($1,000.00) without the Artist's prior approval. Not withstanding the foregoing, in the event that Manager does not submit a detailed written request for expense reimbursement within ninety (90) days of such expenses being incurred, Manager waives his right to receive reimbursement for such expenses. In the event that Manager incurs expenses on Artist's behalf which also benefit Manager's other clients, Manager shall pro-rate the amount by which he is to be reimbursed.

The added language protects you from runaway or unexpected expenses and also makes the manager think twice about incurring expenses unless there is a compelling reason to do so. Although the time limit on reimbursement is difficult to get in an agreement, it protects you from getting slapped with a hefty bill covering expenses incurred more than three months prior, and also gives the manager incentive to issue timely expense statements.

KEY PERSON CLAUSE / ASSIGNMENT

If your manager owns or is employed by a company, your agreement will be between you and the company, not you and the manager himself. This is fine, but you must ask for a keyperson clause in this situation or you may find yourself bound to the company after your manager leaves, sells out or is terminated. The relationship between artist and manager is extremely personal. Without a key person clause, you will be forced to work with any replacement the company designates, and this could be disastrous. You must also make certain that your manager cannot assign or sell his right to be your manager to another person or company. The following language should protect you:

(a) Manager shall not assign this Agreement or any rights or obligations hereunder without Artist's consent, except that Manager may assign this Agreement without Artist's consent to any parent, subsidiary or other related or affiliated company or to any other person, firm or corporation acquiring a significant portion of Manager's stock or assets or entering into a merger or joint venture with Manager.

(b) Notwithstanding anything to the contrary contained herein, in the event that [name of actual manager] is not an officer, employee, partner or active consultant of Manager or its assignee and that [name of actual manager] is not personally responsible for the supervision of Artist's career on behalf of Manager or its assignee, Artist shall have the right to terminate this Agreement by sending Manager written notice within thirty (30) days of the date on which [name of actual manager] ceases to be so involved with Manager or its assignee.

LEAVING MEMBER

Another clause you want to pay close attention to regards so-called "leaving members." If you are a band rather than a solo artist, and if each member of the band is signed to the management agreement, the agreement will usually stipulate that each person signing is jointly and severally liable to the manager and that if a member of the band quits or is fired, the manager still has the right to manage (and collect commission from) that leaving member. Take a look at the following provision:

As used herein, the term "Artist" shall be deemed to refer to the entertainment unit presently known as "[band name]" (the "Group"), as well as to each individual member of the Group who is a signatory hereto. In the event any such member should leave the Group or pursue a solo career while remaining a member of the Group, this Agreement shall continue to be binding with respect to such member during the Term hereof. In the event Artist wishes to add a new or additional member to the Group, Artist shall cause such member to accept the terms and conditions of this Agreement and such member shall be deemed a signatory hereto. This Agreement shall be binding jointly and severally upon said persons and the Group. Wherever required, the singular shall include the plural and, unless the context otherwise requires, the masculine gender includes the feminine and the neuter.

"Joint and several liability" means that each member is liable for 100% of any obligation to the manager. This means that if you breach your agreement with the manager and the band owes him $1,000,000 in commissions, the manager can sue one or all members for the entire amount owed. Of course, if you end up being the only member with money and are forced to pay the manager the entire amount yourself, you may in turn sue the other members for their pro-rata share of the payment.

There is much more to be said about management agreements, but I think that the foregoing should arm you with enough knowledge to have an intelligent conversation with your attorney and any professional manager. For more specifics and commentary on the management agreement, check out the sample agreement I have so thoughtfully provided for you in Appendix B. Also, read my interview with **Jackson Haring** of Bill Graham Management in Appendix A.

3. AGENTS

The role of a music business booking agent is much different than that of a motion picture or sports agent. The latter are actively involved in seeking out and negotiating all kinds of deals for you. In the music business, agents seek out and negotiate agreements for your live appearances only. Lest I understate the importance of a good agent, you should understand how absolutely critical touring is for ninety-nine percent of all artists in the music business. Touring sells records, it's that simple. In speaking with managers, I am continually struck by the fact that sales invariably go up (even if just a little) in a market where an artist has just played or plays frequently. For this reason, you cannot succeed without a good agent. Hell, even ultra DIY bands like Superchunk and Fugazi have agents. Agents generally fall into two classes.

MAJORS

There are essentially only a handful of major agencies in the music business. The big three are The William Morris Agency, ICM and CAA. These agencies are involved in all areas of entertainment, not just music. The big three agencies typically work only with artists that command nice big fees, although they are starting to take on baby bands due to the explosion of so-called "Alternative Music." These agencies are in really cool buildings with ridiculously expensive art. The agents that work in these cool buildings are always ready to liquidate their fat expense accounts in an effort to curry the favor of hot new artists, managers and attorneys (and for this I am thankful). Major agencies have their plusses and minuses. On the plus side, they have clout. These agencies wield a lot of power in the industry, especially in motion pictures and TV. As a result, managers and other agents are loathe to piss them off and are keen to do them favors (in the hope that the favor will be returned one day). The major agencies can also get you involved in movies and TV if you are inclined to move into these areas. For instance, a major agency might represent a director who is putting together a big movie soundtrack. Your chances of getting a cut on that soundtrack are enhanced if you are represented by the same agency. On the minus side, these agencies tend to have huge rosters. When a nice slot on a hot tour (or *any* tour, these days) opens, you might find yourself competing with fifteen other acts who are also represented by the agency. Also, all those promises of crossing you over into movies might be a load of crap. Despite the minuses, you will probably end up at a major agency when your career starts to boom.

BOUTIQUES / INDIES

As with law firms, there are a number of relatively small, music only agencies commonly referred to as "boutiques." These agencies typically employ three to four agents and a few assistants. Most are anchored by a few major clients, and nearly all are more willing than the majors to take on new artists. The boutiques have a reasonable amount of clout in the music world, but would seem to have very little in the world of TV and motion pictures. Foremost among boutique agencies are Monterey Peninsula Artists, Artist Direct and FBI.

In the realm of indie rock and "Alternative Rock™," the indie agencies are king, although several formerly independent agencies (such as Venture Booking and Twin Towers) have been sold to major agencies over the past few years. This is where nearly all artists who record for independent labels start out. Most start as one person operations with a handful (maybe 5-10) of clients. These agencies tend to be more in touch with small clubs and dives, because these are the only places new bands can get booked. I like indie agents. The touring business is extremely competitive at all levels these days, and the indies tend to have small rosters. Accordingly, you are much more likely to get a shot as an opener on a good tour if you don't have to compete with fifteen other similarly-situated acts on the agent's roster. Foremost among indie agencies are Flower Booking, The Billions Corporation, Leave Home and CPG.

HIRING AN AGENT

You will find this a fairly difficult task these days. The majors won't even look at you unless you are already established or have a huge buzz. The boutiques can ill afford too many new artists, because they don't have the size or overall income that the majors have. The indie agents can be great, but you will find that they are very choosy because they do not have the capacity to book too many acts. Remember, booking a tour is an extremely time-intensive task. Relationships between the agents and clubs are very important, and the agent must always be careful not to sell a club booker on too many acts that don't draw well. You will find that your manager, attorney and label can be helpful in hooking you up with an agent. After all, the success of your record depends a great deal on touring, and booking your own tour leaves you little time for making music.

AGREEMENTS / FEES

The agreements are fairly straightforward and standardized, because the activities of agencies are governed by two unions, the AFM (American Federation of Musicians) and AFTRA (the American Federation of Television and Radio Artists). The unions limit an agent's take to ten percent of your gross income, without any deductions. Although most agencies would like to have signed agreements with their artists, it is my experience that most will work on a handshake. For example, I have represented hundreds of artists over the years, and only a few have signed agency agreements. However, if you do get presented with a written agreement, it is most likely a union form agreement. Have your attorney look this over.

GIG CONTRACTS

Again, these are fairly standard. The big points are: 1) When do you "load in" (arrive at the venue with your gear); 2) When do you (or do you even get to) sound check; 3) When do you go on-stage (opening, middle or headlining); 4) How long do you get to play; 5) How much do you get paid (a flat fee "guarantee," percentage of box office receipts, or a combination of both); and 6) What is on your "rider." The rider is the part of the gig contract which specifies the goodies you get backstage. This typically includes beverages (beer, soda, water, hard stuff, etc.) and food. When you start out, you will be lucky to get a six pack and a bag of chips. When you move up to headliner, you can usually get premium beers, liquor and edible food. Some bands and agents get very creative with riders. I have witnessed riders which include socks (don't laugh — clean socks can keep a band together), smokes, rolling papers, pre-stamped postcards, condoms and disposable cameras. Get creative, and don't let the hangers-on drink all of your beer. Another tip — when the headliner is onstage, raid their dressing room. They usually have the good stuff.

4. ACCOUNTANTS & BUSINESS MANAGERS

WHAT THEY DO & WHEN TO GET ONE

As you may have guessed, these guys deal with your money. Accordingly, you don't really need one until you have some coming in. The accountant or business manager is usually the last player to make your team, and you will likely be referred to him by your attorney, manager or another artist. This may seem obvious, but you should take great pains to check out your accountant or business manager before you bring him aboard. Check his references and his background, because your money and your future will soon be in his hands.

Before we go on, you should note the distinction between accountant and business manager. An accountant is usually a CPA, which means he has studied accounting and has passed difficult exams to become certified. An accountant usually only takes care of your taxes, whether they be for you individually, your partnerships, your LLCs or your corporations. "Business manager" is a term I will use to describe an accountant who does much more than simply prepare your taxes. He may or may not be a CPA (although I strongly recommend that you choose a CPA). In either case, I cannot overstate how important it is to have one of these guys onboard once you have money coming in. This means you should probably engage one before your record deal is done so that you will have a bank account to put the money into at the very least. The level of service you get from your business manager depends on your needs and your willingness to relinquish control over your financial empire, but most offer the following services:

TAXES

This is the most obvious and basic function of a business manager. Look, you have to pay your taxes, and you don't want to end up like Willie Nelson (at least in the fiscal sense), so even if you are only making slave wages, your money man will sit down with you and plan your financial year. At this point, he will give you the sad news that you are going to have to set aside a good-size chunk of your advance for the tax man, since

33

the record company sees you as an independent contractor and does not take taxes out of your advance check. He will also tell you that you can deduct damn near any expense related to the music business from your taxable income. In other words, save your receipts whenever you spend money on musical equipment, records and rehearsal space time.

MONEY MANAGEMENT

If you can't be bothered to deal with bank accounts and bills, you may want your business manager to handle these things for you. If you choose this option, he will arrange for your bills to be sent directly to him and simply pay them on your behalf (with your money, of course). You will have access to your money through an ATM, or you may periodically pick up a check from his office. Of course, it is up to you to spend your money wisely. To ensure this, a business manager will likely put you on a monthly or weekly allowance which you can use for your day-to-day expenses. At the early stages, I heartily recommend this kind of arrangement. In any event, you should ask for a monthly statement from your business manager which clearly indicates what has come in and where it has gone. If you don't understand the statement, schedule an appointment and ask him to walk you through it.

INVESTMENT ADVICE

You may even want your business manager to invest your money for you or help you find someone who is a specialist in that area. Be very careful here — make sure that your business manager or the person he recommends is an experienced professional, because some kinds of investments are very risky.

TOURING/INSURANCE/MISCELLANEOUS

Business managers are very invloved in your touring operation, and they will be glad to help you buy, rent and lease all kinds of vehicles for your professional and personal use. They will also help you to insure your vehicles and musical equipment. I cannot overstate the importance of insurance. I don't know how many times I have heard sad stories about theft, accidents and other mishaps on the road. Inevitably they involve a van break in or a theft of equipment from a venue. MAKE SURE YOU HAVE GOOD INSURANCE. Your business manager will know who to call. A business manager can also set you up with prepaid credit cards and calling cards (even if you have bad credit) and these things can really help when your transmission blows up in the middle of nowhere. The business manager must also deal with state and foreign taxes whenever you venture into a foreign territory. When you start to make a lot of money on tour, your business manager may send an accountant to accompany you on the road. Having an accountant on the road with you will make it much easier to collect money and pay your bills.

ROYALTY STATEMENTS & AUDITS

Your business manager should be familiar with the ins and outs of royalty statements. When a statement is received, he will review it to make sure the statement jibes with the royalty structure the attorney has negotiated. If things look fishy, or if you have sold a ton of records (usually a million or more), he will likely recommend an audit of the company's books and records. It is important to note that a great many qualified business managers will farm out audits to specialists, and that audit fees are generally *in addition to whatever fee you are paying your business manager.*

FEES

The fee structures for business managers are similar to those employed by attorneys. Most charge by the hour, via a monthly retainer or a percentage. Go back to the section on attorneys and review these options, and do not be shy to ask your business manager about fees up front.

RETAINER AGREEMENTS

Some of the high-rolling business managers will require you to sign an agreement. I think some kind of agreement is advisable so that you will know exactly how much you are being charged, but most relationships are handshake agreements.

In conclusion, I want to reiterate that you should choose your business manager or accountant very carefully. As with attorneys, make sure they specialize in music or general entertainment. For further insight into a business manager's duties, read the interview with **Larry Einbund** of Provident Financial Management in Appendix A.

Congratulations, you have made it through Chapter One. Hopefully, you have a good understanding of what managers, attorneys, agents and business managers can and cannot do for you. Follow me to Chapter Two, where we will learn about copyright law.

CHAPTER TWO

A Copyright Primer

Please take the time to read and understand the copyright concepts I have outlined for you in this chapter. Armed with this knowledge, the chapters on recording agreements and music publishing will make much more sense to you.

WHAT IS COPYRIGHT?

The Copyright Act of 1976 is Federal law that came into effect on January 1, 1978. The 1976 Act superseded the 1909 Act. The U.S. Congress created copyright law to give "authors" a limited monopoly in tangible "original works of authorship." In the context of the music business, an "author" can mean any person or group of persons who write a song or contribute to the creation of a sound recording, or a publisher or record company that commissions a song or sound recording as a "work made for hire" (more on this later). For our purposes, an "original work of authorship" is a song or a sound recording fixed in a tangible medium that has not been copied from another song or recording. Of course, many other works of authorship are covered by copyright law (such as photographs, paintings and computer software) but we are only talking about the music business, so I am not going to deal with anything other than songs and sound recordings from this point forward. In creating copyright law, Congress wanted to give creative people like you a degree of control over the songs and sound recordings you create. The idea is that if people can control how and where their works are exploited, they can make money by selling, trading or licensing certain rights to such works. This is supposed to encourage you to create wonderful things like songs and sound recordings.

HOW TO SECURE A COPYRIGHT

In order to secure copyright protection for your song or sound recording, you simply need to create it and fix it in a tangible means of expression. In other words, if you write down the words and music to your original song on a piece of paper or record it on an audio or video tape, that song is now copyrighted and you are the author (unless you are creating the song as a work made for hire). **That's it** — you need not register your song or sound recording in order for it to be protected by copyright law. However, registration does have its benefits.

BENEFITS OF COPYRIGHT REGISTRATION

★ Registration is necessary before you can sue another party for infringement of your work.

★ Registration establishes a public record of the copyright claim.

★ If registration is made within three months after publication of the work or prior to an infringement of the work, the copyright owner may seek statutory damages and attorney's fees in any infringement action. Otherwise, the copyright owner is limited to an award of actual damages and profits.

★ If you register your work before or within five years of publication, the court will view your registration as *prima facie* evidence of the validity of the copyright and the facts stated in the registration certificate. In other words, the court will assume that you are the author of the work in question and have the right to sue for infringement, and the burden of disproving your copyright in and to the work in question will fall on the other party.

★ Registration allows the owner of the copyright to record the registration with the U.S. Customs service for protection against importation of infringing copies.

WHAT ARE YOUR RIGHTS AS COPYRIGHT OWNER?

The Copyright Act gives a copyright owner the following exclusive rights (although only the first four apply to music):

★ To **reproduce** the copyrighted work in copies or phonorecords. For example, no one can dub a copy of your four-track demos, put your song or recording in a movie or make copies of your CD without the copyright owner's consent.

★ To **prepare derivative works** based upon the copyrighted work. If some one wants to take one of your copyrighted songs and make material changes in the lyrics or basic melody, thereby resulting in an essentially different but similar song derived from your song, he must get your consent. For example, if you take a Bob Dylan song and change all of the lyrics, you have created a derivative work. You cannot do this without Bob's consent. When you make a new song or recording using copyrighted "samples," you are creating a derivative work.

★ To **distribute copies or phonorecords** of the copyrighted work to the public by sale or other transfer of ownership, or by rental, lease, or lending. This is separate from the right to reproduce. For example, assuming you give someone the right to make copies of your demos, that person does not have the right to publicly distribute those copies to the public without your consent.

★ To **perform the copyrighted works publicly.** No one can play your sound recordings or perform your songs in a bar, in a motion picture shown in a

U.S. movie theater or at Dodger Stadium (or in any other public area) without your consent. This includes radio and TV broadcasts. There are exceptions to this general rule, and they are as follows: First, bona fide record stores (i.e., stores that count record sales as their primary business) may perform recordings of songs, without permission and without payment of performance license fees, to promote record sales. For example, Tower Records would be deemed a record store for the purposes of this exception, but Wal Mart would not, since Wal Mart is really a department store with a record department. Second, jukebox owners can get compulsory jukebox performance licenses for commercially exploited songs whether you like it or not, but they still have to pay license fees to the performaning rights organizations. Finally, a fairly recent amendment to the Copyright Act provides that owners of "small vending establishments" which are 2,000 square feet or less, and "food service or drinking establishments" which are less than 3,750 square feet can play recordings from radio, TV cable or satellite without acquiring performance licenses or paying any performance license fees. Of course, it is virtually impossible to control how and where your songs or recordings will be performed, so songwriters join performing rights organizations like ASCAP, SESAC and BMI to enforce their performance rights and collect their public performance royalties. More on performing rights organizations later.

★ To **display the copyrighted works publicly.** Inasmuch as you can't see a song or a sound recording, this doesn't have much application in the music world, except that now, with the advent of music videos, in theory this could be a consideration. However, this right applies more to photographs, paintings and other visual works.

The exclusive rights granted to a copyright owner are separable. For instance, you can give someone the right to make copies of a work without giving them the right to distribute that work, and an exclusive licensee will have standing to sue for violation of their respective right(s). The copyright owner may also spread these rights over different territories. For instance, DreamWorks Records has the exclusive right to reproduce and distribute new George Michael records in the United States, while Virgin Records has the rights to these recordings in the rest of the world.

EXCEPTIONS TO THE EXCLUSIVE RIGHTS

Now that you know all about your exclusive rights, you need to know about a few very important exceptions to some of them: the first sale doctrine and compulsory licenses.

THE FIRST SALE DOCTRINE / RECORD RENTALS

The so-called first sale doctrine is an exception to the exclusive right of distribution. Once a legally made copy of a work is sold or given away, the copyright owner ceases to have any claim or control over what happens to that copy thereafter. For example, let's assume that you have purchased a CD of the latest Garrison Starr record, *Eighteen Over Me*. You look on the back cover and you see that the copyright in and to the sound recording is owned by Geffen Records, Inc. Up until the moment that Geffen sold that CD to the One Stop or major chain that put the record into the store where you purchased it, Geffen owned and controlled that copy. Now that you own it, you can do whatever you want with it. You can sell it, destroy it, or loan it to someone else. However, you cannot copy it or prepare a derivative work from it.

Of course, there is an exception to this exception, and this concerns the rental by a "commercial establishment" of records containing sound recordings of musical works. You cannot rent records in the United States (unless you are a non-profit library or school). Why is the rental of records prohibited while the rental of books and videos is not? The record companies (through their trade association, the Recording Industry Association of America, or RIAA) are well represented by influential lobbyists to Congress, and they do not like the idea of people making copies of rented records rather than buying them, especially with the advent of cheap digital recording devices.

COMPULSORY MECHANICAL LICENSES

This is going to come up again and again, so pay close attention: In order to reproduce a song in a record you need a mechanical license. The mechanical license and any other kind of license pertaining to the song is granted by the copyright owner or administrator (that entity is called the publisher). The mechanical license specifies the royalty to be paid for every record distributed or sold. We call this royalty the mechanical royalty. In certain situations, the Copyright Act compels copyright owners to issue mechanical licenses, even if the copyright owner is adamantly against issuing such a license. For instance, let's say your band wants to cover "Sad Eyed Lady of the Lowlands" by Bob Dylan on your new record. Even if Bob or Bob's publisher doesn't want you to issue your recording of this classic on a record, you may do so if you get a compulsory mechanical license.

A person can obtain a compulsory mechanical license if the following three requirements are met: First, the song must be a "non-dramatic musical work." In other words, you cannot get a compulsory mechanical license for an opera, a piece of music from a Broadway musical or a movie score or soundtrack. Second, a recording of the song in question must have been "distributed to the public in phonorecords." This means that a recording of the song has been commercially released (not just recorded) and that copies of a phonorecord embodying the recording of that song have been made available to the public. In the world of copyright law, "phonorecord" means an audio-only mechanical playback device, whether it be vinyl, CD, tape, whatever. Consequently, you cannot get a compulsory mechanical license for a song that is embodied in sheet music or a movie but has not been released on a phonorecord. Note also that the recording of the song need not be a version recorded by the songwriter — for instance, many of Bob Dylan's songs first saw the light of day as "cover recordings" performed by other artists. Third, your use of the song must be limited to phonorecords. If you want to make a video or put the song in a movie or a CD-ROM, you must get Bob's permission.

Also, it is important to remember that even if you are able to get a compulsory mechanical license, you cannot alter the basic melody, lyrics or harmonic structure of the song. You may arrange the song to fit your style — for instance, if you are a hard core punk rock band, you may speed the song up as long as you don't change the lyrics or the basic melody and structure of the song. If you step over the line and want to change these aspects of the song, you are now creating a derivative work, and you must again go back to the copyright owner for permission, or you run the risk that your song will be deemed an unauthorized derivative work in violation of the copyright holder's exclusive rights under the Copyright Act.

HOW TO OBTAIN A COMPULSORY MECHANICAL LICENSE

It's not so simple, I am afraid. If the three threshold requirements have been met, you must then file a notice of your intention to obtain the compulsory license with the Copyright Office. You then pay mechanical royalties (at the statutory rate) on every record distributed each month. The statutory mechanical royalty rate is established by the Copyright Office and is occasionally updated to reflect cost of living increases. The most recent increase went into effect as of January 1, 1998. This increase (and pre-negotiated increases that will take place every two years over the next eight years) can be attributed to the combined lobbying efforts of the National Music Publishers' Association, the Songwriters Guild of America and the RIAA. Let's take a look at the various rates in effect from 1978 to the present and beyond (the rate was 2 cents per song from 1909 through 1977):

Effective date of new rate	Cents per song	Cents per minute
January 1, 1978	2.75	0.5
January 1, 1981	4	0.75
January 1, 1983	4.25	0.8
January 1, 1984	4.5	0.85
January 1, 1986	5	0.95
January 1, 1988	5.25	1
January 1, 1990	5.7	1.1
January 1, 1992	6.25	1.2
January 1, 1994	6.6	1.25
January 1, 1996	6.95	1.3
January 1, 1998	7.1	1.35
January 1, 2000	7.55	1.45
January 1, 2002	8	1.55
January 1, 2004	8.5	1.65
January 1, 2006	9.1	1.75

WHY ARTISTS AND RECORD COMPANIES THINK COMPULSORY MECHANICAL LICENSES SUCK AND WHY THEY PREFER TO OBTAIN MECHANICAL LICENSES DIRECTY FROM THE PUBLISHER

If you are a record company, or an artist covering a song, compulsory mechanical licenses are a drag. There are three primary reasons for this: First, you have to pay royalties at the statutory mechanical royalty rate. Let's assume you have now jumped through all of the hoops with the Copyright Office and have obtained a compulsory mechanical license for "Sad Eyed Lady of the Lowlands." If you distribute 1,000 copies of a record embodying your recording of this song in January of 1996, you need to pay Bob's publisher a mechanical royalty on every record distributed equal to 6.95 cents or 1.3 cents per minute of the recording, whichever is greater. Uh-oh. "Sad Eyed Lady of the Lowlands" is an epic song if there ever was one. Bob's version clocks in at 11:19, so let's assume that your version clocks in at 11:00. That's 14.3 cents for every record distributed, my friend — 1,000 times 14.3 cents is $143.00.

Had you covered the relative short Dylan composition "Jet Fighter" instead (Dylan's version runs less than a minute) you would have to pay 6.95 cents per record distributed, or $69.50. This may not seem like much of a difference, but if you put out an entire LP of lengthy covers, you or your record company are going to pay a lot of money in mechanical royalties if you rely on compulsory mechanical licenses. For this reason, record companies do not like to use compulsory mechanical licenses. In fact, most record companies don't even want to pay 100% of the *minimum* statutory mechanical royalty rate: in most cases they pay mechanical royalties based on 75% of the minimum statutory rate. Why? Simple greed. Record companies find other ways to reduce the mechanical royalties it must pay, but we'll explore this topic in great depth in Chapter Four.

The second problem with compulsory mechanical licenses concerns accounting: you or your record company must account to the publisher (via the Copyright Office) on a monthly basis. Most record companies account for mechanical royalties every three to six months. Asking them to account every month will make their brains explode.

The third and final problem with compulsory mechanical licenses concerns the number of copies you must pay mechanical royalties on. Most record companies will only obligate themselves to pay you mechanical royalties on records *sold and not returned*. The compulsory mechanical license requires them to pay mechanical royalties on *every record distributed*. What's the difference? Let's say a record company ships or gives away (as promotional copies) 10,000 copies of your record. The record sells ZERO copies. Nonetheless, if the record company has secured a compulsory license for the Dylan cover on the record, they will ultimately have to pay a mechanical royalty for that song at the statutory rate on every one of the 10,000 records, despite the fact that no copies sold. Conversely, if Bob's publisher issues a mechanical license which provides for payment of mechanical royalties only on records sold, the record company ultimately owes Bob's publisher nothing. Of course, the negatives I just outlined are positives for publishers and songwriters. However, compulsory mechanical licenses are kind of a drag for publishers too, if only because the publisher must go through the Copyright Office to collect its royalties. Do you want the government handling your royalties?

For these (and other) reasons, the compulsory mechanical license is rarely used. If you want to cover a Dylan song, you go to Dylan's publisher. If the publisher doesn't want to grant you a mechanical license, you must attempt to secure the compulsory mechanical license. For more information about this process, you can contact the Copyright Office Licensing Division (see Appendix C). The terms of a compulsory mechanical license are non-negotiable. Accordingly, you hope that Bob's publisher will save everyone a little trouble and agree to grant you a mechanical license directly.

When the publisher issues a mechanical license, the terms are completely negotiable. The typical "regular" mechanical license will require you to account quarterly (every three months) and pay royalties only on records sold (and maybe on 50% of LP "free goods"). The "rate" (the percentage of the statutory rate you agree to pay) is also a big point of negotiation. You will want to pay mechanical royalties based on 75% of the statutory rate and without regard to the playing time of the recording. Bob's publisher will probably only issue a mechanical license based on 100% of the statutory rate.

If you don't quite understand the concept of mechanical royalties at this point, don't worry too much. We will revisit this topic in Chapters Four and Six. For now, just remember that there are two types of royalties payable on every record: the record royalty is paid to the recording artist; the mechanical royalty is payable to the publisher of the songs recorded on that record. Got it? Let's move on.

WHO'S THE OWNER? JOINT WORKS & WORKS MADE FOR HIRE

You already know that copyright ownership initially vests in the author of the work. But what if you write or record a song pursuant to an employment agreement? What if you write or record a song with other people? Depending on the circumstances, you may have a joint work or work made for hire on your hands. As we shall see, the classification of a work has serious consequences.

WORKS MADE FOR HIRE

A work made for hire is a work that you may actually create, but because of an agreement or the terms of your employment, your employer is deemed the author of the work for purposes of copyright law. How does this apply to you? Let's fast forward to the copyright ownership provisions of a standard major label recording agreement. With very few exceptions, these provisions provide that any sound recordings you make during the term of the agreement are "works made for hire" for the record company. This means that the record company owns the copyright to the sound recording despite the fact that you are the person that actually authored the recording. The same cannot be said for songs you write for a publisher under most standard songwriter or co-publishing agreements, although these agreements typically require you to assign fifty to one hundred percent of the copyright in and to your songs to the publisher after the songs are written (as you soon see, songs which are assigned after creation rather than created as works made for hire are treated differently under the Copyright Act). To get technical for a moment, the Copyright Act defines a work made for hire as either:

1) A work prepared by an employee within the scope of his or her employment. Suppose you work in the mail room at Warner/Chappell (a giant music publishing company) and you have written a few songs on the job when things are slow. Is Warner/Chappell the "author" of these songs under the Copyright Act? The answer is no, because songwriting is not included in the "scope of your employment." Your job is to operate the Pitney Bowes machine, Xerox flyers for your shitty band and steal CDs from the mail. They don't ask you to write songs. Contrast this with songs written by a songwriter who is specifically employed (via a written agreement) by a publisher to write songs as works made for hire and happens to write these songs in an office provided by the publisher.

or

2) A work specially ordered or commissioned for use as one of the following:

- a contribution to a collective work (e.g., an anthology or encyclopedia)
- as a part of a motion picture or other audiovisual work
- as a translation
- as a supplementary work
- as a compilation
- as an instructional text
- as a test
- as an atlas

In any case under subdivision (2), the parties must expressly agree in a written instrument (signed by both parties) that the work shall be considered a work made for hire.

CONSEQUENCES OF CLASSIFICATION OF A WORK AS A WORK MADE FOR HIRE

What does any of this mean to you? If you don't own the copyright to a song you have written or a sound recording you have made, you generally don't have any say over what happens to it. Of course, recording and publishing contracts (as we will soon see) may have provisions which give you the right to make sure that your songs or recordings are not exploited or changed in certain ways, but absent such provisions, these matters are out of your hands. Beyond mere ownership, the classification of a work (joint work, work made for hire or just plain work) determines the duration of the copyright and affects certain termination of transfer rights. We'll get deeper into some of these issues in a little bit.

JOINT WORK

The Copyright Act defines a joint work as "a work prepared by two or more authors with the intention that their contribution be merged into inseparable or interdependent parts of a unitary whole." In addition, for people to be considered "joint authors", each author must have made more than a "de minimis" or insignificant contribution. I hope the following examples are illustrative.

Example 1 – You have written a poem. As you wrote the poem, you had no intention or desire that the poem ever be combined with music to constitute a song. Across town, Lucy (whom you have never met) is writing some music. Lucy has written her music with the hope that she can find suitable lyrics at a later date. The two of you meet a few weeks later and combine the poem with the music to create a song. This is *not* a joint work under the Copyright Act, because at the time you wrote the poem, you did not have the intention to merge it with music and make a song out of it. Accordingly, the song created under this example is a derivative work rather than a joint work.

Example 2 – Same scenario as above, but you wrote your poem with the intent to merge it with someone's music at some point in order to create a song. We now have a joint work, because each composer intended to create a joint work at the time they created their separate components. It does not matter that the authors were unknown to each other at the time of creation.

Example 3 – You and your band write a song during rehearsal. Each of the four members contributed something to the music and the lyrics. This is a joint work, because all four authors clearly intended that their contributions be merged into a single song.

Example 4 – You and your "writing partner" intend to write a song together. You write the whole thing, music and lyrics, and your "partner" just contributes the title: "Physical Climber." Unless you are really generous and you and your partner have an agreement to the contrary, your partner, by contributing only a title, which is not a form of protectable expression, would *not* be deemed a joint author under Copyright Law.

Confusing, no? That's why we get the big bucks, people. Anyhow, the key here is that all of the authors involved must have the INTENT to create a joint work when they create their contribution.

CONSEQUENCES OF CO-OWNERSHIP:

Administration – The authors of a joint work are deemed to be tenants-in-common of the work. This means that each author has an undivided ownership in the entire work. Let's go back to Example 3. In this example, each member of the band (as a co-owner) can license or exploit the entire song as he wishes. The only catch is that the other co-owners must be paid an equal share of the proceeds from such license. Note, however, that no co-owner may (without the consent of the other co-owners) assign (sell) the entire work or grant an exclusive license to the work without the other co-owners' written consent. For example, let's say your drummer wants to assign the entire copyright to the song to a movie producer for use in a big movie. Since this is a transaction that would transfer all exclusive rights in and to the song to the studio for the duration of the copyright, the drummer cannot legally complete this transaction without the consent of the other three co-owners. However, the drummer can give the studio a non-exclusive license to use the song in connection with the movie, as long as he pays the co-owners their share of the license fee. Let's contrast this with the derivative work that was created in Example 1. With a derivative work, each author owns only the portion that he contributed. Consequently, if Lucy wants to license the song in question, she needs your permission. Conversely, she may license the music only without your consent and she may keep all of the proceeds.

Ownership – Let's go back once again to Example 3, which is the most likely scenario you will encounter. Although each member of the band contributed something to the lyrics and music (I realize that this is unlikely, but humor me), some members contributed less than others. Let's say that the bassist and guitarist actually wrote about 40% each, while the drummer and keyboard player chipped in with 10% each. Guess what? Absent a written agreement to the contrary, each co-owner owns an equal 25% of the copyright. In other words, if you want more than your pro-rata share of a song copyright, you'd better get the new "publishing splits" down in a written agreement signed by all of the co-owners. In fact, drop the book, call your attorney and deal with this straight away — you will thank me later.

HOW LONG DOES A COPYRIGHT LAST?

It depends on a number of factors. Copyright law was substantially overhauled when the Copyright Act of 1976 took effect on January 1, 1978, and that is the dividing line when it comes to determining duration of a copyright.

WORKS CREATED ON OR AFTER JANUARY 1, 1978

★ **Regular Works**: Life of the author plus 70 years.

★ **Joint Works**: Life of the last surviving author plus 70 years.

★ **Works Made For Hire, Anonymous and Pseudonymous Works**:
   The shorter of 95 years from first publication (distribution to the public)
   or 120 years from creation.

WORKS PUBLISHED AND REGISTERED BEFORE JANUARY 1, 1978

Under the 1909 Act, copyright owners were entitled to a first term of protection equal to 28 years with a renewal term of 28 years. Failure to renew injected the work into the public domain. *Renewal is now automatic* for works still in their first 28 year term of protection as of 1/1/78. The 1976 Act (as recently amended) mandates the following copyright duration for all works published and registered prior to 1/1/78:

★ **Copyrights in First Term on 1/1/78** – 28 year first term and a 67 year
   renewal term for a total of 95 years.

★ **Copyrights in Second Term on 1/1/78** – 95 years total (original 28 year
   term plus 67 year second term).

GOVERNMENT WORKS

You say you feel the need to put some cool NASA Apollo moon mission footage in your next video, but you're daunted by the prospect of complicated licenses and heavy licensing fees? No worries — works owned by the United States Government or created by U.S. Government employees acting within the scope of their employment are not subject to copyright protection — they are in the public domain. However, whenever you use any government work in phonorecords "consisting preponderantly of one or more works of the U.S. Government" the notice of copyright is supposed to indicate that Government material is being used. You have been warned.

THE PUBLIC DOMAIN

You can use any public domain work to your heart's content without charge and without permission. How does a work find its way into the public domain? Think of the public domain as the place where old copyrights go after their term has expired or has been terminated. You will also find all of the aforementioned Government Works as well as what I like to call "stillborn works"— works that would have enjoyed copyright protection had their careless owners not botched the registration and publication formalities in place under the 1909 Copyright Act. Once a work is in the public domain, it's in there forever. We are not likely to see any well known rock/R&B/soul songs or sound recordings enter the public domain for many years, since "the modern era" of music didn't begin until the late Fifties or early Sixties.

NOTICE

Go and pick up a record. Somewhere on the back cover you will see some very small print that looks something like this:

©℗ 1997 Vandelay Industries.

When a work is published under the authority of the copyright owner, the owner should place such a notice on all copies of the work that are intended to be distributed to the public. I emphasize the word "should" because as of March 1, 1989, notice is no longer required on a publicly distributed copy of any work and the omission of notice will not result in that work being "injected" into the public domain. The main reason people affix copyright notice to records these days is to let people know who owns what. Copyright notice makes it much easier for a professional to get in touch with the right person if they need to license a song, a sound recording or some artwork on behalf of one of their clients. The notice is also supposed to put potential copiers or infringers on notice that there is a valid copyright in and to the work, although I find it hard to believe that a bootlegger will be "frightened" enough by the notice to stop running off bogus cassettes. Whatever — put the proper notice on anything you create. This prevents an infringer from asserting a defense of "innocent infringement" during litigation, which will not insulate an infringer from liability, as copyright infringement is a "strict liability" offense, thus even if you don't know you are doing it, you are guilty. However, "innocent infringers" are treated much less harshly by courts in assessing damages in copyright infringement litigation.

You have probably always wondered what the difference is between the © symbol and the ℗ symbol. The type of symbol used depends on the type of work involved.

© – VISUALLY PERCEPTIBLE COPIES

You should use the © symbol whenever you are publishing "visually perceptible copies." In the case of a record, this would include printed music, lyrics and album artwork, since you can see these copyrighted works. There are three required elements in the notice for visually perceptible copies:

★ The © symbol. The word "copyright," or the abbreviation "Copr." will also suffice;

★ The year of first publication of the work; and

★ The name of the copyright owner.

℗– SOUND RECORDINGS

The ℗ symbol should be used whenever you are distributing copies of sound recordings to the public. Since you cannot "see" sound recordings (absent first rate hallucinogens and a $10,000 hi-fi rig), the © symbol won't work. Wasn't it nice of Congress to give sound recordings their own special symbol? There are three required elements in the notice for sound recordings:

★ The ℗ symbol;

★ The year of first publication of the sound recording; and

★ The name of the copyright owner.

INFRINGEMENT

So you have a valid copyright and you think someone is ripping you off — what do you do? Hire an attorney, of course! Infringement occurs when someone else exercises one or more of your exclusive rights without your consent. To sue, you need to (A) show that you are the owner of a registered copyright (remember, registration is not mandatory to own a copyright, but you must register before you sue someone for infringement); and (B) show that the defendant copied your work. To prove that someone has copied your work, you must show that the defendant had *access* to your work and that his work is *substantially similar* to your work. Absent direct evidence of copying, you can show that the defendant had access to your work and that his work is substantially similar to your work. For example, the publisher of the song "He's So Fine" successfully sued George Harrison for using the melody of that song in Harrison's song "My Sweet Lord" without a license. I could spend the next three hundred pages writing about these two requirements, but suffice it to say that any attorney specializing in copyright litigation will know all about them and how to prove them, so let's move on to what you can hope to receive from the defendant if your infringement suit is successful.

REMEDIES

The Copyright Act provides a number of possible remedies to the successful plaintiff in a copyright infringement action. They are as follows:

Preliminary Injunction – The court may, in its discretion, grant both a preliminary and permanent injunction. An injunction is a court order preventing the defendant from continuing its pattern of infringement and/or "forcing" the defendant to do certain things (e.g., to hand over all of his infringing goods).

Seizure and Destruction of Infringing Articles – The court may order the seizure of any records, tapes, CDs, masters, stampers, etc. used in connection with any infringing activity. This remedy comes in very handy in the case of bootlegging, obviously. The court may order destruction of these materials at final judgment, unless it makes sense for the plaintiff to recover these items.

Damages and Profits – The infringer is liable for either (1) the copyright owner's actual damages and any additional profits made by the infringer, or (2) statutory damages (if the copyright owner registered his copyright within three months after publication of their work or prior to an act of infringement). The plaintiff may choose either option prior to final judgment. Since actual damages are hard to prove, successful plaintiffs usually choose to go after statutory damages or the infringer's profits. If the plaintiff chooses statutory damages, the amount of damages awarded is within the court's discretion. The range of statutory damages (per infringement) is $500 at the low end and $20,000 at the high end. If you can prove that the defendant *willfully and knowingly* infringed your copyright, the court may award up to $100,000. Conversely, a court, at its discretion, may also lower minimum statutory damages to $200 for cases of innocent infringement. In practice, it is extremely difficult to show that infringement is innocent. First of all, the burden of proof is on the defendant, who must show that he had a good faith belief that there was no infringement. Moreover, that belief must be reasonable. Keep in mind that when someone rips off part of your song and the song infringing your copyright gets played 1,000 times a week on the radio, this is still only one infringement for the purposes of calculating statutory damages.

Attorney's Fees /Court Costs – A prevailing party in a copyright infringement action may be awarded (in the court's discretion) "reasonable" attorney's fees and court costs.

Criminal Penalties – If the court finds that the defendant has infringed a copyright "willfully and for the purposes of commercial advantage," he shall be guilty of a misdemeanor under federal law. This can carry with it jail time and a stiff fine.

WHAT IS NOT PROTECTED BY COPYRIGHT

Band Names and Logos. Here's another common voice mail message from one of my clients: "Uh, Bri, I think we need to copyright our name, cuz I saw in *Flipside* that there's another band called "Lawn Chocolate" in Portland, and they just put out a seven inch." WRONG, Ringo — you'd best stick to drummin'. Copyright law has nothing to do with protection of your band name or any logo you design in connection with your name (except to the extent that you have a copyright interest in the artwork for your logo, but that's a whole 'nother can of worms). This is covered by *trademark law*, and we'll get to this soon enough, so keep your shirt on.

INTERNATIONAL COPYRIGHT

There is no such thing as international copyright law. Everything you have read up to now generally applies only in the United States to works copyrighted in the United States. However, most countries have signed treaties granting a measure of reciprocal protection to U.S. works. Before you make any deals to publish or license your songs or recordings outside of the United States, you may want to find out a little bit more about the copyright laws in the territory concerned. Let me know what you find out.

SOUND RECORDINGS AND PUBLIC PERFORMANCE ROYALTIES

Believe it or not, sound recordings were not eligible for Federal copyright protection until 1972 (though pre-1972 works were and still are protectable under the common law and, in some cases, statutes enacted by certain states). Even so, owners of sound recordings (unlike publishers and writers of musical compositions) have not been entitled to any royalties for the *performance* of their works. This changed somewhat when President Clinton signed into law the Digital Performance Right in Sound Recording Act of 1995. The Act (which became effective on February 1, 1996) is extremely narrow in scope, inasmuch as it applies only to digital audio transmissions of sound recordings that are part of an interactive service for which the subscriber pays a fee. The operators of such services are now required to obtain licenses and pay royalties in connection with the performance of masters. What does any of this mean to you? Not much, due to the limited scope of the law. However, it is a step in the right direction.

SAMPLING

I am sure that you all know what a "sample" is. Bottom line: if you are sampling a copyrighted song or sound recording, think long and hard before you try to "sneak it past" the copyright owner. You may be thinking, "Gee, we only used two snare hits off of that Led Zeppelin record, what's the big deal?" The big deal is that publishers and record companies hire people to listen for and seek out unauthorized samples of their songs and recordings. If you want to use a sample, hire a clearing house or alert your attorney. There are no compulsory licenses for samples of musical compositions. If you steal a melody line from somebody's song, they can sue you for infringement and they don't have to give you a reduced mechanical rate, so be careful out there.

Since this chapter actually deals with real laws and not just my arrogant musings on the music business, I strongly suggest that you use it only as an introduction to the most basic copyright concepts. Men and women far brighter than I have devoted their life's work to the study of copyright law, and laws change over time, so if you are inclined to learn more, take a trip down to your local law library and ask the librarian to point you in the right direction. Check out *Nimmer on Copyright*. If you need general information on copyright law or registration information, write to:

The Copyright Office
Publications Section, LM-455
101 Independence Ave. SE
Washington DC 20559-6000

While the Copyright Office is not allowed to give you legal advice, they will send you a variety of publications, registration forms and "circulars" which are actually written in plain English and can be quite helpful. Many of these items are available for downloading online from the Copyright Office website at: http://www.lcweb. loc.gov/copyright.

CHAPTER THREE

Record Companies and Distributors

In order to understand recording agreements, you need to know a little bit about record companies and distributors. Please note that I will be using the terms "record company" and "record label" interchangeably.

RECORD COMPANIES

In the United States, there are essentially two kinds of record companies: majors and independents ("indies").

MAJOR LABELS

In 1998, the line between indie and major is kind of blurry. For our purposes, we'll call any record company owned in whole or in part by one of the five major music conglomerates a *major label*. What follows is a far from exhaustive list of major labels and their associated distribution companies:

Bertelsmann Music Group (BMG)/BMG Distribution – Arista (Arista Nashville, Bad Boy, Dedicated, LaFace & Time Bomb), RCA, CMC International

EMI Music/EMI Music Distribution and Caroline Distribution – Angel, Capitol (Matador, Grand Royal), Blue Note, Capitol Nashville, Chrysalis, SBK, EMI, Pendulum, Virgin (Charisma, Point Blank, Caroline, Astralwerks, Noo Trybe, Pitch-A-Tent)

Sony Music/Sony Music Distribution – Columbia, American Recordings, Ruff House, So So Def, The WORK Group, Epic, Immortal, Cold Chilln', Okeh, 550, Relativity

Universal Music Group/UNI Distribution – Geffen/DGC, DreamWorks, Outpost, Interscope, Almo Sounds, Universal, GRP Records, Rising Tide, MCA (Gasoline Alley, Chess, Coral, Curb, Decca, MCA Nashville, Radioactive, Uptown), ABKCO, A&M, Polydor, PolyGram Classics & Jazz, Blue Gorilla, Def Jam, Mercury, Fontana, Island, Megaforce, Mercury Nashville, Motown, Antilles, Verve

Warner Music Group/WEA and ADA Distribution – Atlantic (Big Beat, Lava, Rhino, Modern), Elektra/EastWest, Warner Bros./Reprise (4AD, Dark Horse, Duck, Revolution/Giant, Luaka Bop, Maverick, Sire), London/Slash (FFRR)

INDEPENDENT LABELS

Independent labels are generally privately owned and distributed by independent distributors. Here's a list of a bunch of them:

Alligator, Alternative Tentacles, Alias, American Gramaphone, Amphetamine Reptile, Antone's, Ardent, Bar/None, Barking Pumpkin, Bellmark, Cargo, Cherry Disc, CMC International, Continuum, Cruz, DB, Dischord, Empty, Epitaph, Estrus, Fantasy, Flydaddy, Flying Fish, Frontier, Hollywood (Mammoth, Ideal), Ichiban, Jive/Silvertone, Justice, K, Lookout!, Merge, Mesa/Bluemoon, Metal Blade, Mute, Palm Pictures, Restless, Rykodisc, Shanachie, SpinArt, SST, Sympathy For The Record Industry, Touch and Go, Triple X, TVT, Volcano, Zero Hour.

Over the last few years, many of the larger independents have been bought (in whole or in part) by major labels. For instance, did you know that Time/Warner owns 49% of venerable Seattle "indie" Sub Pop, or that Capitol owns 49% of Matador? Indie giant Caroline really isn't so indie — it's 100% owned by Virgin (which is owned by EMI). Even though many of these "indie" labels are in bed with the majors, most still function independently in that they have their own staff and sell their records primarily through independent distributors or direct to stores. The staff makeup is similar to that of a major label, but whereas a major label may have a staff of ten promotion people, an indie may have only one or two. This isn't the case with major independent labels such as Hollywood (owned by Disney), Jive and Rykodisc.

Nearly every independent label starts with limited cash and a few or no employees. Some keep things small and manage to function just fine, but many find that they need more cash and better distribution, so they hook up with the majors. While everyone likes to make money, I have found that many indie labels are much less concerned with massive profits than major labels. Many of you will find yourselves much more comfortable at an indie, at least at the start of your career.

ANATOMY OF A RECORD COMPANY

Now that you know all about record companies and distributors, let's take some time to meet the staff of a typical record label:

A&R

Stands for "Artists and Repertoire." What do A&R people do? The ones I know get into the office about noon, order coffee, smoke some pot, listen to a few tapes, make a few calls and then go to lunch. Just kidding (kind of). A&R people are charged with the responsibility of seeking out new talent for the label to sign. Consequently, these are the first "label people" you are apt to meet. Most A&R people spend their time doing the following:

1) Listening to solicited and unsolicited material – As you can probably guess, major labels are inundated with thousands of tapes and CDs a year. Many are unsolicited (i.e., the label did not ask for them) or through industry professionals (such as attorneys, managers and publishers). Frankly, it's unlikely that an A&R person will give your material a listen unless it is sent in by one of these professionals. It also helps if your attorney or manager has some kind of relationship with the A&R person. A&R people also occasionally listen to material which they have discovered on their own.

2) Seeing artists play live – This is an essential step in the A&R process, and it goes hand in hand with listening to recorded material. An A&R person may love your demo, but he wants to see what you look like and whether you can cut it live.

3) Selling the company on an artist – So let's say that the A&R person likes your tape and live show enough to consider signing you. For most A&R people, the next step is getting the senior executives from the company to pay attention. This may entail flying the band into New York or LA to play a show and meet said senior executives, or it may simply mean sending copies of your material around the company. The extent to which this protracted process is necessary depends on the A&R person's clout within the label. For instance, if A&R person X has a long track record of signing credible and/or successful (read: profitable) artists, they may have "signing power."

"Signing power" generally means that the A&R person has attained Vice President status and can sign you even if others at the company have reservations about the quality or commercial viability of your music. I know several A&R people who have signing power but will nevertheless refrain from signing an artist unless there is widespread support for the signing at the label. This is wise, because the people who will try to *sell* your records (promotion people, marketing people and product managers) have a fair degree of discretion as to which records they "push," and they typically have MANY RECORDS to push at the same time to the same radio stations and retailers. Accordingly, it helps if they share the A&R person's enthusiasm for an artist. Other A&R people may have little or no clout (these are generally referred to as "A&R representatives/directors" or "A&R Scouts"). These A&R people usually need a senior A&R person to shepherd them through the same process.

4) Selling the artist on the company – This is not as easy as it sounds. There is intense competition among the major labels for the services of talented artists, and the best A&R people possess the ability to make the artist want to sign with the label. Typically, the A&R person will go to great lengths to show how well he "gets" what the artist is trying to do with his music. The A&R person will also parade the artist through the company to meet with every department (we call this the "dog and pony show"). This task is especially difficult for A&R people who work for shitty labels.

5) Making the record – OK, so everyone loves each other and the ink is finally dry on your shiny new record deal. The next step is making the record. At this point, the role of the A&R person may vary depending on just how much he knows about actually making records. I know what you are thinking — "Gee, don't all A&R people know how to make records?" NO. I don't want to get into too much trouble, but I wouldn't trust some A&R people with making toast, let alone a $200,000 record. Some A&R people have an ear for talent and songs and nothing more. Some A&R people may not be able to spot talent but are great at making records because they are actually producers and/or musicians. Some A&R people combine all of these skills. It doesn't matter what kind of A&R person you have as long as he helps you make good records. This may entail helping you find producers and musicians or selecting the songs you want to record. Look out for the A&R person who has experience making records but is so heavy-handed that he interferes with your vision (unless you're looking for such guidance, of course). Also try to avoid the A&R person who doesn't know the first thing about making a record yet wants to pretend he is Phil Spector or Butch Vig. In any event, there are certain administrative duties the A&R person may have to deal with as well, such as putting together a recording budget with your manager and producer and scheduling recording sessions. These days, most major labels have "A&R administration" departments to deal with these aspects of the recording process.

6) Shepherding your record throughout the company – Once your record is done (maybe even before), you and your record are assigned to a product manager. A product manager is the person who is supposed to make everyone else at the company so excited about your record that the company will kill itself trying to make it sell. I mention this here because at some labels (Geffen Records comes to mind) your A&R person is also your product manager. Other labels (Warner Bros. Records comes to mind) have a whole team of product managers.

For more insight into the responsibilities of an A&R person, read my interview with **Lenny Waronker** of DreamWorks Records in Appendix A.

PRODUCT MANAGER

As I mentioned mere seconds ago, product managers (be they A&R persons or full-time product managers) run around the building and get the marketing, sales and promotion people excited about your record. Accordingly, you should be very nice to your product manager. Flip to Appendix A and read the interview with **Lorrie Boula**, a product manager at Warner Bros. Records.

PROMOTION

These people perform a variety of functions: They help pick the "singles" off of your record which have the best chance to get played on the radio and MTV/VH1/The Box, etc. This may entail doing a "radio edit" of a track if it is felt that the track stands a better chance of getting played in an edited form. The primary job of a "promo guy" is to get radio stations to "add" your single to its playlist and to make sure it gets as many "spins" (plays per day, week, etc.) as possible. This is the tricky part, of course, because a given radio station has limited airtime and every single promotion person is vying to get their record played. You may make the greatest record of all time, but if your label doesn't have a decent promotion staff for each format, your chances of success are slim. This is one of the two areas (publicity is the other) where "independents" are very influential. There are several independent record promotion firms in the country that have a lot of clout with radio stations. Accordingly, you may want your record company to hire one of these indies to work your records even if the record company has a competent promotion department. See the interview with **Chuck Arnold**, formerly of The Want Adds for more insight.

MARKETING

The people in the marketing department try to get retailers (record stores) excited about records and artists. They work closely with the product managers and the artist development staff to establish an identity for the artist. Many labels have marketing personnel in every major region across the country. The regional marketing people are in constant contact with the record stores in their region. They set up in-store promotions with artists and oversee advertising. They may also accompany the artists to interviews, in-store appearances and live appearances.

PRESIDENT

The head honcho, the big cheese. This person is responsible for overseeing the operation of the entire label. Some presidents (such as Interscope's Tom Whalley) started in A&R and are very hands-on when it comes to signing and developing talent. Other presidents are more business-oriented and defer more to the A&R department when it comes to creative decisions. More and more we are seeing label presidents who have a background in promotion. For instance, Sylvia Rhone (president of Elektra Entertainment) and Phil Quartararo (president of Warner Bros. Records) started out in promotion. Others are former managers (such as Tommy Mottola of Sony). Clive Davis (Arista Records) started out as an attorney. Nick Gatfield (former President of Polydor Records and PolyGram Music Publishing) was in Dexy's Midnight Runners. I'm not kidding. The powers that be at the helms of the giant corporations that own the major record companies feel that these individuals possess the necessary combination of management skills, instincts and relationships to run giant record companies. If a label is hot on signing you, you will very likely get at least a brief audience with the president of the company. Check out the interview with **Bob Biggs**, President of Slash Records, in Appendix A.

ART DEPARTMENT

You get an artwork budget for each album, and some labels will allow you to create your own album artwork. If you don't feel like doing it yourself, all major labels have art departments of varying quality staffed with people who can assist you in bringing your vision to life. The art department also puts together advertisements and designs promotional items.

ARTIST DEVELOPMENT

These guys spend a lot of time on the road with new and developing artists. They have a lot of say when it comes to divvying out tour support money and will make sure you get to the in-store (promotional appearance at a record store) in Topeka on time. Remember the Artie Fufkin character in the movie *Spinal Tap*? Artie was an artist development guy (and he was modeled after a now-retired Warner Bros. executive).

BUSINESS AND LEGAL AFFAIRS

These guys take care of the day-to-day business and legal affairs for the label. This entails negotiating and drafting agreements with artists and other companies and dealing with a variety of other general problems that pop up. Some labels have a large business and legal affairs department staffed with attorneys and non-attorneys, while other labels rely heavily on outside counsel.

ROYALTIES/COPYRIGHT

This department deals with your royalty statements and handles mechanical licensing of the songs on your records.

INTERNATIONAL

If you are signed to a worldwide deal, these guys will get the foreign affiliates excited about your record. Not as easy as it sounds, as we will see later.

PUBLICITY

While most superstars (and indie acts) rely on independent publicists, major labels still provide the services of one or more in-house publicists. Their job is to get the media (newspapers, magazines, TV shows) to cover your activities, review your records and feature you on TV shows such as *Saturday Night Live, The Late Show with David Letterman, Late Night with Conan O'Brien* or *The Tonight Show*. A positive review, a blistering TV performance, or a nice feature in a major magazine or newspaper can do wonders for your career, so try to cooperate with your publicist, okay? See the interview with **Mitch Schneider** of the Mitch Schneider Organization in Appendix A.

SALES

Very important. These people deal with major retailers (such as Tower, Wal Mart and Blockbuster) and try to make sure that they order enough of the company's records. They may negotiate special deals on pricing in order to get a particular record better positioned in each store.

VIDEO

The video department is responsible for making music videos. They give you "reels" (tapes of videos by various directors) to look at when you are deciding who you would like to direct your overpriced music video. They typically have a fair degree of input on the creative aspects of the video. They oversee production of the video and service it to MTV and local video shows in each market.

DISTRIBUTORS

Once a record has been completed, the production person at the label ships the production master and artwork off to the pressing plant, where the record is manufactured. The records are then shipped to the distributors. The major distributors (BMG, EMD, UNI, SONY and WEA) have distribution warehouses all across the country, while most independent distributors (Caroline, RED, Alliance, A.D.A., I.N.D.I., REP, Mordam, and Revolver to name but a few) focus more on specific regions and independent label records. Both types distribute their records via the following methods:

1) Directly to the retailer – The big chains (Best Buy, K-Mart, Wal Mart, etc.) deal in high volume and sell lots of records, so they buy directly from the distributors and get the best prices. Many independent labels (Sub Pop, Drag City and Matador come to mind) sell directly to small, mom-and-pop stores.

2) One-stops – These are essentially "middle men." The one-stops (so named because small stores can get all the records from any major or indie distributor in one place) buy from the big five distributors and independents and then sell to the smaller mom-and-pop stores. If you have a small independently owned record store in your town, this is where it gets most of its records. Because there is a middle man, prices are higher for the mom-and-pop retailer, and the retailer will likely pass this cost on to you. This is why you can get a better deal on that Pearl Jam CD at Best Buy than you can at Chumley's Record Wigwam.

3) Rack Jobbers – Rack jobbers buy records directly from the major and independent distributors and sell them at major department stores like Target, K-Mart and Sears.

4) Record Clubs / Direct Mail / Internet Stores / TV Sales – Records also find their way to the consumer by these methods. In the case of record clubs ("8 CDs for One Penny!") and TV sales (K-Tel records, "Freedom Rock," etc.), the labels actually license these companies the right to manufacture and distribute whole albums or selected tracks (as part of a compilation album).

How do the distribution methods of the majors and independents differ? The majors have the sheer muscle and size to get mass quantities of records into stores across the nation in a hurry. The majors have branch warehouses and fulfillment centers in every major region of the country, thereby allowing them to fill large orders overnight. Very few independents have such vast coverage. However, independents are able to get certain records into a lot of stores and markets that the majors cannot. Of course, independents are less likely to get your record into every major chain store, but they may actually have better relationships with mom-and-pop stores and specialty retailers. For more on distribution, go to Appendix A and read the interview with **Russ Bach**, former President of EMD.

DOING IT YOURSELF

Of course, you can always put out your own records. I would not recommend this unless you enjoy calling record stores, stuffing envelopes and spending all of your time moving giant boxes of unsold records around your apartment. If this sounds like loads of fun to you, go for it. Putting out cool records that may not otherwise be heard is a truly noble endeavor and many great labels started this way. Unfortunately, this book is not about doing it yourself, so if you want to follow this path, I heartily recommend Gary Hustwit's fine book *Releasing an Independent Record*. If you don't, turn the page and start reading Chapter Four, which covers record deals with major and independent labels.

CHAPTER FOUR

Anatomy of a Record Deal

This is really what it's all about. Unless you want to put out your own records, you need a record deal. This chapter dissects the provisions you will find in most recording agreements. Before we start, I suppose I should attempt to define a few of the terms I have been using thus far. When I refer to a *record*, I am referring to any physical object that can carry an audio signal. This includes albums, singles and EPs in all existing formats (vinyl, CD, DAT, analog cassette tapes, mini-discs, DVD, etc.) and any other format the major labels may attempt to ram down our throats in the future. All records are comprised of master recordings, or masters. A master is a sound or sound and video recording of a song. Got it? Good.

To reiterate, this book is not a "do it yourself" guide to music industry contracts. If you are about to enter into a recording agreement of any kind, do yourself a favor and retain the services of an experienced attorney. DO NOT attempt to negotiate a deal aided only by this book. Why? I don't want you to sue my Scottish ass when you realize that the deal you negotiated "all by yourself" with the help of this flimsy volume is a complete piece of crap, that's why.

Additionally, I'm not stupid enough to make myself and my beloved colleagues obsolete by revealing all of our secret negotiating tactics. No, dear reader, you'll have to retain my services to get that information. I realize that you've heard this rap before, but it bears repeating as we get into the kind of agreements that deal with potentially valuable intellectual property you create — masters and songs. These deals are long and complex, and they typically assign the rights to your masters and songs to the record company or publisher in perpetuity (that is, forever). Accordingly, use the information I am about to foist upon you to get a grip on the terms and concepts you will come across in a recording agreement, but leave the negotiating to the pros. Let's get started.

I. MAJOR LABEL DEALS

TERM & RECORDING COMMITMENT

This is one of the first issues addressed in a recording agreement. The *term* is the length of time you are obligated to make records exclusively for the record company. The term is comprised of *contract periods*. The length of the term depends on three factors:

★ The recording commitment — The number of albums you are required to deliver in a given contract period.

★ The number of optional contract periods the record company has negotiated for itself.

★ The dates upon which you deliver each record.

This is kind of confusing, so let's take a look at some language I yanked out of a major label recording agreement:

> Company hereby engages Artist's services for producing and recording master recordings embodying Artist's performances for an initial period commencing as of the date hereof and expiring nine (9) months after the delivery of the Second Album (as herein defined). Artist hereby grants to Company three (3) separate, consecutive and irrevocable options, each to renew the term of this agreement for a period commencing upon the expiration of the immediately preceding period of the term and expiring nine (9) months after Artist's delivery to Company of the last Commitment Album (as herein defined) to be delivered during such period of the term in satisfaction of the Recording Commitment (as herein defined) therefor. Each such option period shall be upon all of the terms and conditions applicable to the initial period, except as otherwise specifically set forth herein. Each such option shall be exercised, if at all, by Company giving Artist notice at any time prior to the expiration of the then-current period of the term. During the initial period and each option period of the term hereof, Artist agrees to cause to be recorded and delivered to Company the number of Masters set forth below (the "Recording Commitment"):

Period of the Term	Recording Commitment
Initial period	2 albums
First option period	1 album
Second option period	1 album
Third option period	2 albums

Under this deal, you would be required to deliver two albums during the initial contract period. If you are a new, unproven artist, this is good, because the record company is obligated (in theory) to let you make a second record. This may not seem like a big deal, but if your first record is a total stiff, you get a second shot. The initial contract period ends nine months after delivery of the second album. At any time prior to the date nine months following delivery of the second album, the record company may send a written notice to you or your attorney stating that they are exercising their option for an additional contract period. If they fail to send such a notice, the deal is over. It is important to note that *these are options that can be exercised by the record company only*. In other words, you do not have the option to tell the record company that you no longer wish to make records for it. Record companies would rather commit to recording only one record in the initial contract period and like to get as many options as possible. Back in the day, most record companies required seven or eight option periods. These days, they will usually agree to five or six. If you are involved in a "bidding war" for your services, you might be able to get them down to two or three options.

Fewer options are better for you. Let's look at a real life example to see why: You sign a low money, low royalty rate recording agreement that requires you to deliver one record in the initial contract period. The deal also gives the record company seven options for additional albums and contract periods. Fortunately, your first album sells a million copies and your second album goes triple platinum (three million). Now you are a superstar with a crappy record deal. Unless the record company is willing to renegotiate your deal (and they don't have to) you will have to record as many as six more albums for the record company before you can secure the kind of recording agreement that takes your success into consideration (in the form of much higher royalties and advances). To be fair, many record companies will renegotiate your deal at this point just to keep you happy, but they will surely ask for even more options in exchange. Conversely, had you agreed to give the record company only two options for additional albums, you would be sitting pretty. With only one more album left to deliver on your deal, the record company will be begging *you* to renegotiate. You are in control — you can renegotiate with your present label or sign a new deal with another label (as long as you fulfill the recording commitment under your present deal).

"FIRM" RECORDS & "PAY OR PLAY" CLAUSES

The recording commitment albums you are required to deliver in any contract period in effect are commonly referred to as "firm" albums. Going back to our example, the record company has promised to allow you to make two albums in the initial period. Let's say you put out your first album under this deal, and it stiffs really badly. At this point, the company may not want you to make your second album. Unfortunately for the record company, you have a "two firm" deal. Does this mean that the record company must allow you make your second album? Of course not. However, it does mean that they will have to pay you something for the privilege of breaking the promise. Exactly what they have to pay you is addressed in what we commonly refer to as the "pay or play" clause. The most common "pay or play" clause I have encountered provides that the record company will pay the artist the *difference* between the recording fund(s) for any *unrecorded* "firm" albums and the *recording costs* for the last album you made. Applying this formula to our example, let's say your recording fund for the second album is $250,000, and you spent $100,000 in recording costs in connection with your first album. Thus, the record company may break their promise to let you record the second album by paying you the sum of $150,000. If you don't have much bargaining power when negotiating your deal, the record company may try to dispense with the formula approach and instead specify a fixed sum for any unrecorded "firm" album. If this is the case, you want that sum to be as large as possible.

Some would argue that a "pay or play" clause gives the record company an incentive to stay with an artist after a poor-selling first or second album, because the company will have to write a fat check to terminate the agreement. Others feel that "pay or play" clauses encourage record companies to give up on artists early if letting the artist record another album will be more expensive than simply writing a check and terminating the agreement. The bottom line is this: If you have a "two firm" or "three firm" deal and the record company wants to drop you without allowing you to fulfill your recording commitment, your fate will likely hinge on whether the cost of the "pay or play" payment is less than the cost of recording and releasing the as yet unrecorded "firm" album(s). Getting cashed out and released is better for you than wasting eleven or twelve songs on an album that will never be promoted or widely distributed by your estranged label, so get as many firm albums as possible.

EXCLUSIVITY

The majority of major label recording agreements are *exclusive*. This means that you are bound to make records exclusively for your record company until the term of your agreement expires or is terminated. This makes sense, since the record company is investing a lot of money in you. Of course, you can (and should) try to carve out some exceptions, and we will look at some of these later on.

ADVANCES/RECORDING FUNDS

Most artists that sign with major labels these days are given an *all-in recording fund* for each album in lieu of separate cash advances and recording budgets. Out of this fund, the artist is responsible for paying all recording costs. After recording costs are paid, the artist may do whatever it pleases with the remainder of the fund (if any). The entire recording fund is deemed an *advance* under a recording agreement.

DO YOU HAVE TO PAY BACK ADVANCES?

Yes and no. Think of the record company as a bank. Your recording fund is little more than a loan from the record company. You need the loan/recording fund to make your record, buy guitars and pay your rent. However, this particular "bank" won't require you to send in a payment on the first of every month. Instead, the record company will simply apply any record royalties you earn from the sale of your records against the advances it has paid to you or on your behalf. This little trick is called *recoupment*, and your contract will specify which advances and costs are *recoupable* and which are not.

Let's look at a simple example: You get signed and receive a $250,000 recording fund for your first album. Assuming that 100% of the entire recording fund is deemed recoupable under your contract (which it almost always is), you will not receive an actual royalty check from the record company until you have earned more than $250,000 in royalties. If you only earn $100,000 in royalties, you have an *unrecouped balance* of $150,000. You also need to keep in mind that you will only have one royalty account with your record company. This means that royalties generated from the sale of one record can (and will) be applied against any unrecouped advances on your royalty account, even if the unrecouped advances are attributed to another record. For instance, if your first record recoups before you make your second record, you will start getting royalty checks every six months. However, if your record company gives you a $500,000 recording fund for the second record and the record flops, the nice royalty checks from the sale of the first record will stop showing up in your mailbox. Instead, those royalties (and the minimal royalties from the second record) will be used to recoup the $500,000 debt you incurred in connection with your second record.

Before we get into what is and isn't recoupable, allow me to make one last distinction between a bank loan and an advance under a record deal: If you take out a loan to open a bagel shop, the bank will expect regular payments whether or not your business is a success. Conversely, if your records stiff and you get "dropped" (released from your contract), the record company will not ask you to repay any unrecouped advances. Of course, they will still have the right to apply any future royalties against this unrecouped balance, but what do you care?

OK, WHAT'S RECOUPABLE?

Excellent question! Damn near everything, I am afraid. By definition, anything deemed an "advance" under your recording agreement must be recouped from your royalties before you start to see additional royalty checks. Accordingly, your attorney needs to pay very close attention to the definition of "advance" in your recording agreement. Advances are almost always 100% recoupable. I say "almost" because there are more record companies than there are talented artists out there these days, and some desperate labels are willing to pay *non-recoupable signing bonuses* in order to induce artists to sign to their label. These bonuses (I won't call them advances because they are not an "advance against royalties") can range from five thousand to several hundred thousand dollars. *Recording costs* are also deemed recoupable advances. Recording costs include all costs of recording, from tape and equipment to mastering, studio rental, producer advances, sample clearance payments, hotel costs and per diems (if you or the producer are staying in a hotel during the recording of the album), rehearsal space time, and "all other costs and expenses incurred which are now or hereafter generally recognized as recording and mastering costs in the phonograph record industry." Finally, tour support payments, video production expenses, independent promotion, independent marketing and independent publicity expenses are customarily recoupable to some extent. We will explore these areas in greater detail a bit later on.

DAMN. IS ANYTHING NON-RECOUPABLE?

Yes! Most major labels cover the cost of preparing album artwork. Conversely, many indie labels want the artist to cover these costs outright or will recoup the costs from your royalties. This is kind of harsh, especially in light of the fact that the recording funds for indie records tend to be on the small side. Regular advertising costs are borne solely by the label, although they will ask you to contribute (typically via a reduced royalty) if they mount a major television or radio advertising campaign to promote your record. The cost of manufacturing your records is not recoupable, but you end up paying the "packaging costs" of each record in the form of packaging deductions (more about this later). Most record companies will deem only 50% of music video production costs recoupable from record royalties. If you have sufficient bargaining power, a portion of tour support may be deemed non-recoupable. Finally, most labels will hold you responsible for only 50% of monies expended for independent promotion and publicity.

HOW MUCH MONEY CAN I GET?

Admit it — this is all you really care about. The amount of money you can squeeze out of the record company depends on your bargaining power. While other commentators take great pains to map out advance ranges for new, mid-level and "superstar"

ng goes these days. One of my loose-lipped colleagues
deal for one of his clients that will pay the band a seven
first album alone. This band has never released a record
eptional, and it is also a testament to the extremely com-
music business in the late '90s. There are a lot of labels
tists making hit records. Accordingly, whenever "the next
labels line up and are more than happy to mete out siz-
ou find yourself with only one suitor, you have to take
bel may pay only a few thousand dollars per album, while
y at least $50,000 for the first album, and more for each
recording agreements, the recording funds for all albums
lated by using a formula based on the U.S. sales of your
ormula is 2/3 of the royalties generated from the sale of
aring the nine to twelve month period following its initial
to note that this formula does not take into account any
ales outside of the U.S., nor does it take into account any
(such as singles and EPs). Note also that the total amount
e subject to prenegotiated minimums ("floors") and maxi-
e a look at a hypothetical recording fund clause from a
rtist deal:

	MINIMUM	MAXIMUM
	$200,000	$400,000
Third Album	$250,000	$500,000
Fourth Album	$300,000	$600,000
Fifth Album	$350,000	$700,000

Now let's apply the standard 2/3 formula to some hypothetical sales scenarios:

EXAMPLE 1 – Your first album is a smash and generates $1,000,000 in U.S. royalties within the first 9 months following its release. Two-thirds of $1,000,000 is $666,666, but you will only be entitled to a recording fund of $400,000 for album two since that is the maximum amount payable under your deal.

EXAMPLE 2 – Your first album does pretty well, generating $500,000 in U.S. royalties within the first nine months of release. Two-thirds of $500,000 is $333,333, and that will be your recording fund for album two, since it falls between the minimum and maximum amounts.

EXAMPLE 3 – Your first album stiffs, generating $10,000 in U.S. royalties within the first nine months of release. Two-thirds of $10,000 is $6,666, but you are still entitled to the minimum fund of $200,000 for album two.

EXAMPLE 4 – Same facts as Example 3, but your first album generates a combined $3,000,000 in record royalties *outside* of the U.S. Unfortunately, the record company does not take these sales into consideration when calculating your next recording fund, so your fund for album two is still a measly $200,000.

Please note that the foregoing examples do not take into account the phenomenon of "reserves." You will learn more about reserves when we get to the subject of royalties, but for now all you need to know is that reserves will very likely reduce your recording fund in Examples 1 and 2.

HOW AND WHEN ARE THE RECORDING FUNDS PAID?

How much of each recording fund is paid to the artist before recording begins depends on the size of the fund and how much of the fund the artist budgets for recording costs. In an average new artist deal, a portion of the entire recording fund is paid to the artist within a few days after the contracts are signed. The artist can do anything he wants with this money (after he pays the attorney, the manager, the business manager and the IRS, of course — more on this in a minute). The balance of the fund is usually held in reserve by the record company and is used to pay the recording costs for the record involved. After the record is finished and delivered, any monies left in the fund are paid to the artist. Let's look at an example:

Recording fund for Album One	$350,000
MINUS Signing Advance	- $75,000
MINUS Recording Costs for Album One	- $200,000
Advance payable to Artist on Delivery of Album One	$75,000

In this example, the artist gets a total cash advance of $150,000 for the first album. Keep in mind that $350,000 is an above average recording fund for a first album. For subsequent records, a portion (usually ten to twenty percent) of the recording fund is usually paid to the artist in cash just prior to the commencement of recording for the second album. Sometimes labels prefer to pay a portion of the recording fund to the artist in the form of a monthly salary, but I like to get the money in one chunk, thereby allowing the artist to earn interest on the money.

REALITY

At this point, a few words of caution: Unless you have secured a truly incredible deal, do not assume that the advances you draw from your recording funds will afford you the lavish lifestyle you feel you so richly deserve. Let's see how much pocket change you are left with after signing a slightly less robust (yet still above average) major label deal:

Recording Fund for Album One	$250,000
MINUS Recording Costs	- $175,000
Gross Advance to Artist	$75,000

Before you start making your shopping list, please don't forget those who have toiled diligently behind the scenes to get you where you are:

MINUS Legal Fees	- $10,000
MINUS Manager's 20% (of $75,000)	- $15,000
MINUS Business Manager's 5% (of $75,000)	- $3,750
Net Advance to Artist	$46,250

If you are a solo artist, you might be able to live on this for a year or so. Unfortunately, you will also have to pay your hired band members with this money. If "you" are a four person band, a four way split leaves each member with $11,562.50 BEFORE TAXES. Can you live on less than $9,000 a year? Do you like Top Ramen?

Now let's look into how you are going to recoup the advances, recording funds and recoupable costs paid by the record company.

RECORD ROYALTIES

The royalty provision is the most important part of the recording agreement because it dictates just how much money you will make from each record sold. *Record royalties* are the royalties the record company will pay you (or credit to your royalty account against unrecouped prior advances) on the sale of records embodying your performances. You must distinguish record royalties from *mechanical royalties*. Record royalties are paid to the artist playing and singing on the record, while mechanical royalties are paid to the songwriters and publishers of the song on the record. Both royalties are paid on the basis of records sold. In most cases, the artist is also the publisher and songwriter, but this isn't always so. For instance, you may choose to record songs written by another songwriter. In this case, the record company will pay the mechanical royalty for those songs directly to that songwriter's publisher, while the record royalty for your recording of that song will be paid to you. Get the distinction?

As crazy as it may seem, inexperienced attorneys often gloss over the fine points of royalty provisions when negotiating recording agreements. If the advance is high enough and the royalty rate is "in the ballpark," that is good enough for them. Of course, that's not good enough for YOU, dear reader, and by the time you finish this section, you will have a good understanding of how royalties are calculated and why a 10% royalty under one deal may actually put more money in your pocket than an 11% royalty does under another deal.

How much money you put in your pocket at the end of the day depends on three factors:
   ★ The royalty base price of each record
   ★ The royalty rate
   ★ The number of records sold

THE ROYALTY BASE PRICE

In a nutshell, the royalty base price of a record is the suggested retail list price (SRLP) or wholesale price of a particular record, minus packaging costs. Since the wholesale price is generally 1/2 of the SRLP, your royalty rate in a wholesale scheme should be double what it would be under a retail scheme. In light of the fact that only a few major record companies utilize the wholesale price as the royalty base price, we will be using the SRLP for the purposes of exploring record royalties. The SRLP of a particular record varies, but most record companies price their album length records within three ranges, also called *price lines*.

TOP LINE

$15.98 to $17.98 for CDs; $10.98 for cassettes. Nearly all albums comprised of new material are earmarked for initial release in this price range. You can usually get the record company to agree that all of your albums will carry a top line SRLP upon initial release unless you agree otherwise.

MID-LINE & DEVELOPING ARTIST LINE

Mid line albums typically carry an SRLP which is 20% to 30% less than the top line SRLP. The record company and distributor will sometimes move an album from top line to mid line if they feel that they can sell more copies at this price. Some record companies have had success selling albums by new artists at mid line prices, and the logic is simple: A record buyer is more likely to take a chance on a record by a new artist if the price is relatively low.

BUDGET LINE

Budget line albums typically carry an SRLP which is 30% to 50% less than the top line SRLP. This is where old albums go when they stop selling at the mid line price.

Ultimately, the SRLP of an album is determined by the people in the sales and marketing departments at the record company. If you want to see the SRLPs for the top selling albums in the country, take a look at the Top 200 in *Billboard Magazine*. The retail price for the cassette and CD is listed in parentheses just to the right of the record company name.

PACKAGING DEDUCTIONS

The record company makes you cover the cost of the packaging of each record. They achieve this by reducing the SRLP by a percentage. Typical major label packaging deductions are 25% for CDs, 20% for cassettes and anywhere from 10% to 20% for vinyl albums. Of course, the packaging of a standard CD costs nowhere near $4.25 (25% of $16.98), but (once again) the record companies are greedy and this deal point is non-negotiable, so settle down.

THE ROYALTY RATE

As with any other material deal term, what you get depends on your bargaining power. For new artists, most major record companies will initially offer a 12% or 13% "all in" base royalty rate on albums. "All in" means that any record royalties you are obligated to pay a producer, musician or other royalty participant are your problem and must come out of this "all in" royalty. More on this later. The base royalty rate applies to top line U.S. retail sales. Your royalty rate for all sales that do not fall into this category will probably be reduced (more on this in a second). If you are a new artist involved in a "bidding war," you can expect to secure a base album royalty rate in the 14% to 18% range. Royalty rates for established platinum or multi-platinum artists can creep into the 20% to 22% range. If you haven't sold any records and only one record company wants to sign you, take what you can get. I would try to get at least 12% in any event. The royalty rate on singles and EPs usually hovers around 60% to 80% of the base album royalty rate.

ROYALTY RATE INCREASES

Record companies often agree to increase your U.S. base album royalty rate in two different ways: First, the base royalty rate on a particular album may increase as certain sales plateaus are reached. For example, most record companies willingly grant artists 1/2% escalations at U.S. retail sales of 500,000 albums and 1,000,000 albums. Assuming you have a base album royalty rate of 13% with the 1/2% escalation I just mentioned, and assuming that the record company manages to sell 2,000,000 copies of this album, you will be paid 13% on the first 500,000 copies sold, 13 1/2% on copies 500,001 to 1,000,000, and 14% on every copy thereafter. In addition to sales-based escalations, the base album royalty rate may increase with each album you release. For example, the base album royalty rate on your second album might start at 14% instead of 13%, while the base album royalty rate for your third album may start at 14 1/2%, and so on.

MULTIPLE RECORD ROYALTIES

The base royalty rate only applies to "single" albums. If your album is so long that it requires a second (or third) CD or LP, you have released a "multiple record album" and your contract may specify a different royalty rate. The royalty rate for a multiple record album generally depends on the royalty base price of the multiple record album. If your new album is a two CD set and the SRLP is two times the normal top line SRLP, your royalty rate will probably be the same. However, a $34.00 SRLP is pretty steep for most retailers and consumers, so record companies tend to sell multiple record albums for less. If this is the case, most record companies use the following formula to calculate your royalty:

> If the SRLP of any Multiple Record Album is less than twice the highest top line price, then the applicable royalty rate for such Multiple Record Album will be equal to the otherwise applicable royalty rate multiplied by a fraction, the numerator of which is the SRLP of such Multiple Record Album, and the denominator of which is twice the highest top line price.

Let's assume that your base album royalty is 14% and that your next album is a two CD set. If the SRLP of a top line CD is $16.98, you must set the SRLP of your album at $33.96 to maintain your 14% royalty rate. Of course, your record company will probably decide that this price is too high and that record buyers will balk at this price. Accordingly, you decide to reduce the SRLP to a more reasonable $24.98. What is your royalty?

14% times ($24.98 ÷ $33.96) = 10.3%

COMPILATION ALBUM AND SOUNDTRACK ALBUM ROYALTIES

This is as good a place as any to introduce the concept of *pro-ration* of royalties. At some point in your career, it is inevitable that one of your masters will be released on an album along with masters recorded by other artists. This is called *coupling*. If you only have one master on a soundtrack album or other compilation album, your per record royalty rate depends on the number of masters by other artists on that record. For instance, if one of your masters appears on the soundtrack album to the next Batman movie (and let's hope it does), you or your record company will probably be offered a base royalty of 12% to 14% of the SRLP. That base royalty will be multiplied by a fraction, the numerator of which is one (because you have one master on the album) and the denominator of which is the total number of masters contained on the album. Assuming that you have a 13% royalty and that there are 14 masters total on the album, your royalty will look like this:

13% times (1 ÷ 14) = .93%

The same math generally applies to other kinds of compilation albums, although some record companies will simply dispense with the math and agree to pay you a non-pro-rated royalty rate of one or 1/2 percent per record. Other companies will make it even simpler and simply provide that you will receive 15 or 16 cents per record sold.

Keep in mind that you will probably have to split whatever royalty you end up with 50/50 with your record company if the master in question is released by a record company other than the one you are signed to.

LICENSING OF MASTERS FOR NON-RECORD USE

When your record company licenses one of your masters for use in the soundtrack to a movie, TV show or advertisement (as opposed to a record), they are paid a one-time *master use fee* instead of a royalty. These fees vary depending on your popularity and what kind of use will be made of the master, but the important thing to remember is that you will once again split the royalty with your record company 50/50. We will more fully explore the licensing of masters and songs for movies and TV in Chapter Nine.

VIDEO ROYALTIES

If you start selling some records, your record company may decide to compile the music videos you have made for them on a video cassette, laserdisc, or DVD and sell these to the public through record and video stores. These cassettes and discs are commonly referred to as *home videos*, and for some reason the royalties are calculated in an entirely unique way. In any event, how you are paid depends on whether the home video is released or distributed by your record company or whether the video is licensed to a third party. The royalty rates break out this way:

HOME VIDEOS LICENSED TO THIRD PARTIES

You get 50% of your record company's "net receipts" or "adjusted gross video receipts." See the sample recording agreement in Appendix B to find out what these terms really mean.

HOME VIDEOS SOLD BY YOUR RECORD COMPANY

You will be paid anywhere from 10% to 25% of the wholesale (generally 1/2 of retail) price of the disc or cassette. The royalty rate should increase for more expensive titles. What's a decent royalty rate? If your royalty for lower priced home videos starts at 15% and increases as the prices of the videos increase, you're doing pretty well. In any event, don't kill yourself over this point, inasmuch as home videos aren't huge sellers.

ROYALTY RATE REDUCTIONS:

CDS AND NEW FORMATS

Although the CD is hardly a "new" format, many record companies persist in reducing base album royalty rates for records sold in this format. The reduction is usually around 15% to 20% for CDs and 30% for other "new formats." Let's see what a 15% rate reduction does to your basic 14% royalty rate:

Cassette Royalty Rate	14%
Vinyl Royalty Rate	14%
CD Royalty Rate	11.9%

Why do record companies do this? In the early 1980s, cassette and vinyl were the only viable formats. When CDs came along, no one had any idea that they would become so popular so quickly, and there were no manufacturing plants equipped to make them in the U.S. Accordingly, manufacturing costs for CDs were relatively high compared to cassettes and vinyl. At that time, a royalty rate reduction was reasonable. Unfortunately, when CDs became easy and cheap to manufacture, the record companies resisted raising the royalty rate. This phenomenon is known as "Greed." A reduced royalty rate for CD sales is even more painful in light of the fact that the royalty base price is typically reduced by a 25% packaging deduction. While it is virtually impossible to negotiate around the packaging deduction, some record companies will succumb and pay CD royalties at 100% of the base royalty rate.

Once again, whether or not you get a "100% CD rate" depends on your bargaining power and the company's general royalty policies. I should also mention that some record companies do not pay CD royalties based on the SRLP of the CD. Rather, they create a "special" "CD only" retail price by multiplying or "uplifting" the subdistributor (or "box lot") price of the CD (which ranges from $10.30 to $11.35 these days, depending on the distributor and the retail price of the CD) by a percentage. This percentage can also vary, but it is usually around 120-130%. Assuming that the subdistributor/box lot price of your CD is $10.50 and the "uplift" is 130%, the "CD only" retail price (pre packaging deduction) is $13.65. You can do the math if you like, but suffice it to say that the "uplift" method of computing CD royalties tends to leave the artist with an even lower royalty per unit than the artist would receive under a standard SRLP CD royalty calculation. Why do some record companies employ this bogus "uplift" method of calculating CD royalties? Simple — it confuses novice attorneys and allows the record company to pay you even less. It also allows them to make your attorney feel like he's getting something when he successfully negotiates a "100% CD rate" on your behalf, even though you're getting paid on less than 100% of the CD SRLP. It's a wonderful world, isn't it?

When it comes to "new formats," the going gets a little tougher. As I noted mere moments ago, your recording agreement will likely state that your base royalty rate will be reduced (usually by 30%) on any record sold in a "new format." Of course, most new formats are rejected by the record-buying public and don't sell anyway (just look at the DCC). On the flip side, cassettes and CDs fell into the "new medium" category at one time, and (as you have just learned) most artists are *still* forced to live with lower royalty rates on CD sales. While it is difficult to avoid getting stuck with a reduced royalty on "new format" sales when that "new format" takes over the marketplace, some record companies will agree to a contract provision that increases the royalty on a "new format" if and when the company adopts a "general policy" of paying non-reduced royalties with respect to that format.

FOREIGN SALES

The base royalty applies only to U.S. sales. In almost every deal, the record company will reduce your base royalty rate for sales occurring in territories outside of the U.S. Their argument is that they have to split royalties with companies in the other territories (whether or not the foreign companies are owned by the same parent company as the U.S. label) and that they must pay you less to recoup some of this loss. What can you expect? It varies, but a quick look at a foreign royalty provision from a recent deal I negotiated should give you some idea:

(a) On Records sold for distribution through normal retail channels outside the United States, the royalty rate for such sales shall be the indicated percentage of the base United States album royalty rate for retail sales of Records as provided herein, and shall not escalate:

(1) Canada – 85%
(2) United Kingdom, the countries of the EEC, Australia, New Zealand and Japan – 75%
(3) ROW (rest of the world) – 60%

Note also that your foreign royalty will typically not escalate, even if your deal provides for an escalation of your royalty on U.S. sales. If you don't feel like swallowing these reductions, you can try to strike separate deals for each territory outside of the U.S. However, this means that you will probably receive a smaller advance for your U.S. deal.

RECORD CLUBS

Record clubs license albums from record companies and manufacture their own CDs and cassettes to sell through the mail. Nearly all major label recording agreements provide that your base album royalty rate will be reduced by 50% for the sale of albums through these clubs. To make matters worse, you probably won't get paid on any of the "bonus" CDs the clubs give away (does "Get 12 CDs for $1.00!" ring a bell?). Record clubs piss off record retailers because the record clubs pay only $4 to $5 for a CD, while retail stores must pay $10 or more for CDs, even if purchased in extremely large quantities. Since many people obtain hot-selling records through the record clubs, retailers lose a sure sale.

What can you do about it? Not much, but if you have bargaining power, you can get paid your reduced royalty on 50% of the "bonus" records (instead of the standard 0%) or get 50% of your record company's net receipts instead of a reduced royalty. Some attorneys also like to make the record company withhold any club sales until the date that is nine to twelve months following the release of a record. You should know that a handful of record companies will not license their records to clubs. As I write this, the National Association of Record Merchandisers (NARM) is considering filing anti-trust charges against the clubs, so it will be interesting to see what transpires.

NON-RETAIL SALES & PREMIUMS

Your royalty rate will typically be reduced by 50% for records sold through the mail (such as "K Tel" type records sold via TV campaigns) or as premiums. The royalty base price for these records is usually reduced as well. A "premium" is a record sold in conjunction with an unrelated product. For example, a clothing chain might offer a free CD with the purchase of an item of clothing. This type of program ostensibly serves the dual purpose of enticing the consumer to purchase the clothing while exposing the consumer to the music of a particular artist. Be aware that you can usually get the right to approve any use of your music as a premium..

MID-PRICE & BUDGET REDUCTIONS

No, I am not repeating myself. Record companies reduce your royalty rate on sales of records in these reduced price categories. Typical royalty rate deductions run from 25% for mid-line records to 50% for budget records.

We've covered a lot over the last few pages, so let's recap before we move on. The amount of money you put in your pocket for each record sold depends on three factors:

★ The royalty base price of each record
★ The royalty rate
★ The number of records sold

We just covered the first two, so let's move on to the third item.

THE MEANING OF "SOLD" / SALES BASIS

I hate to be the one to break the bad news to you, but you are not going to get paid on every record you sell. Rather, you will be paid on "Net Sales" of records. Most record contracts define Net Sales as follows:

> "Net Sales" means sales of Records paid for and not returned, less returns and credits, after deduction of reserves against anticipated returns and credits.

Before we get into this, do not assume that Net Sales = 100% of sales. Some companies (A&M, Island and Atlantic come to mind) only pay royalties on 90% of the records they sell. This brilliant idea was borne out of the fact that old shellac records tended to break during shipment. Although no such "breakage" occurs in 1999, these record companies continue to pay on 90% of actual sales. Say hello to our old friend greed! If this really sticks in your craw, get your "pennies" somewhere else in the deal — make the record company raise your base royalty rate by 10%. Alternatively, if the CD rate is 90% or less, make the record company raise it by 10% (of course, this won't help your royalty rate on cassettes or vinyl, but it's better than nothing).

FREE GOODS AND PROMOTIONAL COPIES

There are two kinds of free goods: regular free goods and special free goods. Regular free goods are the records that the record companies give to retailers at no cost as a way to induce them to stock your record. For example, if Joe retailer wants 100 Lawn Chocolate CDs, the distributor will give him 100 but only charge him for 85 — a 15% discount. Since the other 15 copies are technically not paid for, they are not deemed sold for the purposes of computing your royalties. The record company avoids paying royalties on regular free goods in one of two ways: 1) They deduct 15% from your Net Sales (which, as we have seen, may be 90% or 100% of actual sales) as a "free goods allowance"; or 2) They agree to take no free goods allowance, but instead simply pay you on only 85% of Net Sales at the outset. Either way, the numbers come out the same. What can you do about it? Make sure that the record company is not allowed to take a regular free goods allowance greater than 15% of albums distributed and 23% of singles distributed. The same amount is deducted regardless of whether such discounting actually takes place, so don't think that your record company will reduce the free goods deduction just because they didn't actually give a discount to the retailers.

In addition to regular free goods, companies will also ask that you accept additional deductions for special free goods. These special free goods are sold at a substantial discount to the retailer for "sales programs of limited duration" and the idea here is that if the retailer can make 10% more selling your record than he can selling another record, he will stock more of your records and put them in a highly visible location in his store. While attorneys customarily ask for and receive contractual provisions that limit special free goods programs, many record companies are asking artists to let them have more latitude when it comes to special free goods programs (especially for CD singles). Many record companies feel that these programs are necessary to break a new artist because retail shelf space is scarce and the competition for that shelf space is so fierce.

PROMOTIONAL COPIES

Promotional copies are the records that are given away to DJs, writers and taste makers. These records are usually "drilled" or stamped with PROMOTIONAL so that they cannot be returned to retailers for credit (this would be theft, but it still happens). Since these records are not sold, you don't get paid a royalty on them. This makes sense since the record company isn't making a profit either. Unfortunately, a large number of promotional copies end up in "used" bins at mom and pop record stores. This totally screws the artist and songwriter (not to mention the record company), of course, since there are no royalties payable on these copies. But hey, that's life . . .

RESERVES AND RETURNS

Do you ever wonder what record stores do with the records they can't sell? They return them to the distributor. The record companies and their distributors have to accept *returns* to ensure that they can get enough records into the stores to meet demand and to develop new artists. Otherwise, record stores would only stock titles by artists that are established sellers and they wouldn't take chances on new artists. The return privileges granted to retailers put the record companies in a difficult position: On the one hand, they don't know if the records they have shipped out are actually sold or if they will be returned; on the other hand, they are contractually obligated to pay royalties to their artists every six months.

Allow me to illustrate: Let's say the record company ships out 10,000 copies of your record. Six months pass, and it's time to pay royalties (we'll assume that your royalty account is in a recouped position and that there are no free goods for the purposes of this example). Assuming that zero records have been returned, the company is obligated to pay you royalties as if all 10,000 copies have been sold. The company dutifully sends you a royalty check for sales of 10,000 copies. Four months later, 5,000 copies of your record are returned to the record company. Congratulations — the record company overpaid you. Since there is no way in hell any record company can convince an artist like you to promptly return any overpayment of royalties, the concept of *reserves* was born. A reserve is the retention of a portion of royalties otherwise payable to the artist in anticipation of returns. Let's revisit the previous example, but this time let's assume that instead of paying you royalties on 10,000 records, the record company maintains a 50% royalty reserve and sends you a check for sales of 5,000 records. Because of the reserve, there is no overpayment when 5,000 records are returned. Let's look at the same example yet again, but this time assume that only 1,000 copies have been returned. If the record company has maintained a 50% reserve, you have been underpaid. Is there a way to keep you and the record company happy in this situation? Not really, but you want the reserve to be as low as possible, and you also want the record company to pay you the reserved royalties (to the extent that the records have not actually been returned, of course) within two years after the reserve was first maintained. This is called "liquidation" of the reserve. In the case of new artists, record companies like to allow themselves the right to maintain "reasonable reserves." This will most likely lead the record company to maintain a reserve of 50% or more. If you have a proven track record or a little bargaining power, you can usually get the record company to agree not to exceed a fixed reserve of 30% or so.

SOUNDSCAN®

The advent of SoundScan® has made it much easier to estimate how many records have actually sold. SoundScan® is a computerized system installed at most record retailers in the U.S. which allows record companies to get weekly printouts of the sale of any record with a UPC code. When you hear someone at a record company say a record has "scanned 300,000 copies," that means that at least 300,000 records have actually been sold to consumers. In fact, if a record has "scanned" 300,000 copies, it is very likely that it has sold more copies than that, simply because not all record stores are equipped to report sales to SoundScan®. Nevertheless, the availability of this incredibly accurate information makes it harder for record companies to justify a large royalty reserve.

Case in point — about two years ago, I received a royalty statement for one of my artists. According to SoundScan®, this artist had sold approximately 500,000 copies of its latest record in the period covered by the accounting statement. Nevertheless, the record company maintained a 50% royalty reserve on this statement, because the prior albums by this artist did not sell nearly as well. I placed a call to the head of business affairs at the label, pointed out the SoundScan® figures, and the reserve was immediately liquidated. It turns out that the band's original record deal (which was negotiated by another attorney years ago) did not place a limit on reserves. Naturally, the record company decided to maintain a 50% reserve, even though the record was selling like hot cakes. The moral of this story is as follows: While you may not be able to place a limit on reserves, you should ask the record company to immediately liquidate reserves to the extent that SoundScan® shows that records have been sold. They probably won't go for this, but it's worth a shot.

HOW MANY PENNIES PER RECORD?

Now that you know how the royalty base price, royalty rate and sales basis are determined, let's run through some hypothetical royalty/sales scenarios.

EXAMPLE 1 – Let's assume that you have 15% base album royalty rate with a 25% packaging deduction and a 15% CD royalty rate reduction. Also assume that your record company uses the SRLP of the CD for the purposes of computing your CD royalties, and that the SRLP of the CD is $16.98. Assume that your record company has "sold" 100,000 copies of your album.

$16.98	SRLP of Album-Length CD
- $4.25	25% Packaging Deduction for CD
$12.73	ROYALTY BASE PRICE
15%	Base Album Royalty Rate
- 2.25%	15% CD Rate Reduction
=12.75%	Your Adjusted Royalty Rate for CD Albums

$12.73 x 12.75% = $1.62 PAYABLE TO YOU PER ALBUM SOLD

100,000	CDs sold
- 15,000	Minus 15% regular free goods
85,000	NET RECORDS "SOLD"

85,000	
x $1.62	
$137,700	Gross Royalty Payable
- $41,310	Reserve (30%)
$96,390	NET ROYALTY CREDITED TO YOUR ACCOUNT

EXAMPLE 2 – Assume the same facts as in Example 1, with two exceptions: There is no CD royalty rate reduction, and royalties are paid on 90% of album sales.

$16.98	SRLP of CD
- $4.25	25% Packaging Deduction for CD
$12.73	ROYALTY BASE PRICE

15%	Base Royalty Rate
- 0%	No CD Rate Reduction
15%	YOUR NET ROYALTY RATE

$12.73 x 15% = $1.91 PAYABLE TO YOU PER ALBUM SOLD

100,000	CDs sold
- 15,000	Minus 15% regular free goods
85,000	Gross Sales
- 8,500	Minus 10% (90% Sales Basis)
76,500	NET RECORDS "SOLD"
x $1.91	
$146,115.00	Gross Royalty Payable
- $ 43,834.50	Reserve (30%)
$102,280.50	NET ROYALTY CREDITED TO YOUR ACCOUNT

The foregoing examples should illustrate that not all royalty rates are created equal (even when they appear to be equal!). Now just for kicks, let's take the royalties you earned under Example 2 and see how your royalty statement might look after the record company has spent some money on you:

$102,280.50	NET ROYALTY CREDITED TO YOUR ACCOUNT
- $250,000	ADVANCES & RECORDING COSTS
- $100,000	50% OF COST OF TWO VIDEOS
- $50,000	50% OF COST OF INDEPENDENT PROMOTION
- $75,000	TOUR SUPPORT
- $372,719.50	**YOUR TOTAL UNRECOUPED BALANCE**

You sold 100,000 records (which is not bad at all) and yet you are unrecouped by nearly half a million dollars. Keep in mind that it could be worse — these examples don't take producer royalties into account, and most major labels spend at least $500,000 when they really want to "push" a record. Don't quit your day job.

ACCOUNTING / AUDITS

Most major record companies send you statements which indicate the royalties credited to your account and recoupable expenses racked up for each semi-annual period of the year (January through June and July through December) within 90 days following the end of each semi-annual period. Make sure that your contract specifies that these statements are sent to your attorney as well as your accountant or business manager. If your advisors think there is something wrong with your statement, they may advise you to conduct an *audit*. An audit involves a meticulous review (usually by a CPA trained in these matters) of the record company's books and records pertaining to the sale of your records. While most record companies will allow you to conduct such an audit, they will limit your rights in the following ways:

1) You must give at least 30 days written notice prior to the commencement of an audit;

2) The audit must be conducted at a time and place agreeable to both parties;

3) You may audit a particular statement only once;

4) The audit must be conducted within one to three years (it's negotiable) following your receipt of the statement concerned; and

5) The audit must be conducted by an attorney or CPA.

The time limit referred to in item 4 is the most heavily negotiated aspect of the accounting provision in a recording agreement, and for good reason. If you do not conduct an audit of a particular statement within the specified time limit, most recording contracts specify that you will not be able to sue the record company for unpaid royalties that may be discovered by an audit of that statement. In other words — you snooze, you usually lose.

MECHANICAL ROYALTIES / CONTROLLED COMPOSITIONS

You already know a little about mechanical royalties from reading Chapter Two. If you haven't read it, please go back and do so now. Mechanical royalties are the royalties payable by the record company to the publishers of the songs which have been "mechanically reproduced" on a record. Accordingly, in order to distribute your records in the U.S. and Canada, the record company must obtain a mechanical license for every song you record on a record, whether or not you are the writer or publisher of that song. Problem: As we discussed in Chapter Two, record companies do not like to pay mechanical royalties at the full statutory rate and find the task of obtaining compulsory mechanical licenses from the government cumbersome and costly. Solution: The *controlled composition* and the *controlled composition clause*.

CONTROLLED COMPOSITION CLAUSE

A controlled composition is typically defined as a musical composition written or controlled, in whole or in part, by the artist signed to the recording agreement. Some record companies will also deem songs written or controlled by your producer as controlled compositions. Every recording agreement contains a controlled composition clause that specifies the terms upon which you will be obligated to license your controlled compositions to the record company. Invariably, these clauses allow the record company to pay your publisher less on controlled compositions than they would have to if they had to get a compulsory mechanical license for each composition. Let's look at the key components of a standard controlled composition clause:

1) The mechanical rate payable on controlled compositions will NOT be the U.S. statutory rate at the time the record is distributed. Rather, the rate will be *75% of the minimum* statutory rate in effect *at the time of delivery* of the master recording embodying the controlled composition. This simple language reduces the mechanical royalties you might otherwise be paid in three ways:

75% – Right off the bat, you are getting 5.33 cents per song and NOT 7.1 cents. Why 75%? Just another way to pay you less. If you have bargaining power, you can increase this "controlled rate" all the way up to 100%. As a compromise, try getting the record company to increase the rate as your record sells more copies. For instance, you might negotiate an 87.5% rate for every copy sold between five hundred thousand copies and one million copies, and a 100% rate for every copy of that record sold thereafter. This is a deal point most record companies do not like to compromoise on, but they seem to be a bit softer on it these days.

<u>Minimum</u> **statutory rate** – I highlighted the word minimum because of the so-called "long song" provision found in the Copyright Act. As we know, the statutory rate as I write this is 7.1 cents for each song or *1.35 cents per minute of playing time (including fractions of a minute), whichever is greater.* The record companies don't want to deal with long song formulas, and they certainly don't want to pay your publisher higher mechanical royalties just because your songs are lengthy, so this language eliminates the long song problem. This provision is difficult to get around, so focus on increasing the controlled rate instead.

at the time of delivery – Guess what? If and when the statutory rate increases, your mechanical royalties won't. As you know, the statutory rate is increased from time to time to reflect the increase in the cost of living. Of course, the record companies don't care about your petty problems, so they *freeze* your rate at the rate in effect on a pre-negotiated date. This date is typically the date of *delivery* of your completed album (or the last date the album should have been delivered under the contract if it is late). Accordingly, if the rate increases by 500% in ten years, you will still be paid mechanicals based on the rate in effect when you delivered your record, no matter when the records are sold. This makes me feel kind of bad for some songwriters who are still being paid only 2 cents per song (the rate from 1909 until 1977). The best you can hope for (unless you are a superstar) is that the record company will base your rate on the statutory rate in effect at the time of initial *U.S. release* of the record embodying the controlled compositions. This may seem a like small victory, but if your record sits on the shelf for any appreciable amount of time prior to release, the rate may well have increased in the meantime.

2) Instead of paying mechanical royalties on all records distributed, the record company will pay only on *records "sold" and not returned*. Unfortunately, "sold" has the same meaning when it comes to mechanical royalties as it does with respect to record royalties. Fortunately, most record companies will agree to pay mechanical royalties on 50% of album length free goods if you have some bargaining power.

3) No matter how many songs are on your album, the record company will pay mechanical royalties on a *maximum* of ten or eleven songs (whether or not they are controlled compositions). We call this a *cap* on mechanicals. Thus, if your album has thirteen controlled compositions, and your controlled composition clause says you only get paid a 75% controlled rate on a maximum of ten controlled compositions per album, your publisher will be paid about 4 cents per controlled composition and not the 5.33 cents per composition you would get if you had a 13-song cap. The total mechanical royalty payable per record (53.25 cents) would be the same whether you have 10 or 20 songs on your record. The cap for singles is usually two or three and the cap for EPs is usually four or five.

4) Noncontrolled compositions can kill you. Let's say your album has ten compositions, seven of which are controlled compositions. The other three songs are *noncontrolled compositions* (songs written by a person not signed to your record contract). The publisher of the noncontrolled compositions does not have to issue mechanical licenses to the record company on the same onerous terms that you do. In fact, you know from reading Chapter Two that the publisher doesn't have to issue you a mechanical license at all unless a record embodying the composition in question has been commercially released. Let's assume that the publishers of the noncontrolled compositions agree to issue mechanical licenses, but at 100% of the minimum statutory rate. Let's do some quick math:

7 Controlled Compositions at 75% of the minimum statutory rate – (7 x 5.33)	37.31 cents
3 Noncontrolled Compositions at 100% of the minimum statutory rate – (3 x 7.1)	21.30 cents
Total Mechanical Royalties Payable by Record Company	58.61 cents

Since the controlled compositions clause of your recording agreement stipulates that the record company is obligated to pay mechanical royalties on a *maximum* of ten compositions at a 75% rate (53.3 cents) you are short by 5.31 cents. Guess who pays the difference? That's right, YOU do. Since you just HAD to record those noncontrolled compositions, the record company is going to *deduct the amount of excess mechanical royalties payable with respect to noncontrolled compositions from the mechanical royalties which would have otherwise been paid to you.* Thus, in this example, you will be paid on a per composition rate of approximately 4.57 cents. Remember when this was 7.1 cents? How can you avoid this problem? Don't record noncontrolled compositions. This won't be much of a problem if you write your own material, but almost everyone records a cover or writes a song with someone else at some point. Otherwise, you can try to get the record company to increase your "cap" to 12 or 13. Finally, try to get a provision in your controlled composition clause that allows you to include as many noncontrolled compositions as possible without reducing your mechanicals. We call this "protection." For instance, if the record company gives you *"protection"* on up to two noncontrolled compositions per album, this means that you can include two noncontrolled compositions on your album (even if the record company has to pay mechanicals on these compositions at 100% of the statutory rate) without cutting into your mechanical royalties.

OTHER REDUCED MECHANICAL ROYALTY SITUATIONS:

MULTIPLE VERSIONS ON ONE RECORD

If you put different mixes or versions of the same composition on a record (as many artists do these days, especially on 12" vinyl or CD singles) the record company will only pay mechanicals on the composition once.

VIDEOS

Record companies don't want to pay mechanical royalties on controlled compositions embodied in home videos (videotapes, laserdiscs or DVDs). Some record companies will offer a one-time flat fee of $500-$1,000 in lieu of the standard per-unit mechanical royalty, but you should try to get a per unit royalty, even if it's only a few cents per composition for every video sold. Then again, don't kill yourself over this, since music videos don't really sell in big numbers.

MID PRICE / BUDGET / RECORD CLUB SALES

As we discussed, the record company charges less for these records, so in addition to paying a reduced record royalty, they will ask you to accept a further reduction on your mechanicals, usually in the form of reducing the 75% rate by an additional 25%. This leaves your mechanical royalty rate at a little over 50% of the statutory rate.

COMPOSITIONS SHORTER THAN ONE MINUTE

Some record companies refuse to pay mechanical royalties on songs that are less than one minute long. I don't know why this is so, but it shouldn't be a problem unless you write a lot of really short songs.

MULTIPLE RECORD ALBUMS

If you release a multiple record album, the retail price of that album will be higher (as will the record company's profit). However, just because you have a 10 or 11 song cap on mechanicals for single record albums, don't assume that your cap will increase to 20 or 22 songs on double albums. In situations such as these, the record company will likely increase your cap in proportion to the increase in the retail price of the multiple record album. The record company will multiply your per album cap (let's say it's 10) times a fraction, the numerator of which is the retail price of the multiple album in question (let's say $22.98 for a double CD) and the denominator of which is the record company's "then prevailing retail price" for company's newly released top line single albums (let's say $16.98 for a single CD). Let's (once again) do the math:

$$\$22.98 \div \$16.98 = 1.35 \text{ times } 10 = 13.53$$

Thus, you will get paid on 13.53 compositions on your double CD instead of 10.

HOW AND WHEN ARE MECHANICAL ROYALTIES PAYABLE?

CROSS-COLLATERALIZATION

You already know that you won't receive record royalty payments until you have recouped your advances, recording costs and other recoupable expenses. Conversely, most record companies will not cross-collateralize your mechanical royalties against the unrecouped balance of your record royalty account. In other words, mechanical royalties are typically payable to you from the first record sold (or "from record one," as we like to say). Let's look at an example. Assume that you have sold 100,000 copies of your album, and that you wrote all of the songs on the album. Also assume that you are unrecouped by $500,000 (from advances, recording costs, tour support, etc.) You will receive two separate accounting statements from the record company – one for record royalties, and one for mechanical royalties. They will look something like this:

RECORD ROYALTY STATEMENT

$150,000 – Record royalties on 100,000 albums sold
-$500,000 – Advances, recording costs, tour support, etc.
Record royalties payable: $0

You don't get a check until your royalties exceed the unrecouped balance. In this case, you need to earn another $350,000 in royalties before you will see a check.

MECHANICAL ROYALTY STATEMENT

$53,250.00 – Mechanical royalties on 100,000 albums sold

Mechanical royalties payable: $53,250.00

In the foregoing example, your record royalty account is still in the red, and the record company may still be losing money on you, yet they have to write you a check for $53,250 in mechanical royalties. Now you can see why record companies love to reduce mechanical royalty payments as much as possible. Keep in mind that if you have signed a publishing deal, your co-publisher will be entitled to recoup these mechanical royalties against the advance it paid to you, but we'll get into this in Chapter Six.

EXCEPTIONS

There's always a catch. Your recording agreement will probably allow the record company to apply (cross-collateralize) your mechanical royalties against your unrecouped record royalty account under certain circumstances, so let's look at a few of them:

OVER BUDGET

If you manage to spend more on your album than your recording agreement allows, most record companies will cover this "overage," but they will penalize you by applying any mechanical royalties which would have otherwise been payable to you against this overage. Here's how it works:

Final recording costs for album	$250,000
Amount budgeted for recording	- $200,000
Overage – paid by record company	$50,000
Record royalties on 100,000 albums sold	$150,000
Mechanical royalties on 100,000 albums sold	$53,250
Minus overage – paid by record company	- $50,000
Record royalties payable (unrecouped)	$0
Mechanical royalties payable	$3,250

Do you see what happened? Since you exceeded your recording budget by $50,000 the record company applied your mechanical royalties to the overage until it was paid off, leaving you with a measly $3,250. Possible ways to avoid this calamity: Before you exceed your recording budget, check to see if you have enough money left in your recording fund to pay the overage. If not, ask the record company to send you a letter stipulating that they will not cross-collateralize your mechanical royalties in any event. Of course, they don't have to do this, so you are pretty much at their mercy.

NONCONTROLLED COMPOSITIONS

We already discussed this. If the mechanical royalties payable on your album exceed the maximum allowed under your recording agreement, the excess will come out of your mechanical royalties and/or your record royalties.

SCUMBAG RECORD COMPANY

Some record companies (usually shady independent labels) will cross-collateralize your mechanical royalties with your unrecouped record royalty account balance even if the prior two exceptions do not apply. This is totally uncool and you should not sign any deal that allows the record company to do so.

ACCOUNTING

Most major record companies will account for mechanical royalties owed within forty-five days following the end of each calendar quarter. Contrast this with record royalty accountings which take place only twice per year.

CANADA

The record company will need mechanical licenses to sell your records in Canada as well. Most agreements provide that your mechanical royalties will be based on the Canadian statutory mechanical rate. The current rate established by the Canadian Musical Reproduction Rights Agency (CMRRA) is 7.1 cents per song where the playing time per song is five minutes or less. For each additional minute (or part therof) 1.42 cents is added to the rate. The same reductions and restrictions applicable to your U.S. mechanical royalties will apply to your Canadian mechanical royalties.

FOREIGN TERRITORIES

Our entire discussion thus far applies only to the U.S. and Canada. Elsewhere, record companies pay mechanical royalties to local mechanical rights collection societies. These societies retain the royalties until you or your publisher makes arrangements with the society to collect the royalties. Outside the U.S. and Canada, mechanical royalties are based on the retail selling price of a record or the published price to dealers (PPD). For instance, if the mechanical rate in the European Union is 9.01% of the PPD, and the PPD for an album is $15.00, the mechanical royalty payable on that album is $1.35. In any event, there's nothing to negotiate on this point in your record deal, so we'll cover this topic in greater depth in Chapter Six.

CREATIVE CONTROL & THE RECORDING PROCESS

Most new artists seem to believe that the record making process goes something like this:

STEP 1 – Artist signs recording agreement.
STEP 2 – Record company hands over check for $200,000 and tells artist to come back with a great record in three months.
STEP 3 – Artist delivers great record.
STEP 4 – Record company loves record and releases it.
STEP 5 – Record sells millions and everyone gets rich.

It just doesn't work that way, my friends. When entering into contract negotiations with a major record company, keep in mind that *the record company will try to exert as much influence over the record-making process as possible.* Why? Because your record company doesn't want you to hand in a three hour, one song tribute to John Cage produced by your plumber and recorded on a Fisher-Price cassette recorder, that's why. Okay, that's an extreme example, but since I am assuming that most of you want the record company to have as little influence as possible, you must address creative control issues in your recording agreement. The extent to which you are able to get creative control written into your recording agreement depends (once again) on your bargaining power. Let's take a look at the major creative control issues addressed in recording agreements.

CHOICE OF PRODUCER/MIXER

Record companies will want the right to approve your choice of producer. If you have bargaining power, you may be able to choose the producer or self-produce your records with the approval of the record company. The most common compromise is *mutual approval.* Under this arrangement, you can choose your producer, but the record company can veto your choice, and vice versa. This can result in months of back and forth until the two of you agree on someone.

RECORDING STUDIO/LOCATION OF STUDIO

The record company will usually approve just about any legitimate "First Class" recording studio, so don't sweat this too much.

SELECTION OF SONGS TO BE RECORDED

This is an often overlooked yet vitally important deal point, but not for the reasons you might think. Presumably, you like your songs, and the ones you don't like you won't play for the record company. However, you don't want the record company telling you to record a cover if you think it's lame (and believe me, plenty of artists have been forced to do this). Also, you don't want them telling you that you can't go into the studio to make your next record because "your songs aren't ready." If the record company has the contractual right to approve the songs to be recorded, they can use this to keep you out of the studio indefinitely, even if your songs are perfectly good. I should add that even if you have the right to designate the songs to be recorded, most recording agreements will require you to record new songs written by you, recorded in a studio (no live albums, please) and not previously recorded by you. They will also forbid you from delivering an entire album of covers, instrumentals or "seasonal" songs (e.g. Christmas or Hanukkah songs). You can live with the "live" and "seasonal" restrictions, but fight like hell to choose what songs you record.

RECORDING BUDGET APPROVAL

The recording budget specifies exactly how much you intend to spend making your record, from pre-production through mastering. The record company will try to make sure you don't budget too much or too little of your recording fund. It also wants to make sure that you aren't getting ripped off and that you are complying with all of the musicians union regulations (see the sample recording agreement and recording budget in Appendix B for more info on unions). You can usually get the record company to pre-approve any budget that doesn't exceed 80% of the available recording fund, provided all of the other non-monetary budget elements are in order. They want to make sure you have left a reasonable buffer for mastering and any unexpected costs, such as remixing.

TECHNICALLY SATISFACTORY VS.
COMMERCIALLY SATISFACTORY MASTERS

This is very important. In 1975, a guy named Lou Reed delivered an album entitled *Metal Machine Music* to RCA Records. If you haven't heard it, this two record set consists primarily of amplifier feedback and other noises. Although many claim to love this record, it apparently didn't thrill RCA too much, and for good reason: it bears no resemblance to *Sally Can't Dance* or *Rock and Roll Animal* (Reed's prior studio LPs) and people tend not to buy records of this ilk (although they *do* tend to buy records that suck far more than *MMM*, of course). In response to such "groundbreaking" and "innovative" recordings like *Metal Machine Music,* record companies began requiring that artists deliver *technically* and *commercially* satisfactory recordings. The technically satisfactory part is easy enough to deal with — just make sure that your recordings are properly recorded and EQd and you should be fine. So what does commercially satisfactory mean? It means that the label thinks that there is some possibility that it will sell. I got a good laugh recently whilst arguing with an A&R person at a certain major label regarding the "commerciality" of a certain batch of recordings. He claimed that the recordings were not commercially satisfactory. However, when I pointed out that he had bought more records in his lifetime than any of his signings had sold, he realized that he had never, in fact, demonstrated any ability to determine whether or not a record is in fact "commercial." Defeated, he agreed to release my client's record.

That's a funny story (I think), but the problem here is that the record company can use this subjective "not commercial" argument any time it wants to keep you out of the studio or reject a record you have turned in, even if your songs are perfectly good. This can lead to the termination of your contract. Nevertheless, I understand that record companies can't do much with *Metal Machine Music*-type records, so if negotiations on this point reach a stalemate, I will usually agree to a substitute provision that requires the artist to "use good faith efforts" to deliver commercially satisfactory masters. This just means that you can't intentionally record and deliver "non-commercial" masters. To address this problem, some record companies put language in their recording agreements which requires artists to deliver recordings "reasonably consistent in style to artist's prior recordings." This means that a speed metal band can't shift gears and suddenly turn in a country record. We can probably thank good ol' Neil Young for this clause. In 1981, Neil left Reprise Records and signed a new deal with Geffen Records. Geffen expected Neil to deliver "classic Neil Young type" records. Neil had other ideas. Let's quickly review the first three records Neil delivered to Geffen:

Trans – a record featuring extensive use of synthesizers and the vocoder — not
    exactly Neil's trademark sound..
Everybody's Rockin' – a "rockabilly" record.
Old Ways – a very subdued country record.

Geffen got so pissed off by Neil's new-found eclecticism that they actually sued Neil Young for not acting (or recording) like Neil Young! The case was eventually settled, whereupon Neil returned to Reprise and started making "classic Neil Young type" records again.

MERCHANDISING

We haven't talked about this yet, but when I use the term merchandising, I am referring to the use of your name(s), logos and likenesses in connection with t-shirts, hats, posters and the like. We call this stuff "merch" for short. Merchandising is covered in greater detail in Chapter Seven, but for now you should know that some record companies will attempt to take your merchandising rights in your record contract. Do not allow the record company to use your name, likeness or logo for any purpose other than selling and promoting your records. You can make a great deal of money keeping these rights yourself or selling them to the highest bidder later on. That being said, most record companies will ask for the right to manufacture and distribute a limited amount of shirts, hats and the like for promotional purposes (meaning that they will be given away and not sold). As long as you can approve these items, this is perfectly fine. I should mention that one very large record company will strongly suggest that you give their merchandising company a matching right with respect to your merchandising rights. The concept of a matching right is going to come up again later, so I might as well talk about it now.

Let's say you sign to a record company and they require you to give them a matching right with respect to your merchandising rights. This does not mean that you no longer control your merchandising rights. You may continue to sell your merch yourself as long as you want, but as soon as you decide to open the bidding to third parties, you must give the record company's merch company the right to match the terms of any deal offered by another party. If they refuse to match the other party's offer, you can make the deal with the third party. If not, you have to sign with the record company's merch division or no one at all. I realize that this sounds kind of screwy, and I certainly don't like any provision that restricts your right to sell your merch rights on the open market, but matching rights are only really a problem if the company that has the right to match is a piece of crap.

TERRITORY

Every major label will want to sign you for the entire universe. This means that you will have one record deal which covers every imaginable territory on (and off) the planet. Signing a worldwide deal has its ups and downs, but I am finding that my clients are growing increasingly interested in the idea of signing separate recording agreements in each major territory. There are pros and cons to this approach.

THE UPSIDE

If you sign a universe-wide deal with a U.S. record company, there is a good chance that one or more of the U.S. company's foreign affiliates may not care for or see the commercial potential in your music. If this is the case, it is unlikely that they will release your records. This particular problem can be obviated somewhat if you are able to negotiate a firm release commitment for the territory in question (we'll cover this topic next), but wouldn't you really rather be with a label that is excited to work with you? If you exclude key foreign territories from your U.S. deal, you have a better chance of making this happen, because you can then make separate deals with companies who give a shit. Another advantage to making separate deals in each territory concerns your record royalties. If you recall, U.S. labels typically reduce your base royalty for sales of records outside of the U.S. If you sign directly to a separate label in each territory, you won't have to accept a reduced royalty, because there is no "middleman" label.

Finally, none of the separate deals you strike will be cross-collateralized against each other. For example, let's say you have signed two separate record deals, one covering the U.S. and Canada, and one for the rest of the world. If your record is selling like mad in the U.K. but stiffs in the U.S. despite the fact that the U.S. spent a million dollars promoting the record, you will see royalties from the U.K. despite the fact that you are massively unrecouped in the States. Had you signed a worldwide deal, you would have a single royalty account, and all of your U.K. royalties would be applied against your massive U.S. debt.

THE DOWNSIDE

What are the disadvantages of signing separate deals for each territory? Assuming all territories are available, U.S. record companies are extremely reluctant to sign artists for anything less than the Universe. If you insist, they will either pass on you entirely or pay you much less (depending on the foreign territories you want to "carve" out of the deal). Additionally, multiple record deals mean higher legal and accounting fees for you, since there are multiple deals to negotiate and multiple accounting statements to scrutinize. Some managers and artists also find it a bit cumbersome to deal with multiple record companies, but I would argue that they have to deal with different affiliates and licensees of the U.S. label in different territories even if the artist is signed to a worldwide deal, so what's the difference?

RELEASE COMMITMENTS

Just because you deliver your record on time doesn't mean that the record company has to put it out right away. In fact, unless you negotiate *release commitments*, they can put the record out whenever they want to (or not at all). Since you have a career to think of, here's what you need to get in your deal:

U.S. release within 90 days of delivery – 90 days is just a suggestion. If your record hasn't been released within the specified time period, you send a letter to the record company notifying them of their failure to comply with the agreement, and they then have 30-60 days to effect such release. Note that for the purposes of counting the 90 days, most record companies *do not count the months of October, November and December.* This is because these are tough months to release records by new artists (the companies typically try to release their "superstar" records during the November-December period to take advantage of the massive consumer spending on music during the holidays). Accordingly, if you have a 90-day release commitment and you deliver your record October 15, the record company doesn't really have to release it until April of the following year.

Failure to release in U.S. results in right to repurchase masters and terminate agreement – If your record company fails to release your record even after you wait 90 days and send notice, you have a problem. If they refuse to release it, you'd better hope that your attorney has negotiated a provision whereby the record company must sell you back the record (usually for a sum equal to the actual recording costs) and allow you to terminate the agreement. Otherwise, the record may never see the light of day.

Foreign Release within 90 days of U.S. release – If the territory of your deal extends beyond U.S. borders, you want to be sure that your record actually gets released in these territories.

Failure to release in foreign territories results in reversion of that territory to artist OR triggers right to license record to company of artist's choosing – It's funny: U.S. record companies pretty much demand that the deal extend to the entire universe, yet they don't like to promise that they will release your records in every major foreign territory. Why? Two possibilities: 1) They may feel that your record hasn't got a chance in hell in a certain territory, and they don't want to waste their money putting it out there unless it makes sense. Usually, they will wait until your record goes gold (500,000 copies) in the U.S. before they put it out overseas. In any event, record companies don't like having to deal with strict time limits imposed by foreign release commitment provisions. They will tell you "Hey man, [fill in foreign country of your choice] is a different kind of market – we need time to set this record up properly. Trust me!!" 2) If the foreign affiliate of your U.S. record company really hates your record, the U.S. record company won't force the issue with the foreign affiliate, because they need to be able to count on the foreign affiliate when they hatch their plot to break the next shitty American band worldwide.

In any event, you need to be able to get your records out overseas, so go for the release commitments, and if you can't get the non-release territories to revert to you (meaning that your record deal no longer applies to that territory and that you now own your record there) at least try to get the right to license your records to the label of your choice. Some U.S. record companies have zero presence outside the U.S., so this is very important.

VIDEOS

I am finding that many record companies are not very interested in doing videos for developing artists these days. Let's face it — outside of *120 Minutes*, MTV doesn't really seem that interested in even showing them any more. While the initial playlists of the nascent M2 are promising, it probably won't be long before that channel is running *Singled Out* 24 hours a day. The upshot is that record companies aren't really into spending $100,000 to make a video that gets shown on MTV twice (if at all) and I can't say I don't see their point. However, I still try to get the following provisions in my clients' agreements:

> One or two guaranteed videos per album.
> Minimum budget of at least $50,000 per video.
> Only 50% of video production costs are recoupable from record royalties.
> Artist must approve director and concept of video.

TOUR SUPPORT

Let's say your agent calls and tells you that your band has been offered the opening slot on the next Dave Matthews Band tour for $500 per night. Unfortunately, it will cost your band $1,500 a night to tour, what with the van rental and road crew.

Should you blow off Dave? Hell no! Choice tours like this are hard to get, and your record company knows this. Accordingly, most major record companies would be happy to give you tour support in this situation. Tour support is the term we use to describe the additional advances the record company will (hopefully) give you to help you tour, and it takes two forms:

- Money paid to purchase or lease touring vehicles and equipment; and
- Money paid to you to eliminate the deficit you will incur on your tour (such as the $1,000 per night deficit you will incur opening for Dave).

In the first instance, your record company may agree to give you tour support money before your tour so that you can buy the van and equipment (such as road cases, amplifiers, etc.) you need before touring begins. In the second instance, your record company will most likely want to see a detailed tour itinerary before they cut you a check. Some won't cut you a check until AFTER the tour, and only then if you can document that you lost money. If your tour resulted in a loss of $5,000 (and believe me, that's not bad) they will (hopefully) write you a check for the same amount to bring you back to zero. In any event, *get as much tour support guaranteed in your contract as possible*. If you are a new artist, I think a minimum of $75,000 to $100,000 per album is pretty good.

APPROVALS / MARKETING RESTRICTIONS

Try to get the following provisions in your agreement:

Approval over licensing of masters. – Remember that your record company owns your masters and can do anything it wants with them unless you have the contractual right to veto their plans. Accordingly, ask for the right to approve any license of a master recording for a radio or TV commercial, a movie, a TV show or another record (such as a sampler or a soundtrack album). If you can't get outright approval rights, at least try to get approval when it comes to licenses for more "controversial" uses, such as liquor, tobacco, birth control or feminine hygiene ads and political advertisements. If you strike out completely, keep in mind that any party that wants to use your masters for non-record purposes also needs to get a synchronization license from the publisher of the song embodied in the master. If you wrote the song and you still control the publishing rights (or have the right to veto any licenses in your publishing deal) you essentially have veto rights on non-record use licenses.

"Holdbacks" on sale of your records on Mid Price or Budget price lines – As we discussed earlier, these records sell for less and you are paid a lower royalty on them. While the record company is not likely to reduce the price on your record until sales flatten, you should ask that they not go to Mid Price or Budget price without your consent until at least 18 or 24 months after initial U.S. release of the record at the Top Line price.

Approval over premiums – I bet you vegetarians wouldn't be thrilled to see your next record being given away at Burger World. Plus, you get paid reduced royalties on these records. Accordingly, you should try your best to get absolute approval over any use of your masters on premium records.

Approval of photographs, likenesses and biographies – During the term of your contract, the record company will have the exclusive right to use your name, photograph, likeness and biography in connection with the sale of records. We've all seen horrendous promo photos and read inane biographies, so why not get the contractual right to approve them before they are sent out to the public? Most record companies will ask you to submit photos and bios you like, while others will submit the same to you for your approval. Either way, you generally only have five days to approve or disapprove before the record company interprets your silence as approval and does whatever it wants, so be prompt.

No exploitation of demos, outtakes or live recordings without your consent – Demos are recordings you make to get signed or to play for your A&R person before you go into make "master quality" recordings. They are not usually intended for commercial release, although the quality of inexpensive recording equipment has improved so dramatically in recent years that demos often find their way onto "proper" albums. Outtakes are masters recorded for possible commercial release that are left off the record for one reason or another. Your demos or outtakes may be genius or they may suck to high heaven, but you don't want the record company putting them out without getting your permission. This will come in very handy when you become hugely successful and move to another label. When this happens, your former label will scour the vaults for every shred of tape in the hopes of rushing out a shoddy and shameless "compilation" record. You can foil those greedy bastards if you get the right to approve such uses in the first place.

Approval over album cover artwork – You want this regardless of whether you are interested in actually creating or assisting in the creation of the album cover. To reiterate, all art preparation costs should be paid for by the record company on a 100% non-recoupable basis.

Selection of "B" sides of singles & EPs – Why not?

Sequencing of masters on album – A&R people tend to want to put all of the "hits" up front. You might have other ideas.

GREATEST HITS / COMPILATION ALBUMS

You may be shocked to learn that absent a contractual prohibition to the contrary, your record company can put out as many "Greatest Hits" or "B Sides and Outtakes" records as they want to. While you may welcome this, some companies really milk it. At the very least, try to limit the record company to two such records overall. You may also want to only allow the release of one such record during the term of your agreement. In any case, they will often ask for the right to require you to deliver one or two new recordings to make the album more appealing to buyers. This is fine as long as they make the following promises (the dollar figures are just suggestions):

★ Advance of $50,000 for each new master.

★ Advance of $250,000 upon release of any greatest hits or compilation album.

★ Royalties – Try to get the highest royalty possible, perhaps linking the royalty for the Greatest Hits album to the highest royalty achieved by any of your regular albums

★ Mechanical Royalties – Try to get the *current* mechanical rate to apply (and not the rate in effect when the master was first released)

★ Approval of masters to be included on the album

INDEPENDENT RADIO PROMOTION / PUBLICITY

The radio promotion and publicity departments at some record companies may not be to your liking, or they may be overwhelmed with twenty other releases. This is where the independents come in. Independent radio promotion is crucial these days, and it doesn't come cheap. If you are leery of your label's chances of scoring you a hit record, make them commit to spending money on an indie radio promoter (although they probably will anyway). Publicity is also a highly specialized area. While the label's publicist may be diligent and well intentioned, there are several indies that kick ass and can deliver key magazine interviews and television appearances that in-house publicists cannot. (In defense of label publicists, the opposite is often true.) Indie publicists cost money too, so get it in writing. Most record companies will treat any monies spent on indie promoters and publicists as 100% recoupable, but you can usually get this reduced to 50% if you ask.

OWNERSHIP OF MASTERS

The majority of recording agreements stipulate that the record company owns the copyright in and to the master recordings you create during the term of your agreement. Remember that masters are called sound recordings for the purposes of U.S. copyright law. There will be a page or two of language in your agreement which states that the record company owns the copyright to the masters because you are their employee and/or the masters are works made for hire. Many clients come to me and ask if it is possible to get the copyright to the masters back at some point. Unfortunately, unless you are R.E.M or the Rolling Stones, this probably isn't going to happen. Copyrights are extremely valuable, and record companies are not likely to allow them to revert to you.

RE-RECORDING RESTRICTIONS

Every major label recording agreement includes a *re-recording restriction*. This provision is "standard" and essentially non-negotiable, and it means that once your recording agreement has ended, you cannot re-record and commercially release a record embodying new recordings of any of the songs you recorded for your former label at any time prior to the *later* of the following dates: The date five years after the date of delivery to the record company of the last master embodying such song, or the date which is two years after the expiration or termination of the term of your recording agreement. You may be able to lower these time periods a little, but it's not easy. If you have some leverage, you may be able to limit the restriction to songs that have been commercially released during the term of your agreement. Some record companies will also seek to prevent you from re-recording a song for a non-record use, such as an advertisement or a movie.

HEALTH INSURANCE

Nearly all of my clients ask me if the record company will provide them with health insurance. The short answer is "no." Record companies see you as independent contractors, not employees. When I ask for health and dental insurance in a negotiation, the record company attorney politely tells me that the artist should pay for it out of the artist's advance. Of course, advances are not usually large enough to allow this. There are a few labels who have made efforts to help with health insurance (Sub Pop comes to mind), but you are pretty much on your own. Alternatives? If you are a vocalist signed to a major label, you will likely be required to join the American Federation of Television and Radio Artists (AFTRA). This union offers a relatively cheap insurance plan to its members, but your annual earnings must exceed a certain amount before you are eligible. If you aren't a vocalist, you may be able to get insurance through the American Federation of Musicians (AFM), another union that your entire band will have to join if you sign to a major. Unfortunately, the monthly premiums are relatively high and the coverage isn't as good as that offered under the AFTRA plan. Finally, the performing rights organizations ASCAP and BMI now offer their members access to health insurance plans, so be sure to explore these plans if you are a songwriter or publisher.

OUTSIDE ACTIVITIES / MOVIES / SIDEMAN EXCLUSIONS

As I mentioned earlier, most record companies will require you to grant to them the exclusive right to your recording services. This means that you cannot perform as a recording artist for anyone else during the term of your deal. The reasoning behind this is obvious, given the vast amounts of money that record companies spend developing new artists these days and given how much money a successful artist can make for the label. However, the record company will usually add a provision to your deal that allows you to perform as a *sideman* and/or a *producer* on recordings by other artists for other record companies. Your label will ask only that you don't render a "step out" performance or a featured vocal. In other words, you must be a background musician and vocalist. If you want to do a duet with Nick Cave or Polly Jean Harvey, you will have to ask for special permission. In any case, your record company will also ask for a courtesy credit on the liner notes, usually in the form of "Joe Blow appears courtesy of Thrifty Scot Records."

Recording a song for a *motion picture* and/or a *soundtrack album* is another story. Your record company does not have to allow you to do this unless you have negotiated a provision that gives you the right to do so. Movie soundtracks are very big business these days, however, and your record company may be eager to get you onto the soundtrack of the next big budget "event" movie (e.g., *Batman*, *The X-Files*, etc.), since the soundtrack albums released in conjunction with these (and other) pictures have fared very well commercially. We'll talk more about this in Chapter Nine.

GROUP ISSUES / LEAVING MEMBERS

If "you" are a group and not a solo artist, your recording agreement will be a little fatter, due to *leaving member provisions*. These provisions spell out what will happen if and when one or more member leaves the group or the group disbands entirely. In each case, the record company will typically require you to give them formal notice of the personnel change or break up. Within a relatively short period of time following their receipt of your notice (30-90 days), the record company typically has the right to do the following:

★ Terminate the recording agreement as to the leaving member(s) AND the remaining members.

★ Terminate the recording agreement as to some of the leaving members and/or remaining members while retaining the rights to other leaving members and/or remaining members.

★ Require any leaving member to record anywhere from 2 to 5 demos for their review. After submitting the demos, the record company has an additional period of time (usually 30 days) to drop or retain the member(s).

If the company decides to terminate the recording agreement with respect to any or all leaving members, those members are free to sign another deal with any other company; Any retained members are still signed to the record company. Depending on the terms of the recording agreement, the major deal points (advances, royalties, number of albums owed to record company, etc.) may or may not change. They typically do, and here's how:

★ Royalties for records recorded by leaving members will be reduced.

★ Advances/recording funds for future records will be reduced.

★ The record company may require an additional option or two for more albums.

★ Royalties generated from the sale of leaving member records will be used to satisfy 100% of the debt the group incurred before the departure of leaving members. Ideally, you want any royalties generated from the sale of leaving member records applied only against your pro-rata share of the group debt (for instance, if there were four members of the band including you, the royalties generated from records you record as a leaving member in the future can be used to recoup only 25% of past group debt).

Of course, 100% of the royalties generated from the sale of the existing group records will always be applied against 100% of the group debt.

Fortunately, the leaving member provisions are somewhat negotiable. Let us assume that you are the lead singer and sole songwriter of your band, and that you decide to leave the band and make your way as a solo artist. Your attorney sends a letter to the record company notifying them of this, and the record company promptly writes a letter back informing you that they would like to retain you as a solo artist. Where does this leave you contractually? It depends. If your attorney was aware of your important role in the group, he should have asked the record company to deem you a key member. Just what this special designation will get you varies according to your bargaining power, but in an ideal scenario, a key member's solo recording agreement won't be changed in the unfortunate manner I outlined above.

If you are unable to secure designation as a key member when your recording agreement is negotiated, you may still be able to avoid the royalty and advance reductions once the band splits through careful negotiation and cooperation with the record company. If not, you'll have to live with the terms of the original deal, but at least you won't have to split the advances or royalties with any of the other members. This is one of the arguments record companies will throw at you to justify lower advances and royalties for leaving members. The record company will also argue that a solo artist (or a leaving member's new band) is essentially a new artist and that the costs of marketing and promoting any new artist are higher than those involved in marketing and promoting the next umpteenth album by the leaving member's former group.

The whole leaving member scenario brings up a lot of internal band issues with respect to royalties, debts, trademarks and the like. These issues will be dealt with more fully in Chapter Eight.

DEMO DEALS

A demo deal is a short term, low risk (for the record company) recording agreement between you and a record company that isn't really sure that it wants to sign you. Some of these deals are based on a handshake, and some are in writing. They all work something like this: A&R person who can't pull the trigger gives you some money (usually $500 to $7,500) to go into a studio and record a few songs. You record the songs and hand the tapes over to the record company. The catch? For a period of 30 to 90 days after your delivery of the demos, the record company will ask for the exclusive option to sign you to a full-on recording contract. During that period, you are not supposed to play the demo tape for any other record company. If they like the demos and decide to go forward, you start negotiating. If the 30 to 90 days end and you can't agree on a deal, you can play the tape for other people and solicit other offers, but the record company paying for the demos will have the right to match any deal offered to you.

A business affairs executive from a top label called me the other day to inform me that the label was passing on one of my artists who had recently done a demo deal with them. In closing, she said "Y'know Bri, they should call these deals *kiss of death* deals." She's right. Demo deals suck. I have negotiated many demo deals for clients over the years, and not one of them has evolved into a full-on long-term recording agreement. The upside of the demo deal is that at least you have a tape to shop. The downside is that when labels "pass" on you, the industry tends to label you as undesirable. This is due to the fact that many A&R people are sheep. They may like your tape, but then they think, "Gee, I want to sign them, but if they're so good, why did Thrifty Scot Records pass on them? Well, I'm not going to chance it by actually relying on my ears and instincts, so I guess I'll pass too." This scenario plays out in the offices of record companies all too often, dear reader. If you need to get your songs down on tape, find some way to do it without signing a demo deal. However, if you must sign one, try to follow these basic guidelines: Make the record company's "review period" as short as possible. If they like you enough to do demos, they will be able to evaluate the demos in a week or so. 90 days is way too long. If the record company passes, make them give you the masters (and the copyrights thereto) for free. At least you can put out a single or something. If you can't get them for free (cheap bastards!!) promise that you'll pay back the recording costs if and when you get a major label deal. They will usually go for this.

PRODUCTION AGREEMENTS

I call these "middle man" deals, and most of them are inadvisable. A "production company" is usually a record producer or just a couple of people with some spare cash who "want to get into the music business." A production company will approach you as a record company would. They tell you how great you are and they convince you that they can get you a great record deal because of "who they are" and their "connections." Of course, before they put you into the studio, they will want you to sign the production agreement. If they are real scumbags, they will try to convince you to sign the first draft without letting an attorney take a look at it. After all, you're all friends, right? Who needs an attorney? This should be a major red flag to you. A production agreement is just like a recording agreement except that instead of signing directly to a record company, you sign to the production company. The production company then owns your ass and can shop you to any label. Once they find a taker, the agreement is between the record company and the production company. The production company simply warrants and represents that it has the exclusive rights to furnish your services to the record company. What does this mean to you? It depends on the deal you signed with the production company. Most production agreements provide that you must split your royalties and advances with the production company. The usual ratio runs from 50/50 to 90/10 (in favor of the artist).

Why would anyone sign a production agreement? Good question. Some of you probably don't think that you can get a record deal without someone else making it happen. This may be true, but a competent manager or attorney is perfectly capable of helping your music reach the right ears. However, most managers and attorneys aren't willing to put up the money to put you into the studio. Moreover, they don't really have much to offer you in the way of production assistance. If you have tried everything else and have been unable to generate any heat, signing a production agreement with an experienced record producer is better than never getting a deal at all. If you have decided to sign with a production company, heed this advice:

Give the production company a time limit for getting you a major label deal. If the production company can't get you a deal within a year, they probably can't get you a deal at all. If twelve months have passed and no deals are in the offing, you should have the right to terminate the production agreement.

Limit the production company's share of your record royalties. If the production company gets you a deal with a 12% royalty and a $25,000 advance, a 50/50 split will leave you with a 6% royalty and a $12,500 advance. This isn't much, so try to get at least a 75/25 split.

Limit the duration of the production company's participation in your record royalties. As the years go by, the role of the production company will very likely be reduced to cashing the royalty and advance checks and sending you your portion. Accordingly, a reduced participation in your earnings is reasonable and fair.

Whatever you do, **DON'T LET THE PRODUCTION COMPANY TAKE ANY OF YOUR PUBLISHING.**

Try to arrange for direct accounting from the record company of your share of the advances and royalties. Otherwise, the production company will receive all of the advances and royalties and forward them to you in another 30 to 60 days. Why should you have to wait?

Make sure that you (not the production company) can make the call on any creative approvals and marketing restrictions.

Make sure your attorney has a right to co-negotiate the record deal with the production company's attorney.

There are many other things you need to worry about when it comes to production agreements, but this should give you a good idea of what to expect. Be careful.

2. INDEPENDENT DEALS

While most independent (or "indie") label recording agreements look a lot like major label recording agreements, some independent labels take a different approach. For instance, some do not even "believe in" written agreements. Other labels use extremely brief "homemade" forms. Major independent labels use agreements more closely resembling major label agreements. In any event, pay close attention to the following deal points:

TERRITORY

Very few independent labels have international affiliates. Most indie labels started as regional labels, putting out music by artists from a specific area. Accordingly, it may not make sense for you to sign for the whole world when you are making an independent deal. If you do, your U.S. label will very likely just license your record to other companies in other territories. Why allow this (and take a 50% cut in royalties) when you can do this yourself? If you cut ten separate deals for ten territories with ten different companies, you have ten separate advances and ten separate and non-cross collater-alized royalty accounts. Of course, if you can't or don't want to do this yourself, then by all means sign for the world. Cutting ten separate deals for one record can be time consuming and expensive, and you may not even be able to find a suitable record company in every territory. Plus, some indie labels have great relationships with foreign record companies and this may give you a better shot in that territory. Just weigh your options before you sign up for the world.

TERM

Major labels are able to sign artists for up to six or seven records because they are investing hundreds of thousands of dollars in you. While some indies expend a great deal of money on their artists, most don't have the money of staff to justify this kind of long-term deal. Accordingly, you should think twice before signing up for more than two or three records. This advice should be taken very seriously if it is your intention to move up to a major label deal sooner than later. While you may think that recording three or four records for an independent is a good idea (and it may well be), you may be dismayed if a major comes along flashing wads of cash two weeks after your first indie record comes out. More on this later.

EXCLUSIVITY

Indies tend to be a bit more lax about this issue. This once again can be traced back to the relatively small amounts invested in your career by an indie, but I think it is also consistent with the spirit of the independent label community in the U.S. Labels like Sub Pop, Merge, Drag City and Touch and Go have never had a problem with allowing their artists to put records out on other labels, and as a consequence, these labels frequently issue records by artists signed to other labels. The records usually take the form of split singles or "supergroup" records.

ADVANCES

Some indies don't pay advances or cover recording costs. In these situations, I think you should insist that you retain all ownership rights in and to your masters. By maintaining the copyright to your masters, you can *license* your record to the label for any period of time you can agree upon. License terms of three to seven years seem to be the norm. If the label is willing to pay an advance, try to get as much as you can.

ROYALTIES

This is where indie deals can differ greatly from major label deals. You already know that major labels pay royalties based on a percentage of the retail or wholesale selling price. Many independents employ this method as well, but here are some alter-native methods of calculating royalties employed by other indies:

PROFIT SPLIT DEAL

This kind of deal is very popular among many of the important indie labels in the U.S., such as Touch and Go, Merge, Drag City and Chainsaw. Instead of paying you on each record sold and not returned, you get paid a percentage (anywhere from 30% to 60%) of the net profits generated from the sale of your record. This means that the label doesn't have to pay you anything until it recoups from its gross receipts all of the costs associated with making, manufacturing, distributing and promoting your record. After all of the costs are covered, you split the profits in accordance with the deal you struck. Make sure that you get reimbursed for any costs you have shouldered in making the record (such as recording costs) before you and the record company split the dough. Also note that your share of the profits is usually inclusive of mechanical royalties, so take this into consideration before you go looking for a publishing deal. There are two reasons indie labels like to use this method: First, it makes accounting fairly simple — you just need to know how much you've spent and how much you've collected. Second, it allows the label to avoid paying royalties until there is an actual profit. This method can be really good or really bad for you depending on your cut of the profits and how much money the label spends. If they spend a ton of money on promotion and the record still doesn't sell, you may have been better off with a royalty deal. On the other hand, if the costs are low and the record sells a lot of copies, you may earn a royalty as high as three dollars a unit or more. This is a better royalty than most major label superstars receive.

FLAT ROYALTY PER RECORD

I know of at least one major independent that simply pays a flat fee per record sold, regardless of the retail or wholesale price. This makes a lot of sense, as long as the amount you are receiving is competitive with the money per record you would receive under a straight royalty deal. Mechanical royalties may or may not be included in the per-record flat royalty.

YOU GET A PERCENTAGE OF THE PRINT RUN

Under this method, the label will simply give you a percentage (usually 10 percent to 20 percent) of the entire print run to sell on your own. You keep all profits from the sale of your share of the print run, and the label keeps the money it makes from its share. This method is usually utilized by indie labels in the case of 7" singles, but I know of a few (usually very small) labels that utilize it for full-length records as well. This can work well if you sell all of your records on tour (limited edition singles tend to sell well on tour), but I don't recommend it unless you want to be your own record company. You also have to trust your record company to tell you exactly how many records it has pressed.

CREATIVE CONTROLS

Many artists prefer to record for independents because there tends to be little or no unwanted interference with the creative process. Many indie labels will simply ask you to turn in your art and your masters when you have finished recording. If absolute creative control is what you seek, you should probably record for an indie.

MECHANICAL ROYALTIES

Before you sign to a label that employs an unorthodox method of royalty accounting, make sure that you reach an understanding as to how and if mechanical royalties will be paid. If the label wants to lump the mechanical royalties in with your share of net profits or fixed per record royalty, do the math and make sure you're not getting screwed. This will become very important later on if you decide to do a co-publishing deal, because your big-time corporate publisher wants to collect your mechanicals every quarter, and they don't like having to jump through hoops to do it.

DISTRIBUTION

Before you sign with an indie, make sure that they have legitimate distribution.

CHANGING LABELS – THE BUYOUT

Before we move into the next chapter, I want to touch briefly on the subject of buyouts and overrides. Let's say you sign a four record deal with Thrifty Scot Records, a hypothetical small indie label. Your first record comes out and it's great and it even sells a little. Pretty soon, all of the major label A&R people who passed on you already or missed you entirely are offering you giant bags of money to sign with them. You fall in love with the staff of 321 Records and decide to sign with them. Not so fast — you owe Thrifty Scot three more records.

What can you do? It depends. Since this book isn't about suing your way out of a record deal, we will assume that your contract with Thrifty Scot is valid and enforceable. Assuming that Thrifty Scot is amenable to it, the most common way to move on to 321 is by way of a *buyout and/or override*. In exchange for letting you sign with 321, Thrifty Scot will ask for a cash sum (the buyout) and royalties (the override) on the records you record and release with your new label, 321. The size of the buyout and override is subject to negotiation, but you can bet that a four record buyout will cost more than a one record buyout.

Some of the most popular artists of our time have been bought out of their record deals. For example, Geffen Records paid Sub Pop Records a pretty penny for the right to sign Nirvana. More recently, Virgin Records (UK) and DreamWorks Records (U.S.) paid a huge sum of money to buy George Michael out of his world-wide recording contract with Sony Music. If you find yourself in a buyout situation, just try to make sure that some or all of the cash and royalties payable to your old label come out of your new label's pocket (and not yours). Whether or not you can get them to eat this depends (once again) on your bargaining power.

Remember that every recording agreement is different. Also, there are many issues that I have skipped in this chapter that are discussed in the footnotes to the sample recording agreement in Appendix B, so check it out.

CHAPTER FIVE

Producers, Mixers and Engineers

Once you've finished making your record deal it's time to start thinking about making a record. Part One of this chapter is an overview of the record-making process, from selecting a producer to mastering. Part Two covers artist/producer agreements

1. PRODUCERS AND THE RECORD-MAKING PROCESS

SELECTING A PRODUCER

Record producers are the creative and administrative overseers of the record-making process. While many artists "self-produce" their recordings, even the most respected and visionary artists of today (Radiohead, Dylan, Beck, U2, Nine-Inch Nails, etc.) typically engage one or more producers to help realize their artistic vision. Whether or not you can self-produce or select the producer for your album depends on the terms of your recording agreement and/or the level of confidence your label has in your creative vision. As we discussed in Chapter Four, most record companies will demand the right to approve any producer or mixer you select. If you do not have a particular producer in mind, your A&R person will be more than happy to suggest a few. In any event, you should make sure that you are familiar with the producer's work and recording methods before you head into the studio.

MAKING A RECORD

There are five phases to the record-making process: Pre-production, tracking, overdubbing, mixing and mastering. The producer is typically involved in every phase. Let's take a quick look at each phase:

1 – PRE-PRODUCTION:

CREATIVE ASPECTS

Prior to entering the studio, a producer wants to get familiar with the artist's songs and the people who will be playing on the record.

While most artists have an over-abundance of songs, others are less prolific. Some rely on outside material entirely. Accordingly, it is the producer's task to compile a manageable selection of songs prior to entering an expensive recording studio (a "state of the art" recording studio can cost anywhere from $1,000 to $2,000 per day). Many producers are also musicians and songwriters, and producers with this background are likely to get heavily involved in selecting, dissecting and arranging the songs with the artist. The producer's input may result in a fairly minor change to the structure of a song, or it might result in a co-writing credit. Many producers are essentially glorified engineers — they are less likely to mess with your songs and are more concerned with getting a particular sound or simply selecting the songs to be recorded. Before you select a producer, you and your A&R person should decide just how much songwriting input you want from your producer.

Producers also use pre-production to determine whether or not all of the musicians in your band are up to the task. You would be shocked to know how many records are made with studio musicians or "hired guns" instead of the actual band members. If you don't have a band, the producer will work with you to select the appropriate musicians for the project.

ADMINISTRATIVE ASPECTS

In addition to his role as the general creative overseer of the record-making process, the producer is usually charged with certain administrative duties. Most of the producer's administrative work is done during pre-production. Producers are supposed to work with your manager and A&R person in selecting recording studios, putting together budgets and dealing with the unions. These days, most producers leave these tasks to their management (yes, producers have managers, too). Alternatively, the producer may try to get your manager or A&R person to deal with these matters. In any event, it is essential that you figure out who will be dealing with these matters early on, especially if you have a weak or inexperienced A&R person.

2 – TRACKING

Tracking is kind of like laying the foundation for a house. At this stage, the producer and engineers focus on recording good, solid drum and bass tracks and perhaps some "scratch" (read: temporary) vocal, guitar and keyboard tracks (these are collectively referred to as the "basic tracks"). Since drum sounds are crucial to a good recording, most producers like to track in studios that have at least one large room with good acoustics, a nice selection of microphones and a good-sounding recording console (or "board"). Tracking on a typical album project usually takes no more than ten days to complete.

3 – OVERDUBBING

At this stage, any basic tracks that are deemed inadequate are overdubbed. A large or acoustically "happening" room is not really needed for overdubbing, since the drum tracks have already been recorded. Overdubbing is typically the longest and most labor-intensive phase of the recording process — it can last from mere days to several months, depending on how long it takes to get good performances out of the artists.

4 – MIXING

Most recordings are recorded on twenty-four or forty-eight track tape machines. Mixing is the process by which the multitrack recording is reduced to a two-track recording. In many cases, the producer is not involved in the mixing process (more on this later). Mixing is usually done at yet another studio, and most producers, mixers and engineers have favorite places to work. In selecting a mixing studio, producers, mixers and engineers tend to focus on the mixing console (most producers, mixers and engineers seem to prefer computer automated consoles by Neve and SSL) and outboard gear (such as limiters, reverb units, monitors, eq's and other effects).

5 – MASTERING

Mastering is the final phase of the record-making process before manufacturing. The mastering engineer takes the mixed two-track stereo master tape and uses varying amounts of equalization to prepare the master for production. For vinyl releases, this means cutting a lacquer, from which a stamper is made. For CDs, this means transferring the mix to a DAT or a 1630 cassette. The stamper or 1630 cassette is then sent off to a manufacturing facility where the records and CDs are made. A botched mastering job can make an excellent recording sound like shit, while a good mastering job can make a so-so recording sound quite a bit better. Please keep in mind that even the finest mastering engineers cannot turn a bad recording into *Dark Side of the Moon*. Any producer worth a damn will insist on attending the mastering session because it is the last time the recording can be manipulated before it is sent off to the pressing plant.

For more insight into the producer's role in the recording process, read the interview with **Rick Rubin** in Appendix A.

MIXERS, REMIXERS AND ENGINEERS

MIXERS

As I mentioned earlier, some artists, record companies and producers choose to engage a person other than the original producer to mix the finished multitrack recordings. Why? Let's look at a few scenarios:

★ The producer is not available to mix due to other commitments.

★ The producer mixes the record, but the artist and/or the record company hate the mixes.

★ It was never contemplated that the producer would mix the record— he was hired only to coax good performances out of the artist.

Whatever the reason, know that a gifted or "hot" mixer may ask for a substantial advance and royalty to work on a project, thereby increasing your recording budget by as much as $5,000 per track.

REMIXERS

Remixes are becoming increasingly popular and important, especially in the hip-hop, R&B and electronic world. A remix is not supposed to replace an original "album" mix — it's just another person's interpretation of a particular track. Accordingly, some remixes retain very few elements of the original recording and may well embody several new samples, drum beats and vocal parts. Other remixes are very similar to album mixes and may only differ in that the vocals or drums are louder (this type of remix is aimed at getting radio airplay). The practice of remixing album tracks began in the disco era when extended, rhythm-heavy versions became popular in nightclubs and discotheques. These days, remixes are commissioned for a number of reasons: The record company may need extra tracks for a single or EP; the artist or record company may decide that the original mix of a track may not be suitable for release as a single; or the artist may simply want another talented individual to re-work his track in the name of art (imagine that). Take Beck's *Odelay!* album, for example: Tracks from this record have been remixed by Aphex Twin, Noel Gallagher, Mario Caldato, Mickey P, Butch Vig and The Dust Brothers. Remixers of this caliber can command handsome fees for their work.

ENGINEERS

Many producers and nearly all mixers and remixers start out as engineers. The engineer is responsible for setting up mikes, getting "sounds" and the task of actually running the equipment to make sure that everything sounds as it should. Engineers are rarely asked to provide any kind of input into the songs or performances — they simply follow orders from the producer and artist. Engineers are paid a flat or hourly fee for their work (these fees are deducted from your recording budget as a recording cost). Some producers will bring in their favorite engineers to help them with a project, while others are content to work with the engineers that are employed by the recording studio where the record is being made. The latter are referred to as "house engineers," and their fee is typically included in the fee you pay to rent the studio.

Now that you have some concept of what producers, mixers, remixers and engineers can do for you, let's talk about how you're going to pay them.

2. PRODUCER AND MIXER AGREEMENTS

In most cases, the artist is responsible for hiring and paying the producer, engineer or mixer. Once a producer or mixer is selected, the artist's attorney and manager negotiate a written agreement with the attorney or manager representing the producer or mixer. Occasionally, the record company will offer to negotiate the producer or mixer agreement on the artist's behalf. This is fine (and it will save you some legal fees) but you should make sure that you have the right to approve all of the important (i.e., financial) deal terms — after all, it's your money. Let's take a look at the key terms found in a typical producer agreement (mixer and remixer agreements are essentially the same):

NUMBER OF TRACKS

For an album project, most producers will agree to produce masters "sufficient to constitute an album" and will record as many tracks as time and money permits. However, many top producers will agree only to a specific number of tracks — say fourteen or so for an album. If the producer is asked to produce more tracks, he will ask for a larger advance.

ADVANCE

The size of the advance depends on the number of masters you want the producer to produce and the stature of the producer. Quality producers don't come cheap, and you can expect to pay an experienced producer an advance in the range of $25,000 to $100,000 for an entire album. This advance is deducted from your recording fund, so the less you pay the producer or mixer, the more you get to keep. In most cases, the producer must recoup 100% of his advance from his producing royalty before he is entitled to additional royalty payments. More on this later.

RECORD ROYALTIES

The size of the royalty goes hand-in-hand with the size of the advance. Top producers command no less than a 3% royalty (calculated on the suggested retail list price) on the records they produce, and a few get as much as 5% or 6%. Once again, these royalty points are deducted from yours, so if your record deal specifies an "all-in" royalty of 15% and you have to pay your producer 3%, you are really only getting paid 12%. In very rare circumstances, the record company will agree to pay the producer or mixer out of its pocket, thereby leaving your royalty rate intact. Make sure that the producer's royalty is calculated in the same manner that your royalty is calculated, e.g., the producer shouldn't be paid on records for which you don't receive a royalty (such as free goods), and the producer's royalty should be reduced as your royalty is reduced with respect to foreign sales, CDs, singles, etc. You should also make sure that the producer's royalty is pro-rated to the extent that a record contains tracks not produced by the producer.

ROYALTY ESCALATIONS

Most producers will ask that their royalty be escalated as certain sales levels are reached (500,000 and 1,000,000 units sold are common benchmarks, inasmuch as most artist royalties increase at these levels). If you are entitled to such royalty "bumps" under your record deal, this isn't a big problem, but try not to let the producer take your entire royalty escalation. For example, if your producer demands a 1/2% royalty bump at 500,000 (gold) and 1,000,000 (platinum) units sold, and if your record deal gives you a 1/2% royalty bump at these sales levels, it strikes me as unfair that the producer should get the benefit of the entire bump. Suggest a 1/4% bump, or better yet, a pro-rata bump (see the sample producer agreement in Appendix B to see how this works). Of course, you might be happy to give the producer your entire escalation if his services are in high demand.

ROYALTY REDUCTIONS FOR THIRD PARTY PRODUCERS AND MIXERS

Remember when we were talking about mixers a few minutes ago? Let's say your producer's mixes just don't cut it, so you decide to bring in a hotshot mixer to remix your album. Problem: you agreed to pay the producer a 3% royalty, and the remixer wants a 1% royalty. You are now faced with paying one more royalty point than you thought you would have to. Solution: You're probably stuck this time, but next time add a provision to your producer agreement that allows you to engage other producers and mixers, and allows you to deduct any royalty payable to the new producer or mixer from the producer's royalty. Of course, sneaking this provision into a producer agreement isn't as easy as it sounds. I have found that most non-superstar producers will agree to this kind of conditional royalty reduction, provided that the reduction does not exceed 1/2% to 1%.

RECOUPMENT

Here's where things can get tricky. After you pay the producer his initial advance, you need not worry about paying him additional royalties until his royalty account is recouped. There are two stages of recoupment in the average producer deal: First, the recording costs for the masters produced by producer must be recouped at the "Net Artist Royalty Rate." The Net Artist Royalty Rate is equal to the artist's basic royalty rate minus the producer's royalty rate. After the recording costs have been recouped at the Net Artist Royalty Rate, the producer is entitled to receive royalties (at the producer royalty rate, not the Net Artist Royalty Rate), but only to the extent that the producer's royalties exceed the advance previously paid to the producer. At this point, you need to understand that producers typically get paid for every record sold (or "from record one" as we like to say) following recoupment of recording costs, while artists do not. Thus, assuming recording costs get recouped at the Net Artist Rate, the producer will eventually get paid on every single copy sold while the artist only gets paid on the copies of records sold after recoupment of all recording costs. Moral of the story: sell your guitar and become a producer.

I sense that you are completely confused at this point, so let's look at some examples: Let's say you have a $200,000 recording fund for your next record. After the record company sends you a check for $50,000 as an advance, you are left with $150,000 to make your record.

EXAMPLE I – 100% OF PRODUCER ADVANCE RECOUPABLE FROM PRODUCER ROYALTY.

The recording budget for this example might look something like this (keep in mind that I am over-simplifying for the sake of clarity):

PRODUCER ADVANCE	$40,000.00
TRACKING/OVERDUBS	$50,000.00
MIXING	$30,000.00
TAPE, EQUIPMENT	$5,000.00
TRAVEL, HOTELS, ETC.	$3,000.00

ENGINEER FEES	$5,000.00
MASTERING	$3,000.00
UNION SESSION FEES	$14,000.00
TOTAL RECORDING BUDGET	$150,000.00

For purposes of calculating the producer's royalties, we need to divide the total recording budget into two categories:

RECORDING COSTS	$110,000.00
PRODUCER ADVANCE	$40,000.00

Assume that your base royalty is 13% and that the producer's royalty is 3%. This means that the Net Artist Royalty Rate is 10%. Let's also assume that each royalty point is worth 10¢. Accordingly, the Net Artist Royalty per album is $1.00 (10% royalty x 10¢) and the producer royalty per album is 30¢ (3% royalty x 10¢). Now let's look at some numbers:

# OF ALBUMS SOLD	NET ARTIST RATE ROYALTY	PRODUCER ROYALTY
100,000	$100,000	$0
110,000	$110,000	$33,000
130,000	$130,000	$39,000
140,000	$140,000	$42,000

At 100,000 albums sold, the producer is entitled to no royalties, because recording costs have not yet been recouped at the Net Artist Royalty Rate.

At 110,000 albums sold, the recording costs have been recouped at the Net Artist Royalty Rate. Accordingly, the producer now gets paid his 3%/30¢ royalty on all 110,000 albums sold. At 30¢ per album, the producer has earned $33,000 in royalties. Alas, our producer already received an advance against this royalty of $40,000, so he is still unrecouped by $7,000.

At 130,000 albums sold, the total producer royalty is $39,000 and he is still $1,000 short of recouping his advance.

At 140,000 albums sold, the producer is in the black. 140,000 times 30¢ is $42,000, and this exceeds the producer advance by $2,000. Accordingly, the artist owes the producer $2,000, bringing the producer's total take (including the advance) to $42,000.

EXAMPLE 2 – SAME FACTS AS EXAMPLE 1, BUT ONLY 50% OF PRODUCER'S ADVANCE IS DEEMED RECOUPABLE FROM PRODUCER'S ROYALTY.

Many producers have the clout to negotiate a deal whereby only 50% of the advance is recoupable from the producer royalty. The other 50% is deemed a non-recoupable engineering fee. I believe that this practice started when a number of engineers became producers and started arguing that half of their work is actual production while the other half is engineering. Since engineers get paid non-recoupable fees, the argument is that part of the producer/engineer's advance should be non-recoupable as well. This is fair as long as the producer's dual talents actually allow you to do without a bona-fide engineer. Otherwise, it's just a way for producers to earn additional royalties earlier than they otherwise might under traditional deals where 100% of the advance is recoupable. Let's take a look at a revised budget:

PRODUCER ADVANCE	$20,000.00
TRACKING/OVERDUBS	50,000.00
MIXING	30,000.00
TAPE, EQUIPMENT	5,000.00
TRAVEL, HOTELS, ETC.	3,000.00
ENGINEER FEES	25,000.00
MASTERING	3,000.00
UNION SESSION FEES	14,000.00
TOTAL RECORDING BUDGET	$150,000.00
RECORDING COSTS	$130,000.00
PRODUCER ADVANCE	$20,000.00

Compare this budget with the budget from Example 1. The total dollar amount is the same, but in Example 2, the producer advance is reduced to $20,000 and the other $20,000 is allocated instead to the engineering fee category. Let's see how this can affect how a producer is paid:

# OF ALBUMS SOLD	NET ARTIST RATE ROYALTY	PRODUCER ROYALTY
100,000	$100,000	$0
110,000	$110,000	$0
130,000	$130,000	$39,000
140,000	$140,000	$42,000

As in Example 1, the producer is entitled to no royalties at 100,000 albums sold because recording costs have not yet been recouped at the Net Artist Royalty Rate.

At 110,000 albums sold, another $20,000 of recording costs needs to be recouped at the Net Artist Royalty Rate before the producer is entitled to royalties.

At 130,000 albums sold, the recording costs have been recouped at the Net Artist Royalty Rate and the producer is entitled to receive his producing royalty of 3%/30¢ on all 130,000 units. 130,000 times 30¢ is $39,000, a sum which exceeds the producer advance of $20,000 by $19,000, which is the amount of the check you must now write to him. Accordingly, the producer has been paid a grand total of $59,000 at this point — $20,000 in engineering fees $20,000 in advances, and $19,000 in additional royalties. Contrast this with Example 1, where the producer has been paid only $40,000 at this sales level — a difference of $19,000.

At 140,000 albums sold, the producer is entitled to an additional $3,000 (10,000 times 30¢), bringing his total take to $62,000. At the same point in Example 1, the producer has been paid only $42,000.

If the foregoing examples confuse you, don't worry about it. That's what attorneys and accountants are for. Just know that producers and mixers are in a better position than the artist is when it comes to recouping advances and receiving additional royalties. Like I said, put down your guitars...

NON-RECORD ROYALTIES

As you know from your careful reading of Chapter Four, your recordings may well earn you royalties for non-record uses (e.g., movie soundtracks, radio and TV advertisements, etc.). The artist is entitled to a portion (usually 50%) of the record company's net receipts for these uses. Of course, producers want their piece of this money too, and there is a fairly simple formula for calculating the producer's take: Multiply the artist's share by a fraction, the numerator of which is the producer's base royalty and the denominator of which is the artist's base royalty. The resulting sum belongs to the producer. For example, let's say your record company licenses one of your recordings to Coca-Cola for use in a TV ad campaign for a fee of $75,000. The record company takes 50% off the top, and credits your royalty account with $37,500. What is the producer's take? If your "all in" base royalty is 15%, and the producer's base royalty is 5%, the producer is entitled to one-third of your royalty, which in this case would be $12,500. The only exception to this formula applies to home video device royalties, where the producer is typically entitled to receive only 50% of the otherwise payable share of net receipts. The argument here is that since the home video is comprised of an audio and a visual element, the producer of the recording shouldn't get a full royalty.

ACCOUNTINGS/LETTERS OF DIRECTION

The bad news: the artist is contractually responsible for paying advances, fees and royalties to producers, mixers and engineers. The good news: as an accommodation to the artist, most major record companies will assume these tasks on your behalf. To make sure this happens, your attorney should lobby for a clause in your recording agreement that obliges the record company to accept irrevocable *letters of direction*. The letter of direction is a two or three-page letter from the artist to the record company which gives the record company permission to make advance and royalty payments for you. These payments are deducted from your advances and royalties. I have included a sample letter of direction with the sample producer agreement in Appendix B.

WHY YOU NEED A LETTER OF DIRECTION

I don't really want to walk you through any more confusing examples, so I'm just going to tell it to you straight: If you make an album that sells respectably but not well enough to recoup your overall royalty account with your record company, there's a good chance that you will find yourself owing a nice chunk of change to the producer (and possibly mixer) of the album despite the fact that you don't have enough money in your pocket for a trip to Starbucks. Unless you (a) managed to put away a nice chunk of your advance, or (b) are independently wealthy, you are up shit creek. However, if your record company accepts a letter of direction, you can rest easy, because they will pay any royalties owed to the producer and simply tack this payment onto your unrecouped royalty account balance. If not, you'd better find the money, because I can guarantee you that the producer will not be sympathetic to your financial plight. Frankly, the kind of nightmare I just described doesn't happen that often, because most producers won't even agree to work with you unless they are guaranteed direct accounting from the record company. If your record company agrees to accept a letter of direction, try to word it so that they can't use your mechanical royalties or future album advances to make royalty payments to the producer. This isn't always possible, but it is important, because you don't want your future album advances reduced and publishing companies are less likely to sign you if the record company has first claim on your mechanical royalties.

CONTROLLED COMPOSITIONS

Remember when I told you that some producers end up co-writing some or all of the songs on the albums they produce? Remember the controlled composition clause we talked about in Chapter Four? Make sure that there is a clause in your producer agreement that compels the producer to issue mechanical licenses to the record company on the same basis that you are obligated to do so. In other words, if you have to live with a three-quarter rate and a ten-song cap, so should the producer. Otherwise, the producer's portion of the co-written compositions may make you exceed the maximum aggregate mechanical royalties figure specified in your record contract. In this case, the excess mechanical royalties will be deducted from your mechanical royalties, and that sucks.

SAMPLES

The task of clearing samples is a fu**ing nightmare, and it's an even bigger nightmare if your producer or remixer throws a bunch of samples onto a track and fails to tell you or the record company about them (not that I have any experience with this…). Once a record embodying an unauthorized sample is released, the owner of the sample has a gun to your head. How to avoid this calamity? At a minimum, make sure your agreement with the producer or remixer obligates them to keep a detailed written log of all samples used in a particular track. This log should include the best possible information on the owner of the copyright to the sampled song and the sampled master. At a maximum, try to make the producer or remixer contractually responsible for clearing and paying for any samples that are put onto a track at their suggestion. Finally, be very wary of the producer who says, "there are no samples *that we need to worry about* (wink-wink)" on a track. If the producer refuses to identify a sample, ask him to either take it off or clear it. Unless you are 100% sure that a sample is in the public domain or that it does not otherwise constitute copyright infringement, take it off or clear it. This is really important, and it can save you lots and lots of money down the line. It will also cut back on your attorney's Maalox® bill (trust me).

Kind of makes you want to self-produce, doesn't it? Before you go down that road, read the **Rick Rubin** interview in Appendix A and browse through the sample recording budget, producer agreement and letter of direction in Appendix B.

CHAPTER SIX
Music Publishing

Music publishing is a complex topic that requires a good grasp of copyright law, so I strongly encourage you to read or review Chapter Two before reading any further.

In Chapter Four we explored the kinds of deals that relate to your master recordings and your services as a recording artist. This chapter deals with the related yet distinct topic of the songs you write, the money you can earn from exploitation and performance of your songs, and your contractual relationships with third party music publishers and performing rights organizations. Given the breadth of this topic, I have divided the chapter into four parts: Part One takes a look at songwriters and publishers and explains what they do. Part Two looks at the different sources of music publishing income and explains how the money gets divided between the songwriter and the publisher. Part Three breaks down the different types of publishing agreements you may encounter. Finally, Part Four gives you some tips on setting up your own publishing company.

I. PUBLISHERS AND SONGWRITERS

THE ROLE OF THE SONGWRITER

Songwriters write songs. Duh. If you are a songwriter and your songs are being performed and/or commercially exploited, you need to take at least one of the following steps to ensure that you collect all the royalties to which you are entitled:

1 - Form your own publishing company; or
2 - Enter into an agreement of some kind with an existing publishing company.

Actually, you should probably form your own publishing company whether or not you intend to enter into an agreement with another publisher down the line. The reasons for this will become clear when we look at publishing agreements in Part Three. In any event, you will almost surely end up doing business with a third party publishing company at some point in your career, so let's talk about them for a minute.

THE ROLE OF THE MUSIC PUBLISHER

The music publisher is the business entity that owns and/or controls musical compositions and the copyrights thereto. Many songwriters (through the formation of their own publishing companies) function as their own publisher. Other songwriters assign all or part of their songs to third-party publishers.

WHAT A PUBLISHER IS SUPPOSED TO DO FOR THE SONGWRITER/CO-PUBLISHER

Advances – If you enter into an agreement with a third party publisher, you will probably receive a recoupable cash advance in exchange for a negotiated share of publishing income. More on this later.

Licensing – A publisher issues mechanical licenses to record companies and synchronization licenses to companies that want to use your songs in movies, TV shows, advertisements, video games, karaoke discs or tapes. If your publisher does not print sheet music or songbooks, it will engage a third-party print music publisher to do so on its behalf.

Collection – A publisher collects all of the income generated from the licensing of your songs and pays the appropriate share of royalties to writers and (if you have a co-publishing agreement) your own publishing company on a quarterly or semi-annual basis.

Song Plugging – Most publishing companies (and certainly all major publishing companies) employ one or more people whose job is to get your songs covered by other artists. These publishers also have departments devoted to pitching songs to advertising agencies, motion picture music supervisors and TV producers in the hopes of placing your songs in a commercial, movie or TV show, thereby generating synchronization license and performance income.

Copyright Registration – A publisher performs the mundane (but important) task of registering your songs with the Copyright Office. As I noted in Chapter Two, your songs are still "copyrighted" if not registered, but your publisher cannot take legal action against infringers unless the copyrights are registered.

Registration of Songs with Performing Rights Organizations – In order to collect performance rights royalties, the publisher needs to register each song with the appropriate performing rights organization.

Protection Against Copyright Infringement – A good publisher is always on the lookout for unauthorized uses of its songs. Since the publisher owns and/or controls all or part of the copyright in and to the songs in its catalog, it has the right to take legal action against any such infringer.

Career Development – Many publishers sign new, unknown and unsigned artists and songwriters to publishing deals. While these deals usually call for relatively small advances compared to the advances payable under deals for established artists and songwriters, such advances can buy an artist or songwriter enough time to develop his craft to the point where he can secure a recording agreement or have songs covered by other artists. Most publishers also provide their writers with access to publisher owned recording studios so that the writer can demo his songs.

There are tens of thousands of music publishing companies around the world. Here's a short list of the big ones:

Almo/Irving - Rondor Music Int'l.
BMG Music Publishing
Cherry Lane Music Publishing
Chrysalis Music
Disney Music Publishing
EMI Music Publishing
Famous Music Publishing
MCA/PolyGram Music Publishing
Peermusic
Sony Music Publishing
Warner/Chappell Music Publishing
Windswept Pacific
Zomba Music

Most of these companies are owned by one of the five major music conglomerates or another large entertainment company. Accordingly, all of these companies have offices and affiliate companies around the world. Of course, there are many independent music publishers with song catalogs and business operations of varying sizes.

2. MUSIC PUBLISHING INCOME

PUBLISHER'S SHARE & WRITER'S SHARE

There is much money to be made in music publishing. Understanding how the money gets divided is not always easy, and you need to understand the distinction between the *writer's share* and the *publisher's share* of music publishing income.

The publisher's share is the share of income allocated to the owner of the copyright in and to a song. The publisher's share is equal to 50% of all music publishing income.

The writer's share is the share of income allocated to the writer or composer of the song, whether or not the writer owns all or part of the copyright. Historically, the writer's share is equal to the publisher's share of income (with the exception of print income).

I sense your confusion, so let's look at some really basic examples using the following facts: Vandelay Industries releases an album comprised entirely of your original songs and it sells well enough to generate $1,000 in mechanical royalties over a six-month period.

EXAMPLE 1 – You formed your own publishing company, Lawn Chocolate Music, which owns 100% of the copyrights in and to your songs. The record company sends Lawn Chocolate Music a mechanical royalty check for $1,000. The money is divided like this:

LAWN CHOCOLATE MUSIC (100% of Publisher's share)	$500
SONGWRITERS (Writer's share)	$500

EXAMPLE 2 – You formed your own publishing company, Lawn Chocolate Music, which originally owned 100% of the copyrights in and to your songs. You needed money, so you sold 100% of the copyrights in and to your songs to Thrifty Scot Songs, a big-time music publisher. When the record company sends Thrifty Scot a mechanical royalty check for $1,000, Thrifty Scot divides the money like this:

THRIFTY SCOT SONGS (100% of Publisher's share)	$500
SONGWRITERS (Writer's share)	$500

EXAMPLE 3 – You formed your own publishing company, Lawn Chocolate Music, which originally owned 100% of the copyrights in and to your songs. You needed money, so you sold 50% of the copyrights in and to your songs to Thrifty Scot Songs. When the record company sends Thrifty Scot a mechanical royalty check for $1,000, Thrifty Scot divides the money like this:

THRIFTY SCOT SONGS (50% of Publisher's share)	$250
LAWN CHOCOLATE MUSIC (50% of Publisher's share)	$250
SONGWRITERS (Writer's share)	$500

Still confused? Don't worry, you'll get the hang of it soon enough. Just remember that traditionally, the songwriter is entitled to receive the entire writer's share of income, which equals 50% of gross income, regardless of who owns the copyrights in and to the songs that generated the income. Once again, this is not true in the case of print income, but we'll get into that later. I don't know how or why this writer's share/publisher's share nonsense got started, but that's the way we divide most music publishing income in this business, so just accept it. Now that we've got that covered, let's look at the different ways you can make money with your songs.

SOURCES OF MUSIC PUBLISHING INCOME

The two primary sources of music publishing income are *mechanical royalties* and *public performance royalties*. However, income from *synchronization licenses* and *printed editions* of your songs can be substantial as well. Let's look at each in turn.

MECHANICAL ROYALTIES

For most publishers and songwriters, mechanical royalties represent the biggest piece of the music publishing income pie. If you don't know what these are you didn't read Chapters Two and Five. Now is a good time to review the pertinent parts of those chapters. To recap, mechanical royalties are the royalties payable by the record company to the publishers of the songs which have been "mechanically reproduced" on a record. How they are paid and collected differs depending on the terms of the mechanical license and where the record is sold.

U.S. & Canada – In order to distribute records in the U.S. and Canada, a record company must obtain a mechanical license from the publisher of every song on the record (unless the song is in the public domain). Accordingly, the record company negotiates the terms of the license with you and your publisher and the publishers of any "outside" songs on the record and the publishers issue mechanical licenses to the record company. Remember that all recording agreements contain *controlled composition* clauses that effectively pre-negotiate the mechanical license terms with respect to your own songs. You will find a sample mechanical license in Appendix B if you're interested. The record company then pays the appropriate publishers the mechanical royalties due for each record sold in accordance with the terms of the mechanical licenses. The standard mechanical license requires the record company to make these payments at the end of every calendar quarter.

Under certain circumstances, the record company may obtain a compulsory mechanical license from the U.S. Copyright Office instead of the publisher, but for the reasons I outlined in Chapter Two, this rarely occurs. You should also know that some publishers hire the Harry Fox Agency (HFA) to issue mechanical licenses and collect the resulting income for them. The HFA is a subsidiary of the National Music Publishers' Association. Over 17,000 music publishers currently engage the HFA to issue mechanical licenses and collect and distribute royalties generated from the mechanical reproduction of the publishers' songs. The HFA also issues synchronization licenses for the use of songs in movies, TV, home videos and advertisements, although most major publishers use the HFA for mechanical licenses only. The HFA charges a fee equal to 4.5% of all mechanical royalties collected. The HFA will not issue a license at less than the full statutory rate without the publisher's consent.

Why do so many publishers use the HFA to deal with mechanical licensing? In many cases, it's more economical to farm this work out than to hire people to do it in house. Additionally, the HFA is very aggressive when it comes to auditing the books of record companies. These audits often unearth sizable amounts of unpaid mechanical royalties, and these royalties often exceed the 4.5% commission charged.

Outside the U.S. and Canada – Collecting mechanical royalties generated from the sale of records outside of the U.S. and Canada presents a different challenge for publishers. There is no per-song "statutory rate" in these territories. Rather, a rate is established for each territory via an agreement between record company trade organizations and mechanical rights bodies. For example, the continental European mechanical rate and mechanical royalty payment structure was recently overhauled via a fiercely negotiated agreement between the International Federation of Phonographic Industry (IFPI) and BIEM, the European mechanical rights body. This rate is applied to the retail or wholesale selling price of the record concerned. For instance, in continental Europe, the current rate is equal to 9.01% of the Published Price to Dealers (PPD). If the PPD in continental Europe is equivalent to U.S. $10.00, the total mechanical royalty payable on that record would be 90¢. The royalties are paid to the publishers of the songs on each record in pro-rata shares based on a twenty-song "cap" per album. The record companies calculate these royalties and pay them not to the publisher but to the mechanical rights society for the territory concerned. It is then up to your publisher to notify the various mechanical rights societies around the world that they are entitled to collect these royalties. If your publisher does not have an office in a particular territory or a subpublishing agreement with a publisher in a territory, then your mechanical royalties will remain with the mechanical rights society until they are collected. If the royalties go unclaimed for an appreciable period of time (usually 2 to 3 years) they will disappear into what is known as the black box. This is bad for you, because black box royalties are ultimately distributed amongst the society's local members, leaving your publisher empty handed. Avoid this calamity by making sure your publisher is equipped to collect royalties in every major territory. If you are self-publishing, make a subpublishing deal with a foreign publisher or an administration deal with a U.S. publisher. At the very least, get the HFA to collect your foreign mechanical royalties. The HFA has agreements with 23 mechanical rights societies in over 100 territories. The upside of using the HFA to collect your foreign mechanical royalties is that they take a smaller piece of your royalties than a third party publisher does. The downside is that they don't act as a real publisher in the sense that they won't try to get your songs covered or included in movies, TV shows and commercials in the territory concerned — they will simply collect the royalties, take a fee off the top and remit the remainder to you.

PUBLIC PERFORMANCE INCOME

Public performance income represents the second biggest piece of the publishing income pie for most publishers and songwriters. The exclusive right of public performance, also referred to as the performing right, is one of the five exclusive rights enjoyed by the copyright owner of a song. U.S. law currently does not confer a similar public performance right for sound recordings (although this may change someday). Accordingly, those who want to publicly perform your songs (this includes TV, radio and cable broadcasters, bars, restaurants, clubs, elevators and any place or business that plays music in the background) need to secure a performance license. Of course, no publisher has the time or resources to issue individual licenses to each user around the world. Enter ASCAP, BMI and SESAC — the three U.S. performing rights organizations.

What Do Performing Rights Organizations Do? Performing rights organizations issue licenses for the non-dramatic public performance of the songs written and published by their members. These licenses are known as blanket licenses and they entitle the holder to publicly perform all of the songs in the society's repertoire for a flat fee. The performing rights organization then attempts to determine the number of times each song is performed during a particular period, and then pays the performance royalties (in equal shares) directly to the writer and publisher. Performing rights organizations are NOT music publishers.

When Should You Affiliate With A Performing Rights Organization? While each organization has its own eligibility requirements, you should think about affiliating before your songs are publicly performed. For most of you, this won't happen until your songs are recorded and commercially released. If your songs are being performed but aren't registered, you won't get any performance royalties.

How do Performing Rights Organizations Pay Royalties? As we will learn, every organization is different, but they all pay the writer's share and publisher's share of public performance income directly to the writer and publisher. Contrast this with mechanical royalties and synch license fees, where the combined writer's share and publisher's share is paid to the publisher. Accordingly, if one of your songs generates $1,000 in public performance royalties, the organization that administers the performing rights for the song will send separate checks for $500 each directly to the writer and publisher. Let's take a look at each performing rights organization:

ASCAP

Founded in 1914, the American Society of Composers, Authors and Publishers currently represents over 75,000 writers, composers and music publishers. ASCAP has offices in New York, Chicago, Los Angeles, Nashville, Puerto Rico and London.

How to join ASCAP – Call up the closest office, get a membership packet and fill out the application. Writers and publishers must apply separately. Specific membership requirements are as follows:

To become a writer member, you must have any one of the following:

- A published composition available for sale or rental;
- A commercially recorded song; or
- Proof that your song was publicly performed in a venue licensable by ASCAP (TV, live concert, radio, etc.). Proof may come in the form of a playlist, program or a letter of confirmation.

To become a publisher member, you must:

- Apply as a partnership, corporation, or as an individually-owned publishing company.
- Prove that you meet any of the writer member eligibility requirements.
- Verify that your publishing company is "regularly engaged in the music publishing business," or that you publish songs which are performed regularly by ASCAP's licensees.

Upon becoming an ASCAP member, you must immediately register any existing songs that are being performed. Thereafter, every new song that you write should be registered prior to its anticipated performance or as soon as a record embodying the song is released. You must also notify ASCAP if a song is used in a movie or a TV show. Always get a cue sheet from the producer of the movie or TV show and send a copy to ASCAP. If your publisher doesn't register your songs, you won't get credited with performance royalties on them.

How long is the ASCAP Membership Agreement? The ASCAP writer/publisher agreement has a year to year term, meaning that you can terminate it at the end of any given year. The ASCAP writer and publisher agreements are identical in this respect.

How much does it cost to join ASCAP? While it doesn't cost anything to apply, annual dues are $10.00 for writer members and $50.00 for publisher members.

How Does ASCAP Track Performances? It's kind of complex, but I'll give it a shot. With respect to radio, ASCAP randomly tapes thousands of hours of programming by different radio broadcasters. From these tapes, ASCAP determines the number of times its songs are performed, and calculates your royalties based on frequency of performance and a bunch of other factors. In addition to tapes, ASCAP uses written logs of songs performed on various stations, as well as information provided by Broadcast Data Systems, or BDS. BDS is kind of like SoundScan for the airwaves — BDS computers somehow determine the number of "spins" each song receives on participating stations. With respect to TV, ASCAP conducts a census, or minute-by-minute survey of the major networks (ABC, NBC, CBS, Fox, UPN and WB) and cable networks (HBO, Cinemax, Showtime, the Movie Channel, Nickelodeon, the Disney Channel, the Nashville Network, MTV, USA, Lifetime, TNT and A&E).

ASCAP also uses *cue sheets* to determine how often a song is performed on TV. A cue sheet is a piece of paper that lists the songs performed on each TV program. The cue sheets list the duration of the performance and specifies whether or not the song was used as background music or whether the song was performed "on screen" (like when the Flaming Lips played "She Don't Use Jelly" on *Beverly Hills 90210* a few years back). TV stations and network program producers are supposed to send cue sheets to ASCAP (and BMI and SESAC, for that matter) and the cue sheets help determine how often a song is performed on TV. In addition to radio and TV, ASCAP surveys performances on airlines, background music services such as MUZAK, and at certain live performances (we're talking top-grossing tours and other "major" live performances only). Note that performances of songs in U.S. movie theaters aren't surveyed by any of the performing rights organizations.

What About Foreign Performance Royalties? There are numerous performing rights organizations currently operating outside of the U.S., and ASCAP currently has reciprocal agreements with 54 of them. ASCAP licenses the songs of the members belonging to these affiliated organizations, and they in turn license the songs of ASCAP members. Note that if your publisher has a subpublishing agreement (I'll explain what this is in Part Three of this chapter) in a foreign territory, that subpublisher will collect the publisher's share of public performance royalties for that territory, and ASCAP will collect only the writer's share. If your publisher doesn't have a subpublisher or an affiliate in a territory, ASCAP will collect the publisher's share from its foreign affiliate as well.

How Often Will I Receive Statements From ASCAP? ASCAP pays domestic royalties every calendar quarter. In addition to these statements, ASCAP accounts for foreign performance royalties three times a year: in April, August and December.

Does ASCAP Keep Any of My Royalties? Yes and no. ASCAP is a nonprofit organization, so every penny is distributed to members after all overhead expenses are covered.

Will ASCAP Pay Me an Advance against My Performance Royalties? No.

Does ASCAP offer any other Services? In addition to collecting your performance royalties, ASCAP provides the following services to its members:

Showcases – ASCAP frequently sponsors performances by its members in clubs and concert halls around the country. These showcases tend to attract a large number of A&R people and publishers, and ASCAP does a pretty good job of promoting them.

Equipment and Tour Liability Insurance – ASCAP offers its members a "low cost" insurance plan to cover gear. ASCAP now also offers access to discounted tour liability insurance which may cover your ass in the event that you are sued for negligently causing personal or property damage on tour.

Medical/Dental/Life Insurance – ASCAP offers its members access to group medical, dental and term life insurance plans.

Access to Credit Unions – Credit unions are way better than most banks, so check it out.

Access to Tax-deferred Investment Services – Regular Joes have access to these programs, but musicians typically do not. It's never too early to start thinking about retirement.

See my Interview with **Ron Sobel** of ASCAP in Appendix A.

BMI

Founded in 1940, Broadcast Music, Inc. currently counts over 200,000 songwriters, composers and music publisher members. BMI's main offices are located in New York, Los Angeles, Nashville and London.

How to join BMI – Call the closest office and fill out an application. You must apply separately as a writer and as a publisher. You are eligible for BMI membership if you have written or co-written a song, and the song is either commercially published or recorded or is otherwise likely to be performed. Upon becoming a BMI member, you need to register your songs just as you would if you joined ASCAP.

How long is the BMI Membership Agreement? Unlike ASCAP, BMI has different agreements for writers and publishers. The term of the BMI writer agreement is two years. The term of the BMI publisher agreement is five years. Note that writer and publisher agreements are automatically renewed at the end of each term unless the writer or publisher gives written notice of its intention to terminate the agreement at least three months prior to the renewal date for the agreement.

How much does it cost to join BMI? It costs nothing to join BMI as a writer. It costs $100 to join as a publisher. Thereafter, there are no dues. However, there is a $50 fee for changing the name of your publishing company.

How Does BMI Track Performances? BMI monitors a "scientifically chosen cross-section of radio stations" on a quarterly basis. These stations provide BMI with written airplay logs that purportedly reflect over 500,000 hours of airplay annually. BMI feeds this information into a really expensive computer system that spits out a statistical approximation of performances for each song on U.S. radio. For TV performances, BMI utilizes cue sheets in addition to a nationwide computer listing of all local TV stations. With the exception of certain contemporary classical music performances, BMI does not survey performances of songs at live concerts.

What About Foreign Performance Royalties? BMI collects foreign performance royalties in the same manner as ASCAP, via affiliations with foreign performing rights organizations.

How Often Will I Receive Statements From BMI? BMI sends statements for broadcast, cable and background music performances every calendar quarter. Additionally, BMI sends statements relating to commercials and "live concerts of serious music" once a year. Statements relating to foreign performance royalties are issued twice a year.

Does BMI Keep Any of My Royalties? Like ASCAP, BMI is a non-profit organization. Accordingly, monies collected are distributed to members after overhead expenses are paid. However, BMI only pays guaranteed rates to its members. After royalties are distributed according to these rates, BMI pays "voluntary bonuses" to writers. I guess these bonuses are a plus if you are a recipient; I am not sure to what extent they reduce monies otherwise payable to BMI members. Perhaps you should ask them.

Will BMI pay me an Advance against My Performance Royalties? No.

Does BMI offer any other services? In addition to collecting your performance royalties, BMI provides the following services to its members:

Showcases – BMI sponsors showcases and at music conferences such as SXSW, NXNW and CMJ. These showcases tend to be well attended by music industry professionals.

Workshops – BMI sponsors a number of workshops for songwriters. There are workshops for Jazz composers, songwriters interested in film and TV music and various other types of workshops.

Insurance – BMI offers access to medical, life and equipment insurance programs.

Direct Deposit – BMI can deposit your royalties directly into your bank account.

See My Interview with **Rick Riccobono** of BMI in Appendix A.

SESAC

The Society of European Stage Authors and Composers was founded in 1930. Although it is the second oldest U.S. performing rights organization, it is by far the smallest in terms of membership and repertoire.

SESAC is Privately Owned – Unlike ASCAP and BMI, SESAC is a for profit venture. SESAC retains nearly half of the performance royalties it collects for its own profit.

Can Anyone Join SESAC? No. SESAC is a "selective organization," meaning that an otherwise qualified applicant may be rejected.

How much does it cost to join SESAC? Nothing.

How Does SESAC Track Performances? Like ASCAP and BMI, SESAC uses broadcast logs and airplay monitoring to track performances. Unlike those organizations, SESAC relies heavily on chart information gleaned from trade publications such as Radio & Records and Billboard. SESAC was the first performing rights organization to employ Broadcast Data Systems (BDS) data to monitor radio airplay.

What About Foreign Performance Royalties? SESAC is similar to ASCAP and BMI in this area.

Will SESAC pay me an Advance against My Performance Royalties? In some cases SESAC pays advances against future public performance royalties. The size of the advance depends on how often your songs are likely to be performed.

WHICH PERFORMING RIGHTS ORGANIZATION IS BEST FOR ME?

Good question. I am tempted to say, "flip a coin," but you should choose your performing rights organization very carefully. Ask your colleagues about their experiences. Take the time to meet with representatives of each organization — they will be happy to answer your questions and will do their best to show you why you should join their society. Just make sure that you affiliate and register your songs as soon as possible.

GRAND RIGHTS

Before we move on, a few words about grand rights. Grand rights are the rights granted to anyone who wants to perform your songs in a "dramatic" context. Accordingly, if someone wants to incorporate your songs into a ballet or a Broadway show, they need to acquire grand rights from the songwriter or the publisher, depending on whether or not the songwriter granted the right to license grand rights to the publisher.

SYNCHRONIZATION FEES

Let's say a movie producer approaches you and wants to use a recording of one of your songs in his next movie. In order to do so, he must secure two *synchronization (or "synch") licenses:* one from the owner of the master recording, and one from the publisher of the song. These licenses are called synchronization licenses because they grant the licensee the right to "synchronize" a master or a song in timed relation with a visual image (whether the image is in the form of a movie, TV show, videocassette or commercial). Since there is no such thing as a compulsory synchronization license for songs and master recordings, movie and TV producers are pretty much at the mercy of the publisher when it comes to these licenses. Publishers can charge anything they want for these licenses, and the fees are often enormous. Many factors go into just how much money a publisher can expect to receive in exchange for a synch license, but I'm going to hold off on a full exploration of this topic until Chapter Nine. For now all you need to know is that income from synch licenses for musical compositions is paid to the publisher, who customarily pays half of the income to the songwriter (the writer's share) and divides the publisher's share in accordance with the agreement it strikes with the songwriter and the songwriter's publisher (this is usually a 50/50 split in a copublishing agreement).

SHEET MUSIC/PRINT ROYALTIES

Writers and publishers are paid royalties for the sale of printed editions of their songs. Since print royalties represent a relatively small percentage of music publishing income, most publishing companies choose not to manufacture and sell printed editions of their songs. Fortunately, there are a handful of specialized print music publishers who are up to the task. For instance, the Hal Leonard Corporation of Milwaukee, Wisconsin, is one of the largest print music publishers in the world. In addition to selling printed editions of songs, Hal Leonard also publishes and distributes many books on music and the music business, including the book you are holding. This has been a paid advertisement. Print royalties are calculated and paid in a manner unlike any other type of music publishing income. Let's take a quick look at the different forms of print music and the corresponding royalties:

Sheet Music – A song printed on an unbound sheet of paper that contains the music and lyrics of the song. The standard royalty for a single piece of sheet music is a sum equal to 20% of the retail price. Accordingly, if a piece of sheet music retails for $4.00, the royalty payable to the publisher is 80¢.

Folios – A folio is a compilation of sheet music bound into a single volume. They are commonly referred to as songbooks.

Matching Folio – A matching folio is a folio of songs that matches a product like a CD or a movie soundtrack. Royalties on folios vary from company to company, but 12 1/2% of the retail price of the folio seems to be the industry average.

Mixed Folio – A mixed folio is a folio of songs by different writers, publishers and artists. The standard 12 1/2% royalty will be pro-rated to the extent that the folio contains songs from other writers, publishers and artists.

Personality Folio – A personality folio is a folio of songs by the same writer or artist with pictures of the artist and/or songwriter. The standard royalty for a personality folio is 5% greater than the mixed or matching folio rate. The extra royalty is paid to cover the right to use the likeness of the artist or songwriter.

Fake Books/Educational Editions – These are folios aimed at the "beginners" market. Do you remember *Roy Clark's Big Note Guitar Book?* No? Do you remember Roy Clark? No? In any event, the standard royalty for these printed editions is 12.5% of the retail selling price.

3. PUBLISHING AGREEMENTS

If you don't want to be bothered with the task of collecting all of the income derived from your songs, you need to think long and hard about entering into a publishing agreement of some kind. Publishing agreements are written agreements between copyright owners (you and/or your publishing company) and a publishing company. In return for the right to share in the income generated by your songs, the publishing company typically pays you an advance against future royalties and agrees to perform some or all of the tasks I outlined in the first part of this chapter. (See "The Role of the Publisher.") Let's take a look at the three most common types of publishing agreements: the standard publishing agreement, the co-publishing agreement and the administration agreement.

THE STANDARD PUBLISHING AGREEMENT

The *standard publishing agreement* (some people call this a songwriter agreement since the songwriter's publishing company is not involved) works something like this: Songwriter assigns 100% of the copyright in and to his songs to the publisher in exchange for advances against future royalties. This kind of deal leaves the songwriter with 100% of the writer's share of income only. In the old days, standard publishing agreements were the norm. These days, co-publishing agreements (which we will get to in a second) are much more common. Accordingly, standard publishing agreements are no longer standard, despite our terminology. Comprende? Excellent! Standard publishing agreements fall into two categories: the single or individual song agreement and the exclusive songwriter or "term" agreement.

Single/Individual Song Agreement

Under this type agreement, the songwriter assigns 100% of the copyright in and to one or a specific number of songs to the publisher. The songwriter is not obligated to deliver more songs to the publisher and may enter into agreements for other songs with any publisher.

Exclusive Songwriter/Term Songwriter Agreement

If a publisher believes that a songwriter will continue to write valuable songs in the foreseeable future, the publisher will likely offer this kind of agreement. Under an exclusive standard publishing agreement, 100% of the copyright in and to any song written by the songwriter during the term of the agreement is automatically assigned to the publisher. As with any agreement, the term varies from deal to deal, but the typical deal provides for an initial contract period (usually one year) and gives the publisher the option to extend the term for additional contract periods. Typically, the publisher has two or three options for additional one-year contract periods.

THE CO-PUBLISHING AGREEMENT

When I refer to a *co-publishing agreement*, I mean an agreement whereby the songwriter's own publishing company assigns only a portion of the copyright (usually 50%) of its songs to the third party publisher (whom we will call the co-publisher in this context), leaving the songwriter with 100% of the writer's share of income and the songwriter's own publishing company with a negotiated portion (usually equal to the percentage of copyright retained) of the publisher's share of income. As I mentioned earlier, the co-publishing agreement is the most common type of publishing agreement entered into by new songwriters and artists. Like standard publishing agreements, the co-publishing agreement takes two basic forms: It can cover only a specified number or type of songs, or it can cover all songs written during the term.

THE ADMINISTRATION AGREEMENT

You say you want someone to look after your publishing, but you don't want to give up any of your copyright ownership? An administration deal might be just the thing for you. Under these agreements, the administrating publisher takes care of licensing and collection and keeps a percentage of all income collected as a fee. This fee can range from 5% to 25% depending on the value of your copyrights. Administration deals offer a great deal of flexibility to the writer and the writer's own publishing company, because the term is usually short (from two to five years, depending on the publisher) and you keep ownership of your (hopefully) valuable copyrights. You can also strike a separate administration deal for each territory. Administration deals outside of your home territory are commonly referred to as subpublishing agreements. The downside to administration/subpublishing deals? Don't expect a huge advance unless your catalogue is full of valuable copyrights. I find administration deals particularly appealing for my clients who are willing to wait until their publishing has more value before they enter into a co-publishing deal. While most administration agreements cover only specified songs, some cover all songs written by a writer during the term of the deal. Once again, whether you can avoid this is a matter of leverage and how large your advance (if any) is.

CONTRACT PROVISIONS COMMON TO (NEARLY) ALL PUBLISHING AGREEMENTS

As with recording agreements, the deal terms of any publishing agreement are highly negotiable depending on the bargaining power of the writer and the writer's own publishing company. Let's walk through key provisions that you will find in nearly all publishing agreements.

Exclusivity/Compositions subject to the Publishing Agreement

This is simple enough if the deal specifies only one or a specified number of songs. Under an *exclusive* deal, the publisher or co-publisher will want to publish or co-publish all songs currently in your repertoire, as well as any songs written during the term of the agreement. If you can't limit the agreement to a specified number or type of songs, but if you have bargaining power, you may be able to negotiate the following limits on which songs are subject to the agreement:

Exclude songs written expressly for other artists. This is tough to avoid, I'm afraid.

Ask for a reversion of songs which are not recorded (whether by you or another artist) or *commercially exploited* during the term (or within a few months following the end of the term). Just how the term "commercially exploited" is defined will be subject to negotiation. For instance, you might suggest that songs are not "commercially exploited" unless they have been covered by another artist on a major label or included in a TV production, advertisement or motion picture for a fee of $5,000 or more. This prevents the publisher or co-publisher from issuing free synch licenses just to keep the song in its catalogue.

Exclude songs that you write expressly by you for inclusion in a motion picture. As we will see in Chapter Nine, most major motion picture studios and some big time movie producers will try to share in the publishing of any song they place in one of their movies. Accordingly, you want to be free to give them those rights, inasmuch as having one of your songs in a major motion picture can do wonders for your career and your bank account.

DELIVERY TERM/MINIMUM DELIVERY COMMITMENT

With the exception of single song or individual song agreements, most standard publishing and co-publishing agreements are structured like recording agreements in that they provide for an initial contract period with options for additional contract periods (usually no more than two or three). Keep in mind that when we speak of the "term" in this context we are not talking about the length of time a publisher owns or co-publishes a song with you — that period of time is called the *retention period* and we'll get to that in a minute. In this context, the "term" refers to the time period that you are obligated to exclusively deliver songs to your publisher or co-publisher.

For artists signed to a major label, the term is typically tied to the commercial release of each regular studio album. For plain old songwriters, the term is usually year to year. In any event, the average exclusive songwriter publishing or co-publishing agreement will stipulate that a contract period does not end until the *minimum delivery commitment* for that contract period has been satisfied. For signed artists, the minimum delivery commitment for a particular contract period is usually defined as an album released by a major label on which at least x% of the songs are subject to the publishing or co-publishing agreement. The actual percentage is negotiable, but most major publishers will extend your existing contract period (meaning that you don't advance to the next contract period) unless 70-80% of the songs on the album you release are written by you and therefore subject to the agreement.

Some deals (typically deals for songwriters as opposed to songwriter/recording artists) don't specify a percentage, but instead require you to have a minimum number of songs commercially exploited on a major label album (this is commonly referred to as a *record and release* requirement) during a particular contract period. This number is negotiable, but a minimum of eight or nine songs per contract period is fairly typical. In either case, keep in mind that if you co-write any of these songs with outside song-writers, only your fractional share of those songs will count towards your minimum delivery commitment.

ADMINISTRATION RIGHTS

Remember that administration rights belong to the copyright holder. Accordingly, since standard publishing agreements convey 100% of the copyright to the publisher, the publisher automatically has the right to administer 100% of the rights for any song covered under the agreement. Despite the fact that co-publishing agreements call for only a portion the copyright to be assigned, these agreements usually give the co-publisher the right to administer 100% of the rights to a song as well. Administration agreements convey these rights by definition, even though no copyright interest is assigned. 100% control of administration gives the publisher the unfettered right to:

- Issue mechanical licenses
- Issue synchronization licenses
- Authorize samples
- License performance rights (although ASCAP, BMI or SESAC administers these rights under most circumstances)
- License a song title or lyrical plot for dramatic use
- Authorize lyrical/melodic changes to your songs
- Authorize changes to the titles of your songs
- Authorize foreign translations of your songs
- Manufacture and distribute or sublicense the right to manufacture and distribute printed copies of your songs
- Take action against infringers of your copyrights
- Do anything else it wants with your songs.

Some publishing agreements spell out these and other administrative rights in great detail, while other agreements will simply state that the co-publisher "will have exclusive worldwide administration of all songs subject to this agreement."

LIMITATIONS ON ADMINISTRATION RIGHTS & MARKETING RESTRICTIONS

As you just learned, the standard publishing/co-publishing agreement gives the administrating publisher the right to do anything it wants with your songs. Accordingly, it is essential that you carve out some restrictions (often called *marketing restrictions*) on this right so that you have some control over how your songs are used. Specifically, you want to make sure that the administering publisher or co-publisher does not do any of the following things without your prior written consent:

Make any changes to your songs, whether lyrical or musical. The publisher or co-publisher might ask for the right to make foreign translations of songs, and this is not entirely unreasonable.

Change the title of any song.

License the title of any song independent of the song itself.

License any song for use in any motion picture, TV show or advertisement. Unless you have leverage, it will be tough to get this approval. However, many co-publishers will allow you to approve or veto any use of a song in a motion picture rated "X" or "NC-17." When it comes to advertisements, try to get absolute approval. Failing that, try to get approval over the use of any song in a commercial for booze, cigarettes, political candidates or issues, male or female hygiene or contraception products, or any other kind of ad you may not want to have your songs associated with.

Issue a mechanical license for your song at less than the minimum statutory rate (unless it is for your own record, in which case you want the publisher or co-publisher to comply with the provisions of the controlled composition clause in your recording agreement).

Issue a "first use" mechanical license to a third party. Remember that no one can release a recording of your songs without your consent until the song has been commercially released on a record. Accordingly, you don't want your publisher or co-publisher allowing another artist to get first crack at your own material without your permission. If you are a songwriter and not a recording artist, this point is somewhat moot, since your primary goal is to have your songs recorded by others.

Issue any licenses for "grand rights." We discussed grand rights in Part Two of this chapter.

Commercially exploit any demo recording. Many publishing companies will provide you with money or studio time to make demo recordings of your songs for one purpose or another. Since these recordings are of "demo quality" by definition, you don't want them to see the light of day without your permission.

GRANT OF RIGHTS

This is the provision of the agreement whereby the writer/publisher assigns all or part of the copyright in and to its songs to the publisher or co-publisher. Once again, this percentage is typically fifty percent (50%) in a co-publishing agreement. In a standard publishing agreement, this percentage is one hundred percent (100%). Remember that no copyrights are transferred in an administration agreement. Before we move on, try to avoid signing any agreement whereby the songs you write under the deal are deemed "works made for hire." As you recall from your careful reading of Chapter Two, your employer is deemed the author of works made for hire for purposes of copyright, and this will eliminate your right to reclaim the copyrights at a later date.

RETENTION PERIOD/REVERSION OF COPYRIGHTS

The *retention period* is the length of time a publisher or co-publisher administers and/or owns all or part of your songs. Under most standard publishing and co-publishing deals, the retention period is equal to the *duration* or "life" of copyright. However, if you have bargaining power, some publishers will agree to a *reversion* of copyright under certain circumstances. This is very good for you, because it allows you to keep your copyrights or make another deal for your songs. There are several kinds of reversion:

Reversion of all songs at a specified date following the end of the term of the agreement – The shorter, the better, obviously. Realistically, you can't expect to get your songs back earlier than five years after the end of your deal. Some publishers will also require you to be recouped before any reversion takes place. If this is the case, try to negotiate a provision whereby you can effect reversion if you pay back any unrecouped advance.

Reversion of unexploited songs – We talked a little bit about this earlier. If a publisher can't get a song covered or used in a movie, commercial or TV show, ask them to return it to you.

Reversion of right to administer your 50% publisher share of copyright and writer's share of income – Under this scenario, you have the right to administer or allow someone else to administer your 50% of the copyright. You also get to collect your writer's share of income directly.

In most cases, the publisher or co-publisher will require you to send a notice to effect any kind of reversion, but if you have bargaining power, your deal will provide for automatic reversion. Once all or part of the copyrights revert to you, the publisher will ask that it be given an additional period of time (known as the *collection period*) to collect any publishing income that was earned during the retention period. This is reasonable, inasmuch as it can take a minimum of six months and sometimes several years to collect publishing income after it is earned.

TERRITORY

When it comes to territory, most publishers will ask for the universe, but you may only want them to have rights in Zimbabwe or the EEC. These days, many successful U.S. writers/publishers prefer to make ex-North America subpublishing deals instead of worldwide co-publishing deals, since it's relatively easy to administer a catalogue in North America. The bottom line is that it will be tough for you to carve territories out of a co-publishing deal unless you have leverage or are willing to accept a smaller advance. For reasons we discussed in connection with recording agreements, making a number of deals instead of one worldwide deal may or may not make good business sense for you.

ROYALTIES/DIVISION OF INCOME

This is the most crucial provision of any publishing agreement. Let's recap a little bit before we start: Remember that the writer of a song is entitled to receive the *writer's share* (50%) of any and all publishing income, while the publisher is entitled to receive the *publisher's share* (the other 50%). In order to understand how income gets divided, you need to learn a few new terms: Gross income and net income.

GROSS INCOME

Gross income is equal to all monies received by the administering publisher from licensees and performing rights organizations in connection with the exploitation and performance of your songs. This covers the combined writer/publisher share of mechanical income, the publisher's share of public performance income (since the writer is paid the writer's share directly), and the combined writer/publisher share of any other income (such as synch license fees and print income).

Foreign Income: Net Receipts vs. At Source Accounting – Note that gross income does not always equal 100% of all publishing income earned from the exploitation of a song. Most major publishers are international publishers. EMI, Warner/Chappell, Sony, MCA, BMG and PolyGram have wholly owned companies in all "major" foreign territories. These companies are known as *affiliates*. However, some major publishers contract with non-affiliated local publishing companies to administer their publishing interests in certain territories. These non-affiliated companies are sometimes referred to as *subpublishers*. It is important to determine whether your U.S. publisher uses an affiliate or a subpublisher to collect foreign publishing receipts, because subpublishers are in this to make money too, so they charge your U.S. publishing company an administration fee before remitting gross income to the U.S. Accordingly, if your publisher or co-publisher makes a deal with a non-affiliated subpublisher in the U.K. to collect U.K. publishing income, that subpublisher will charge them a fee, typically ranging from 10% to 25%, of gross income, prior to sending monies to the U.S. Some publishers will try to deduct this fee even if they use wholly owned affiliates.

Let's look at an example: You sign a co-publishing deal with a major U.S. publisher. Your co-publisher then makes a deal with a non-affiliated subpublisher to collect publishing income in the U.K. Assuming the subpublisher charges your co-publisher a 20% subpublisher fee, and assuming the subpublisher collects $100,000, your co-publisher receives only $80,000 in gross income from the U.K. The U.S. co-publisher then pays royalties to you based on gross income of $80,000 instead of $100,000. How to avoid this? Ask that all foreign receipts be calculated on an "at source" basis instead of a "receipts" basis. If they agree to this, they will have to calculate your royalties at 100% of actual gross income without regard to reduction by any subpublisher. Of course, they will resist this whether or not they actually use a subpublisher instead of an affiliate, but it is essential that your attorney get to the bottom of this before you sign on the dotted line. These days, most major U.S. publishers will agree to an "at source" calculation of foreign receipts if you are a superstar writer/artist or if you are an extremely sought after new writer/artist. If not, you may be able to get your U.S. co-publisher to agree to limit subpublishing fees (sometimes called *collection fees*) to a certain percentage, regardless of what they have to pay.

If things get heated, one compromise is to allow a subpublishing fee only as long as you are unrecouped. Alternatively, some publishers will reduce the maximum subpublishing fee as each contract period passes or as certain gross income levels are achieved. Bottom line: fight like hell to get an "at source" calculation, especially in territories where your U.S. publisher has wholly-owned affiliates.

NET INCOME

Net income is calculated by subtracting the following from gross income:

Writer royalties – The writer's share of income (50%) is deducted from gross income and credited to the writer. If you have a standard publishing deal and not a co-publishing deal, this is usually all you get.

After writer royalties are deducted, your co-publisher is left with 50% of gross income. From this 50%, the following costs are deducted to arrive at net income:

Administration fee – This is a fee (usually 10% to 15%) calculated on gross income or net income, depending on the deal. Either way, the fee is usually deducted after the writer's 50% share of gross income is paid, since it is not the writer's job to administer. You might be asking yourself, "Gee Bri, I thought we gave up half of our copyright to cover administration costs? Why do we have to pay an additional fee on top of that?" You shouldn't. The administration fee is just another way for the administering co-publisher to take money from you. My esteemed colleague Larry Kartiganer would call an admin fee "viguerish." Most major publishers do not deduct an administration fee if you protest, but they still try. Try to get this provision removed from your deal, especially if your publisher is not calculating your foreign income on an "at source" basis. If you can't knock the "admin fee" out of the deal, make sure it gets deducted from net income instead of gross income. Let's look at a quick example to see what a difference this can make. Assume that you have a co-publishing agreement with Thrifty Scot Songs whereby the publisher's share of income is split 50/50 between your publishing company (Lawn Chocolate Music) and Thrifty Scot Songs. Assuming that the deal provides for a 10% administration fee, and assuming that Thrifty Scot receives $10,000.00 in U.S. mechanical royalties, here's how the numbers look:

	10% deducted from gross income	10% deducted from net income
Writer's Share	$5,000	$5,000
Lawn Choc. Music	$2,000	$2,250
Thrifty Scot Songs	$3,000	$2,750

Remember that the administration fee typically does not diminish the writer's share even if the fee is calculated on gross income — the non-administering publisher must eat the whole fee. Moral of the story: If you can't avoid the admin fee, make sure it is calculated on net income instead of gross income.

Collection costs – Collection costs may include commissions payable to the Harry Fox Agency for issuing and collecting on mechanical licenses and any other costs incurred pursuing or suing third parties for publishing income. You want to make sure to limit these costs to "actual and reasonable out-of-pocket collection costs" just to keep your publisher honest.

Copyright registration costs – It costs a few bucks to register copyrights with the copyright office.

Lead sheet costs – A lead sheet is a printed copy of a song containing the melody line, lyrics and harmonic structure notations. Before the Copyright Act was overhauled in 1976, you needed to submit a lead sheet in order to register a song for copyright. These days, you may submit a recording instead.

Demo costs – Costs incurred in making demo recordings of your songs.

Let's recap: Gross income equals 100% of income received by your publisher or co-publisher. Net income is equal to gross income minus the writer's share of royalties, administration fees (if any), collection costs, copyright registration costs, lead sheet costs and demo costs. Simple, right? Now that we know how net income is calculated, let's look at some more examples to see how publishing income received from various sources is divided between the songwriter, your own publishing company, and the publisher or co-publisher. Let's assume that the copyright is owned in equal shares and that the basic royalty split between publisher and co-publisher is 50/50 in the case of co-publishing deals.

MECHANICAL ROYALTIES

Standard Publishing Agreement – The publisher collects all income (gross income). The publisher then pays 50% of the gross income (the writer's share) to the writer and retains 100% of the net income/publisher's share.

	$10,000	Gross Income
MINUS	$5,000	Paid to songwriters (the writer's share)
=	$5,000	Net Income - Retained by publisher.

Co-publishing Agreement – The co-publisher collects all income (gross income). The co-publisher then pays 50% of gross income (the writer's share) to the writer and deducts the various collection costs. to arrive at net income. The co-publisher then pays 50% of net income to your own publishing company. Thus, you and your publishing company end up with a combined writer/publisher share equal to roughly 75% of gross income, while the co-publisher ends up with roughly 25%. Let's assume that your band sells enough records to generate gross income of $10,000.00 in U.S. mechanical royalties. The gross income is paid to the administering co-publisher and then divided as follows:

	$10,000	Gross Income
MINUS	$5,000	Paid to songwriters (the writer's share)
=	$5,000	Net Income
	$2,500	Paid to your publishing company (50% of net income)
	$2,500	Retained by administering co-publisher (50% of net income)

Of course, administration fees and other costs can vary these figures slightly.

Administration Agreement – As we discussed, the administration fee in this type of agreement ranges from 5% to 25%. Let's assume that the administration fee is 15%. The administering publisher collects all the gross income then deducts customary expenses and 15% from the gross income. The remainder is paid to your publisher, who is responsible for paying the writer's share of gross income to the writers. Some administrating publishers will agree to pay the writer's share directly. Assuming that you earn $10,000 in mechanical royalties, let's see how the money gets divided:

	$10,000	Gross Income
MINUS	$1,500	Retained by administering publisher as an administration fee (15% of gross receipts)
=	$8,500	Net Income – Paid to your own publishing company.

Out of this, you must pay the songwriters:

$5,000	Paid to songwriters (100% of the writer's share)
$3,500	Retained by your own publishing company

Accordingly, the writer/publisher ends up with 85% of the combined writer/publisher share of income. Depending on your leverage, some publishers will agree to an administration fee that is lower than 15%. If you do not receive an advance or if your publishing catalog contains one or more hit songs, you may be able to reduce the administration fee to as little as 5%.

COVERS

A quick note about covers (recordings of your songs by other artists): Your publisher, co-publisher, subpublisher or administering publisher will try to get a bigger piece of the pie on mechanical and performance income derived from cover recordings of your songs which originate in the territory covered by the agreement (we call these *local cover recordings*). Depending on the territory, try to avoid this. At the very least, you should agree to a lower royalty only in cases where the publisher actually pitched the song to an artist and was responsible for the recording. If the publisher can prove this, agree to pay a little more. If not, the split should be the same that applies to mechanical royalties payable from the sale of your own recordings.

PUBLIC PERFORMANCE ROYALTIES

Standard Publishing Agreement – Remember that performing rights organizations account directly to writer and publishers. Accordingly, under a standard publishing agreement, 100% of the publisher's share of public performance income is paid to and retained by your publisher. You get your writer's share directly.

Co-publishing Agreement – The administering co-publisher collects 100% of the publisher's share of public performance income and pays 50% of this to your own publishing company. Thus, your combined writer/publisher share of all public performance income is 75% while the co-publisher ends up with the other 25%, or 50% of the publisher's share.

Administration Agreement – Once again assuming a 15% administration fee and $10,000 in performance royalties, the money gets divided as follows:

	$5,000	Paid directly to songwriters by performing rights organization (100% of the writer's share)
	$5,000	Paid to administering publisher by performing rights organization (100% of publisher's share)
MINUS	$750	Retained by administering publisher as an administration fee (15% of publisher's share)
=	$4,250	Paid to your own publishing company by administering publisher.

Since the writer's share of public performance income is not included in gross income for the purposes of calculating the administering publisher's take of royalties, the writer/publisher ends up with 92.5% of the combined writer/publisher share of public performance income. Note that some writers and publishers succeed in excluding public performance income from the scope of their administration deals, since this type of income is relatively easy to collect.

COVERS

As with mechanical royalties, publishers, co-publishers, subpublishers and administering publishers will endeavor to secure a larger stake of performance royalties generated by cover recordings. The problem unique to performance royalties is that it is impossible to determine from your performance royalty statement whether a performance is an original recording or a cover recording. This is not the case with mechanical royalties, because you can see which version sold. Yet another reason to resist giving up increased royalties on covers.

SYNCHRONIZATION FEES AND ROYALTIES

Standard Publishing Agreement – These fees are generally split 50/50 between the writer and the publisher, although some publishers will try to secure an extra 10 to 15 percent. Resist this, and at the very least, agree to the extra percentage only in cases where the publisher is directly responsible for securing the synch license. Some publishers are very active in pitching songs to movie and TV producers and advertisers, while others are not.

Co-publishing Agreement – The split is typically 50% to the writer, 25% to the co-publisher and 25% to your own publishing company, but once again, some publishers will try to get a larger piece of the action whether or not they actually secured the synch license.

Administration Agreement – The administering publisher retains a portion of any synch fee equal to the administration fee agreed upon in the deal. These guys will also try to get a bigger piece for synchs they secure.

SHEET MUSIC/PRINT ROYALTIES

Before reading further, go back and review our brief discussion of sheet music and print royalties in Part Two of this chapter.

STANDARD PUBLISHING AGREEMENT

Sheet Music – Remember that the publisher typically receives a royalty of 20% of the retail price for a single piece of sheet music. Accordingly, if a piece of sheet music retails for $4.00, the royalty payable to the publisher is 80¢. Unfortunately for you writers, the major publishers have historically paid writers a royalty of 6¢ or 7¢ per copy instead of 50% of gross income. This leaves the publisher with 73¢ to 74¢. Why does this gross inequity persist? Ask an old guy — I don't know and I'm too tired to find out why. Just accept it and try to make sure that you get a "most favored nations" provision in your deal.

Matching Folio/Mixed Folios – Things get better with folios. If the publisher receives a 12 1/2% of retail price royalty, they will likely agree to pay the writer a 6 1/4% of retail royalty. Some publishers (Warner/Chappell comes to mind) will pay the writer a royalty of 12 1/2% of *wholesale*, but since the wholesale price is generally 1/2 of retail price, the numbers usually work out the same. In other words, if the publisher is paid $1.00 in folio royalties, the writer gets 50¢ and the publisher keeps 50¢.

Personality Folios – If you're the artist and it's your likeness, you keep the same as above plus 5%.

Fake Books/Educational Editions – The publisher is paid 10% of retail. The publisher then pays the writer 10% of wholesale or 5% of retail, which, as we just discussed, is more or less the same royalty.

CO-PUBLISHING AGREEMENT

Sheet Music – In addition to the whopping 6¢ or 7¢ per copy you will receive as a writer, you get 50% of what is left over. Using the example from above, if the publisher is left with 74¢ after paying the writer, the publisher pays you half of that, or 37¢, as your co-publisher share, bringing your grand total to 43¢ or 44¢ per copy.

Matching Folio/Mixed Folios – You get your writer's share (50%) of the 12 1/2% retail royalty (6 1/4%) plus 50% of the remaining 6 1/4%.

Personality Folios – If you're the artist and it's your likeness, you keep the same as above, just add 5% to the royalty before dividing it up.

Fake Books/Educational Editions – If the publisher is paid 10% of retail, the publisher pays the writer 10% of wholesale or 5% of retail, which, as we just discussed, is more or less the same royalty. The remaining royalty is split between the publisher and co-publisher.

Administration Agreement – If you are going to do an administration agreement, you might as well exclude print rights from the deal. It's easy to make a print-only deal with one of the four major print music publishers (if your sheet music is worth anything, that is). Otherwise, the administering publisher will do this for you and will deduct the agreed-upon percentage from the gross print income it collects. Accordingly, if you have a 15% admin deal and receive 80¢ per piece of sheet music, you pay the administrator 12¢ a sheet and keep 68¢. The admin/subpublishing percentage also comes off the top of other kinds of print royalties.

ADVANCES

Hard to believe it took me nearly 30 pages to get to the money, but we're finally here. Let's face facts — most songwriters and publishers enter into publishing agreements for the up-front cash. The size of the advance depends on the nature of the deal and (once again) on our old friend, bargaining power.

Standard Publishing Agreement – The advance for a single/individual song agreement varies wildly depending on the stature of the songwriter. Songs that are already hits will obviously bring higher advances than unexploited or non-hit songs. The advance under this kind of deal is typically paid on signing of the agreement. Conversely, advances under an exclusive songwriter agreement are likely to be higher, because the publisher is getting all of your songs for the agreed upon term. If you are a songwriter (but not a recording artist), your advances under an exclusive songwriter agreement might be paid on a monthly or annual basis, kind of like a salary. Some deals pay a specified advance per song delivered. If you are a recording artist, advances will probably be keyed to the delivery and release of your next album.

Co-publishing Agreement – Since this is the type of publishing agreement you are most likely to encounter, let's look at an example. Your band signs a co-publishing/exclusive songwriter deal with Thrifty Scot Songs and the advance provision in the contract looks like this:

> The advance for the First Qualifying Album shall be $150,000, payable $50,000 on signing with the balance on initial U.S. release of such album. In the event that we exercise a renewal option, we shall pay you an amount (payable upon initial U.S. release of the subject Qualifying Album) equal to 70% of your combined U.S. writer/publisher mechanical royalties from the immediately preceding Qualifying Album as of the end of the calendar quarter preceding the calendar quarter during which the subject Qualifying Album is released, but not more or less than the following:

Qualifying Album	Minimum	Maximum
2nd	$150,000	$200,000
3rd	$200,000	$400,000
4th	$250,000	$500,000

Advances shall be prorated to the extent that any Qualifying Album does not consist of 100% previously unrecorded compositions that are written by you and subject to this agreement.

The last paragraph is important. Under this deal, the minimum delivery commitment per contract period is an album comprised solely of your songs. Thus, if you deliver an album with songs written by other writers, you don't get the full advance. For instance, if you end up writing only 50% of the songs on the First Qualifying Album, your $150,000 advance is now a paltry $75,000. Moral of the story: Get the minimum delivery percentage lowered (75% is good) or don't record other people's songs. The minimum/maximum formula should be familiar to you if you read Chapter Four. If not, it works like this: Let's say your first album generates $100,000 in U.S. mechanical income prior to delivery of your second album. Since this is a co-publishing deal, your combined writer/publisher share of this income is $75,000. 70% of $75,000 is $52,500. However, the contract says that your minimum advance for the second album is $150,000, so that's what you will receive (assuming you wrote 100% of the songs on the album). If your first album generated $500,000 in gross income, your combined writer/publisher share is $375,000. 70% of $375,000 is $262,500, but you will only receive an advance of $200,000, since that is the maximum allowed by the deal. Of course, you would also be recouped at this point, so your publisher might be willing to pay you a larger advance anyway. If not, you'll have to wait until your next statement arrives in the mail. Most publishers account twice a year, but some account every quarter.

Before we leave the land of advances, remember that you must recoup them out of your combined writer/publisher share of royalties before you can expect to see a non-contractual royalty check. Let's say you are advanced $300,000 over two records under a standard 75/25 co-publishing agreement. If your co-publisher collects $300,000 in gross income, you are still unrecouped by $75,000, since only your combined writer/publisher share of royalties ($225,000) goes against your unrecouped balance.

LEAVING MEMBERS

If you sign an exclusive songwriter publishing or co-publishing agreement as a band, your publisher will insert language into the agreement which gives it the right to keep individual members on as a writer/publisher in the event that they leave the group or in the event that the group disbands. The reasons behind this and the steps you must take to protect yourselves in this situation are similar to those behind leaving member provisions in recording agreements, so I'm not going to bore you with more examples — just something to think about.

WHY SIGN A PUBLISHING AGREEMENT?

1) Money – As you know from reading Chapter Four, you probably won't be able to maintain a reasonable quality of life on the money you get from your record deal alone. In general, the more you give up (in terms of copyright, number of songs, exclusivity, etc.) the larger your advance will be. Of course, if no one likes your songs or if your records don't sell, you may have trouble getting any kind of deal at all.

2) Money – Remember, it's not about the money, it's about the money.

3) Administration – We covered this in the first part of this chapter. Go back and read it again.

4) Career Development – Publishers are often instrumental in getting their writers signed to recording agreements.

5) You have no choice – Many record companies (especially independent record companies) will "strongly suggest" or even demand that you assign part or all of your copyright in and to your compositions to the label's publishing company. You should avoid this unless it makes sense. At the very least, make sure that (a) the publishing company is in fact a real publishing company that can actually administer your catalogue effectively; (b) your controlled composition clause calls for U.S. mechanical royalties to be paid at a rate equal to 100% of the current statutory mechanical rate; (c) your mechanical royalty account and your record royalty account are not cross-collateralized; (d) the term of the publishing deal ends when and if the record deal ends; and (e) the royalty rates and advances are competitive with those that might be offered by non-affiliated publishers. Of course, you should always try to get a reversion.

WHEN IS THE BEST TIME TO SIGN A PUBLISHING DEAL?

You should consider signing any deal that you and your representatives feel will better your career. At the very least, you will probably need to consider an administration deal of some kind after your songs start getting made into records. The million-dollar question is whether or not you should sell all or part of your copyrights, via a standard publishing agreement or a co-publishing agreement. There are a few basic approaches to consider:

Bet Against Yourself: Sign Early – Let's face it, success in the music business is a crap shoot. Accordingly, if a publisher offers you a reasonable amount of money for your songs before you have had a significant degree of success, you should think long and hard about doing the deal. If there is any residual hype left from the record deal bidding war, a good attorney can roll the hype over into a bidding war for your publishing. The downside to signing early: if you ultimately become a huge star, you are giving up a substantial piece of change to your publisher or co-publisher. The upside: If your career goes nowhere, at least you got an advance. Who cares that your publisher lost a bundle?

Bet On Yourself: Wait and Sign Late – If you are sure that you are going to sell a billion records, your best bet is to wait until you are well on your way to doing so. If you have a hit record (or even if it just looks like it could be a hit), the major publishers will be lining up to sign you and will offer large advances and favorable deal terms, because the risk is lower — they already know that you are getting airplay and selling records and will take a chance that you will continue to do so. On the other hand, if you pass on a nice deal early on, and your records stiff, you can bet that those early offers will evaporate in a hurry.

4. DO IT YOURSELF

As we discussed, most of you will end up forming a publishing company whether or not you ultimately decide to sell your publishing. Here's how you do it:

1) If "you" are a band of songwriters, you need to decide whether or not you will form one publishing company for all the writer members, or form separate companies for each member. If you decide to have one company, you need to draw up an agreement that specifies how the company is to be managed and how royalties and advances are to be split. This agreement may take the form of a partnership, a corporation or an LLC (limited liability company). Ask your attorney and accountant to help you with this.

2) Choose a performing rights organization. Take the opportunity to meet with a representative of each organization to help you decide.

3) Pick A Name. You need to come up with a unique name for your publishing company. Don't submit "Steve's Songs," because it's probably already taken. No two publishers can have the same name. Clear the name with the chosen performing rights organization and affiliate as a writer and a publisher

4) File a DBA ("doing business as") notice in a local paper, get a federal tax ID number and open a bank account.

5) Register your copyrights.

6) Collect publishing income.

7) Cash your royalty check, go to a bookstore and buy another copy of this book for a friend.

It's just that simple!

CONCLUSION

I've already said too much. If any of this is confusing to you, read it again, write down your questions and ask them of your attorney. If you don't have an attorney, get one. In the meantime, take a look at the sample co-publishing agreement in Appendix B, and for additional publishing wisdom read my interview with legendary songwriter **Mike Stoller** in Appendix A.

CHAPTER SEVEN

Merchandising and Trademarks

Merchandising is a huge and often lucrative business — who among you hasn't purchased a T-shirt, program or hat at a concert? The first part of this chapter covers the different kinds of deals you can enter into to sell your merchandise. Since merchandise involves trademarks (band names, logos and the like), the second and final part of the chapter is a very brief primer on trademark law.

I. MERCHANDISING

WHAT IS MERCHANDISE?

Merchandise (or 'merch') is any non-record product bearing your name, image, logo or likeness. The bulk of merch sold in the music business is clothing (T-shirts, hats, sweatshirts, etc.), but calendars, programs, lighters and posters are also popular items.

HOW TO SELL IT

Do it Yourself – You can screen your own T-shirts, or you can hire someone to do it for you. It really helps to have someone available to ship new supplies of merch to you on the road when you run out. You will also need someone to help you sell the merch at the venue (unless you feel like selling it out of the van after the show). While selling your own merch can be profitable, you may find that doing it yourself can be quite cumbersome and expensive. If so, you should consider signing a merchandising agreement with a merchandising company.

Sign a Deal with a Merchandising Company – There are only a few full-service merchandising companies in the U.S., and, predictably, most are owned or co-owned by the major music conglomerates:

> Sony Signatures (Sony)
> Great Entertainment Merchandising (owned by PolyGram/UMG)
> Nice Man Merchandising (co-owned by BMG)
> Winterland Productions
> Giant Merchandising (owned by Warner Music Group)

There are also a number of independent merchandisers, although only Tannis Root (based in North Carolina) comes to mind.

HOW TO GET A MERCH DEAL

Shop Around – The merch companies will come to you if you are selling a respectable amount of records and touring on a regular basis. If they don't come calling, ask your manager or attorney to call them.

Surprise! You Already Have One: Record Deal Tie Ins – Some recording agreements contain provisions that grant the record company merchandising rights in addition to your exclusive recording rights. While many record companies ask for exclusive merchandising rights, others (Epitaph and Revelation, for example) will only ask for the right to sell a few designs through their mail order catalogs and retail accounts. The latter isn't such a bad thing, as long as the royalties you earn are fair and not applied against any debts you have accrued with respect to records (recording costs, advances, etc.). A less onerous (yet still annoying) provision in recording agreements relates to matching rights and rights of first and last negotiation. For example, nearly all PolyGram owned or affiliated record companies will require you to grant GEM some kind of matching right or first/last negotiation right. As I mentioned back in Chapter Four, GEM is a fine company, but you'd rather be free to sign with the company of your choice if and when it comes time to sell your merch rights. Accordingly, try to eliminate or limit the scope of any merchandising provisions in your record deal, and *never* sign over all of your exclusive merch rights (especially if the record company has no ties to a legitimate merchandising operation).

MERCHANDISING AGREEMENTS

Merch deals take three forms: Tour only, retail only and tour/retail. Let's look at the most important provisions in each.

TOUR AGREEMENT

This kind of agreement gives the merch company the right to sell merch bearing your marks at your shows.

Rights Granted/Creative Control – A typical tour merch agreement grants the merchandising company the exclusive right to sell any merchandise (other than records, of course) bearing your name, photo, likeness, logo, artwork, etc. (we call these things your 'marks') on any merchandise, including T-shirts, shorts, sweatshirts, underwear, lighters, posters, coffee mugs, tour programs, calendars, etc. If you care what kind of merch the company sells or what it looks like, make sure you have the right to approve this in your deal - it's usually not a problem.

Term – Most merch agreements span one or two contract periods. Each contract period is typically defined as one or two "album cycles" instead of years or months. An album cycle stretches from the first show following the release of your next album until the last show prior to the release of the following album. Accordingly, a contract period can last anywhere from six months to three years, depending on the success of your record and how much you like to tour. However, most merch deals will provide that each contract period will last at least one year, while other deals allow the merchandising company to extend each contract period to the date you recoup your advances (even if the album cycle has concluded). You want to avoid this if you can. If you cannot, try to get the right to end the deal by paying back any unrecouped advances. If your deal is for one contract period only, the deal ends at the later of: one year, the end of the tour cycle or (if applicable) recoupment of advances. Most merch companies will try to get an optional contract period out of you, but you can usually avoid this if you are a superstar. If the merch company can't get an outright option for your next tour cycle, they will probably ask for a right of first negotiation coupled with a matching right.

Territory – As with any other kind of deal, the merch company will ask for the world. If you have relationships with merchandisers outside the U.S., or if the merch company is weak outside the U.S., it may make sense to make separate deals for different territories.

Tour Obligations/Performance Guarantees – Most tour merch agreements require the artist to commit to a tour where the artist will play to a minimum number of concertgoers over the course of a tour. Let's look at some language from a recent deal proposal made to one of my clients:

> ARTIST will guarantee that during the Album Cycle, ARTIST will perform as a so-called 'headline' act before an aggregate of 200,000 paid attendees at venues throughout the Territory (the 'Performance Minimum'). In the event that the Performance Minimum is not achieved, MERCHANDISER may demand that ARTIST repay to MERCHANDISER the full amount of unrecouped Advances paid to ARTIST. In the alternative, MERCHANDISER may deem any unrecouped Advances as additional Advances to ARTIST with respect to the subsequent Album Cycle, in which event the amount of such additional Advance shall bear interest at a rate equal to the prime interest rate of Citibank, N.A. calculated from the date upon which MERCHANDISER originally paid such Advance.

In other words, if your tour does not go as well as expected, your attorney may receive a letter politely asking for the return of the unrecouped portion of your advance. Of course, this doesn't always happen - some companies don't go after you unless you break up or you otherwise make them feel truly burned by the deal. As you can see, the merch company will asess interest on your unrecouped balance in any event. If you have some leverage, you may be able to work in a provision that obligates you to pay back only a pro-rata portion of your unrecouped advance. Here's how that works: If your performance minimum is 200,000, and you only play to 100,000 paid attendees during the tour cycle, you owe only 50% of the unrecouped balance, since you achieved 50% of the performance minimum.

Advances – Advances are based on your popularity, your prior sales history and the scale of your tour plans. Most agreements call for an advance on signing or commencement of touring with additional 'rollover' advances as certain sales levels or performance minimums are met. Get what you can, but don't be stupid: Remember that the merch deal is the only type of deal you are likely to encounter which may require you to repay advances out of your own pocket if things don't go well.

Tour Royalties – Tour merch royalties are based on a percentage of net sales. 'Net sales' in the context of the merch trade is typically defined as gross receipts (all monies paid to or received by your merch company) minus local sales tax, credit card fees, value added taxes and import duties. Let's look at a royalty schedule from an actual deal:

United States	31% of net sales
	33% of net sales after recoupment of advances
U.K./Canada	30% of net sales
Australia/NZ	29% of net sales
Japan	29% of net sales
EEC	27% of net sales
ROW	26% of net sales

Assuming your T-shirts sell for $30.00 on your U.S. tour, you will receive roughly $9.30 for each shirt sold before recoupment and $9.90 thereafter. The royalty rates in this example are respectable for a new artist. Some deals start at less than 25% in the U.S., while few deals start higher than 35%. Royalty rates for superstar acts often exceed 50%. Royalties for sales outside the U.S. are lower because of customs duties and VAT (value added tax, which doesn't apply to U.S. sales).

Leaving Member Issues – If a member of your band leaves or your band breaks up completely during an album cycle, many merch companies will ask for the right to terminate the agreement and require you to repay any unrecouped advances. This makes sense, since it is impossible to sell any merch if there is no tour. If a member leaves and the tour continues, some agreements will require you to give the merch company the continued right to use the leaving member's likeness, so you want to be sure that you have this right. This issue is usually dealt with in the band agreement (which we will discuss in Chapter Eight). Try not to allow the merch company to have merchandising rights with respect to the solo career of a band member.

RETAIL AGREEMENT

A retail-only agreement gives the merch company the right to sell merch bearing your marks at retail outlets and sometimes via mail order.

Retail Royalties – Retail merch royalties for products manufactured by the merch company are based on the wholesale selling price of merch sold by the merch company. The wholesale price is the price at which the merch company sells merchandise to retailers. The average royalty for this product runs from 10% to 16% of the wholesale price in the U.S. Accordingly, if your merch company sells a T-shirt to K-Mart for $2.00 and your royalty is 12% of wholesale, you get 24¢ for that sale. Keep in mind that many merch companies will sublicense the right to manufacture and sell certain types of retail merch which they do not ordinarily sell. You will likely receive 60% to 80% of your merch company's net receipts from these sales. Foreign retail royalties typically run 10% to 20% lower than U.S. royalties.

Advances – Depends on the artist. On the whole, advances are lower for retail deals.

Term – Unlike tour merch agreements, retail deals usually run a year or two. Some deals don't end until advances are recouped, and some allow the artist to buy out the unrecouped portion of the advance.

Mail Order – You may wish to sell merch through your fan club, your website or through a newsletter, so make sure your merch deal allows you to do this.

TOUR/RETAIL AGREEMENTS

Many artists sign deals which cover touring and retail. The big downside here is that this allows cross-collateralization of advances and royalties.

That's merch in a nutshell. Check out the sample merch deal proposal in the Appendix B.

2. TRADEMARK BASICS

WHAT IS A TRADEMARK?

A trademark is a symbol, word, phrase or design (or a combination of any of them) that identifies the source of goods and services and allows the consumer to distinguish the source of the goods and services among different parties. Contrast this with copyright, which protects original works of authorship, such as songs, master recordings and photographs. Trademarks (such as a name or a logo) can identify goods (such as records and T-shirts) while *service marks* identify the source of a service. In the world of rock and roll, the same mark can be both a trademark and a service mark. Need an example? Let's say your band is called Lawn Chocolate. When you sell goods (such as records and T-shirts) under that name, Lawn Chocolate is a trademark. When you provide entertainment services under that name (by playing a concert or appearing on a TV show) Lawn Chocolate is a service mark. Keep in mind that there are different 'classes' of goods and services in which marks must be registered. For instance, Class 9 covers records, Class 25 covers clothing, Class 16 covers paper goods and Class 41 covers entertainment services. Accordingly, if you want to protect your mark in connection with CDs, T-shirts, posters and live performances, you need to register your mark in each of these classes and pay a separate registration fee for each class.

HOW TO ESTABLISH TRADEMARK RIGHTS

Contrary to popular belief, federal registration is not necessary to establish trademark rights. Trademark rights arise from *actual use* of a mark or the filing of a proper "intent to use" application with the United States Patent and Trademark Office ('USPTO'). While you don't necessarily need to register your mark before or after you use it, federal registration confers many extra benefits on the trademark owner. We'll explore those benefits in a minute, but for now let's focus on the meaning of actual use. Actual use means using your mark "in interstate commerce." For example, if Lawn Chocolate conducts business in more than one state, whether via touring, selling records and/or radio airplay, it has succeeded in using its mark in interstate commerce, thereby satisfying the actual use requirement.

FEDERAL TRADEMARK REGISTRATION

While actual use of a mark confers certain rights, federal trademark registration confers many additional rights and is recommended. As with copyright registration, federal trademark registration puts other users on constructive notice that the owner of the mark has the exclusive right to use the mark nationwide. More importantly, registration establishes a presumption that your mark is being used nationwide and gives you priority over all other users except for those that can establish prior use. Federal registration also gives the owner the right to sue infringers in federal district court (although holders of unregistered marks can sue infringers in federal court on the basis of common law rights).

LAWN CHOCOLATE V. LAWN CHOCOLATE

Let's look at a hypothetical. Let's say your band Lawn Chocolate formed in Phoenix, Arizona in 1994. Over the ensuing years, the band plays many live shows as Lawn Chocolate in Arizona, New Mexico and Utah. Additionally, Lawn Chocolate (AZ) puts out several albums, copies of which sell in neighboring states. Due to financial constraints, no federal trademark registration is filed, but all of this activity arguably amounts to use of the "Lawn Chocolate" mark in interstate commerce. Accordingly, Lawn Chocolate (AZ) has established trademark and service mark rights through actual use. In 1997, another band called Lawn Chocolate forms in Brooklyn, New York. Lawn Chocolate (NY) has no idea that Lawn Chocolate (AZ) exists. Lawn Chocolate (NY) establishes trademark and service mark rights in the name Lawn Chocolate through actual use and then proceeds to file trademark and service mark applications in all appropriate classes with the USPTO. Assuming Lawn Chocolate (NY) secures federal trademark registrations, which band has rights to the name Lawn Chocolate? Both do, although Lawn Chocolate (AZ) may only use the name in the Phoenix area and the natural zone of expansion therefrom. Lawn Chocolate (NY) may use the name throughout the country, except for the region where Lawn Chocolate (AZ) has exclusive rights. Moral of the story: if you aspire to become a 'national act,' file an intent to use application or establish trademark rights through actual use and then register your mark with the USPTO as soon as possible.

BEFORE YOU REGISTER . . .

Before you file your registration or intent-to-use application, you should make sure your mark does not infringe an existing mark, because you don't want to get sued for trademark infringement and because the USPTO won't refund your registration fee if your application is denied. How does the USPTO determine whether there is a conflict between two marks? They determine whether there would be a likelihood of confusion regarding the source or origin of the goods or services. In other words, if the USPTO thinks that your mark, although unique, may confuse the consumer as to the source of goods or services, they may reject your application.

In any event, the USPTO weighs several factors in their analysis, chief among them being: 1) The similarity of the marks; and 2) the commercial relationship between the goods and services identified by the marks. Conflicts can (and have) been found in instances where the marks are not identical and in instances where the goods or services are not the same. Of course, the mere fact that the USPTO approves your registration application does not mean that you cannot be sued for infringement. Accordingly, you should conduct a thorough search and review the results with an attorney before you file your application. There are a number of research avenues available to the trademark applicant. For instance, many applicants engage a company called Thomson & Thomson to conduct thorough domestic trademark searches. In exchange for a few hundred dollars, Thomson & Thomson will run a fairly comprehensive search of various trademark databases. The results of the search are summarized in a written report, which is utilized by the applicant or applicant's attorney to make a determination as to whether a particular mark could potentially infringe on an existing mark. If you don't have the scratch for this kind of search, check out the free search service at the USPTO website (the address is in Appendix C), but keep in mind that the search results provided by the USPTO website are three months behind. You can also perform your own search in the USPTO public search library in Arlington, VA. If you don't feel like traveling to Virginia, you can visit a patent and trademark depository library (call the USPTO or visit their website to find the closest one) to scan CD-ROMs containing the trademark database of registered and pending marks. Happy searching!

THE APPLICATION PROCESS

There are two kinds of Federal trademark registration applications: Intent to Use applications and Actual Use applications. Which should you file? Read on!

Intent to Use – Your band isn't ready to record or play live shows just yet, but you have decided that 'Lawn Chocolate' is the perfect name. How do you protect the name without using it? If you have a bona fide intent to use the mark, you can file an intent to use application (cost: $245.00) with the USPTO. This gives you six months to use the mark in commerce and fulfill the requirements of registration. Once you actually start using the mark, you file a Statement of Use with the USPTO, and this costs another $100.00 per class. If you don't actually use the mark within the initial six-month period, you can renew your application for additional six-month periods by filing a Request for a Six-Month Extension of Time for Filing a Statement of Use, and this also costs $100.00 per class. If you don't use the mark and file the Statement of Use or get a six-month extension, anyone can file an application to register your mark.

Actual Use – If you have established actual use of a mark, you should file an Actual Use application. Please note that the USPTO is very strict when it comes to registering marks for use in Class 9 (the class that applies to records and CDs). For some reason, they won't let you register your mark in this class until your second release.

How Do I Register My Trademark or Service Mark? After you have done your research and determined what kind of application your should file, you need to get a hold of the appropriate applications. Check the Appendix for info on the USPTO, but I suggest getting on-line and utilizing the USPTO website. This informative website has all of the information, instructions and applications you need to register your marks. If you are lazy and feel like contributing to an attorney's mortgage payment, hire an attorney. It will cost a lot more, but can you put a price on peace of mind? No? I can suggest a figure . . .

How Much Does It Cost To Register A Trademark or Service Mark? The USPTO charges $245 per mark per class. Legal fees vary from attorney to attorney.

How Long Does a Trademark Last? Trademark rights can last indefinitely as long as the owner uses the mark to identify goods and services without any serious time lapses and takes reasonable steps to stop non-authorized users from utilizing the mark. The actual term of federal trademark registration is 10 years, with additional 10 year renewal terms. However, between the fifth and sixth year after the date of initial registration, the trademark registrant must file an affidavit setting forth certain information to maintain the registration. If you don't file the affidavit, the registration is canceled.

What Do ® and ™ Mean? Only owners of federally registered marks may use the registration symbol ®. You are not supposed to use this symbol with your mark until you have confirmation of registration. Conversely, anyone claiming rights in a mark may use the TM (trademark) or SM (service mark) designation to put the public on notice to your claim on the mark.

CONCLUSION

This is a really sketchy overview of a complex and super gnarly area of the law, so be sure to consult an experienced attorney if you have serious trademark issues to contend with.

CHAPTER EIGHT

Business Entities and Band Agreements

Whether you are a solo artist or a band, you need to choose a sound structure for your music business operation. In Part One of this chapter we'll look at the most common types of business entities favored by artists, songwriters, publishers and labels in the music business. Part Two is for bands, and it outlines the issues you need to contemplate before you put together a written band agreement.

I. BUSINESS ENTITIES

Assuming that you want to make a living in the music business, it is imperative that you structure your business properly before any money starts flowing in or out. The way you structure your business is important because it affects, among other things, your liability to others and the way you are taxed. There are many factors to consider in choosing a structure for your business, among them: whether you will operate it alone or with your fellow partners or shareholders, the kind of risk of personal liability with which you are comfortable, and the most appropriate tax treatment. Let's look at each of these factors as we explore the four most common business entities: the sole proprietorship, the partnership, the corporation and the limited liability company (LLC).

SOLE PROPRIETORSHIP

In a sole proprietorship, a single person (the sole proprietor) owns 100% of the business and is personally responsible for all liabilities. This is a common business structure adopted by solo artists for their recording and publishing enterprises. It may surprise you to learn that many "bands" are actually nothing more than a single person acting as a sole proprietor who has hired other musicians to act as "band members."

Liability – As a sole proprietor, you and your business are one and the same. Accordingly, you are personally liable for any losses or debts you incur as a sole proprietor. For example, if you put out your own record and are sued for copyright infringement because one of the tracks on your record includes an infringing sample, the party suing you can go after your personal holdings and possessions as well as any holdings of your business. This is one of the primary reasons why artists, labels and songwriters tend to avoid this structure as they get more successful and have more assets.

Tax Issues – In a sole proprietorship, any net profits or losses from the business are reported on the sole proprietor's personal income tax returns. If you intend to have employees, it is a good idea to obtain a federal tax ID number (also known as an Employer Identification Number, or EIN). You can obtain an EIN by calling the IRS at 800-829-3676 and asking for Form SS-4. Note that an EIN number is mandatory for partnerships, corporations and LLCs.

How to Form a Sole Proprietorship – It's fairly simple, actually. If you do not have a partner and choose not to incorporate, you are a sole proprietor. However, if you want to operate your business under a "fictitious name," you will need to register your sole proprietorship with local or state authorities. For instance, let's say you want to start a record company. Assuming you don't want to use your legal name as the name of the record company, your business will operate under a fictitious name. After some thought, you settle on "Fred's Hit Records." Your next step is to head down to city hall to file a "doing business as" or DBA statement in the name of your business with the county clerk. Please note that some states may have different procedures for filing DBA statements, but a few calls to local government offices should get you started. In California, you must publish a legal notice in a local paper that states that you have established your business under a fictitious name. This doesn't cost much and the idea is that it allows any interested party to know the real identity of the sole proprietor. Your final step is to open up a bank account. If you are not operating under a DBA, this can be your personal checking account. Otherwise, it's a good idea to open a separate account under the name of your business.

GENERAL PARTNERSHIP

A general partnership is legal agreement by and between two or more people or business entities in which each party agrees to furnish a portion of the capital (such as cash and equipment) and labor necessary to conduct business, and by which each partner shares in profits and losses in the manner specified in the partnership agreement. A partnership agreement can be oral or written, but I suggest putting it in writing. You and your partners can run your partnership virtually any way you like, but if your partnership is in California, for example, and the partners plan to operate it as anything less than a true democracy, the partners should execute a written partnership agreement. Otherwise, all partners will have equal voting rights, equal rights to profits and assets, and equal liability.

Liability – Written partnership agreement or not, the entire partnership is liable for all acts of any partner (even if the written partnership agreement does not allow the partner to take action without a partnership vote). For example, if your band operates under a partnership, and your guitar player books a gig for the band without running it by the other band members, the entire partnership is liable for breach of contract if the band doesn't show up for the gig. Assuming the promoter goes to court and is awarded $10,000 in damages, this money must come first from partnership assets. If the partnership has only $5,000 in assets, the promoter can then reach into the pockets of any or all partners to claim the rest of the money. Bummer. Here's another good one: Your guitar player decides it would be fun to chuck a beer bottle into the audience during a show. Unfortunately, someone gets injured and sues the band. Who is liable? That's right, the entire partnership is liable, as are the individual partners. The injured party can seek to recover all of its damages from one partner or any combination of partners. Keep in mind that partnership liability extends only to acts or omissions within the scope of partnership business. For instance, if your bass player decides to rob a bank while on vacation with his family, the partnership should not be liable for the consequences of his actions.

Tax Issues – The partnership itself does not pay taxes. Instead, partnerships are required to file a partnership informational tax return which tells the IRS and state tax authorities how much the partnership made or lost and how such profits or losses were divided amongst the partners. Each partner then reports his share of any partnership profits or losses on his personal tax return.

How to Form a General Partnership – As I have already mentioned, a written agreement is not required to form a partnership, but this doesn't allow for much flexibility when it comes to the kind of decisions you will need to make. So hire an attorney and get it in writing. You will also need to get an Employee Identification Number and open a partnership bank account. Depending on where you live and the name of the partnership, you may also need to file a DBA statement with your city or county.

CORPORATIONS

A corporation is a legal entity having its own rights, privileges, and existence independent of and distinct from those of its shareholders. While incorporating your business is a great deal more costly and complicated than forming a sole proprietorship or a partnership, incorporation offers something that neither of those entities offer: a potential shield against personal liability. Corporations are comprised of shareholders and governed by a board of directors. The directors are elected by the shareholders. Day to day management of the corporation is handled by corporate officers (the president, secretary, etc.) who are selected by the board of directors. When bands incorporate, each member is typically issued a certain number of shares in the corporation. These band members turned shareholders usually elect themselves as the directors and officers of the corporation. Prior to incorporation, you will have to decide whether you wish to incorporate as an S corporation or a C corporation. The main difference between that S corporation and a C corporation lies in how and a what level corporate income is taxed. We'll get to that in a moment.

Liability – We already talked about the downside of partnerships when it comes to the risk of personal liability. The beauty of a corporation (S and C corporations are alike in this regard) is that unlike a partnership, one shareholder generally wont be held personally liable for the actions or omissions of the corporation or of another shareholder as long as all of the formalities of corporate existence and maintenance are complied with on an ongoing basis. In a nutshell, corporate formalities generally include (among other things) holding regular meetings, electing directors and officers, issuing stock, opening a bank account and maintaining sufficient capitalization in light of potential liability. Let's look at a hypothetical scenario which assumes that your band is incorporated and that all corporate formalities have been complied with: If your drummer drives the band's van into a troop of Girl Scouts on the way to a gig, the other shareholders probably won't be held personally liable to the victims or their families. If we change the example so that the band operates as a general partnership, all of the partners would be personally liable. Naturally, there are limits to the protection a corporation affords. For example, your drummer is still personally liable for the consequences of his poor driving, even though he is a shareholder in the corporation. Also be aware that some states will hold certain shareholders liable for unpaid employee wages and failure to withhold income taxes from those wages. Finally, remember that every state has different corporate laws, so what may be true in one state may not be true in another.

Tax Issues - With respect to corporations, tax liability differs greatly depending on the type of corporation that is formed.

S Corporation – While S corporations must pay minimal annual taxes, profits and losses from the business of the corporation flow through to the shareholders (band members), and the shareholders report these profits and losses on their personal income tax returns.

C Corporation – Unlike sole proprietorships, partnerships, LLCs and S corporations, C corporations file and pay corporate income tax on the profits of the corporation. After corporate tax is paid on profits, the officers of the corporation may elect to distribute the remaining profits to shareholders as dividends. Shareholders must report dividends as income on their personal income tax returns. So if your band is incorporated as a C corporation, the dividend each member receives as a shareholder has been taxed twice — once at the corporate level and once at the personal level. Not good. For this reason, most bands that incorporate choose the S corporation. So why even think about forming a C corporation? There are a few good reasons: First, a C corporation may be able to deduct the cost of certain fringe benefits (such as a health care plan) from corporate taxes, while S corporations are limited to deducting only a small percentage of these costs. Second, corporate tax rates can be lower than personal tax rates, at least initially. Accordingly, if you don't distribute any corporate profits to shareholders by way of dividends, you avoid double taxation and pay less in tax. Of course, each shareholder will eventually want to take his profits, so "double taxation" is probable with a C corporation unless you get creative with your accounting, and that's not my department.

How to Form a Corporation – First, come up with $2,000 or so (to cover legal fees, filing fees, etc.). Next, hire a competent corporate attorney or experienced corporate paralegal. Your attorney and accountant or business manager can then help you determine in which state you should incorporate and what kind of corporation you should form. Every state has different laws and regulations governing corporate formation, taxation and liability. For instance, Delaware and Nevada are popular places to incorporate businesses because these states have adopted laws that can be favorable to corporations. Ask your attorney and accountant whether or not it makes sense for you to incorporate in a specific state. Next, you need to choose a unique name for the corporation, file the articles of incorporation with the state, pay the necessary fees and taxes, and sign the corporate bylaws your attorney has drafted for you. (The bylaws spell out how the corporation will be managed.) You may also want to consider entering into a shareholder's agreement which can place further restrictions on the management of the corporation and the transfer of shares of the corporation to persons you would want as your fellow shareholders. Your corporation may also want to have employment agreements with each band member, although these aren't necessary to form the corporation. As I mentioned earlier, there are a number of corporate formalities you will need to comply with to maintain the corporation over the ensuing years, but your attorney can fill you in on these. Just know that if you fail to comply with these formalities, you may lose your protection against personal liability in certain situations.

LIMITED LIABILITY COMPANY

A limited liability company (LLC) is a relatively new type of business entity that allows members to enjoy the tax benefits of a partnership and the limited personal liability of a corporation. In light of the foregoing, it shouldn't come as a surprise that many bands are now structuring their businesses as LLCs instead of partnerships or corporations. LLCs are creatures of state law which, as you know by now, varies from state to state.

Liability – The rules differ from state to state, but let's look at my home state of California. In California, the members of an LLC are liable in the same way that shareholders are liable in a corporation. Accordingly, members in California LLCs must comply with certain formalities to maintain their shield from personal liability (much like they would as shareholders and officers of a corporation).

Tax Issues – As in a sole proprietorship, partnership, and S corporation, LLC members report business income and losses as personal income for tax purposes, although some states may impose a minimum tax on gross revenues at the LLC level.

How to Form an LLC – States that recognize LLCs require LLC members to sign an operating agreement. The operating agreement is similar to the partnership agreement and corporate bylaws in that it spells out (among other things) how the LLC is managed and how profits and losses are divided. You will need to hire an attorney or paralegal to draft this for you. Like corporations, LLCs must comply with state and federal rules governing formation. This will likely entail filing a series of forms and other paper work with the state and the IRS. In light of the foregoing, the cost of forming an LLC is pretty much in line with what you would pay to form a corporation.

WHICH TYPE OF BUSINESS STRUCTURE IS BEST?

General partnerships are relatively easy and inexpensive to form and manage, but LLCs and corporations offer significantly more protection from personal liability. This protection is worth the expense if you can afford it. Of course, these entities are more expensive to form and maintain. Bottom line: consult with your attorney (and an attorney in your home state if your primary music attorney doesn't practice in the state where you are forming your business) and your accountant or business manager. Most of my clients operate under partnership agreements, while a few of the more successful artists may have several different corporations and LLCs to protect their assets.

2. BAND AGREEMENTS

KEY PROVISIONS TO CONSIDER IN ANY KIND OF BAND AGREEMENT

Regardless of the type of business entity you form, and no matter how sure you are that there will never be a dispute among band members about anything, you and your band members should have a written agreement (partnership agreement, LLC operating agreement, or shareholder agreement) which addresses the following issues:

WHO OWNS THE BAND NAME?

The name of your band (and any associated trademarks or service marks) is an asset just like an amplifier or a van. Your band agreement should specify who can and cannot use the band name in the event that the band dissolves or members depart. This is not easy to discuss, but it is important, because if you do not spell out who owns what rights in and to the name, any member of the band can perform and record under the name. Some of the bands I work with have adopted a simple solution: the key members have exclusive rights to use the name no matter who they play with. Other bands agree that no one (including the remaining members) can use the name without the consent of the leaving member. Still others agree that leaving members have no rights to the band name once they depart or are fired. Whatever - it's your call. Just make sure you get it in writing.

THE MONEY

Unless you want to share all income equally (and you may want to), you'll need to spell out a different division in your band agreement. Let's look at the different sources of income and some hypothetical scenarios:

Record Royalties – Most bands split record royalties equally. However, this isn't always the case. If there is one person in your band that plays all of the instruments on your records, he may argue that he is entitled to more than his pro-rata share of record royalties. Here's something else to think about: making the record is only the first step in becoming successful and selling millions of copies. The real work lies ahead in the form of endless touring and promotion. Accordingly, you may want to include a provision in your band agreement that specifies that any band member who doesn't complete an entire album cycle of touring and promotion will have his share of royalties reduced. To what extent the departing/non-touring member's royalty is reduced is negotiable, but 30% to 50% seems to be the norm.

Publishing Royalties – Almost all bands have internal arguments about the distribution of publishing and songwriting royalties at one time or another. For this reason, it's really important to establish a clearly defined policy regarding this issue as soon as possible. If all band members contribute equally to songwriting you don't really have a problem. Unfortunately, this is rarely the case. In fact, most bands seem to have one or two primary songwriters. In this situation, it's a matter of whether or not the songwriters care to share their royalties with non-writing members or not. While I *never* get involved in this discussion, here are some commonly adopted arrangements:

- Songwriters keep all of the copyrights and publishing income separate from the band, and the other band members get nothing.
- All songwriting and publishing income is divided equally amongst all band members, whether or not they contributed to songwriting.
- Same as the last example, but non-writing members forfeit their right to share in songwriting and publishing income when they leave or are forced out of the band.
- Songwriters keep 100% of the writer's share of income and all band members (including non-writing members) split publisher's share equally.

The beauty of a written band agreement is that the band members can make any kind of arrangement they like. But remember that copyright law provides us with very specific rules regarding ownership of songs written by more than one person. (Go back and review Chapter Two if you forgot them already.) If the songwriting and publishing income splits you have in mind for co-written songs vary from the splits imposed by copyright law, by all means get them down on paper and get all of the co-writers to sign off on the new splits as soon as possible. You will thank me later.

Live Income – Most bands split this equally amongst all performing members. However, I have heard of one very well-known band that still pays a percentage of all live income to a founding member who has only played with the band a handful of times over the last ten years. In other words, it's negotiable like anything else.

TANGIBLE GROUP ASSETS

In addition to intangible group assets such as trademarks, service marks, copyrights and the right to receive royalties, most bands accumulate tangible assets such as recording equipment, musical instruments, PA and lighting systems and motor vehicles. Your band agreement needs to specify what monies are to be used to acquire these assets. More importantly, the agreement should specify what happens to these assets when the band breaks up or a member departs. For example, you might decide that leaving members are entitled to the cash value of their percentage share of the assets, subject to depreciation, of course. Alternatively, you might decide to give the leaving member the van or some equipment instead of cash.

MANAGEMENT AND CONTROL

The band agreement should specify how key decisions are to be made. Most bands make decisions by a majority vote, but your band agreement can mandate other kind of decision-making procedures. Here are some examples:

- Two founding members have two votes each while the other two members have only one vote;
- One member has absolute power to carry out any actions on behalf of the band;
- Four band members have one vote each, and the manager or attorney votes in case of a tie.

In deciding how you want to manage the partnership, you should give some thought to the kind of decisions you will inevitably have to make, among them:

Creative decisions – Which songs to record; which producer to hire.

Business decisions – Incurring major expenses (such as equipment, etc.), hiring and firing of managers, attorneys, agents and accountants; which record company/publisher to sign with.

Touring decisions – What tours to take, who to take on tour as an opening act, when to tour, what kind of production to mount.

Band membership decisions – This is a big one. Think long and hard about the vote required to add new members, dissolve the band or terminate existing members. Some band agreements contain clauses which allow members to be ousted if they are disabled due to drug or alcohol abuse or a major illness.

Keep in mind that you are free to mandate different kinds of voting schemes for different kinds of decisions. For instance, hiring and firing of band members and choosing a record company are obviously decisions that carry long term consequences, so you might want to require a unanimous (or near unanimous) vote in these circumstances.

WHAT IF THERE IS NO WRITTEN AGREEMENT?

Let's say your band has played together for years, but you never quite got around to signing off on a written partnership agreement. Where does this leave you in the eyes of the law? In this situation, your band is presumed to be a general partnership operating under an oral agreement. In the absence of a written partnership agreement, the Uniform Partnership Act imposes the following legal presumptions:

– All partners have an equal vote in partnership management. A majority vote is needed to make partnership decisions.

– Each partner is entitled to an equal share of profits and is liable for an equal share of any debts or liabilities.

– Each partner is entitled to an equal share of band assets, including the name.

– If a partner quits, dies, or is forced out, the partnership automatically terminates, even though the remaining partners may want to continue on. They can, of course, just by forming a new partnership, but they will first have to settle the affairs of the old partnership.

Even if this sounds like a good way to manage your band, I still recommend that you go to the trouble and expense of putting together a written band agreement. This can be a painful process, because it's difficult for a band (especially a newly formed band) to acknowledge that the shit may hit the fan at some point ("Because we're, like, all such *good friends*, y'know?"). But hit the fan the shit invariably will, so you should think long and hard about everything you just read.

SIDEMAN AGREEMENTS

As I mentioned earlier, some artists prefer to hire musicians to play and record with them on a song by song, album by album, gig by gig or tour by tour basis. This allows artists to exert a great deal of control over all of the creative and business aspects while maintaining a professional quality act. Since these musicians are not legally part of the band, they need to be engaged as employees. If you are curious about what one of these agreements looks like, there is a sample in Appendix B.

CONCLUSION

I cannot overstate the importance of setting up your business properly. A significant part of setting up your business is negotiating and executing a written band agreement or (if applicable) sideman agreement. If you put it off, you can count on an ugly settlement or lawsuit when band relations go sour. In any event, take a good look at the sample band partnership agreement I have provided for you in Appendix B.

CHAPTER NINE

Movies, TV and Advertisements

We briefly touched on the topic of licensing master recordings and musical compositions for use in media other than records in Chapters Four and Six. Since this can be a great source of income for artists, record companies, publishers, and songwriters, I felt it deserved a chapter of its own, so here we are. This chapter takes a look at the various licenses and agreements that govern the use of musical compositions and recordings in movies, TV productions, soundtrack albums, and advertisements.

I. MOVIES

When it comes to movies, music can be divided into three classifications: 1) Existing songs and recordings, 2) Songs written and recorded specifically for a motion picture, and 3) The background underscore (or "score"). Most movies also spawn soundtrack albums that are comprised primarily of songs from the film and/or score. This chapter will focus primarily on the first two classifications.

EXISTING SONGS AND RECORDINGS

If a movie producer decides he must have a particular recording of a particular song in his movie, he needs to secure two licenses. First, he must obtain a license from the publisher(s) of the song. We call this license a *synchronization (or "sync") license* because it gives the producer the right to synchronize the song with the moving images in a movie. Second, he must obtain a license from the owner of the master recording (usually a record company). We call this license a *master recording* or *master use license*.

The Sync License – This license is issued by the publisher(s) of the song. Major publishing companies have licensing departments that do nothing but negotiate and issue sync licenses. If you self-publish your catalog and don't feel comfortable drafting licenses, you can ask the other party to issue a license, or you can ask your attorney to issue a license on your behalf. Also keep in mind that the Harry Fox Agency issues sync licenses on behalf of publishers for a small fee. The fee payable for a sync license is completely negotiable, and the publisher doesn't have to issue a license at all — there is no such thing as a compulsory synchronization license. Fees payable to publishers for sync licenses are usually one time, flat fee payments for all rights contemplated by the license. Publishers generally weigh a number of factors in determining what kind of fee to charge for a sync license, among them: how much of the song is used; how the song is used (for example, does an actor sing the song on screen, or is the song merely heard in the background of the scene); the budget of the movie; whether or not the movie producer wants to use the song in trailers and ads for the movie; whether or not the movie producer wants to include the song in home video versions of the movie; and the popularity of the song itself.

Performance Rights – In addition to sync rights, a movie producer needs to obtain a U.S. theatrical performance license from the publisher of each composition it intends to use in a theatrically released movie. This direct license is necessary because U.S. antitrust law prohibits performing rights organizations (ASCAP, BMI and SESAC) from issuing these licenses for U.S. theatrical (i.e., in a movie theater) performances. This is why publishers and songwriters are not paid public performance royalties by the performing rights organizations for performances of their songs in movie theaters. Instead, the performance right royalty for this type of performance is included in the fee for the sync/performance license. Outside of the U.S., performing rights organizations do issue licenses and collect royalties for theatrical performances of songs synchronized with movies.

The Master Use License – This license is issued by the copyright owner of the recording. You should know by now that this is usually the record company. Much as the publisher is under no obligation to issue a sync license, a record company is under no obligation to issue a master use license. In the event that the record company is interested in granting a master use license, the size of the fee is dictated by the same factors that guide publishers in negotiating fees for sync licenses. In many cases, the master use fee ends up being equal to the sync license fee for the song concerned. Of course, once a movie producer has secured a sync license, he can avoid an expensive master use license by commissioning a new recording of the song. In fact, this is often done these days. Producers seem to like the idea of having a "hot" contemporary artist record a new version of a classic song. We'll talk about the kind of deal a producer needs to make for an entirely new recording such as this in a moment.

SONGS WRITTEN AND RECORDED SPECIFICALLY FOR A MOTION PICTURE

The producers of blockbuster movies (and the record companies issuing the accompanying soundtrack albums) usually want their movies to feature a signature song written with the movie in mind. Need an example? How about "Men In Black" as performed by Will Smith for the film and soundtrack album of the movie *Men In Black*. Some producers prefer new recordings of existing songs. For instance, the *Godzilla* soundtrack features a recording of the David Bowie chestnut "Heroes" as performed by the Wallflowers. The agreements for new songs and new recordings are more complicated than the sync and master use licenses which govern the use of existing songs and masters.

The Song – When a major movie producer commissions a songwriter to write an original song for a movie, the producer will typically require that the song be written as a work made for hire for the producer. This means that for the purposes of copyright law, the producer is deemed the author and publisher of the song. Of course, many successful songwriters are signed to exclusive songwriting and publishing deals, so the songwriter's publisher must give its consent in this kind of ownership arrangement (unless the songwriter wisely negotiated an exclusion for songs written specifically for motion pictures). In any event, the major deal points for this kind of deal are: how much will the songwriter be paid to write the song; will the songwriter and the songwriter's publisher be entitled to administer and/or receive any portion of the publisher's share of income generated by the song; and what songwriter royalties will the songwriter receive. Heavyweight songwriters have the clout to retain 50% of the copyright in some deals. In most cases, these deals look like single song "standard" publishing agreements, whereby the songwriter is paid a fee (which can range from nothing to six figure sums) and is entitled only to his songwriter's share of royalties.

The Master – Most artists are signed to exclusive, long term recording agreements with record companies. Accordingly, if a movie producer wants an artist to record a song for a movie (and, in most cases, the accompanying soundtrack album), the producer and/or the artist needs to get permission from the artist's record company to do so. If the record company waives its exclusivity, it will typically ask for a percentage (sometimes 100%, sometimes 50%) of the fee paid to the artist to record the track. If the record company is in a good mood, they will sometimes allow the entire creative fee to "pass through" to the artist without taking a piece, although this is rare. In any event, the deals usually go like this: the movie producer and artist negotiate a single song recording agreement which pays the artist an "all-in" fund which covers the recording costs for the track and the "creative" fee payable to the artist (and record company, if applicable). Whatever is left over after recording costs are paid goes to the artist/record company. The size of the all-in fee varies depending on the artistic and commercial stature of the artist, but I have worked on deals that pay as little as $500 and as much as $250,000 for a single master. In most of these deals, the movie producer will ask to own the copyright in and to the master. You should resist this, because you don't want the producer using the master for anything more than the movie. If you cannot retain ownership, make sure that the producer's right to use the master is limited to the movie and the accompanying soundtrack album, trailers, ads, etc.

THE SOUNDTRACK ALBUM

Soundtrack albums can be a nice source of income for artists, record companies and movie producers alike. As I write this, the soundtrack album to the motion picture *Titanic* is firmly lodged at number one on the Billboard Top 200 album chart. Most big budget movies spawn at least one (and sometimes two or three) soundtrack albums. The competition among the record companies for the soundtrack rights to certain movies is incredibly fierce, and the deals record companies strike with the movie producers provide for huge advances and recording budgets. How huge? The soundtrack album deal between a movie producer and a record company for a garden-variety blockbuster movie might call for as much as $2,000,000 just to cover recording costs. The producers are often paid separate advances in excess of the recording costs. In light of this, successful recording artists are commanding huge fees and royalties for their contributions to movie soundtracks and soundtrack albums.

If a movie producer wants to put a song written and recorded by your band on the soundtrack of his movie and on the accompanying soundtrack album, he needs to make three deals: one for the use of the song in the movie (via a sync license or a songwriter agreement), one for the use of the master in the movie (via a master use license or a single song recording agreement), and one to put the master on the soundtrack album (the soundtrack album agreement). In many cases, the soundtrack album agreement is included in the single song recording agreement or master use license. What follows is a rundown of the major deal points to be negotiated in a soundtrack album agreement:

Record Royalties – The average artist usually commands an 11% or 12% royalty, but superstar artists can command a royalty as high as 17-18%. Superstars can also require "most favored nations" treatment with respect to royalties so that they can rest assured that they have as good a royalty deal as any other artist contributing to the record. Remember that this royalty is pro-rated and that the artist must pay producers and collaborators out of its royalty.

Advances/Recoupment – In a typical movie soundtrack/soundtrack album hybrid deal (whether the soundtrack album deal is coupled with a master use license or a single song recording agreement), 50% of the total fee payable to the artist/record company is deemed an advance against record royalties. The theory is that the other 50% represents payment for using the master in the soundtrack of the movie. Artists with clout can sometimes cut deals whereby 100% of the total fee payable is nonrecoupable, although this is somewhat rare. Conversion costs (the cost of editing and transferring a sound recording as used in a movie for use on a record) are also recoupable.

What the Artist Gets to Keep – If the soundtrack album is released on a label other than the label to which you are signed, royalties from the sale of the soundtrack album will be paid directly to your record company and will be treated like any other licensing income, which means that the record company keeps 50% for itself and applies the other 50% to your royalty account. If you have clout, you can sometimes get the record company to pass your share of the royalty directly through to you, whether or not your overall royalty account with the company is in a recouped position.

Holdback – If the movie producer owns the master, you and your record company should negotiate the right to use the master on one or more of your records some time in the future at no cost. Most movie producers will agree to this, provided such use does not occur prior to a certain date following release of the movie or soundtrack album. This "holdback" period typically runs anywhere from six to eighteen months following the release of the movie.

2. TELEVISION

See Part One, above. More and more network TV series are "music driven." Record companies and music publishers are often glad to license a track or a song by an up-and-coming artist or songwriter to a show like *Party of Five* or *Dawson's Creek*, because it results in tremendous exposure for the artist or songwriter and can increase album sales. Of course, there are a few differences between TV and movies when it comes to licensing songs and recordings. For one thing, the performing rights organizations are authorized to issue performance licenses for TV broadcast performances of the songs from their respective repertoires. For another, the broadcasters of live TV shows such as *The Tonight Show* and *The Late Show With David Letterman* need only obtain blanket performance or direct performance licenses to synchronize a song with their shows, because when a show is broadcast live there has been no reproduction as far as copyright law is concerned. This is so even if the "live" show is taped for later broadcast.

3. ADVERTISING

It's impossible to turn on the TV these days without encountering an ad that uses a classic song or current hit to sell something. Allow me to illustrate: I turned on the TV 90 minutes ago and during that span I witnessed advertisements for the following products which prominently featured songs performed by the following artists:

> Nike Apparel – The Verve
> Miller Beer – Al Green
> Volkswagen Automobiles – Spiritualized
> AT & T Long Distance – Cracker
> Toyota Automobiles – Sly and the Family Stone
> Microsoft Network – The Dust Brothers
> Chevrolet Automobiles – Bob Seger

I could go on. Bottom line: ad agencies are paying big bucks to use songs and master recordings in ads. In order to do so, they need to get licenses from the publisher(s) of the song and (if applicable) the owner of the master recording. In many cases, advertisers hire studio musicians to record new versions of existing songs, as this usually costs much less than licensing the well-known version. The fee for each license varies based on how the song/recording is used, what territories it is used in, whether the ad is broadcast on TV or radio and how long the advertiser wants to use it. I have heard of publishers and record companies charging as much as $1,000,000 to use a well-known song and recording for six months in a massive TV ad campaign. Ad agencies often commission new, specifically written and recorded works for advertisements. Under these deals, songwriters are typically paid a creative fee that can range from $100 for an unknown to $100,000 for a top-notch composer. These composers typically receive only their songwriter's share of publishing income.

CONCLUSION

We just covered a lot of ground, so please take a look at the various sample licenses and agreements I have provided for you in Appendix B.

CHAPTER TEN

Getting Signed

Now that you know all about the kinds of deals you may encounter during your career, I suppose you are wondering just how to get one of these deals. Read on!

GETTING A RECORD DEAL

Here are some tips for securing a record deal:

1) Write really good or really catchy songs.

2) Spruce yourself up a bit. Appearance counts, and you would be shocked to know how many bands get passed up because they look like hell.

3) It wouldn't kill you to *rehearse* once in a while, would it?

4) Fire your drummer (just kidding).

5) Record a decent demo tape. Your demo doesn't have to be "master" quality, but you should use the best equipment/studio available to you.

6) Get the demo tape to people at record companies. As we discussed, this is usually done through your attorney or manager. However, if there is another way you can achieve this, by all means go for it. Sending the tape in blindly is a long shot, however. My first paying job in the music business was as an assistant to the head of A&R at IRS Records. While submissions from big shot attorneys, managers and publishers went straight to the president of the company, all of the unsolicited material came to me. We received hundreds of tapes a week. After listening to a few hundred tapes, I realized why these artists did not have real managers or attorneys submitting their material: THEY SUCKED. While you shouldn't let my experiences discourage you from blindly sending your material to record companies, you should know that IF your material gets listened to it will probably get about sixty seconds of an intern or low level A&R director's attention. Conversely, material submitted by well-known attorneys and managers will get a more thorough and timely review. No matter how you get your material to the record companies, heres are some general tips: Don't send in a bunch of cheap "promotional" crap (T-shirts, key chains, etc.) with your tape. Record company people have enough of this stuff. Don't put 400 songs on the tape. Give them your three or four best cuts, and put the best or catchiest song FIRST. A&R people are not impressed by endless reams of reviews or photocopies of ads that prove you once opened up for Tonic in Des Moines —putting this junk in your package will only make you look like a BUMPKIN. And please don't send a lyric sheet. Trust me on this one.

7) Play live frequently (but not too frequently — two times a month is good). Try to get decent time slots at decent venues. The venue location is important, because many A&R people are total wimps when it comes to seeing a band at a club like Los Angeles' Jabberjaw (RIP) or Al's Bar (a club in a sketchy neighborhood) just because there is a *slight* chance that they will get killed or that their Range Rover might get stolen. You want them to see you, so book a show somewhere next to a Jamba Juice or near their yoga class or something.

8) Get a publishing deal first. Your publisher can be a big help when it comes to demoing and submitting your material.

GETTING A PUBLISHING DEAL

See 1-7, above. If you sell a bunch of records (or if people think that you will) the publishers will be calling you. If you sign a record deal without an attorney and you haven't read this book, you may have already signed a publishing deal without knowing it! Congratulations!

THE SIGNING PROCESS

Once an A&R person decides that he likes your demo or single or indie record, he will start showing up at your shows. He may then casually wait around after the show and make small talk and compliment your music. If he asks you who your manager or attorney is, that's a good sign. Please remember that this doesn't mean that he has the actual authority or "green light" to sign you. Lunches, dinners and drinks may follow, and if these casual get-togethers evolve into meetings at the label offices, you're doing well.

When and if the record company actually decides to make an offer, it's time to get the attorneys involved. Here's how a typical deal goes down:

STEP ONE – THE PHONE CALL

Record Company: "Hey Bri! — It's Artie Fufkin. I'm the head of business affairs over here at Vandelay Industries! Brian, the whole label just loves your client, Lawn Chocolate, and we think that they are the next [fill in the blank — Oasis, Savage Garden, Verve Pipe, Smashing Pumpkins, whatever]. How can we get this deal done right now?

Me: "Uh, send a messenger over with a contract and a really big bag of money."

Record Company: "Ha ha — you crazy nut! Why don't you just fax me a deal proposal?

Me: "Actually, I would prefer that *you* fax me a deal proposal, Artie."

Record Company: "Well Bri, we don't really like to do that, but since you and I are such good friends, I'll fax something over."

When the offer comes through the fax machine, it will probably bear little resemblance to what you have in mind unless you are in a serious bidding war. Record companies don't like to negotiate with themselves — if they send over a fat offer, it may well exceed what your attorney would have asked for (although this is not likely with respect to the attorneys I know). After reviewing the record company's initial proposal with you and your management, your attorney then sends a counter-proposal to the record company, outlining what he thinks the deal should look like. Your attorney and the record company then go back and forth until all of the "major" points of the deal (advances, royalties, number of "firm" records and options, etc.) are agreed upon, or until it looks like a deal cannot be made.

STEP TWO - THE CONTRACT

While some record companies will issue abbreviated "short form" contracts at this stage, most record companies prefer to go straight to the negotiation of the "long form" recording agreement. These agreements can run anywhere from forty to one hundred pages in length. Keep in mind that several weeks may elapse before your attorney actually receives the contract. Once received, your attorney will spend several hours going through the contract and "marking it up" with his comments. The attorney then sends the marked up contract back to the record company (and to the client) and the negotiation process begins anew. This process can take weeks or months depending on how many revisions the contract requires and the availability of your attorney and the record company's attorney. Realistically, most deals take at least four to six weeks to complete on average.

STEP THREE - SIGNING THE CONTRACT

This is pretty self-explanatory. The record company will ask you to sign at least four original copies of the contract, so get the band together and get your pens ready.

STEP FOUR - GETTING PAID

Once you send the signed contracts to the record company, it takes a week or so for the advance checks to be cut, so be patient.

NEGOTIATING ETIQUETTE

Clients often ask me if it's kosher to negotiate with more than one record company at the same time. I don't like to do this (unless I think there is a good chance one of the labels may get cold feet), but some attorneys don't have a problem with it. I prefer for the client to choose the label that it wants to sign with, and I like to negotiate with that label exclusively until a deal is consummated or until it appears that a satisfactory deal with that label cannot be concluded. Of course, if you are in a serious bidding war and cannot decide which label you want to sign with, there is no harm in asking the competing labels to submit bids. The offers you receive may help you make up your mind. Just remember that the music business is a small club, and that you must be careful not to alienate people that you may want to (or may be forced to) work with someday.

THE BIDDING WAR

What's that? You say you followed my easy 8-step program, and now every label president is flying you to New York or L.A. for lunch? Excellent! My invoice for 5% of your advance is in the mail. But seriously, if three or four legitimate labels are killing themselves trying to sign you, you have a bidding war on your hands. This can actually be pretty tough on you, because everyone will want a moment of your time and it will be hard to decide which label will have the privilege of releasing your records. The upside, of course, is that a bidding war makes your attorney's job *really easy*. Depending on the number and stature of the labels bidding for your services, you can get a really stupid (that is, grotesquely large and artist-favorable) deal. Here's Uncle Bri's guide to the bidding war:

1) If you are from the West Coast, mention how much you would love to meet the label staffers in the New York office. The label will fly you and your manager (and attorney, if you so choose) to the Big Apple at the drop of a hat. As for accommodations, I recommend the Rhiga or the Soho Grand (24-hour room service). The rooms are too small at the Paramount. East Coast based? No problem! A trip to LA can be arranged just as easily. I like the Chateau Marmont (ask for a bungalow) or the Sunset Marquis. Please call if you need dining or shopping tips.

2) If the label is owned by a giant consumer electronics conglomerate, don't be shy — ask for TVs, camcorders, VCRs, DAT machines, video games, computers, pro recording equipment, whatever. They won't blow the deal over a few thousand dollars worth of consumer electronics, trust me.

3) Ask the label execs to take you shopping for records or clothes — they all have expense accounts at Tower Records, and they wouldn't dream of letting you spend your own money. Barney's is nice, and I find that Zegna suits look real, real fancy on stage or at an awards banquet. Don't be shy!

4) In the event that I ever trade in my attorney stripes for a cushy gig at a record company, please disregard tips 1–3.

Okay, that was my attempt at humor. In all seriousness, a bidding war can be a damaging thing, because it leads to unrealistic expectations. For every artist that succeeds following a bidding war (Nirvana, Green Day, Soundgarden, Beck, Foo Fighters and Jewel were bidding war babies) there are many more that do not (anyone remember Little Caesar, Liquid Jesus, Symposium, Hayden or Greta? How about the Unforgiven?). That's not a knock on any of those artists, it's just a sobering reminder that there is no such thing as a sure thing. If you can get a great deal with a great label without getting into a bidding war, you may have a little more time to develop. Then again, you may not.

CONCLUSION

This marks the end of both Chapter Ten and the first part of the book. Thanks for reading this far, and don't forget to read through the interviews, sample agreements and info I have provided for you in the Appendices.

INTRODUCTION TO APPENDICES

Welcome to the Appendices. When I agreed to write this book, my publisher was pretty much looking for what you get in Chapters One through Ten. But I wanted to make this book a little bit different from other books by adding interviews, sample agreements and a list of resources.

Appendix A contains interviews with twelve music business professionals whom I have a lot of respect for. All of them have interesting things to say about their chosen professions.

Appendix B is a collection of sample agreements, with commentary. If you don't fall asleep while reading through them, you might learn something.

Appendix C is a bunch of phone numbers and addresses (including website addresses — oooh!) for various organizations and companies. They might come in handy.

Hope some or all of this helps and/or entertains, and thanks again.

INTERVIEW: RADIO PROMOTION

Chuck Arnold

Chuck Arnold was the founder and co-owner of The Want Adds, one of the most influential and unique independent record promotion companies in the country. The Want Adds shut its doors late last year.

BHM: Why don't you tell me how you got started in the business and also how you started The Want Adds?

CA: I started at a college radio station back in 1985 and from there on I went to school in Boston and had to take time off and work for a few months, so I opted to come out to Los Angeles to work for Paramount Pictures — at that point I was intending to go into advertising. When I got to Los Angeles, the job wasn't there. So, instead of using my return ticket right away and going back to school in Boston, I started to hit the pavement to see what I could find. I thought that having been a college radio DJ would help me find DJ work at clubs. I wound up working for *Music Connection* (an LA-based music industry magazine) of all places, and there were a bunch of internships available and I thought, "Why not, I could get some kind of crazy bullshit job," which I did. I became an usher (in a polyester suit, no less) at the Henry Fonda Theater when they were still doing live theater back in 1987.

From there I moved on to several internships. I checked out Capitol, and all the other big time labels, but the label closest to my apartment was Triple X Records on Hollywood Boulevard. At that point, they had a tiny little office and I was their first employee. They said, "We've got a record by a new band called Jane's Addiction — promote it." So, that's how I started learning radio promotion — I was 19. After doing that for six months, it was all good, but it was still an internship, so they paid me very little. I also interned for Frontier Records at the same time. After doing that for a while, I asked myself, "Why am I doing this for someone else, when I could do it for myself?" I was 22 in 1989 and I went back to Boston where I knew a lot of bands that were all coming out with records at the same time. At that point it was mostly local bands, mostly independent releases, mostly really bad late '80s rock. I started doing that, and before I knew it, I started scoring more and more records as an independent promoter and getting contracts from record companies to promote records on college radio. At that time, no one else was doing it, now there are about 13 companies in competition with our business.

My biggest break outside of Jane's Addiction was getting a chance to work on the Cocteau Twins' record, *Heaven or Las Vegas* for Capitol. Faith Henschel gave us a shot and it was my biggest break ever. That record went all the way to #1 on the college charts and it totally put our company on the map. Before that I had been working alone with small, independent bands and had just joined forces with Mark Neider. Mark stayed with me for six months, then left for Reprise. Jay Harding then came in, and when he left back in '93, Dave Sanford came in and he is my current partner. We also have one employee and some interns that rotate around. It has gotten to the point where we almost never call out to look for work, we get so much that we have to listen to about 20 different records a week in a multi-hour music meeting. We decide what projects we would like to work with. That's pretty much the entire promotion company in a nutshell.

BHM: What does a radio promotion person do?

CA: The bands make a record, and I get a couple of hundred copies for promotion and then send it to radio stations and try to get them all to play it at the same time so that the record can get a decent chart position — that helps the band get a bigger profile, so that they can tour, so that people will know about them when they go and pitch themselves to a bigger label. They can say that they have a college radio history — it's a stepping stone situation.

BHM: That sounds like a simple job, but it's not as simple as it sounds. There are certain independent promoters that are well-known for being able to deliver what we call "adds" — an addition to a station's play list. The big ones are McCluskey....

CA: On the modern rock level, commercial radio level, there are consultants like McCluskey, McGaffey.

BHM: How do you differ from them?

CA: We pretty much only work with artists we like. We do what we like and that is the most important thing. But, on the modern rock level, I'm more likely to deal with Zeke or Rodney (DJs) at KROQ as opposed to going out to lunch and drinks with Kevin Weatherly (music director of LA's KROQ and other "modern rock" stations). To me it's about the people that I know at the station that believe in the music. I'm not working in some big political structure or some kind of time buy situation. This works effectively for me — I'm not going to be hired to work the new Slayer record to modern rock radio, but I did work the Apples in Stereo to modern rock radio and had relative success with it. So, it is a different kind of promotion.

BHM: So with a band like the Apples in Stereo, you might have been the only independent promotion person...

CA: Right. Quite frankly, I believe I was the only person that could really deliver with that one because I have an "in" with those people from dealing with them on the modern rock level. The difference between those companies and mine is that most of them just do commercial radio and we do college radio almost exclusively.

BHM: What is it about the way you do business and how you conduct yourself that makes your services valuable?

CA: It's all about relationships. I've established myself over the years with these radio stations. Even though it's college radio and the personnel turn over every six months, or a year, my company has a reputation. It comes down to treating people with respect, if you treat people with respect, you'll get respect in return. Also, people know when you are doing something that you believe in, people know when you're giving them schlock... When you're trying to push the new Bryan Adams on them, but then you turn around and say "I'm really into Speculum Fight" — they're not going to believe you, they're gonna know you're full of shit. I make no bones about letting these people know what music I'm into and letting them know that I have a clue. I let them know that I'm a music fan and they appreciate that. That's the difference. It's promoting the music that you love rather than promoting product.

BHM: Tell me about your average day. Do you hit the phones constantly? Do you send records out piece by piece, or do you send radio stations one package a month with all the stuff you're working?

CA: Sometimes I give the major labels my contact list, and they send out the records directly from their office. With most independents, we do the mailing. I tell bands that I can do this cooperative package — the whole package that we send out is a service to make it cheaper for bands. We only charge them 95 cents apiece and it goes out Priority 2 Day. With regard to the phones, we work them as much as we can. We try to reach as many as 50 stations a day.

BHM: Let's say someone has a band and they have a budding label that they're putting together themselves and they start to build a buzz, they start selling a few records and they think it's time to bring someone like you in to help. What kind of deal can you offer a small label where they've sold like 10,000 copies, and what can you do for them?

CA: If a band or label wants to hire us, first of all, we listen to their record at our meeting to make sure that we like it and want to send it out in our package. If we like it, they would give us 300 CDs, we'd put our sticker on it so that people would know that it's affiliated with our package, we'd mark off tracks that we think music directors would like, we'd mark off the songs that have bad language, songs that they can't play on the air — we make it easier for them. The stickers contain detailed information about the music. We make it so easy for them that they'll add one of our CDs quicker than the other 150 CDs that they've never heard that have no description or bios with them. It gives the band an edge. Our mailing list consists of a smaller group of stations that we deal with on a regular basis and are friendly towards independent records. It costs about $250 for an independent label to have three people, full-time calling radio. That includes expenses such as phone bills. As I mentioned earlier, the initial shipping of the record is 95 cents apiece for the cooperative package, they're sharing costs with other bands. If they were to do it themselves it would cost almost twice that much for the postage alone, so it saves them a lot of time and money. In addition to calling radio stations, our staff also keeps in touch with trade magazines, such as *CMJ, Gavin, Hits* and *Album Network*. At the major labels, it's all about getting a high chart position, regardless of whether it's real or it's bought. But here's a good example of what we can do for a band — Babe the Blue Ox (a former indie band now on RCA), they're not concerned with high chart positions, they're concerned with wanting people to know who they are — they want people at their shows. When they're touring, they always have 200-300 people at their shows because they've toured constantly, they put out record after record that does moderately well at the college level chart-wise, but I personally have worked hard to make sure that people know about that band, that the right people have gotten turned on to them so that there's fans at the clubs when they show up. When they get to the radio station, people know who they are. Some major labels take certain steps to obtain high chart positions that are not accurate. The "buying" of chart positions occurs even at the college radio level, believe it or not. That's what it's about for me. If your label buys you a high but fake chart position, don't be surprised if you aren't welcomed with open arms when you get to certain markets.

BHM: The charts in these trade magazines are supposed to reflect what the stations are playing. Are you saying that these charts aren't accurate?

CA: Not always. It depends on the station. Like I said, some stations will take "considerations" from promoters in order to make it appear that certain records are doing better than they truly are. Promoters will fly music directors to conventions and make sure that they have more than just adequate accommodations. They'll fly them out, put them up and hey! More airplay! I've seen the gift giving, the hooker buying, the drug supplying — but the bottom line is that when you just do music that you believe in, you don't have to resort to sleazy, stupid tactics. It's not illegal, there's no actual cash involved. Luckily, we don't need to avoid this situation because our ethical policies prevent us from ever being in that predicament.

BHM: How many different records do you work on at a time?

CA: It rotates all the time. You get, say, ten going on in a week, you might have four of those you've been working from anywhere between four and six weeks already, so they're kind of in a different phase. Three other records might be ones that you're just starting and that's a totally different kind of promotion. They always start at different times, so they're always at different stages, so ten records is a manageable amount even though it may seem large, it makes a lot of sense when you've got records coming and going.

BHM: When The Want Adds started, major labels were not dealing with the type of bands that we've been talking about. With the "alternative music explosion," these labels have hired "alternative" marketing and promotion people. Why would a Warner Bros. or a Geffen still hire you on a project instead of just hiring more promotion people?

CA: Purely because of traffic. There's so much traffic out there now because so many records come out every month. That's because commercial labels realized that money making bands such as U2 and REM can come out of college radio, so they're signing bands at that level, yet they don't have enough experienced staff to handle these additional records.

BHM: That really seems to be the case. Since stations are getting hit with more and more bands and records, how do you convince a station to play one of your artists?

CA: Once again, it comes down to the good music and the kind of relationships you have — and timing. It is feast or famine, and I think we should enjoy the feast. Even though there's more junk you have to go through, we should really appreciate all the good music that's available to us these days. Between five and ten years ago, there just weren't as many bands. I call it the *Nevermind* theory. I think that when Nirvana's *Nevermind* came out, any kid that was fooling around with a guitar and wanted to start an alternative band did. That created a lot of really bad bands, but it also inspired a lot of people who formed good bands.

BHM: I deal with a lot of artists that would have been considered "indie" artists five or six years ago, and more and more are signing to major labels. Do you think it's essential to require a major to commit to independent promotion in their contract?

CA: I think it is great when bands have us, or any independent promotion firm, written into the contract, because a band or a manager is not going to really have a good grasp on what the traffic's going to be like at the time the record finally does come out three, six, nine months later. If you don't opt for independent promotion and it turns out that there is a lot of traffic at the label when your record comes out — tough shit — the promotion department is going to concentrate on those other bands that have a higher priority than you. An independent promotion company truly believes in their artists and is always going to give it their best shot. I personally felt that way with Weezer. My friend Pat Magnarella is their manager, and we were working that record at college and nothing was really happening with that record in modern rock for awhile, but we had that thing hovering at college — I thought we did a pretty good job with that and still to this day believe in that record, I love that debut record — it's great. Of course there's always a team behind each successful record, but I feel that our company really made a big difference by raising awareness of a band that otherwise might have been ignored.

INTERVIEW: DISTRIBUTION

Russ Bach

*At the time of this interview, **Russ Bach** was the President and CEO of EMI Music Distribution (formerly known as CEMA distribution). Bach has worked in the distribution business nearly 40 years and is now a sought-after consultant.*

BHM: You've been in the distribution business for a while now…

RB: Yes, from the time I got out of college in 1960 until today, I've focused on one thing — getting records into the hands of consumers. I've done virtually every job there is to do in distribution.

BHM: When you started, the "Big Six" distributors didn't exist — it was all independents. How has record distribution evolved over the last 36 years?

RB: The independents of 1960 serviced small areas. For instance, when I went to work for a distributor in Chicago, they serviced Chicago, most of Wisconsin, Illinois from Peoria to Chicago, and the upper part of Indiana, but they didn't have Indianapolis. Then, something called trans-shipping started, and I remember my boss being plagued by people in Cleveland and Minneapolis who were shipping into his area. Each territory use to be protected — you got that territory and nobody else was supposed to come in and compete with you. This changed with trans-shipping, and it became a free-for- all. It also changed when the independents weren't really doing the jobs that large companies needed to get done. The independents were there to make money, and they didn't have the number of promotion people the bigger record companies required, or the number of sales people to really cover a territory well, so there was this move to company-owned distribution. From the time I got started in the business, Columbia (now Sony) and Capitol had certain territories where they would handle their own distribution and then they would use independents in other territories. Then they started to take over those independents and began to do distribution themselves.

One of the early labels that did that was Liberty Records. In 1965 when I went to work for Liberty (which was run by Al Bennett at that time), Al had a vision that distribution was very important and he needed to do it himself rather than depending on independent distributors to do it. He fought a lot of battles with the small distributors, but he was very successful. As a matter of fact, Liberty Distribution became Liberty United Artists Distribution, and then when United Artists was bought by PolyGram it became PolyGram Distribution. In the case of the WEA labels, Warner, Elektra, and Atlantic were distributed by different independents in the same cities, and they couldn't coordinate very well. So, in 1971, WEA was formed and the product lines were pulled from the independent distributors. In many cases those independent distributors were also either one-stops or rack jobbers or retailers and there were a lot of threats about losing business.

169

But eventually, everyone saw that it was a better distribution model and that more focus could be given to the artists. Also, at that time, there were a lot of small independent stores that needed to be serviced, whereas we are now seeing massive consolidation. So, distribution has continually evolved as the nature of retail has evolved.

BHM: What's the difference between a branch system and a regional system?

RB: In the beginning most distributors had around 8 branches across the country. The branch system was basically formed by people who came from independent distribution. They generally ran territories that were somewhat larger than the old independent distributors. For instance, the Atlanta branch would also service Florida, North and South Carolina, Mississippi and Tennessee. The Dallas branch generally took care of the entire state of Texas, Louisiana, Oklahoma and Arkansas. As we saw a change in the customer base we decided to move from the branch system, which had been in place since the earliest days of branch distribution, to the more logical regional system. The regional system eliminated a branch manager, whose position was no longer necessary — otherwise most of the things stayed the same. During the earlier days of the customer consolidation however, we did begin removing sales reps as they were no longer needed to call upon the many retailers who had gone out of business. The regional system was more focused on marketing than sales. The new system we just implemented is even more marketing focused with the bulk of our sales staff effort concentrated in the Major Accounts Group.

BHM: In my book, I try my best to explain the differences between "indie" and major distribution. What do you see as the primary differences?

RB: The six major distribution companies (EMD, WEA, UNI, PGD, BMG and Sony) have distribution facilities that reach into every market in the entire United States. EMD and other majors have employees in every major market from Boston to San Diego, from Florida to Seattle. Conversely, many of the independents are in one region or another, they're stronger in one region than another, they're not national in scope. That is one of the major differences. Now RED (Relativity, the independent distribution branch of Sony Music) is national in scope, INDI is national in scope. Caroline (which is owned by Virgin Records) essentially has two locations, New York and Los Angeles, but they do a nice job of covering the entire United States from those two locations. While indie distributors might be more experienced in distributing more esoteric kinds of music, you can't beat a major distributor when it comes to moving millions of copies of a particular record.

BHM: Once you sign to let's say, Virgin, and you make your record and everything's great and it gets pressed up and sent off to the distributor — what does the distributor do to sell that record, aside from manufacturing it and making it available for sale?

RB: I think distribution is the art of getting the right records into the right places at the right time. That's essentially what we do. There are many ways to get the product into the stores. For instance, we might use Southwest Wholesale in Houston, Texas which is a one-stop, to make sure we cover our Latin product; or if it's a country record, we make sure it gets to Anderson Merchandising in Amarillo, Texas. Anderson supplies records to all of the WalMart stores, and in many parts of the country, WalMart is the only place you can buy records. So it's really important to get country records to Anderson. We also have to make sure the records get to the Tower stores and the independent stores in key regions, like Waterloo Records in Austin, TX. Using Austin as an example, EMD has a sales/marketing rep in Austin who sells and markets our product there. The rep meets the buyers at each store, and if a known band like Cracker has a new record coming out, or if the rep is trying to get the buyer to pick up product from a new artist like Menthol or Fatboy Slim, they get in there and explain the marketing plan. They explain how we want to promote the band and drop off a few in-store play copies of the records they are trying to get the store to buy.

The rep then monitors the progress of a record over a period of time as radio, MTV, or the general buzz increases, or as the press starts to pick up on the band. Our reps then interface with the retail stores and make sure more pieces of product get into the store as the buzz or profile of a record increases. They also try to ensure that the record gets good placement in the store — on an endcap or in a special display that is in the sightline of every customer as they enter the store. Don't forget, a lot of records start under "Miscellaneous F." If you get one or two pieces of a record by a new artist under "Miscellaneous F," that's a start and that's the right quantity until a "story" starts developing and it makes sense to get more product into the stores.

BHM: I am always getting irate phone calls from my clients, especially the newer artists, asking why their record isn't in the local store in the town where they are playing a show that night. Does this mean a distributor is doing a crappy job? What should I tell them?

RB: A lot of times the smaller stores cannot afford to stock a piece by a newer, unknown artist until something starts to happen in that area. A lot of times a record is in Tower but not Waterloo, or in Waterloo and not Tower. If our salespersons distribute 15,000 to 20,000 pieces throughout the entire country, they have to spread things thin, and the record is in "Miscellaneous F." That's all you could expect at that point, unless the company has decided to put a $100,000 campaign behind the record. In today's world, I think that set-up is very important and there could be a period of time when there is no product on the market. We begin the buzz, the band is touring, they're talking about in-stores, people are seeing them in clubs, they're opening for somebody. That buzz really helps us to set-up to ship 15,000 or maybe even 30,000 units, whereas with a totally unknown new artist, we may initially ship 10,000 pieces or less. There are a lot of stores that really can't afford to bring records in unless there's something happening. The number of releases from all the companies is absolutely staggering, and the retail store cannot afford to bring in every record of everything that has been recorded. Don't forget, retailers are there for profit. They may love music, but they're there to make a living. Just because your band is cool doesn't mean that they can afford to stock your record. There's this economic proposition — there has to be a reason for stocking the record.

BHM: To what extent do the people at the label interface with the people at the distribution company — how is the decision to ship a lot of units or run a special discount program made? Does the distributor have the authority to make these decisions on its own?

RB: It's always a mutual decision — communication is key.

BHM: Where is the contact point? Which person at the label talks to the distributor?

RB: Usually the vice president of sales or marketing. For instance, at Capitol Records, that person is Joe McFadden. After you and I finish talking, I'm going over to Capitol Records and we're going to talk about how many more pieces of the *Trainspotting* soundtrack we want to get into the stores, because we think we have a unique opportunity. How well will *Trainspotting* play in middle America? Not very. We're not looking to put a lot of pieces in Des Moines, Iowa. But we think it has a chance to do well on the coasts. Right now we're working on a record by a band called Fun Loving Criminals for EMI Records — I've had three or four conversations myself with Davitt Sigerson, the president of the company, about what we need to do. We'll go over where the response has been good and bad, and ask ourselves if we can get more into the Tower in Sacramento for the weekend because 15 records sold there in the last 10 days. You have to stay on top of things — the fun thing about this business is that it changes by the moment, it changes quickly and you have to react quickly. You also can't get sucked into the hype — you'll hear people in the industry say, "Hey! It's a great record, you've got to get it out there." That's fine, and maybe it is a great record, but there are lots of great records that never get heard, and I need to see the marketing plan to make sure that the label is making a commitment to getting this great record to the consumer. I don't care if everyone in the industry thinks the record is great — if it doesn't get to the consumer, it doesn't sell.

BHM: So the record company has to present you with a concrete marketing plan. And then the salesperson from the record company and the marketing people will interface with you and show you their plan and have you implement it.

RB: Right. Then we'll take that plan out and work with the major account group that represents about 70% of our sales, and then the market group that represents the other 30% of our sales. We'll work with those two groups to meet those goals that are set for the project. The goals can be different, maybe this record is going to be set up with our market group first, which focuses on the smaller customers, the hip kind of music that sometimes needs to be worked three to six months before it is ready for the Musicland stores. It depends on where your exposure is coming from — you have to identify heavier airplay and react accordingly. We are familiar with the different markets throughout the United States so we are able to map out a distribution plan that places the appropriate amount of records in the most beneficiary locations. The U.S. is a sophisticated market, but we know how to attack it. There are four main ways to get records into retail stores: 1) through the direct retail stores such as Musicland, Sam Goody, they'll ship into two or three distribution centers; 2) directly to the smaller stores; 3) through the rack jobbers, those who take care of Target, WalMart, K Mart, etc.; and, 4) the one-stop, where retailers can get all their needs fulfilled in "one-stop." In the old days, that's where jukebox vendors got their records — it wasn't practical for them to drive to several different distribution locations just to pick up some 45's, so the one-stops came into being.

BHM: OK, last question. There's an awful lot of hype these days surrounding "alternative means of distribution." You always read these articles in Billboard where some writer will proclaim "In the year 2000, record stores will not exist. People will buy records with debit cards over the Internet or by satellite."

RB: I hate to seem like an old stick in the mud, because I recognize the power of the Internet, and I recognize the power of satellite transmission, but I believe that the average consumer loves going into the record store, loves to be able to browse, loves to be able to look at graphics, loves to talk to a knowledgeable employee about what else is new and interesting. I don't think that the Internet is going to take the place of that, at least not within the next 3-5 years. The Internet is young. The consumer has not responded well to buying from the Internet. Don't forget, the delivery vehicles for satellite downloads are not here yet. There was a great idea that evolved last year called 1-800 MUSIC NOW, but so far that has not been successful. Millions of dollars were spent on advertising this service — you just pick up your phone, order your records and they are delivered to you two or three days later. So far, it hasn't worked and that is far simpler than buying records over the Internet.

INTERVIEW: RECORD LABEL PRESIDENT

Bob Biggs

Bob Biggs is the President of Slash Records, a company he recently merged with London Records, where he also has the title of Senior Vice President. Slash Records started as an independently owned and distributed punk rock label in Los Angeles in the late seventies. Bob signed X, The Germs, Los Lobos, The Dream Syndicate and the Violent Femmes, among others.

BHM: Slash actually started as a punk rock magazine…how did it evolve into a record label?

BB: The magazine was started by a friend of mine, Claude Bessy and a guy named Steve Samiof and their girlfriends, Melanie Nissen and Philomena. Claude was French, Philomena was English, Steve and Melanie were American. They all had various backgrounds that were important to the development of the magazine — Steve had a visual background, Melanie was a photographer, Claude was a poet, and Philomena was… I don't know what — but everyone contributed and it was very good. I was a painter, and they started the magazine in the studio next door to mine. I was in on what they were doing from the beginning and as time went on, I seemed to have the most business smarts and so I ended up doing the business for the magazine. Toward the end I actually published the magazine and Claude went to England with Philomena and Steve started a magazine called *Stuff.* So that was the end of the magazine — that was in 1980. It started in 1977, but in 1978, I put out a single on the Slash label, it was a three song seven-inch by The Germs. Later that year we put out an LP by The Germs. Then I think X followed that, and I just decided I was tired of putting magazines on the stand and them turning yellow and then getting them back and having no money. I thought I would just put out something with a little more shelf life: records. It was no more sophisticated than that.

BHM: You didn't have any plans to become a huge music mogul?

BB: No.

BHM: You just liked the bands...

BB: From my perspective, The Germs were this concrete poetry or something — it was a fine art idea. I just wanted to put it into the marketplace to see how it would do — to see what the whole thing was about. We pressed 1,000 and they all sort of sold or got given away, so I guess in that sense it was a success. I hired a lawyer straight away, you'd be happy to know that, so that when I signed The Germs I had a decent contract.

BHM: Did they have a decent contract?

BB: For those days, it wasn't that bad.

BHM: Did they have a lawyer?

BB: They did have a lawyer, and they had a manager — her name was Nicole, she later became Nicole Panter. Gary Panter was a cartoonist in the magazine. So, my lawyer gave me the contract that he prepared for the deal, and I understood about 20% of it.

BHM: And now you're up to about 30-40%?

BB: (Laughs) 23%. So I tried to figure out what all this "recoupable" stuff was and all these different things. At first I thought it looked to be very scary and very much weighted on my side. I thought, "That's really weird, why don't I just give them this and that…" and then as time went on and I got more educated about the whole thing, I learned what things were there for. I realized how risky the business is and the fact that we sort of have to be a bank sometimes, without any interest. You need to have something on your side. That was pretty much it, and then I signed X and The Blasters and a whole mess of stuff — The Gun Club, The Dream Syndicate.

BHM: How did you distribute your records in the early days?

BB: I did it through (the now defunct) Jem. As we got a little more sophisticated we had a makeshift network of different distributors around the country. Then in about 1981 there was a tremendous crash of all these distributors — out of the ten that we had, about four went out of business — and they took our money. We lost $300,000 which was a lot of money at that point. I decided then and there that the concept of the label was not to be precious, but to get these ideas in the mainstream and to sell as many records as we can — it was really good stuff — that was the organizing idea around starting it to begin with. It was no dilemma to do a deal with Warner Bros. Records. There was no philosophical problem for us.

BHM: I guess a lot of people thought you sold out…

BB: Yeah. Remember, that was a time when there was definitely an "us" and a "them" — "we" were cool and "they" were not, and all of a sudden "we" were getting in bed with "them."

BHM: You were probably like one of the first "cool" indie labels to really do that.

BB: I think so. 415 tried it with CBS and got their head handed to them.

BHM: What kind of deal did you get with Warners? Was it a joint venture? Did you have a lot of control? Looking back, would you have made the same kind of deal?

BB: Many times you make decisions out of what's possible and what isn't possible. At that point we had just lost two or three hundred thousand dollars with these other distributors. We needed distribution, we needed to go ahead and so we accepted a clause which said they got to keep selected artists for ten years. We didn't want to do that, but you know, we needed to keep going. So had I got everything I wanted I wouldn't have done that, but I didn't get everything I wanted, but I did get some other things — it wasn't the worse thing in the world.

BHM: You obviously survived and prospered. Are you directly involved with A&R all the way through with every artist?

BB: Some more than others. My contention is that if you sign a good artist your marketing problems are taken care of, your artistic problems are taken care of, your musical problems are taken care of — everything is in the signing. We were and still are fairly picky about what we sign, because if you do it right, for instance Imperial Teen, or Rammstein, those bands market themselves, we don't have to worry about fixing some sort of marketing scheme or some image — it's already done. The good bands already have a good self-image. So we spend most of our time trying to pick the bands and then sticking with them, and we have been successful so far.

BHM: Does Slash listen to unsolicited material? If someone sends a tape addressed to Bob Biggs c/o Slash Records, what are the chances that that tape will be listened to?

BB: I believe that everyone in the office should be an A&R person — if you hire musical people or people that are into music, you're much better off. For instance, the Violent Femmes sent in a tape, and two people in the office really thought it was great. I didn't hear it at first, but I trusted these people. I was flying somewhere, listening to the tape when it finally hit me, and we bought the material on the tape — the first Violent Femmes LP — for $10,000. We just mastered the demo and put it out. I think it has sold almost 2,000,000 copies to date. That was an unsolicited tape.

BHM: So there is hope for those who don't have high-powered lawyers or managers sending their material in?

BB: It worked for the Femmes.

BHM: When I was doing A&R before I went to law school, I must have listened to thousands of tapes, and not one struck me as worth pursuing.

BB: The overwhelming majority of unsolicited demos are pretty bad. Most of the time what happens is they send a tape and a photo, and if the photo is ridiculous, the music probably is too.

BHM: You and I recently had a discussion about the size of record deals in 1998, and you mentioned that attorneys, managers and bands want more money and bigger deals than they did ten years ago. Obviously, all labels would like to pay as little up front as possible, but the market is very competitive these days.

BB: Obviously from our end smaller deals are better because it takes some of the risk out of it. You're looking at what's good for the label — it's better to have smaller deals, you're not risking so much money. The reason it's better for the band is that if the label's not risking so much, the pressure is not so great to succeed on the first record. Obviously, if you sign a deal for $400,000 dollars on the first record, you're gonna get some pressure to cut a record that's commercial. From the '50s through the '70s, the music was controlled to a great extent by producers and record moguls — they put bands together and made them wear certain kinds of clothes and record covers. In the '80s, things changed and a lot of independent labels cropped up. The bands got to do whatever they wanted to on these labels because the advances and recording budgets were tiny and the risk was so low that these labels stuck with the bands. What happened? Well, bands like the Meat Puppets eventually went gold and Nirvana made their first record for less than $1,000 and their next record sold millions of copies. I don't know what happened, but like 3 or 4 years ago it exploded and there were twice as many labels, and they were going after the same bands. So there's competition, and when there's competition it drives the money up. The pressure to succeed becomes greater. I guess some artists can get away with getting a lot of money and not having a lot of pressure on the art. But there's no way around it because it needs to recoup somehow, some way.

BHM: Let's talk about what a record company spends beyond the advances and recording costs. On the average, for a new band that you're trying to get going — how much extra money are you laying out for promotion, marketing, etc., per record on average?

BB: There are the big costs like videos and advertising campaigns and those kinds of things. There have been a lot of costs that have been going up, like advertising — retailers have less space because there's more product so they demand more money. There's a lot more independent radio promotion, too. There are many expenses just to put a record out. So, if you sign a band for $200,000, you put $100,000 in their pocket, in equipment or whatever, you're going to spend at least another $200,000-$300,000 on marketing the band, tour support, videos. So the label is looking at maybe half-a-million dollars, easy.

BHM: Anything else you'd like to add?

BB: If you're in a band, concentrate primarily on being a band member rather than trying to be a lawyer and a know-it-all about the music business. It's nice to know what's going on to a point, but concentrate on your craft and your art, and let the pros handle everything else.

INTERVIEW: PRODUCER

Rick Rubin

A co-founder of Def Jam Records and the owner of American Recordings, **Rick Rubin** *is also a world class record producer. He has produced records by artists as diverse as Johnny Cash, LL Cool J, Slayer, the Beastie Boys, Tom Petty, Mick Jagger, The Red Hot Chili Peppers, AC/DC and Donovan.*

BHM: How did you get started in the music business?

RR: I started making records as a hobby when I was a student at New York University. I was friendly with a guy named Ed Bauman who owned 99 Records and had a great record shop. He put out independent records. He walked me through the steps of putting out my own independent record. Rap music was going on in New York, but there weren't very many rap records available at that time. The ones that were coming out didn't represent the scene properly. We'd go to the hip-hop clubs and watch what was going on there, and then go out and buy the new hip-hop records — they didn't follow. So, I tried to make records that sounded like what was going on in the clubs — more like a documentary approach to the things that I saw there that moved me about that music. The other rap records that were coming out at that time were more like disco tracks with a guy rapping — what Sugar Hill Records and Oh Joy records put out. These labels put out between six and ten 12-inch singles a year — those were all the rap records we had to go on. That was in 1982 — we started Def Jam and put out our first record in 1984: LL Cool J's *I Need a Beat.* The full concept of the record business — the fact that there were major labels — never entered into my thinking at the time. It was really a hobby; we made records because it was a fun thing to do — we put them out because we made them! Our goal was to sell enough records to make enough money to go back into the studio and make another record. The records started selling, and after putting out seven 12-inch singles independently, Columbia Records came to us and offered us a deal and we accepted. You know the rest of the story.

BHM: What exactly does a record producer do for an artist?

RR: Record producers come from many different backgrounds and do many different jobs — radically different. Even myself, the way I produce rap records is completely different from the way I produce the kind of records I am helping non-rap artists make now. As a rap producer it was understood that it was my job to come up with all the music or the "track," and it was the rapper's job to come up with all the lyrics. Conversely, when I work with a rock band, it's not my responsibility to come up with the music or the lyrics. They already have that, and I just help them make it the best it can be. Some producers come from an engineering background — they're more concerned with how a record sounds. I see my role as a producer differently — my job is similar to what a movie director does. I'm responsible for the overall content — where it all ends up. It starts in pre-production, which usually means sitting down with the songwriters. For instance, with someone like Tom Petty, we'll sit down and Tom will play me a bunch of songs. I'll tell him which ones I like best and why. We'll discuss the components of the songs, like bridges and choruses, and decide what changes should and should not be made — we'll try to get to the root of what the song is all about. I try to do as much as possible with the songs before going into the studio and rolling tape.

BHM: Whenever I hear an artist or a band say, "We're going to write the songs in the recording studio," I think of three things: 1) a bunch of hastily written songs, 2) an out-of-control recording budget, and 3) a really nervous record company.

RR: Yes, it's really important to get the songs together in pre-production. I believe that if you do the pre-production properly, you should have a pretty good idea of what the record is going to be before you ever set foot in the studio. Some people talk about writing and experimenting in the studio, but I don't think that's a good way to start. I don't think there's anything wrong with experimenting once you're in the studio, but that should be supplemental to a strong foundation of songs. If that changes along the way, that's fine. But going into the studio if you are not prepared is a waste of time and money. A lot of bands talk about this spontaneous thing that happens — I understand wanting a certain spontaneity in terms of performance, but in terms of writing, you have to have the groundwork laid. Once you are sure that the artist has a good bunch of songs, the next step is to listen to them for a while and try to get a feel for them. In some cases a song will feel pre-determined because it is so well written. Then you have to try to flesh it out and figure out how to make the most interesting record out of it. There's a difference between a good song and a good record. A lot of bands make good records, but the songs may not be as good as the records are. There was a time when big drum sounds were popular — whoever had the biggest drum sound had the biggest hit. But six months later someone would come out with a bigger drum sound, then six months after that the big drum sound is no longer important. In many cases the artists who focus too much on a particular sound have shorter careers than the artists that start with strong songs do. I prefer to work with the artists in the latter category, obviously.

BHM: How long does the pre-production process take?

RR: It can take a day, it can take years. It starts with the main songwriter, and then you work with the band. You go to band rehearsal and then make suggestions regarding structural changes — lengths, parts not being right, lyrics. Sometimes the lyrics could be better, other times the lyrics are good, but the music doesn't work. Sometimes the song is great, but the feel isn't right, it should be softer, stronger, faster, slower, it should be more swinging, more straight forward, etc. Another interesting thing is that in most bands all the members always play — in other words I turn on the light switch, the song starts, everybody's playing, song ends, everybody stops playing. Sometimes the song is more interesting when not everybody's playing. Maybe the song should start with only drums and bass, or drums, bass and vocal, and the guitar should come in with the chorus. So you have to figure out and build the dynamics of a song from its original structure and also by looking at it after it has been tracked. A mistake that I see other people make is that they'll get their basic tracks down, and they won't be very good, but they'll think that any weaknesses in the track can be "fixed" in the overdubbing and mixing phases of the process. I think that this is a big mistake. Every great record starts with a great basic track. If your basic tracks aren't any good, you've got to start over. Unfortunately, artists sometimes get really attached to sub-par basic tracks. Even if they recognize the flaws, they somehow believe that the track can "magically" transform itself into something better. I just doesn't happen, I'm afraid.

BHM: So how do you get the best performances out of the artists when you get past pre-production and start tracking?

RR: Much like a movie director tries to get the best performances from actors, the record producer sets up conditions where he or she can get the best performance from the band. Sometimes that means recording in a world-class, state-of-the-art studio, sometimes it's going to a little crummy studio. In the case of the Chili Peppers, they had made four or five albums in traditional recording environments prior to working with me. I wanted to make our first record together in a completely different environment. So we rented a big house and put a studio into the house, and the band lived in the house while we made the record. This was an entirely different experience for them. The chance of something magical happening was much greater because it felt special. From the time that we were there, the vibe was totally different and really conducive to making great music. You need to come up with different ways to inspire that special feeling that makes a record unique.

BHM: How involved do you get in the engineering aspect of the recording process?

RR: I am not an engineer, but I know what kind of sounds I want, so it's important to have gifted engineers on my productions. I try to develop a rapport with the engineers I work with so that they are able to quickly translate my ideas onto tape, so I can say very specific things like "I think it should be brighter" or "I think it should be bigger… I think it should be heavier…it has too much ambience…the balance between the drums doesn't sound right…the toms sound too important…the cymbals sound too splashy," etc.

BHM: What do you think differentiates a Rick Rubin-produced record from the other records out there?

RR: I like the fact that my records don't sound like each other. There are some producers who tend to have "a sound," and it's their sound. Certain R&B producers have records that sound exactly the same, the only difference is the singer. I've been making records for quite a while now, and it's more interesting when it's challenging. I'm always trying to do different things. People around me were concerned when I stopped making rap records. It seems like with every project I take on, there's someone out there saying that I shouldn't be doing it, or saying that I should be approaching it in a different way. Fortunately, it usually works out just fine.

BHM: I have to agree with you there. What is the producer's role in the mixing process? It seems like many producers don't even mix their own records these days.

RR: The idea of a producer making this thing, and then handing it over to somebody else doesn't make any sense to me. If the producer you're working with from the beginning is the right person, you hope that they'll see the whole thing through. It doesn't always work out that way, which can be a problem because the mixer doesn't always know what the producer had in mind when it was recorded. Sometimes it can work out well — Brendan O'Brien mixed a Soundgarden record that he didn't produce. One day the artist came in to hear a song and said "That's a backing vocal, what happened to my lead vocal?" Brendan said "I thought that *was* your lead vocal." The song ended up being released as a single with the backing vocal mixed as the lead vocal!

BHM: One last question: Of all the tracks that you have produced over the years, do you have any favorites?

RR: That's too difficult to answer — I don't listen to them too much once they're finished — I'm on to the next thing.

INTERVIEW: PRODUCT MANAGER

Lorrie Boula

Lorrie Boula is a product manager for Warner Bros. Records in Burbank, California. Lorrie has really cool orange dreadlocks and has a great passion for music.

BHM: How did you end up in the music business?

LB: I have always been horribly addicted to music, and it occurred to me at some point that I could actually make a career of it. In the mid-eighties I worked for WEA Distribution at the actual WEA warehouse at which point I met lots of label people, some of whom actually liked music. So, I realized that most of these people could have just as easily been selling shoes, and it made me realize that someone with a clue and a love of music could probably get involved with a good company. Plus, I think I understood the demographic of the kind of music that was just starting to happen, which was "pre-alternative"music. After WEA, I worked at and managed a Tower Records store and a Wherehouse Records store. I made some good connections there and then went to work for World Domination Records, a small indie label. Just before I came to Warner Bros., I worked in alternative sales at Geffen and was the Senior Alternative Marketing Director at Interscope.

BHM: I briefly touch on the role of the product manager in my book, but I think your job is really important to a young artist's success. How are product managers assigned to artists and what do you do for artists once they are signed?

LB: First of all, your readers should understand that not all labels have product managers — at some labels, the A&R person serves (or attempts to serve) this function. In any event, after the artist is signed and makes their first record for us, the artist and management are introduced to the various product managers at the label. After the introductions, it's a collective decision, but certainly if the artist and/or their manager has someone in mind they usually get their way. Similarly, the artist may decide after a few years at the label that a different A&R person or product manager is needed — if it makes the artist happy, it's usually OK with us. It's really important to have your core group of advisors assembled early on because there is so much interaction between the artist, management and the label. After they pick one (or one is assigned to them), the product manager then usually meets with the artist and the management and tries to get a feel for the artist and tries to get a handle on the artist's vision and goals.

At this point, the product manager (along with the artist manager) creates the marketing plan for the record. Most good bands do have a vision of who they are, who they appeal to, where they want to go and how they want to be presented. The marketing plan covers everything from the imaging of the band in their ads to the packaging of their records. The marketing plan encompasses the general strategy for the artist and the record — how they will be promoted, how many records we are going to initially ship, what kind of touring the band will be doing, etc. The product manager is the band's Team Captain or their lobbyist to the label — we interface with the other departments whether it's sales, or radio, advertising or publicity — we micro-manage those areas. When everyone is doing what they're supposed to do, they give us all of the information so that the manager and artist can call us and get an update on what's going on in every department. We speak to the manager or the artist on a daily basis, letting them know where we are on the project and what they can expect. In addition to that, some bands need more imaging, so I'll go to a photo shoot and a video shoot — some bands need less, some bands have a very clear idea of who they are and what they are and how they should be seen. I just try to get them to see that they need to be cognizant of the commercial aspects of this business — we want them to be comfortable with the way they are presented, but they also need to realize that this is a business and that we are investing hundreds of thousands of dollars into each artist, so you've got to give us something to work with.

BHM: To what extent do your duties overlap with the duties of someone in the marketing department?

LB: Marketing starts with the product manager, the artist and management.

BHM: OK. Once the marketing plan is concocted, what happens next?

LB: The marketing department carries out the plan. Obviously, there are different types of plans for each artist. We try to think of different ways to "break a band" which could be anything from trying to get music on a skateboard video or snowboard video to actually buying spots on *The Box*. It really depends on the band and what is right for them. The marketing plan is just an overview of where you'd like to see the band and where the money should actually be spent.

INTERVIEW: BUSINESS MANAGER

Larry Einbund

Larry Einbund is a CPA and business manager at Provident Financial Management. Larry specializes in representing clients in the music, motion picture and television industries.

BHM: How did you get started in the music business and business management?

LE: Believe it or not, I started in the garment industry after I was in college. I always had a love for music and eventually I decided that I wanted to get into the music industry. One day about 13 years ago I came across a classified ad looking for CPAs at an entertainment accounting firm. I applied, and after several weeks of interviewing I was hired as an accountant with this firm here in LA. Over the years we have opened 5 offices and we employ about 150 people. I started at the ground level as a staff accountant and worked my way up to a partner.

BHM: "Business Manager" is different from "Accountant" — most people know that an accountant does your taxes. But a "Business Manager" is much more than an accountant. Why don't you tell the readers what a business manager does?

LE: When a new artist or a band signs a record deal there is usually some kind of a cash advance against royalties from the record company, apart from the recording fund. This money is supposed to be used for living expenses for a period of time — sometimes months, sometimes a year or two, it depends on the size of the advance. All of the money is deposited into a band bank account that is set up at the firm on behalf of the client and all their bills are dispersed from here. We pay the commissions, any legal bills and any other bills that are outstanding. We give these guys a monthly living allowance and withhold the appropriate taxes. Quite frequently, bands will come in that haven't paid their back taxes. We set money aside for delinquent and current taxes. Hopefully there is money left over to give them a monthly living allowance to eat and pay their rent. In addition, we prepare their personal income tax returns, and if there is a partnership, corporation or LLC, we file the appropriate tax return for that entity. As I said earlier we pay the band's bills as well as (in some cases) an individual member's bills. This can be especially helpful when they are on tour, otherwise, there is a possibility that their utilities, phone, insurance and rent won't get paid. We are a full service business management firm — we're the client's central business center. Their business is conducted out of one office while they're touring the world.

BHM: It makes life easier for everyone. At what point does a band need a business manager vs. an accountant?

LE: I believe that an artist or a band needs business management from day one. As soon as a recording advance is paid (because bands usually get 50 to 100 thousand dollars) they are not aware of or don't want to consider that there are taxes and back bills to pay. So if we set them up on an allowance from day one and pay everything, again — commissions, attorney fees, taxes, etc., they get accustomed to having a living allowance, having their taxes taken care of and their entire business is set up properly from day one.

BHM: How do you get paid?

LE: We have three fee structures: 1) a percentage of gross income. Keep in mind that this excludes things such as sound and light expenses and recording costs; 2) on an hourly basis where our account managers and all of the people involved with the account including partners keep track of their time, or 3) or on a monthly retainer, a previously agreed upon flat fee that the client pays every month.

BHM: Have you ever been faced with a situation where you have agreed on a flat monthly or annual retainer but the hourly value of the work you've done far exceeds the retainer?

LE: Sure, that happens, but most bands prefer to go on a percentage basis. A percentage of nothing is nothing, so they don't have to pay much until they really start making good money, and at that point, it's still only 5%, so it's well within their budget. On a retainer we leave it open to suggestions and negotiations at the end of the year. We have gone back to various clients and said, "Our projections were a little less or a little more than the hourly billings," and we try to do what is fair for both sides.

BHM: As a band gets more successful, business managers get more involved with the business aspects of touring. What specific services do you provide with respect to tours?

LE: We are very much involved in touring, it is one of our specialties. We are involved in every aspect of the tour from beginning to the end. Specifically, we prepare tour budgets and prepare all necessary tax documentation to minimize the tax withholding in the various states and countries. In most cases we can greatly reduce or eliminate these taxes. Also, when bands go on the road, payroll needs to be done. It needs to be done for all members in all states — so we prepare the appropriate payroll tax returns, W-2s and 1099s as well as any sales tax returns that need to be done for merchandise. We also look into the insurance and we look into obtaining the best van and sound and light deals we can get.

BHM: Does your firm ever send someone out on the road with an artist if it's a big tour?

LE: All of the partners here have been on the road at one time or another for the bigger tours. We're always available to do it, but nowadays there are tour accountants who go out with the bands, and we can either provide one or help them find one and then coordinate with them so that we know that the tour accountant is on the right track. If there are discrepancies and if we have to go out there and do due diligence or fill in for a couple of days it's not a problem — we're all very familiar with the road.

BHM: In the first chapter of my book I talk about selecting an attorney. I explain that just because your grandpa or your uncle is a big time attorney doesn't mean that he knows how to negotiate a record deal. It's really important to have the same kind of perspective when you're choosing an accountant — there are a lot of different things involved in taxes and other issues — another accountant might be able to do your return but he won't get you the right deductions or know how to deal with various state tax problems or foreign tax problems.

LE: That's exactly right, Bri. These days it is a specialty and there are certain rules and regulations that apply to the entertainment industry. We have to keep current on those as well, and again, from experience we are very familiar with what we can and cannot deduct on tax returns and such.

BHM: Anything else you'd like to say to our readers?

LE: I wish everybody the best of luck. It is a tough business but the upside can be very sweet, so plan carefully and don't quit.

BHM: And save money for your taxes.

LE: That's right. It's very important.

INTERVIEW: BAND MANAGER

Jackson Haring

Jackson Haring is an artist manager and heads up the Los Angeles office of Bill Graham Management. Jackson handles the careers of Cracker, Michelle Shocked, Joe Henry and Menthol.

BHM: How did you get started in the music business and artist management?

JH: I was a DJ at a pretty influential college radio station in San Francisco, KUSF — I think I started back in 1984. As a DJ, I listened to a lot of new music, and one day I picked up a copy of the first Camper Van Beethoven record, *Telephone Free Landslide Victory,* at Tower, and it really blew me away. I assumed that everybody knew about them and that I was late to the party, but it turned out no one had really heard of them, so I kind of took it upon myself to promote them and their music to my friends and listeners. I had an opportunity to interview David Lowery (Camper's lead singer) and we kind of hit it off. It occurred to me that there were a lot of people from my hometown (Portland, Oregon) who would really enjoy the band's music, so I asked them if they had ever toured the Pacific Northwest and they said no, and I said, "Well, I'd love to book a tour for you." I've never told them this, but the main reason I agreed to book the tour was so that my friends from home could see them. Of course, they asked me if I had ever booked a tour before, to which I replied, "Oh yeah, sure, hundreds of tours. You've heard of the Rolling Stones, haven't you?" Basically I lied. I just got into it. Not knowing anything wasn't a barrier. So I got in there and asked for more than I thought they were worth and voila! We went on tour. They actually thought I would go away or something and that it wouldn't come together, but we were all amazed when it did. When we got back they asked me to manage them. I was working at a law firm at the time — you know how much fun that can be — so I said, "What the fuck?" I became the band manager and tour manager.

BHM: What is the role of the artist manager?

JH: Let me simplify it and demystify it for your readers. The manager is a general contractor in that he has a client (the artist) who wants a house (a career) built and they've come to you with the hope that you can build them the best house and save them the most money in doing so. Like a general contractor, it is your job to hire other professionals to cover all the aspects of a successful career, whether it be a tour manager, a sound man, a business manager, an attorney, a label, a publisher, an agent or a publicist. Then it is the manager's job to work with all these people on the team. The manager is the final decision maker when it comes to promoting or marketing your band. There are set things you are going to have to do anyway. The type of artist defines those avenues quite handily for you. "Let's see, I handle Junior Brown, so should I play him at the House of Blues, or should I play him at the Roxy?" You look at the artist and you make some assumption about the type of people that would be drawn to that artist and you pick the best room. If you feel you cannot make an informed decision, you can seek guidance or a second opinion from one of the subcontractors (i.e., the publicist, the booking agent, etc.). I like to consult the artist every step of the way — I let them know what I'm doing and ask them if there's anything that I'm not looking at that they would like to address or if there is a specific way they would like something handled. Not all artists can or want to make those decisions. That's O.K.

BHM: So you have some clients that are much more actively involved in decision making and some that...

JH: "I trust you Jackson. Your way is O.K. with me." Sometimes if I really don't know I'll come back and I'll say it's a hard call and we have to make it together. As you gain experience, decisions are obvious and become so apparent to you that you don't need to go back and bother your artist every single time about it. While I think beginning managers should take baby steps, they shouldn't be afraid to make some decisions without consulting the artist, because that is what the artist is paying them to do. They don't need you if you have to ask them about every little question.

BHM: They don't have the time and they're supposed to be making music.

JH: That's the bottom line. You want to free your artist up to make music and have a life — that's where their music comes from — having a life.

BHM: Is it essential for a manager to have extensive touring experience?

JH: I think it is extremely important. Only then can you appreciate where an artist is coming from when you start heaping stuff on them and they have a problem doing some of it. One has the tendency to think, "Hey you're playing music — you're having a good time — you're doing sound checks and interviews, so what's the problem? Why can't you do ten interviews before 11:00 in the morning?" Well, when you have done a 300-mile drive every day before a 5:00 load in, a 6:00 sound check and then a 12:30 show, you realize that the day starts at 6:00 in the morning and ends at 3:00 in the morning. I think people have the tendency to think touring is all fun and games. It is not!

BHM: When does an artist need a manager?

JH: Most bands think they need a manager before they really do. When an artist comes to me with a line like, "We sound good and we're rehearsing a lot and we need somebody to get us gigs," I tell them they need to call me back when something is really happening. The music will usually take them to a certain degree. When it gets them to a point where there's something going on, people talk, people see bands, A&R people and promoters see bands — word gets around. There are a lot of people in Los Angeles and New York who see bands at home and while visiting other cities. These people talk about these bands even if they don't have a vested interest in them. When you get something happening that is new and impressive, people will start to talk about you. You don't have to be an Adonis or Venus to be successful, but the appearance and presentation of the band are important. None of these things can be neglected. When your songs and your shows reach a certain level, people start offering you deals. That's what I mean by "happening" and that is when you need a manager. Some managers will work with you out of the goodness of their heart beforehand, but all they'll do is put you into a systematized program of gigging until they feel confident to show you to somebody.

BHM: I am sure the readers want to know how they can find a decent manager. Do bands come to you, or do you find them?

JH: There is no mystery to it — it's about networking. In most cases, an attorney or an A&R person will want to get you involved because they have an established rapport with you. You can meet managers at a club — we're not all so gruff and standoffish. Get someone to introduce you, or just say hello. There are so few managers in the business that you get hit on all the time. I get 100 CDs a week from bands with and without managers, bands with and without labels. Some of the music is absolutely frightening — but that's America. I like the fact that you have the freedom to be awful.

BHM: Assuming a band has a legitimate need for a manager, what criteria do you use in determining whether or not to take on an artist? I know that you've passed on established, successful bands.

JH: I can't speak for other managers. I just have to be exceptionally motivated by a band. There's no way that someone trying to curry my favor will know what my private vision is. I know what it is and I don't want to advertise it. I don't put it in the *Yellow Pages of Rock* — "Manager seeks good looking alternarock bands with interesting lyrics." There are things that draw me in. I'm not a public service, I am in business for myself — I follow my own muse. It is a matter of taste and intuition. Not all managers work this way, I'm not saying one way is better than another, it just works for me.

BHM: Do you have any preference for signed artists versus unsigned artists?

JH: With new artists, I like to be involved in making the deals. There is so much competition for talent these days that labels sign bands before they're ready because they're afraid someone else will sign them. If I am involved with a band early on, I will do what I can to make sure they don't get overanxious and sign the wrong deal. Also, I want to have input on the deal terms and the label selection. The attorney will have his or her own agenda about what the deal should be. This usually pertains to term, territory, all the other salient points, money, royalties, etc. Managers have hands-on knowledge of how a record is worked through a particular company in terms of marketing and promotion. I think this knowledge can be valuable to the artist and the attorney when the deal is being negotiated.

BHM: What kind of fee arrangements do you make with your artists?

JH: Generally it is 15% or 20% of gross. Then the lawyers get involved and try to bring that down or modify it.

BHM: When you talk about gross in regards to your average client, do you exclude recording costs?

JH: Yes.

BHM: What about touring? Do you allow the artist to deduct any expenses prior to the calculation of your commission?

JH: If someone puts a dollar on the stage, I get 15 or 20 cents.

BHM: Even if the band is losing money?

JH: That's negotiable. If you're not making more than $250 dollars — forget it — it's not worth it. Early on, touring is about building a band's career. If things go well, that is when you should be taking your commission on gross without deduction. It balances out.

BHM: It's tough when a band is in a deficit situation and the manager sends a band a bill.

JH: 15% of $2,000 is $300. The manager spent more than $300 to get that $300. Get used to it at that stage — it's less onerous later on.

BHM: Do you require your artists to sign contracts?

JH: I have artists that I have written contracts with and artists that I don't have written contracts with.

BHM: Does it come down to how much clout the artist has? For instance, if an artist that has already sold 3 million records comes to you for management, they might not want to sign an agreement. Maybe they figure that you would do anything to manage them.

JH: In that situation, I would require a written agreement. If the artist wants you to be their manager and they already have a preeminent career, then that means they blew out their previous manager for whatever reason. A lot of people bring their family dynamics into this business. It is not like selling shoes or building tables. You're dealing with people, not product, so they bring those same dynamics into their bands. They don't talk to each other, or they are dependent, or healthy or natural or needy, aloof, whatever. If it is an artist that has a reputation for being "difficult" you bet I want a god-damned contract.

BHM: That's a good point. In terms of the contract, let's say you have a 3-year term and the band that you're working with gets a deal for 7 records. The term expires and you and the artist part ways. There are still 4 records left on the record deal. Do you think that the manager should be entitled to receive income from the future records that are going to be made?

JH: (Heavy sigh) It depends on what stage of the relationship you're in. If you were 3 records in, I think it's fair for a manager to get commission in post-term recordings. If you were one record into the deal it would depend on whether I was negligent or not. Two records would entitle you to the records you've worked on, but not post-term recordings.

BHM: Do you ever loan money to your artists?

JH: I've loaned clients money for travel expenses. "Whatever it takes" should be your motto, but I don't do it a lot. I don't think a manager should be a schmuck or an easy touch.

BHM: Up until a few years ago, you worked out of your home or shared a small office. Why did you decide to make the jump to a bigger management company like Bill Graham Management which is one of the biggest management companies in the country?

JH: After working out of my home for seven years, I started to feel limited. I got to the point where I was working the second Cracker record, *Kerosene Hat,* which ultimately went platinum. I was able to do that on my own because I had an excellent tour manager who was totally motivated and committed to making the band happen as well. We were able to cover most of the ground, but I needed someone to help me with things like press and travel and all these ancillary aspects to management that are service oriented. I found that I was less and less inclined to get involved with these tasks, because they required me to expend as much time and energy as the stuff that had to do with how I made my money, such as marketing plans, promotion strategies and the like. I couldn't focus on those things. I had become a glorified travel agent. I realized that I needed to bring in somebody else who was qualified to handle that stuff. I also wanted to add more clients — the nature of management is such that I needed a pool of talent to work with to generate the money in order to stay in business. Suddenly, taking that leap you've got to have a qualified assistant or associate, an office, and all the overhead associated with that. Also, I just wanted a regular paycheck for a change. For all of these reasons, I hooked up with Bill Graham Management, and I have been with them for nearly four years now.

BHM: Are you friends with your clients?

JH: It is difficult not to develop that relationship, but it's not a pre-requisite. I want my artists to sign with me not because they think I'm cool, but because they trust me and believe in my ability. For instance, one of the last clients I signed, their first inclination was "You're so nice,"etc. At that point I quit being nice and tried to be a little abrasive because I thought that was a good chance to test it. I said, "I'm not here to be your friend — I have friends — I'm not lonely, I'm trying to pay my rent and car payment just like you are; I'm in business with you." But if it happens, don't be afraid of it — embrace it. It is a wonderful thing to have a bit of friendly relationship with your clients.

BHM: Right. We talked a little bit about the signing frenzy over the past few years. One of your clients was recently the subject of a small bidding war. Do you think bidding wars are ultimately good for the artist?

JH: I tried to de-evolve it from a bidding war the whole time. I'm not impressed by money — every major label has plenty of cash. I think it is a sad commentary that the labels that cannot impress you with their ability to promote or market an artist end up offering you stupid amounts of cash. I don't want money that way, I want to sell records. That is the healthiest way to look at it. Of course, you can use that leverage to get the kind of deal that will give the artist the best possible chance to recoup and make money. How much money do you need up front? Isn't it better to get it on the back end?

BHM: Well, the advance is just pre-payment of the back end. I'd rather have that money up front rather than let the record company keep it and make interest on it.

JH: Yes, but a big advance brings big expectations. How many new artists come out of the gate selling a million records? Less than one percent. I think that a savvy manager and lawyer can put together a reasonable escalation of advances and royalties based on sales performance — trade off a lower advance for a higher return. But, you need the tools to get the job done. Don't deny yourself that. If you are the kind of artist that needs to spend $250,000 in the studio to realize your vision, then by all means ask for it. If it's a large group, keep in mind that it's very expensive to keep nine people on the road, so don't be afraid to ask for more money up front. If you don't get it up front, you're going to have to go back every time and then you are in the position of dealing with "No."

BHM: Do you think more unscrupulous managers might go for a bigger advance up front even if they think it might be detrimental to the artist in the long run?

JH: Absolutely. This is called "front loading."

BHM: A lot of readers are interested in becoming managers themselves — if you are so inclined and you see a band that you love, what should you do?

JH: Don't deny yourself the dream. Do it. Don't be afraid to manage just one band. You should be prepared for failure, though.

BHM: Thanks, Jackson. Anything else you want to add?

JH: In the words of the great Winston Churchill, "Play for more than you can afford to lose and you will learn the game very quickly."

INTERVIEW: A&R

Lenny Waronker

Lenny Waronker is a legendary record executive and producer. He has worked with Randy Newman, Brian Wilson, Van Dyke Parks, Rufus Wainwright, Rickie Lee Jones, Ry Cooder and many others. After many years at Warner Bros. Records, he (along with Mo and Michael Ostin) formed DreamWorks Records in late 1995.

BHM: I want to talk about your views on the role of an A&R person, but first, why don't you tell the readers how you got started and what you have been doing for the last 30 years.

LW: I was lucky. My father Sy owned Liberty Records, so I went to work for my father. I started at Liberty Records when I was fourteen, and I got to watch all these great people at work. When I was in college, I'd go to work during the summers with Snuff Garrett, who was a producer, a wonderful producer who taught me all about production and songwriting and what a great chorus was all about and why a certain song was a hit and others weren't. He had an amazing ear for that. So that was a terrific experience. I also had the benefit of my father's perspective on music and songs, which had to do with quality and how important it is to go against the grain because that's where you really find success — that was imbedded in me very early. I had a really good pre-education — you don't really go to school for this. I always loved music, and at an early age I was around people who had vision and they made a big impression on me.

Through a series of interesting circumstances I ended up leaving Liberty and moving on to Warner Bros. Records at a very good time. Warners was just starting and I got to be part of that whole scene. I was the youngest person there in 1966. I was like twenty-five years old. I was brought in as an A&R assistant. In those days I was expected to produce. They hired me based on the demos that I was making — I had worked at Liberty's publishing company, so I learned how to make records just because I had to, and in those days again, before it was really a done deal, songs that were written by songwriters had to be demoed mainly because the songwriters were so fearful of what the record producers would do to those songs. They were often ruined so you would have to make these real literal demos in the hopes that they could be copied exactly. You had limited budgets but you could do a lot in those days, paying musicians $15.00 a song and then over-dubbing like crazy. So I learned how to make records based on that. And also being around people like Snuff Garret, and never directly, but indirectly with Phil Spector, Leiber and Stoller, studying that stuff — Burt Bacharach, Carole King…all those people. Being best friends with Randy Newman didn't hurt either, because that kind of major, powerful, creative input and real strength that he had, and continues to have, affected me; it taught me about the difference between a pop record and a great song. Relationships like that really can affect you. I think Randy more than anybody else has affected me not only in terms of introducing me to Ray

Charles and The Beatles, but also introducing me to a true aesthetic about good work and how important that is.

So I took that experience and perspective to Warners and I produced a couple of singles (by the Mojo Men and Harpers Bizarre) that were hits. This immediate success turned out to be a blessing and a curse. At the beginning I thought I was invincible, and after a few stiffs in a row, I realized that I was not. I also realized that I didn't want to be in the studio making pop records, just cutting singles and trying to come up with hits. I was much more interested in artists and living with Randy, literally being with Randy most of the time, I realized that was much more interesting to me. When I ran into Van Dyke Parks and Ry Cooder along with Randy, I realized those were maybe not accessible, but unbelievably challenging and interesting artists who could have an impact. I had limitations in my mind in terms of what I could do in the studio, so I would much rather be associated with something that I thought was really good. That took over in 1967-68.

BHM: I find myself going back to the records you made with Ry Cooder, Van Dyke Parks and Randy Newman a lot more than the hit records you had in the later '60s and early '70s.

LW: Those early Ry Cooder records and the early Newman records or the Parks records still to this day are more meaningful to me and to others than many of the hit records that I produced. I realize that those records affected people, even if it was a small body of people. And this is important for people to understand: that if you're involved with stuff that's really good, even if it's not a big hit, being involved with quality writers and performers really helps you build a career. I knew when I was making those records that I was doing the right thing. I also knew the odds were against them and I wasn't quite sure why I was doing it, except I knew that they'd be good and it's much more fun to be involved with something that's good than some sort of immediate hit — something that'll go away and might even be embarrassing in about five years. You're right — that tough time in the early '70s when there were no hits and just good records — I knew something was right about it. I couldn't quite articulate it, and then later on I realized that, when people like James Taylor and others came to me to produce them based on the fact that I had worked with Randy and Ry and others.

BHM: Do you think that the role of the A&R person has changed since you broke in back in the sixties?

LW: I think the primary role of the A&R person is still the same as it was back then. I want the A&R people I work with to find and make determinations about artists — are they special, do they have the kind of talent that can lead to a long career.

BHM: You started out as a producer. Does an A&R person who works with you need to have production experience?

LW: I keep changing on this — I mean if you look at A&R staffs and A&R people over the years, it keeps changing. In the old days, A&R people were also producers.

They built the studio, found the artists and supervised and produced the artists' records. A&R stands for Artists and Repertoire which means it's about signing artists and finding repertoire (songs). That's changed to a great extent, not totally, but to a great extent because of what has happened in the artist community. We now have singer/songwriters and so now it's being able to spot talent, and so it's changed a bit. I think that knowledge about the creative part of it is important because you're going to have to have a dialogue with the artist that requires some familiarity with the language of songwriting and production, and producers know this language. So, knowing when a song is working and when it isn't working and knowing how to get these opinions across to the artist (and knowing when to keep your mouth shut) — all of those things are really important. I'm not sure, I keep going back and forth, but I don't think it's necessary for an A&R person to know how to make a record. To me, making a record is being in the studio, hiring musicians, saying yes and no to ideas, coming up with ideas, all the things that it takes to make a record in the true sense of the word "make." A lot of people go around saying "I make records," or "I'm making this record with so and so." I know I'm getting hung up in semantics, but in fact, the people that make the records are the artists and producers. A&R people are responsible for putting it together not unlike producers in films. They should know when it's good and when it isn't. To have the absolute creative vocabulary I'm not sure is necessary.

BHM: Right — as long as they can put the artist in the best situation to make a great record.

LW: If you have the right producer, if you have the right situation, and you can be objective and you can keep your mouth shut, and at the same time when necessary have a positive input — positive input meaning either something isn't working or it is working — and being able to communicate to the producer, engineer or artist in a way that helps the project — then you're doing your job. So, knowing whether a specific guitar part works because of the way somebody's playing it or whether something feels busy is a big difference. And just to be able to say, "you know, that doesn't feel right," is sometimes enough. That's how I feel today, I could change my mind. We built an A&R staff at Warners in the early '70s which was made up mostly of producers — but I don't think you can do that now because it is very difficult for somebody to be in the studio all day and then go out at night to look at the bands, or flying across the country or all over the world.

BHM: You have a producer on your A&R staff here at DreamWorks, (Dust Brother) Mike Simpson…

LW: He's unique in that he's flexible, he likes to move around, but when he's in the studio it's hard — it's focused and you have to stay focused. Unless you're really either crazy or gifted, you become obsessed with the project you're working on. It's very difficult not to lose sight of everything once you get involved. So it makes it difficult.

BHM: In the book I talk about how some record companies utilize A&R people not just as talent finders, but as product managers. Do you think that A&R people should fill this role as well? How does that work at DreamWorks, for instance?

LW: At DreamWorks, we are attempting to build a comfortable environment for creative people. We are trying to build a very strong nucleus of creative people in A&R, people that will be involved with not only the signing but also in the molecule. Most of the A&R people that we've hired have certain expertise, whether they come from publicity or other areas of the business. They have a sense of what makes a record work. To be able to really articulate to the rest of the company what the artist is about is a big deal. When I was at Warners, I learned early on that I wasn't going to rival lawyers and accountants in terms of my input. I realized that I would have the best chance of making impact with the company by playing from my A&R/producer background and talking to promotion and sales and other areas of the company about why a record was made, how it was made, all of the fun stuff that everyone is interested in. This was far more impressive to Warners than me trying to become something that I wasn't. I wasn't trying to become some sort of record company president, and that worked best for me. I think that from that experience I realized that you can have a creative philosophy and if you have the right people involved that philosophy can really be part of who you are, it's not just words, it is in fact what you stand for. This way, an artist will come into your company and feel like they are understood — that the people who work for them or who they work with have a real understanding what it's like to be an artist, what it's like to make a record — and what the ups and downs are all about. It makes life a hell of a lot easier, it makes the relationship and the dynamic to be an artist at a record company much better. And, it makes it much more fun.

BHM: Do you give your A&R people "signing power," or do you think signing decisions should be made as a committee?

LW: What we've done so far (who's to say what it'll be a year from now) is not unlike what we do with the artists we're dealing with. Once you sign an artist you have to trust them. You cannot be controlling but you certainly can have input. Similarly, once we bring in an A&R person, if he or she feels really strongly about an artist, regardless of what we think, we're going to try to let that person go after that artist. There's only one way to grow and that's to have the courage and conviction to stand up for somebody you really believe in and to make some mistakes. There is no other way to learn, so you have to be in an environment that allows you to make those mistakes. I think that's hopefully what we'll be about. Not only for A&R people, but for artists too.

BHM: You've mentioned that there are a lot of artists putting out records these days. There also seems to be a glut of new labels. As a result, many artists are getting signed to major labels earlier than they might have a few years ago. Do you think that this phenomenon presents a problem for the music industry?

LW: Yeah, I do. I think this is happening chiefly because there are so many companies out there and there's so much competition for talent. In the old days you could sign somebody and allow that artist to do what they needed to do and what they wanted to do because it wasn't that costly — and put out a couple of records that you knew were just learning vehicles. Now, because deals are so intense and because the competition is forcing that to some extent, you're really forced to put up and it puts the artist in a very odd place. The first two or three records should be released without too much pressure on the artist — we are trying to build careers here, remember. These days, it seems like an attitude of "if we don't get this right now, we're going to be dropped" has developed among artists. I'm not sure that's healthy.

BHM: I know, I get that from some of my clients. I work with a lot of really gifted young artists who sign huge record deals and have everyone telling them that they are going to be instant stars, and then their first record comes out and they sell 10,000 copies and they feel like they've failed. The truth is that they haven't necessarily failed, but the deals are so crazy that anything less than a gold record is looked at as a failure.

LW: In the old, old days there were two schools of thought: One was to make a great record, get great reviews, build a base and record number two will double what we did, so if we did twenty-five thousand we'll get to fifty thousand. If we got to fifty thousand on the first, then we'll get to six figures, which is a victory. And to some extent that still should exist because it is difficult out there. There are a tremendous amount of records being released these days and artists need to learn, they need to learn their craft — not only writing songs and how to develop and grow in that area but also in the record making process. Artists have to understand what that's about. Some learn more quickly than others, but finally you need time and so often it's about immediate gratification and that's not what this is about.

BHM: I think you have a really good point there, and I think that the labels, artists and attorneys should be aware of this when making new artist deals. This philosophy seems to have served you very well over the years.

LW: We all learn, we have our experiences and we learn and some of those early experiences that help us set up our philosophy last forever. I guess that's basically it. I think my father had a lot to do with it too, in terms of just impressing upon me how important it is to do something that's innovative and challenging. Even today at 81 years old he's asking about the Eels, "Does it stand out? Is it unique? Is it interesting?"

BHM: Any parting words for the readers?

LW: Follow your dreams, your musical dreams and your musical instincts. Forget about what's being played on the radio because your brain won't hang onto that no matter what. A lot of your instincts will take over — don't be afraid to take chances, especially when you're young — if you don't, you're dead.

INTERVIEW: PERFORMANCE RIGHTS

Ron Sobel

Ron Sobel is the Assistant Vice President Director of Repertory at ASCAP in Los Angeles.

BHM: When should a songwriter affiliate with a performing rights organization?

RS: As soon as their songs are being performed in public. Playing in clubs doesn't necessarily trigger royalties, but we do survey large venues and successful tours, so even if your music hasn't been recorded, if it is performed in a large venue, it may still generate income. Of course, you should join ASCAP when your songs are recorded, even if they are not getting heavy airplay.

BHM: Assuming a writer or publisher wants to affiliate with ASCAP, what should their first step be?

RS: We are here to make a relationship and we are here to offer services and to introduce them to the world of what ASCAP does and the wider world of what the music industry does. There are membership offices in New York, Nashville, Los Angeles and Chicago, and we are opening two more in 1998. Any prospective member is encouraged to call a membership representative in any one of those offices and engage them in a conversation. We can send them membership forms or set up an appointment and walk them through everything that we can do for them.

BHM: How does ASCAP monitor performances?

RS: In the radio world we employ two methods: First, we survey radio — we literally send folks all over the country to record blocks of radio airplay. They do a random sample that is scientifically designed to take a snapshot of radio airplay across the country. Those people send the tapes to New York and we then identify the music. Second, we receive written logs from disc jockeys that indicate the songs that have been played on a particular station during a particular time period. Between the airplay tapes and the log sheets, we get a very accurate survey of what songs are being played on radio. In the TV world, we conduct a census (minute by minute) survey of music on the major networks and major cable services. For commercial radio, we have a sample size of hundreds of thousands of hours of commercial radio that we take in the form of weekly logs, BDS data and six-hour tape surveys. We conduct surveys of country, religious, classical, ethnic, jazz, Latin, ethnic, urban contemporary and Top-40.

BHM: Why do you think your monitoring methods are better than those employed by BMI or SESAC?

RS: We prefer our method because we've found that airplay tapes can be more accurate than written logs. Logs can have some mis-identifications. A disc jockey can write down the wrong song or wrong artist. Plus, airplay tapes tend to show samples better, you can distinguish between titles of songs better. A title of a song can be misleading. The bottom line is that we think the combination of hundreds of thousands of hours of airplay tapes along with BDS data and written logs gives us what we think is a really accurate sample.

BHM: What is the term of the ASCAP membership agreement?

RS: Both the writer and publisher membership agreements have one-year terms. Accordingly, any member can leave ASCAP at the end of any year as long as they give us notice. Contrast that with BMI, which has a two-year agreement. We're proud that it gives our writers and publishers a bit more flexibility.

BHM: Why don't you tell the readers about other services offered by ASCAP?

RS: We're proud that we've been a leader in innovative services. Most importantly, we pay faster. Domestically we can pay approximately 6-7 months after the performance period. We now pay foreign royalties 3 times a year; BMI only has two foreign distributions a year. In addition to that, we have a Member Services Department, an '800' number that our writers are able to call toll-free from around the country. That department has long hours — it's open from 9:00 a.m. to 8:30 p.m. EST. We encourage our writers and publishers to call any time they have a question about anything — their ASCAP royalty distributions, or services. We have a web site with our ACE clearance system — it allows members to access information 24 hours a day (see Appendix C for address — Ed.). We are innovative with our benefits package. We were the first, and remain the only performing rights organization to offer a credit union with credit cards and loans with favorable rates to our members. We were the first performing rights organization to offer access to health, dental and life insurance programs. And we were the first performing rights organization to offer access to equipment insurance that covers important records, personal computer manuscripts, and computer files in addition to equipment. That program has been quite successful.

BHM: What about workshops and showcases?

RS: We have a variety of career development and educational services. We offer a range of workshops: writer workshops, business workshops, Business 101, Pop, R&B and country writer workshops, film and television scoring workshops. In terms of artist development, there's a range of showcases. Not only do we have showcases in major cities such as New York, Los Angeles, and Nashville, but we also produce them at major regional music conferences, such as South by Southwest, North by Northwest, and CMJ. These showcases allow us to show our best and brightest to the music industry. Publishers, attorneys, managers and record labels are invited to the showcases, and we maintain strong industry relationships. We have had great success in getting writers and artists signed.

BHM: Any other services?

RS: If a member has a problem with the way any of their ASCAP business is being handled, we have an Internal Board of Review that reviews the dispute. This avoids going to court or arbitration. It is a very efficient, inexpensive way for our members to resolve problems. The other performing rights organizations do not offer this service.

BHM: Do ASCAP members have any say in how the organization is operated?

RS: Absolutely. We have annual membership meetings, which BMI does not. Our members vote for our Board of Directors, which is comprised of 12 songwriters and 12 publishers. The BMI Board of Directors is comprised of broadcasters. We are proud that we are created and controlled by our membership and that our Board is comprised of writer and publisher members, as opposed to broadcasters. We also have Advisory Committees, groups of active writers and publishers who meet periodically to inform and advise us — they actually tell us what's going on in the streets, whether it's legislative, creative, technological, etc. There's a great sense of feedback, both structured and unstructured.

BHM: Any parting thoughts?

RS: We're first in service. We are not only innovators, but we offer a broader range of services. We collect and distribute more money than BMI, and we are the first in music as well. We believe that our repertoire is the broadest — we have the leaders in all genres of music. We were the first performing rights society in 1914 and we have maintained that leadership. We are proud of our writers, from Irving Berlin and Johnny Mercer to Mary Chapin Carpenter, LL Cool J, Stevie Wonder, Joni Mitchell, Beck and Madonna.

INTERVIEW: PERFORMANCE RIGHTS

Rick Riccobono

Rick Riccobono is Vice President, Writer-Publisher Relations at BMI in Los Angeles.

BHM: When should a writer or publisher affiliate with a performing rights organization?

RR: At or before the point when their songs are about to be performed. I think you're probably safe to not have to worry about it if you're talking about a local club or something like that, but if there is an opportunity, like television, film, and certainly radio — if that's imminent then it is time to contact a performing rights organization.

BHM: So somebody who has a record coming out should just call the local office and ask for information?

RR: Yes.

BHM: How long is the membership agreement?

RR: It's two years for a writer, five years for a publisher.

BHM: Is it easy to switch from one performing rights organization to another?

RR: Yes. You just have to make sure that you conform to the rules and regulations in the agreement. It's fairly simple — you give notification to your present organization and then at the prescribed date you move from one to the other. It is not an uncommon occurrence — it happens at an even rate from organization to organization. You have to remember that performing rights organizations are here for the betterment of the entire writer/publisher community; we understand that certain people work better with certain personalities and we expect that people will do business with whomever they are most comfortable with.

BHM: How does BMI track performances of the songs in its repertoire and how does your method differ from those utilized by ASCAP or SESAC?

RR: We actually request written logs from radio stations. We get to every station at least once a year and for a 3-5 day period they write down everything that they're playing. In the world of automation it makes it quite a bit easier for them. We not only get the title, but we get the act itself and in some cases the label so it's pretty precise information.

BHM: So, for instance, you're able to determine which version of a song has been played? This can be important, because some publishers retain a larger percentage of performance royalties for covers. Do you think there may be a day when we'll be able to identify each version of every song?

RR: That's still in the future. The problem with that is in the encoding of records.

BHM: Let's talk about foreign collection. BMI has reciprocal agreements with foreign performance societies — how does that work?

RR: For instance, if an American songwriter has performances in England or any of the PRS countries, they would get paid just as a PRS writer would get paid, based on PRS's rules of logging and collection. The foreign performing rights organization then remits the money back to the performing rights organization that the artist belongs to in the U.S. We then remit the royalties to the songwriter through our foreign royalty distributions.

BHM: A lot of artists ask me about advances. I know that SESAC pays them, but I don't believe that ASCAP and BMI do.

RR: Advances are really never a profitable venture for a performing rights organization. Here's why: If you are an A&R person and you have ten bands and decide to give them all an advance, and four of them hit, you're going to be Senior VP and maybe President soon. But with performing rights organizations, you miss six out of ten, and that money really belongs to the other writers and publishers who may not have the same degree of confidence in the staff to be choosing who is going to miss and/or hit. I don't think it is a healthy thing for any performing rights organization to get into. There are certain instances where grants are made to certain types of music that don't fall into our sample. Classical music, some jazz — radio stations are spotty throughout the nation and the performances that we get really don't reflect the impact or actual airplay. It's not really a subsidy, it is a recognition of these forms of music that I think is very fair, and no one is going to argue with it.

BHM: What if a writer or publisher hasn't registered its songs within the nine month period following initial performance?

RR: All the money that we take in is distributed after operating costs are covered. It's a non-profit organization. So if the songs never get registered, the writer/publisher simply misses out on royalties.

BHM: Let's talk about services. Beyond sponsoring showcases at clubs and outreach programs, what services does BMI provide?

RR: We offer access to an insurance program, not only life and health, but for musical instruments and equipment as well. We are now set up to have royalties directly deposited into affiliates' bank accounts. We were the first performing rights organization to have an Internet program that identifies web sites that are playing music and it gives us the address. This allows us to track performances on the Internet. We were the first performing rights organization to pay on college radio performances.

BHM: OK, here's the million dollar question: Beyond what we've discussed, why should a writer or publisher affiliate up with BMI instead of ASCAP or SESAC?

RR: Although I obviously want writers and publishers to choose BMI, I think you'll find that you can't really make a strong argument for choosing one organization over another. ASCAP has as many powerful writers as we have at BMI. I think our catalogue is a little healthier, a little more vibrant than theirs because over the past ten years we've been the choice of a lot of new people. BMI is a mixture of those who have been working for the company for a long time and people who have had relevant careers outside of BMI. I was a music publisher for 12 years. The fellow who runs the New York office was a publisher for 14 years, and the person who runs the national office was one for 15 years. There is more of a feeling that these people know what they are talking about. And, I think we are more service oriented than our competition. Service has been Frances Preston's main focus over the last 11 years that she has been president. It is a legacy at BMI — we were the second performing rights organization (after ASCAP), we were the underdog for many years — we had to try harder, and we still do. We had to take the extra step as far as service was concerned. That's the real difference between the two.

INTERVIEW: PUBLICITY

Mitch Schneider

Mitch Schneider is the President of the Mitch Schneider Organization (MSO), the largest music-only publicity firm in the country.

BHM: How did you get started in the music business?

MS: My background is in journalism. I began writing reviews for *Good Times*, which is a local publication back in Long Island, New York. I graduated to *Crawdaddy* and then to *Rolling Stone*. I interviewed artists, and reviewed shows and albums. I had a good inside look at the process of just being a writer. Eventually I felt that I had said what I needed to say as a critic, so I decided to move into publicity. I was fascinated by the other side of the fence — I was much more interested in working with artists than writing about them. But it was hard to get a publicity gig in New York City in 1979 - keep in mind that there were only nine major labels back then! The business was infinitely smaller than it is now. Since I was unable to secure a job in New York City, I sent a resume out west and I was hired by Solters, Rossman and Friedman, a public relations firm with offices in Los Angeles and New York. I moved to Los Angeles in 1979 and began my career as a publicist. I worked there for about 3 1/2 years — I got laid off because they lost a lot of business — I was kind of unceremoniously booted out without proper notice. I got kind of angry and said "fuck this!" and went back to freelance writing. I contributed to *The Rolling Stone Encyclopedia of Rock & Roll*, and I wrote for *BAM, Creem,* and the *LA Weekly*, but then the publicity urge came crawling again and in 1984 I joined forces with Michael Levine who had just started a PR firm. Michael handled theatrical people, film, TV, all those kind of folks and thought I would be a great addition if I were to do music. I began to sign clients there — I started off with the Everly Brothers, who had just come off their reunion. Danny Goldberg (then an artist manager, now President of Mercury Records) gave me acts like Keel, The Textones, and Bruce Cockburn. I then went on to sign REO Speedwagon and Wang Chung. Astrologically this is proof that the stars can line up! In a 30-day period we signed Ozzy Osbourne, Tom Petty, Fleetwood Mac, and Heart. I can proudly say that they are all still with me. In 1995, I left Levine/Schneider and started this operation. I felt it was time to open up a firm that focused only on music industry clients. My offices are deliberately not in Beverly Hills or Century City, or even Hollywood. — we're here in Sherman Oaks. We just wanted to be separate. We now handle a wide variety of artists — we do the Descendants for Epitaph, we do the Paladins for 4AD Records. We look after David Bowie and Me'Shell Ndegeocello. In fact, we are the publicity firm that is used for all of Maverick Records' acts, which means we also work with Alanis Morissette.

BHM: What does a publicist do?

MS: A publicist brings music to the masses. The way to get music to the masses is to call the gatekeepers of the media — writers, editors — to introduce them to new music, to influence them to write reviews and features and column items about your artists. We pitch anywhere from *Rolling Stone, MTV News,* to *Addicted to Noise,* which is an on-line magazine. Our office is very cyber conscious - we believe that the computer revolution has happened and has changed everything. A good portion of our day is dealing with Internet outlets as well as interactive CD-ROM magazines such as *Blender, Launch* and *Digizine* — they are all a part of the musical menu these days. We get advance cassettes out to writers — we hip them to the music. We put together a biography that captures the essence of the band, we put together press releases that essentially let an editor quickly know what's happening. Editors are constantly getting hit upon by lots of publicists. Right now, there's probably 40% more record labels than there were in 1990. You have to capture people's attention. You have to know how to work the phones — a lot of PR in 1998 is voice mail — there are journalists that don't even answer the phone, they just let it go to voice mail. So the question becomes "How can you capture someone's attention in 20 seconds?" The best pitch I did was for the group The The — Matt Johnson of The The put out a record called "Hanky Panky." This record was his very bizarre interpretations of Hank Williams' songs. I called people up and I said "Hey I'm just calling you about the new The The album, it's called *Hanky Panky* — imagine the music of Hank Williams coming out of a jukebox in a David Lynch film." It produced the quickest amount of return phone calls that I can ever remember on a non-superstar act.

BHM: What about TV? Are publicists responsible for getting an act on the talk shows and music shows?

MS: Yes. Television — we do late night television — *Saturday Night Live, The Tonight Show, Letterman,* and *Conan O'Brien.* Then there's shows — *ABC In Concert, MTV Music News, VH-1 News.* There's local cable shows. When our bands go on tour we can call a local cable show in Detroit to do an interview during sound check. The publicist tries to establish the relationship between the artist and the musical television menu. These relationships are important. Sometimes I take them for granted because our agency is the largest music PR firm in the country. We carry a certain amount of clout just by the phone call. But by the end of the day, it comes down to what act we're pitching. People tend to listen to us because they know that if we deliver a client, there's not going to be any last minute screw-ups. MSO has a good reputation for getting artists to a studio or a rehearsal on time. If it comes down to a show having a choice, I'd like to think that they'd choose an MSO artist because they know that it's always smooth.

BHM: Why would an artist signed to an established major label that already has a publicity staff hire an independent publicist? Do you work in conjunction with label publicists?

MS: Every scenario is different. If I were an artist. I would look at my record company and ask myself "Are they going to totally serve my vision? Which account executive will be assigned to my project?" I would take that into consideration and I would find out if the situation were right for me. Someone would consider MSO for many reasons. I've been in the business since 1979. I was a writer before, and a publicist. Our office is instantly informed by my background which means that since I was a member of the media, I know what they want. I can give them great press releases and non-hyped campaigns. The kind of success we achieve by handling people like Bowie, Alanis Morisette and Tom Petty lets people know instantly that I can deal with superstars, emergencies — tireless, fearless work. We're also very conscious of fanzines, local markets and regional press. I don't want to be presumptuous to say that anything that I do a record company doesn't do, I just happen to think that we bring all the elements together under one roof in a very dynamic way.

We also come up with interesting PR ideas. We were handling Ronnie James Dio, someone who the press was just not keen to write about, and we publicized his tour with a disclaimer that said "This performance does not have any sampling, pre-recorded vocal or musical effects of any kind." That type of performance was a novelty at the time because so many artists were dodgily using pre-recorded tapes and samples, and not in the artistic way artists are using them these days. The whole idea was to make Ronnie James Dio more heroic to his fans. I got that printed in *USA Today*, *The Los Angeles Times* — outlets that do not want to write about Ronnie James Dio. I felt that was a real coup, more so than even securing a cover story for an artist because I really knew that I got inside the consciousness with a creative idea. On the humorous side, the Aerosmith *Pump* Tour — the stage set was an urban rooftop with a clothesline on it. I noticed that during the show people would throw their underwear on stage, so I suggested to the guys that they hang the underwear up on the clothesline. The quote from Steven Tyler was "We've had bras from Wyoming hung up in South Dakota." It was like a traveling shrine to their fans. I think for the sexuality that Aerosmith has in their songs — it was good fun, it was cheeky. And Steven's quote made *Newsweek*. Ozzy Osbourne — who is always attacked by the religious right — although I'm respectful of everybody — a lot of times they tend to have skeletons in their closet too. Remember when Oral Roberts said that he needed seven million dollars or he was going to die? After he collected the money, we had Ozzie send him a dollar bill with a telegram that said "Now that you've collected the seven million, here's a dollar bill for your psychiatric treatment fund." That's the kind of publicity this office is known for — creative ideas. Chris Isaak didn't officially hire us — but I came up with an idea for his last record because he was a nice guy. The record was called *Forever Blue* and he was playing the House of Blues so I suggested that the outside of the club be flooded with blue lights to turn it into a "blue light district." They did, and when he went to Tower Records after the show for an in-store performance, it was all blue light there too. The first paragraph of the *Los Angeles Times* review of the show said that Warner Bros. spared no expense for Chris Isaak. Chris wrote me a very nice note and was very appreciative. That's why you hire us — the blend of creative ideas from a tireless staff.

BHM: Do artists hire indie publicists because the label's in-house publicity department is overwhelmed, or do they do it to get specialized service?

MS: I think artists come to agencies like MSO because we are a "boutique." A record label can have seven releases a month — we don't. We have a lot of clients, but some of them put out an album every 2-3 years and the campaigns are different. We have the time to make sure an artist is taken care of on a year round basis, and many label publicists simply don't.

BHM: How do you get your clients?

MS: Every case is different. Epitaph Records hired us for Offspring, the Descendants and Rancid. Sometimes managers will hire us (much to the chagrin of the record company who feels that they can take care of it), but the manager and artist feel that they need more attention. I also think that if you're paying an indie firm, there is a feeling that you should be able to get these publicists on the phone at any time of the day, including weekends, therefore the artist feels they are a true priority. I think it helps that my front-line people have been with the agency for many years — MSO does not have to re-learn the artist — we know the quirks. Sometimes an artist will be unsure about a particular writer they're doing an interview with— we'll send them writing samples so that they can have an idea of what to expect from a particular interview). I don't look for "puff" pieces, they're not a good thing because the public really doesn't want to read that.

BHM: You mentioned the reaction of some record companies when artists hire you — is it ever difficult for you to get cooperation from the label once you have been brought aboard?

MS: Sometimes it is sticky because the in-house publicists felt that they were working the project and they might harbor some bitterness. But at the end of the day, I try to put out the aura that this decision has been made and the goal is for us to be team players and to create a scenario whereby the artist sells lots of albums and concert tickets and makes money for the record company so that everyone goes home happy.

BHM: One more question: How do you charge your clients.

MS: A flat monthly fee. Our rates do fluctuate depending on the client and the client's needs. It depends upon the amount of time consumption. There could be a superstar who is demanding more time than another band. We do come up with prices we believe reflect time consumption and intensity of a particular project. Sometimes the record company pays, sometimes the artist will pay out of their own pocket.

BHM: Thanks for your time, Mitch.

MS: It's my pleasure.

INTERVIEW: MUSIC PUBLSHING

Mike Stoller

Mike Stoller is one-half of the legendary songwriting team of Leiber & Stoller, the composers of such R&B and pop standards as "Stand By Me," "Hound Dog," "Kansas City," "Ruby Baby," "Is That All There Is?" and countless other classics. Artists ranging from Elvis Presley and the Beatles to PJ Harvey and Donald Fagen have covered their songs. In addition to their efforts as songwriters, Leiber & Stoller were trailblazing record producers (in both a creative and business sense) and music publishers. Leiber & Stoller were instrumental in the careers of such luminaries as Doc Pomus, Phil Spector, Barry Mann, Cynthia Weil, Morty Shuman and many others. As if that weren't enough, Leiber & Stoller are active writers to this day. In their spare time, they oversee the operation of Leiber & Stoller Music Publishing in Los Angeles, a publishing company that administers the majority of their own work as well as thousands of other classic songs. If you get a chance, check out "Smokey Joe's Café," the wildly popular Broadway show that showcases their songs.

BHM: How did you get started as a songwriter and how did you hook up with Jerry Leiber?

MS: Actually those two questions have the same answer. Although I always loved music and wanted to do something with music, or at least from the time I was a teenager I had really fallen in love with boogie-woogie and blues as a child. I first heard boogie-woogie played at an inter-racial summer camp I had attended when I lived in New York. I went to this summer camp for 8 or 9 summers starting when I was 7 years old. My first love in music was really boogie-woogie. Then I became interested in other forms of jazz, and I used to hang out on 52nd Street in the late 40's, the heyday of bebop. It was there that I saw people like Charlie Parker, Miles Davis, Dizzy Gillespie and Thelonious Monk.

BHM: Did you ever see Coltrane...?

MS: I saw Coltrane and McCoy Tyner, all those guys at Birdland — but that was later, when I moved back to New York in 1957. I'm talking about the real early days, when I was 13, 14, maybe 15 years old — I used to tuck a schoolbook under my arm and go in and say in my deepest voice, "I'll have a beer." I moved to Los Angeles in 1949 when I was 16 because my dad had a job opportunity there. I graduated from Belmont High School here in Los Angeles, and in 1950 I enrolled at Los Angeles City College where I majored in music. Around the same time I started to take some private lessons because I knew I wanted to do something in music and I had determined at that time that although I really wanted to be a jazz musician, I finally realized that I just wasn't going to be one — I wasn't good enough. At school I met a guy who was a pretty good piano player, his name I think was Bob Feldman, and one day he told me that he had a piano gig on the following Sunday that paid $3.00, but he got offered another job for $5.00, so he gave me the $3.00 gig. It was in East Los Angeles, a Sunday afternoon dance. I managed to get through it and I got my $3.00 playing piano with a pick-up band. During a break, I was noodling on the piano, and the drummer asked me what I was playing, and I sort of pretentiously answered, "Just something I'm working on." After the gig, he said, "Give me your name and phone number." I thought he would call me for some more gigs and I was looking forward to some $3.00 gigs. Three bucks was three bucks — this was 1950. Instead, it turns out he was a classmate of a guy named Jerry Leiber at Fairfax High School. Jerry was after him to write songs with him, but the drummer had to cancel sessions because he was working after school and so on so forth, so apparently one day when Jerry was accusing him of not being serious, he gave him my name and my phone number and that's when Jerry called me. I was not very eager — I was sure he wanted to write the kind of songs that I wouldn't really like. But Jerry came over to my house, and after he got in the door I took a look at his notebook and saw a line and the ditto marks and a rhyming line — I realized this was 12-bar blues. I said, "This isn't what I thought you meant, — these are blues and I *love* the blues." So we started writing some songs together.

BHM: How long was it before you had any success?

MS: The first song we had recorded was "Real Ugly Woman" sung by Jimmy Witherspoon at a live concert. The first chart record we had was called "Hard Times." It was recorded by Charles Brown on Aladdin Records and it made the Blues and Rhythm chart in *Cashbox Magazine* [a now-defunct music industry trade publication] in 1951. There were a lot of other records after that, but the most important ones were "Hound Dog" by Willie Mae "Big Mama" Thornton, and "Kansas City" by Little Willie Littlefield — both recorded in 1952. Seven years later Wilbert Harrison covered "Kansas City" and it became a big hit. And of course, "Hound Dog" was covered by Elvis in 1956.

BHM: Let's backtrack a little bit — how did you and Jerry go from two guys writing songs together to Leiber & Stoller, the big hit songwriting team?

MS: A fellow named Lester Sill took us under his wing and became our mentor. When we met Lester he was the National Sales Manager for Modern Records which was a Los Angeles based rhythm and blues record company. He set up an interview for us with one of the Bihari brothers who owned Modern Records. On that first occasion, we waited twenty minutes and Jules Bihari didn't show up. I was infuriated so we left their office, which was on Canon Drive in Beverly Hills and we walked up the street grumbling and we looked across the street, and near Little Santa Monica and Canon was another rhythm and blues record company, Aladdin Records, so we went over there. Maxwell Davis was there at the time — he was sort of the musical director, and we played him a couple of songs. He offered us a contract for a few of our songs then and there.

BHM: Let's talk about the contract — was this a co-publishing agreement or did you sign over 100% of the publishing?

MS: It didn't matter with that deal, as nothing came of it, but yes, it was standard procedure to sign over 100% of the publisher's share in those days.

BHM: I guess there weren't any music attorneys back then. Did those deals give the publisher the copyright forever?

MS: Not necessarily. Even then, there were different forms of contracts. When we started out, we usually signed a publishing contract with whoever owned the record company and some of those contracts were more formal than others. For instance, we signed a contract with Modern Records and we discovered years later that we were the publishers and they were the record company! We didn't know that! In most cases you signed a contract that granted the rights to the song, worldwide rights, for the full term of copyright plus renewals. At that time, the term of US copyright was 28 years with a 28-year renewal. Outside the United States deals ran for the full term of copyright, whatever that was and we didn't really know what that was — we weren't really involved in that because it never occurred to us that anybody would be buying a record outside the United States or Canada! There were other contracts, which we found out much later were the Songwriter Guild of America (formerly known as "SPA") contracts. There were two forms of those: the 1939 Form which only was for the first term of copyright — it didn't mention renewals, and the better one, which was for the first term of US copyright throughout the world which gave you your foreign rights back when you got your US rights back. When "Hound Dog" was recorded in 1952, our mothers had to sign with us, since we were only 19. In those days, the publisher and the record company were frequently owned by the same people. The smaller record companies always insisted that you give them the publishing. Beyond that, companies like Federal Records and King Records would stipulate in their contracts that the mechanical royalty rate for your songs released on one of their labels was a 1/4 of a cent instead of 2 cents, which was the statutory mechanical rate at that time.

BHM: How nice! It's almost the opposite now — if the record company's publishing company publishes your song, you usually get an above-average mechanical rate.

MS: Well I don't know about that from personal experience. The standard contracts called for the writers to get 50% of mechanical income and other non-performance income (there wasn't too much money to be made outside of mechanicals and performances at that time). In days earlier, writers like the Gershwin's had signed contracts that gave them only a 33 1/3% share of mechanical income.

BHM: So if you got a 50% royalty on mechanicals, you were actually doing all right.

MS: Well, we were signing the contract that was typical for that day and age, and in most cases it granted both 28 year copyright terms, but in some cases it didn't (fortunately for us) grant the renewal rights.

BHM: Were there any deals in particular that left you feeling ripped off?

MS: We got wise pretty quickly after one incident. A guy named Don Robey (who owned Peacock Records) came in from Texas and gave us a check for $1,200 in exchange for the publishing on "Hound Dog." After we signed the contracts, Robey went back to Texas and stopped payment on the check. We weren't represented by anyone who knew what to do. Most people had no clue as to how the music business was run. The attitude was "take what you can get." In 1954, together with Lester Sill, we started our own record company, Spark Records, and a publishing company. We had a little office on Crenshaw between Wilshire and Pico, and we signed a few acts. The Robins (who evolved into the Coasters) were the main one, a duet called Willy and Ruth, a sax player named Gil Bernal — who I had gone to LA City College with. The most successful record was with The Robins, "Riot In Cell Block #9," "Loop de Loop Mambo," and a couple of other ones. Our last release on Spark was "Smokey Joe's Cafe."

BHM: Did you write, produce, and arrange these tracks?

MS: Yes. Jerry would conduct the session from the booth, and I would conduct it from the floor — I'd play piano and write the charts out, the road maps for the drummers and bass players and guitarists. We rehearsed for weeks before we went into the studio. Pretty soon Nesuhi Ertegun heard our records and sent them back to his brother Ahmet and Jerry Wexler at Atlantic Records and they were impressed enough to come out to LA to meet us. They said, "Make records for us, we'll even pay you a royalty just for making them." According to them, this was the first independent record production deal. That sounded good to us, because we were having trouble selling records east of the Rockies. About a year later we were making records for Atlantic in New York. In the course of moving, we felt our relationship with Lester was going to be difficult because we were three thousand miles away which in those days was the other side of the world. So Lester sold his half of our music publishing company (Quintet Music) to Hill and Range which was owned by the Aberbachs whose main office was in New York.

BHM: They were a big publishing company then?

MS: Yeah, they were very big in country music but they also published some blues and lots of pop stuff. They had deals with Eddie Arnold and Colonel Tom Parker, and that's how they ended up with Elvis. So they made a contract with us for a two or three-year period, and they gave us an advance to be exclusive to Quintet. During that time they broke the exclusivity if doing so worked in their favor. For instance, if we wrote a song for Elvis Presley they would put it into Elvis Presley Music in which we didn't share as publishers. At the same time, we were also producing our own songs on records at Atlantic. We made a copublishing deal at Atlantic when we made our production deal with them. So we now owned 50% of Quintet Music (the publishing company Leiber & Stoller launched at the same time as Spark Records) and Hill and Range owned the other 50%. Quintet Music owned half of Tiger Music which owned the songs we did at Atlantic, and the other half of Tiger Music was owned by Progressive Music (Atlantic's publishing company). So Jerry and I owned 25% or the songs we wrote and produced at Atlantic, the Coasters songs and so on. Years later, through one deal or another, we re-acquired most of the rights in our own songs. In some cases, such as "Kansas City" we bought half of the copyright back. Whenever we could re-acquire one of our copyrights, we did.

BHM: That shows rare foresight — did you realize how much those copyrights would be worth in the future, what with TV, movies and commercials?

MS: It wasn't really foresight. Foresight would have meant insisting on signing only Songwriter's Guild-type contracts back in the 50's — these contracts automatically would have returned the rights to all of our songs after the first 28 year term of copyright. But back then we felt that we were part of the publishing team, so we didn't think it really mattered. After all, we're publishers as well as songwriters. It would have made life much easier if we had signed Guild contracts. We wouldn't have had to swap so many values in order to get our stuff back. We would have just gotten them back. So then, it was obviously a mistake, a lack of knowledge, and a lack of good direction.

BHM: But like you said, back then there weren't any attorneys advising you…

MS: To tell you the truth, we didn't really think that the songs would be worth much after six months, and owning some of the publishing would just earn us a little bit extra during those six months or so.

BHM: It turns out that 30 and 40 years later, a lot of your songs still get played endlessly on radio and television every day, not to mention movies, commercials and Broadway shows.

MS: We had no idea that would happen. As far as we were concerned, all the standards were written, and these were just disposable records that would last a short period of time and then be forgotten. So we just didn't think about things like copyright reversion.

BHM: By the early '60s you had a pretty good handle on the business side of publishing. From that point on, did you own all of your own songs?

MS: In the early '60s, what happened is that when our contract was up with Quintet Music, we started our own company, Trio Music. We still had a deal with Atlantic, but, we were splitting the copyrights 50/50 with their company and Trio. We were able to publish other people's songs at that point primarily because we could get people to record them and put out the records. In addition to Atlantic, we started to produce for United Artists and other labels, and shortly thereafter we started another record company called Redbird, and a subsidiary label called Blue Cat.

BHM: You were doing records with people like Doc Pomus?

MS: We produced a lot of Pomus and Shuman songs — mostly with the Drifters. When a Drifters session was coming up, we'd put out a call to Doc and Morty, Barry Mann and Cynthia Weil, Carole Kind and Jerry Goffin, and Burt Bacharach and Hal David. These teams were writing the kind of stuff we wanted for the Drifters. We wrote some, and we co-wrote some, but as producers we always went for the best song no matter who wrote it or published it.

BHM: Being a good songwriter had a lot to do with picking good songs from other writers. You had a nice string of hits on Redbird, right?

MS: Redbird was somewhat different because we were, for the most part, supervising and producing, but we were also simultaneously training and bringing along young writer-producers like Jeff Barry and Ellie Greenwich, Shadow Morton, Van McCoy, a few other people.

BHM: So it was like songwriter school?

MS: It was like writer-producer school. The artists were The Dixie Cups, The Shangri-Las and the Ad-Libs. We were very successful very quickly on the strength of these singles. We had seven top-ten singles in our first nine months of business. We developed some very talented writers and producers. After two years we gave up the record company, partially out of boredom and partially because it was no longer about the kind of songs we wrote and we found ourselves writing less. The label was featuring the kind of songs that were being written by these young people that we were bringing along. The girl groups were much more pop and less R&B. So we extracted ourselves from the record company and eventually we went into partnership with Freddy Bienstock who had formerly worked for his cousins, the Aberbachs. We took him in, and gave him a desk and a phone. Then, we started to talk about doing things together, and Jerry suggested "Why don't we buy catalogues?" We acquired King, which was Lois Music and all those companies that had been affiliated with King Records. After that we acquired other companies like Commonwealth United and the New York Times publishing company which had acquired Metro Media which in turn had purchased a wonderful catalogue from Tommy Valando, including many Broadway show scores. The New York Times didn't know what to do with the catalogue. They made wrong choices, they spent a lot of money that they didn't have to spend, and therefore were losing money on a catalogue that you couldn't possibly lose money on.

BHM: Again, that shows incredible foresight. These days, catalogue deals and copublishing deals with songwriters and artists can be enormous.

MS: Well, hindsight is 20-20. We just didn't foresee any of this at the time. When we were coming up, the goal for most writers was to get a standard publishing deal. Then the publisher would go out and get the song recorded, and hopefully the record would sell and that was great. As time went by, movies became a great source of income for these old songs. This is how Lester Sill's son Joel became very important in the music industry because he was one of the first to really establish the film score comprised of classic pop records because of the potency of popular music and the instant recognition of the time in which the movie is set. So, that part of the industry became an industry in and of itself. Today, publishers and record companies will try to place brand new pop records into films in the hopes of making the record a hit. Commercials also became a great source of publishing income, because the advertising companies realized how potent these songs were. We've been very fortunate — Citibank used "Stand By Me" for five years and the song is now selling automobiles. So these were usages that were not even conceived of, and we also didn't realize that these usages could yield a substantial royalties. On the other hand, our production contracts didn't call for remuneration for anything but the sale of records.

BHM: So you don't get your share of royalties when the tracks you produced get used in movies and commercials?

MS: Some companies have paid even though the contracts are silent on the subject. They feel that it's appropriate. Other companies say "It doesn't say so in the contract so we're not going to give you a dime." As a record producer, it hurts to watch a movie and hear records you produced emanating from the screen and not see your name on the end credits.

BHM: Does your company continue to acquire copyrights?

MS: Yes, but there is less opportunity today.

BHM: That's really true — there is intense bidding for valuable copyrights. The deals are expensive and highly competitive. It's hard to believe that you guys were picking up these catalogs for what in retrospect is a ridiculously low price. Did you guys manage to repurchase all of your own copyrights?

MS: We own most of our songs. In some cases we copublish them. We don't always own 100% throughout out the world. We just did our best to re-acquire whatever we could.

BHM: Do you have any advice for today's artists and songwriters?

MS: If you are a performer, obviously you want to get a record contract, you want to hold on to your publishing and your masters if you can, but you don't want to let it stop you from getting a foot in the door. You have to give up something to get something. You can't always start out owning everything.

BHM: So giving up some of your publishing isn't necessarily the worst thing you can do?

MS: Not at all. As long as you are getting somewhere. Having a hit is very important — it opens up all kinds of doors.

BHM: Is your publishing company signing any new writers now?

MS: Yes. We recently signed some writers who are doing very well. I wouldn't say that we are making a major effort to sign up lots of new talent, but when we feel someone is exceptional, of course we make an effort to sign them. We used to sign writers back in the '60s when we had record companies, so we were able to offer action. We were able to make records of their own songs, or had them make records of their own songs — we had something to offer them. Today, publishing is often more of a banking affair.

BHM: I take it then that Leiber & Stoller Music Publishing is primarily a vehicle for administering the rights to your catalog. You must get thousands of synch requests and mechanical license requests. Do you use Harry Fox to issue and collect the income for your mechanical licenses?

MS: We do get quite a few requests on a daily basis. We use Harry Fox for mechanical licenses but our synch and commercial licenses are handled in-house. Of course, we have many foreign representatives as well — there is constant action going on.

BHM: Do you use different subpublishers outside of North America or do you have one company that does the administration for you?

MS: We use different companies in different territories. We have separate deals for each territory even if we use the same parent company.

BHM: How do you decide who the best subpublisher is for you in a given territory?

MS: We look at how aggressive they are in collecting and exploiting, what the advances are, what kind of relationship we have with the publisher. All of these things are thrown into a hopper and are discussed with our people and decisions are made accordingly.

BHM: How many people do you have working in your office?

MS: Twelve, or thirteen, top-notch people assembled and under supervision of Randy Poe, the President of our company.

BHM: How many copyrights do you have in the catalogue?

MS: Probably close to 30,000.

BHM: What's your biggest title?

MS: Probably "Jailhouse Rock," or "Stand By Me," maybe "Kansas City," if you mean songs that we wrote.

BHM: Thanks for your time, Mike.

APPENDIX B

Sample Agreements

A WARNING FROM THE AUTHOR AND THE EDITOR

The materials embodied in this book and the sample agreements included in Appendix B are meant to be illustrative and educational, not exhaustive and authoritative. These agreements are NOT the author's "form" agreements — they are merely random samplings of certain types of agreements that one might encounter from time to time. Always remember that no two deals are the same and that these samples should not be used as anything more than educational tools. If you find yourself in a situation where you need to draft or negotiate a contract, do yourself a favor and hire an attorney. In light of the foregoing, the author, editor and publisher are not responsible for anything bad that happens to you based on your use of the materials in this book. What the hell do you expect for thirty bucks?

Also, all the names printed in these samples (including Lawn Chocolate, the law firm of Dewey, Cheatum & Howe, Thrifty Scot Records and any others) are completely fictitious and are not based on any real people or companies.

SAMPLE PERSONAL MANAGEMENT AGREEMENT

AGREEMENT made and entered into as of January 1, 1998 by and between THRIFTY SCOT MAN-AGEMENT, INC., 1234 Main Street, New York, New York 10000 (referred to hereinafter as "Manager") and Fred Johnson and John Doe, professionally known as "Lawn Chocolate" c/o Art Cheatum, Esq., Dewey, Cheatum & Howe, 11111 San Viejo Boulevard, Los Angeles, California 90000 (individually and collectively referred to hereinafter as "Artist").

WHEREAS, Artist desires to engage Manager to represent Artist and to render services to Artist as Artist's sole and exclusive personal manager, representative and advisor throughout the world, in all of Artist's affairs in the Entertainment Industry; and

WHEREAS, Manager desires to act in such capacity and to accept such engagement;

NOW, THEREFORE, in consideration of the premises and mutual promises contained herein, and for other good and valuable consideration, the parties hereto agree as follows:

1. **Services.** (a) Artist hereby engages Manager to be the sole and exclusive personal manager, representative and advisor throughout the world, of Artist (and any company or corporation formed, owned or controlled, directly or indirectly, by Artist) in all facets of Artist's careers in the Entertainment Industry[1]. Artist shall immediately advise Manager of all offers of Employment and of all inquiries concerning Artist's careers.

(b) Manager hereby accepts such engagement and agrees to advise and counsel Artist regarding Artist's careers in the Entertainment Industry and to use its reasonable efforts to promote, develop and advance Artist's careers. Manager's services hereunder are not exclusive to Artist and Manager shall be permitted to perform the same or similar services for other artists or persons during the Term. Manager shall also be permitted to devote such time and efforts to other business activities as Manager may deem necessary or desirable in Manager's sole discretion.

(c) Artist hereby acknowledges that Manager is not licensed under the Labor Code of the State of California as a talent agent or employment agent or otherwise under the Business and Professions Code of the State of California or as a theatrical employment agency or other employment or booking agency under the General Business Law of the State of New York or as any of the foregoing under the laws of any State; that Manager has not offered or attempted or promised to obtain, seek, or procure employment or engagements for Artist; and that Manager is not authorized, licensed or expected to do so. Therefore, Artist shall not look to Manager to procure or provide engagements or employment; provided, however, that Manager shall select, negotiate with and otherwise represent Artist to such agencies and other third parties that seek and procure employment and engagements for artists.[2]

---

[1] This seems a bit broad, inasmuch as you will likely employ other people (attorneys, accountants, psychics, etc.) who may also be advisors. Also, if you want another manager to deal with any non-music careers you may want to pursue, you will have to narrow the scope of this language.

[2] This language is in here because under California law, managers are not supposed to "procure employment" for their clients. Of course, managers do this all the time, usually by booking the odd gig. In these situations, artists may have the right to force managers to disgorge (that is, refund) their commissions. In any event, I'm not really sure that simply putting this language in a management contract really prevents disgorgement from occurring. The best way for a manager to avoid this potential pitfall is to get licensed as a booking agent, and some managers do just that.

2. **Term**. (a) The initial term ("Initial Term") of this agreement shall be for a period of two (2) years from the date first above written. Manager shall have the right to extend the Initial Term for three (3) consecutive one (1) year option periods ("the Option Periods").[3] The first Option Period shall commence immediately upon conclusion of the Initial Term and each successive Option Period shall commence immediately upon conclusion of the preceding Option Period unless Manager gives Artist written notice of its intention not to exercise such option prior to the expiration of the Initial Term or the then-current Option Period. The Initial Term and the Option Periods are collectively referred to hereinafter as the "Term".

3. **Compensation.** (a) In consideration of Manager's services hereunder, Artist hereby irrevocably assigns to Manager and shall pay Manager or cause Manager to be paid, as and when received by Artist or applied on Artist's behalf, a sum ("Commission") equal to fifteen percent (15%) of any and all Gross Compensation.

(b) For the purposes of this Agreement, "Gross Compensation" shall include, without limitation, all forms of income, consideration and compensation relating to Artist's endeavors in the Entertainment Industry, including, salaries, advances, earnings, fees, royalties, partnership interests, shares of stock, bonuses, shares of profits, shares of receipts, music publishing income, recording funds, tour support received from record companies, gifts, income in kind, and other considerations of any kind or nature whatsoever earned or received directly or indirectly by Artist, individually or as a member of a group or by any party or entity on Artist's behalf or by any party or entity which has furnished Artist's services in the Entertainment Industry, regardless of by whom procured. Notwithstanding the foregoing, Gross Compensation shall not include the following:

(i) any actual bona fide recording costs (not including personal advances or wages paid to Artist) paid to Artist or on Artist's behalf pursuant to an agreement for Artist's recording services, up to a maximum of One Hundred Thousand Dollars ($100,000.00) per album;[4]

(ii) all monies paid to Artist as reimbursement for so-called "sound and light" expenses, incurred by Artist in connection with live concert appearances; and

(iii) all monies received by Artist as so-called "tour support" to the extent such monies are recoupable and specifically designated as deficit financing and not used by Artist as a personal advance or for any other purpose.[5]

(c) Manager's Commission shall be payable upon all Gross Compensation as and when such Gross Compensation is paid to Artist or to any third party on Artist's behalf, during the Term or after the Term, as a result of and/or pursuant to:

---

[3] As I mentioned in Chapter One, you may want to insist that some kind of performance plateau be achieved before your manager can exercise an option for additional contract periods.

[4] The artist should seek to have the $100,000 limit removed. Otherwise, the manager is entitled to commission recording costs in excess of such figure, which really isn't fair considering that the artist doesn't get to put this money in his pocket.

[5] The artist should add that monies expended in the production of music videos are not deemed Gross Compensation.

(i)   any and all engagements, contracts, commitments and agreements now in existence or entered into or negotiated during the Term;[6]

(ii)   any and all engagements, contracts, commitments and agreements negotiated and entered into after the expiration of the Term to the extent such contracts, commitments and agreements pertain to master recordings and/or musical compositions recorded and/or written and composed, in whole or in part, by Artist during the Term;

(iii)   any and all extensions, renewals, substitutions, replacements, amendments, additions and modifications of all such contracts, engagements, commitments and agreements referred to in (i) and (ii) above; and

(iv)   any and all judgments, awards, settlements, payments, damages and proceeds relating to any suits, claims, actions or proceedings arising out of alleged breach, non-performance or infringement by others of any of the contracts, engagements, etc. referred to in (i), (ii), and (iii), above.

(d) No expense, cost or disbursement incurred in connection with receipt of Gross Compensation, including, without limitation, salaries, professional fees and booking agency fees[7] shall be deducted therefrom prior to calculation of Commission. In addition to the foregoing, Artist shall reimburse Manager for any and all reasonable bona fide expenditures incurred by Manager on Artist's behalf or in connection with Artist's career or in the performance of Manager's services hereunder within thirty (30) days of such expenses being incurred.[8] It is agreed and understood that Artist will be responsible for all booking agency fees and commissions, union dues, publicity and promotion costs, legal fees and accounting fees and any and all taxes due with respect to Gross Compensation. In the event Manager advances any of the foregoing fees, costs or expenses on Artist's behalf, Artist shall reimburse Manager for such advances within thirty (30) days of Manager's payment and/or in the event Manager does not take or withhold its Commission from Gross Compensation for any reason, such amounts shall be deemed a loan from Manager to Artist. Artist hereby authorizes and empowers Manager to deduct the amount of any such loans and advances from any sums received by Manager for Artist's account.

(e) Any and all agreements between Artist and any corporation, partnership, trust and/or other business entity which furnishes Artist's services or which is owned (in whole or in part) or controlled (directly or indirectly) by Artist or Artist's family shall provide that such entity shall only furnish Artist's services subject to the terms and conditions of this Agreement. Any such entity shall become a party to this Agreement.

4.   (a) Artist shall notify and irrevocably direct and cause any and all third parties for whom Artist renders services in connection with the entertainment industry to pay directly to Manager the Commission due to Manager hereunder, and such Commission shall be payable to Manager immediately upon payment or credit to Artist or to any person on Artist's behalf of the Gross

---

[6] This is too broad, as it allows the manager to commission monies and royalties payable pursuant to all contracts entered into during the term, even if the royalties are generated by songs and recordings created and released after the end of the term. If the manager's commission cannot be limited to records/songs created and released during the manager's tenure, there should at least be some kind of "sunset clause," as I noted in Chapter One.

[7] Try to get agency commissions taken "off the top" prior to calculation of the manager's commission.

[8] There should be a provision here requiring the manager to send artist detailed monthly statements of expenses. There should also be some limits on the manager's unfettered right to incur expenses on artist's behalf.

Compensation upon which such Commission is based. The aforesaid direction to any such third party shall be included in any and all agreements of every kind and nature in respect of Artist's activities in and throughout the Entertainment Industry, including, without limitation, recording agreements, publishing agreements and agency agreements and shall be substantially as follows:

"Artist hereby irrevocably authorizes and directs you to pay to THRIFTY SCOT MANAGEMENT, INC. or its assignee, a sum equal to fifteen percent (15%) of all sums due to, or paid on behalf of, the undersigned hereunder. Such payment shall be made at the same time that payments are due to the undersigned hereunder. Each payment shall be accompanied by a duplicate of the statement rendered to the undersigned."[9]

(b) In the event Artist receives Gross Compensation with respect to which Manager's Commission has not been paid pursuant to paragraph 4(a), above, Artist shall, within fifteen (15) days after the close of each monthly period during the Term of this Agreement and thereafter so long as Artist collects or receives such Gross Compensation hereunder, render a written accounting statement to Manager setting forth all Gross Compensation received by Artist hereunder during the preceding month, specifying the source thereof and Manager's Commission hereunder and including the amount of any expenses and any loans or advances paid by Manager to Artist or on Artist's behalf. Each such accounting statement shall be accompanied by payment to Manager of the sum thereon shown to be due to Manager for such accounting period.

(c) Artist agrees that manager and Manager's representatives may inspect and audit Artist's books and records to ascertain the amounts due Manager hereunder. The aforementioned audits and/or inspections, if any, shall be conducted upon reasonable notice to Artist. "Books and records" as used hereunder shall include ledgers, journals, receipt books, checks and all other records concerning financial matters.[10]

5. No breach of this Agreement on the part of Manager shall be deemed material, unless Artist shall have given written notice specifying the nature of such breach to Manager and Manager shall have failed to cure such breach within thirty (30) days after receipt of such notice if such breach is capable of being cured within such thirty (30) day period and if Manager proceeds with reasonable diligence to complete the curing of such breach. [11]

6. Artist hereby irrevocably authorizes and appoints Manager as Artist's true and lawful agent and attorney-in-fact to execute for Artist in Artist's name and on Artist's behalf, any and all agreements, documents, and contracts for Artist's services. Artist hereby ratifies and affirms all acts performed by Manager pursuant to this power of attorney and confirms that this power is coupled with an interest. [12]

---

[9] Paragraph 4 (a) should be replaced by a paragraph that states that artist's gross compensation shall be paid to artist's business manager, who will then pay the appropriate commissions to the manager.

[10] The artist should have a similar right to audit the books of manager insofar as the same are relevant to the artist's business.

[11] The manager should have a similar obligation to give artist notice and allow artist to cure any alleged breach of the agreement.

[12] This gives the manager way too much power to act on the artist's behalf. The manager should have the right to confirm the booking of one or two night engagements, and that's about it. See Chapter One for a complete discussion of the manager's power of attorney

7. (a) Manager shall not assign this Agreement or any rights or obligations hereunder without Artist's consent, except that Artist's Manager may assign this Agreement without Artist's consent to any parent, subsidiary or other related or affiliated company or to any other person, firm or corporation acquiring a significant portion of Manager's stock or assets or entering into a merger or joint venture with Manager.

(b) Notwithstanding anything to the contrary contained herein, in the event that neither Angus McTavich nor Colin McGee is an officer, employee, partner or active consultant of Manager or its assignee and that neither Angus McTavich nor Colin McGee is personally responsible for the supervision of Artist's career on behalf of Manager or its assignee, Artist shall have the right to terminate this Agreement by sending Manager written notice within thirty (30) days of the date on which both Angus McTavich and Colin McGee cease to be so involved with Manager or its assignee; provided, however, that if at the time of Manager's receipt of such written notice, Angus McTavich and/or Colin McGee become involved in such capacities with the operations of Manager or its assignee, Artist's notice of termination shall be deemed canceled and shall be of no force and effect.[13]

(c) Artist may not assign this Agreement or any of Artist's rights hereunder and any such attempted assignment shall be void. This Agreement shall be binding upon Artist and Manager and shall inure to the benefit of Artist's and Manager's successors. This Agreement shall also be binding upon any entity (including, without limitation, any loanout company that furnishes Artist's services) which directly or indirectly, in whole or in part, through one or more intermediaries, owns or controls, or is under common ownership or control with, Artist. Accordingly, Artist hereby accepts this Agreement on Artist's behalf and on behalf of any such entity.

8. Artist hereby jointly and severally warrants and represents that:

(a) Artist is free to enter into and to perform under this Agreement and is not a party to any presently existing contract that would interfere with the full performance of the terms and conditions of this Agreement.

(b) Artist is over twenty-one (21) years of age and has retained thoroughly experienced and knowledgeable attorneys in the entertainment industry to advise and counsel Artist with regard to this Agreement.

(c) Artist will at all times during the Term devote himself to his career in the entertainment industry and do all things necessary to promote such career.

9. Artist agrees that during the Term Artist will not assign, sell, convey, pledge or otherwise dispose of any property rights in Artist, his trade or personal name, by stock interest, wage assignments, partnerships or percentage or otherwise, without the prior written consent of Manager.

10. As used herein, the term "Artist" shall be deemed to refer to the entertainment unit presently known as "Lawn Chocolate" (the "Group"), as well as to each individual member of the Group who is a signatory hereto. In the event any such member should leave the Group or pursue a solo career while remaining a member of the Group, this Agreement shall continue to be binding with respect to such member during the Term hereof. In the event Artist wishes to add a new or additional member to the Group, Artist shall cause such member to accept the terms and conditions of this Agreement and such member shall be deemed a signatory hereto. This Agreement shall be binding jointly and

---

[13] Whenever "manager" is actually a company or other legal entity (e.g., Thrifty Scot Management), the artist should demand a "key man" clause such as this. Otherwise, the artist may be bound to the management company after the original managers have departed.

severally upon said persons and the Group.[14] Wherever required, the singular shall include the plural and, unless the context otherwise requires, the masculine gender includes the feminine and the neuter.

11. All notices hereunder shall be in writing and shall be given by mail in the United States mail, postage pre-paid or by telegraph with all charges pre-paid at the addresses first indicated above, or such other address as either Artist or Manager may designate by notice to the other and date of such mailing or telegraphing shall be the time of the giving of notice. A copy of all notices to Manager shall concurrently be addressed to: Haring, Smith & Clampett, 321 North Century Way, Beverly Hills, California 90000, Attention: Jed Clampett, Esq.

12.   (a) This Agreement sets forth the entire understanding between the parties with respect to the subject matter thereof, and no modification, amendment, waiver, termination or discharge of this Agreement or any provisions thereof shall be binding upon either party unless confirmed by a written instrument signed by Manager and Artist. No waiver of any provision of, or default under this Agreement shall affect either party's rights thereafter to enforce such provision or to exercise any right or remedy in the event of any other default whether or not similar.

        (b) This Agreement and all of its provisions shall be interpreted and construed everywhere in accordance with the Laws of the State of California applicable to contracts executed and to be performed therein.

        (c) If any part of this Agreement shall be determined to be invalid or unenforceable by a court of competent jurisdiction or by any other legally constituted body having jurisdiction to make such determination, the remainder of this Agreement shall remain in full force and effect.

13. Manager shall have the right from and after execution hereof to obtain insurance on Artist's life, at Manager's sole cost and expense, with Manager being the sole beneficiary thereof. Artist agrees to fully cooperate with Manager in connection with the obtaining of such a policy, including, without limitation, Artist's submission to a physical examination and the completion of any and all documents necessary or desirable in respect thereof. Neither Artist nor his estate shall have any right to claim the benefit of any such policy obtained by Manager.[15]

        IN WITNESS WHEREOF, the parties hereto have entered into this Agreement as of the 1st day of January, 1998.

                        THRIFTY SCOT MANAGEMENT, INC.

                        By:_____

_____

John Doe

_____

Fred Smith
individually and collectively p/k/a "Lawn Chocolate"

---

[14] This "leaving member clause" protects the manager's investment in the artist should a member leave the band and go solo. For instance, if Fred leaves the band to go solo, this agreement goes with him and Thrifty Scot is legally entitled to manage Fred as a solo artist.

[15] Some feel that life insurance clauses are distasteful, but managers feel they are legitimate and warranted in light of the investment they make in an artist's career. If your manager insists on such a clause, make the manager pay for your exam, and make sure that the results remain confidential.

SAMPLE EXCLUSIVE RECORDING AGREEMENT

Thrifty Scot Records, Inc.
1234 Main Street
Anytown, CA 90000

Dated: January 1, 1999

John Doe and Fred Smith, collectively pka
"Lawn Chocolate"
c/o Art Cheatum, Esq.
Dewey, Cheatum & Howe
11111 San Viejo Boulevard
Los Angeles, California 90000

Dear John and Fred:

The following constitutes our agreement ("Contract"):

1. **Services.** During the term of this Contract ("Term") you shall, in accordance with the terms hereof, furnish to us your (hereinafter you shall be referred to as "you" or "Artist") exclusive services[1] throughout the world ("Territory") and the services of one or more producers[2] for the purpose of recording and delivering to us Masters. You accept such engagement and agree to perform this Contract to the best of your ability. Further, upon our reasonable notice to you, you shall render your services at such times and places as we may reasonably designate for the purpose of assisting us in the marketing, advertising and promotion of Phonograph Records hereunder.[3]

2. **Term.** The Term shall consist of an Initial Period which shall commence as of the date hereof and continue until the later of (i) twelve (12) months after the date of the commencement of the Initial Period and (ii) the date twelve (12) months after your delivery[4] to us of the LP to be delivered during the Initial Period in satisfaction of your Recording Commitment. You hereby grant to us seven (7) options.[5] Each such option shall be a separate, consecutive and irrevocable option to renew the Term of the Contract on the terms and conditions hereof. Each Option Period shall commence consecutively upon the expiration of the immediately preceding Contract Period and shall expire the later of (i) twelve (12) months after the date of the commencement of that Option Period and (ii) the date twelve (12) months after your delivery to us of the LP to be delivered during such Option Period in satisfaction of your Recording Commitment. Each option shall be automatically exercised,[6] unless we notify you by written notice at any time prior to the date of expiration of the

---

[1] This means you can't make records or sound recordings embodying your featured performances for anyone else during the term of the contract unless the label waives its exclusivity.

[2] This means that you are responsible for hiring and paying any and all producers, mixers, etc.

[3] This means you have to show up to do press, videos, appearances, etc. more or less when you are asked to.

[4] Twelve months is a bit long - try for eight or nine.

[5] This means that the record company can require you to deliver as many as eight records total, which is probably one or two records too many. The lower the number of options, the better off you are. Also remember that these options belong to the record company, not the artist.

[6] The "automatic option exercise" language is in here to protect the record company from their inadvertent failure to exercise the option.

then-current Contract Period that we do not wish to exercise such option in which event the Term shall expire at the expiration of such Contract Period.

3. Recording Commitment.

(a)   During each Contract Period you shall record and deliver (as that term is defined in Exhibit "A" attached hereto) to us a sufficient number of Masters to constitute one (1) LP.[7] The first album to be delivered in satisfaction of the Recording Commitment for the Initial Period is herein referred to as the "First Album," and the successive albums to be delivered in satisfaction of the Recording Commitment after the delivery of the First Album are herein referred to as the Second Album, the Third Album, etc.

(b)   You shall dleiver the Ffirst Album to us within four (4) months[8] after the execution hereof. Each subsequent album to be delivered in satisfaction of your Recording Commitment shall be delivered no sooner than eight (8) months and no later than eighteen (18) months after delivery of the immediately preceding album delivered hereunder. Time is of the essence in your delivery to us of Masters.[9]

4. Recording Procedures.

(a)   You and we shall mutually designate the producer of each of the Masters, the Musical Compositions or other selections that shall be embodied in the Masters, and the studios at which those Masters shall be recorded ("the Recording Elements"). Prior to the recording of Masters, you shall submit to us for approval a written proposal for the recording of such masters, specifying the Recording Elements, the recording budget of the master(s) in question and any other information reasonably required by us. You shall not commence the recording of Masters unless and until we have approved such proposal in writing.[10]

(b)   We shall pay the Recording Costs for Masters hereunder on your behalf. All Recording Costs shall be deducted from the Recording Fund for the applicable Album, and shall be recoupable from royalties[11] otherwise payable to you hereunder. In the event that we, in our sole discretion, shall pay any Recording Costs for any Masters hereunder in excess of the Recording Fund in respect thereof, you shall repay any such excess upon demand and, without limiting our other rights and remedies, we may deduct same from any monies[12] payable by us hereunder.

---

[7] We discussed the advantages of multiple "firm" records in Chapter Four. Note that this deal provides for only one "firm" record.

[8] You can usually get this increased to six or seven months.

[9] This is a loaded phrase in the legal world. It means that if you turn in your masters even one day late, you have committed a material (i.e. fatal) breach of the agreement. Ask for a notice and cure provision with respect to late delivery of masters whereby the record company must notify you that your record is overdue. Thereafter, you have a prenegotiated amount of time (usually fifteen to thirty days) to get the record done.

[10] This means that the record company essentially has the right to veto your ideas for producer, song selection, etc. This is pretty much standard language. If you have the clout, the record company will give you complete "creative control," which would allow you to designate the Recording Elements without any input or interference from the record company.

[11] You should specify that mechanical royalties shall not be used to recoup recording costs under normal circumstances.

[12] Note that "monies" includes record royalties, mechanical royalties and future advances.

(c)   You shall deliver the Masters to us promptly after their completion. All original session tapes and any derivatives or reproductions thereof shall be delivered to us concurrently, or, at our election, maintained at a recording studio or other location designated by us, in our name and subject to our control. Each Master shall be subject to our approval as commercially[13] and technically satisfactory for the manufacture and sale of Phonograph Records, and, upon our request, you shall rerecord any Musical Composition or other Selection until a Master commercially and technically satisfactory to us shall have been obtained. If we shall make any payments with respect to any Master which shall not have been recorded or delivered in all respects in accordance with the terms hereof, you shall, upon our demand, pay to us the amount thereof and we may, without limiting our other rights and remedies, deduct that amount from any monies payable by us hereunder.[14]

(d)   Each Master shall embody the Artist's performance as the sole featured artist of a single Musical Composition previously unrecorded by the Artist and shall be recorded in its entirety in a recording studio.[15] Each LP shall embody no less than ten (10) Musical Compositions. No Multiple LPs or Masters recorded in whole or in part at live concerts or other live performances shall be recorded or delivered hereunder in satisfaction of your Recording Commitment without our prior written consent.

5.   **Rights.**

(a)   The Masters, from the inception of the recording thereof, and all Phonograph Records and other reproductions made therefrom, together with the performances embodied therein and all copyrights and other rights therein and thereto excluding only the copyrights in the underlying Musical Compositions (individually and collectively, "Works"), and all renewals and extensions thereof, shall for purposes of copyright law, be deemed works made for hire for us by the Artist, and all other persons rendering services in connection with the Masters as our employees for hire and/or contributions to a collective work, and shall be entirely our property throughout the Territory, free of any claims whatsoever by you or any other person, firm, or corporation. Without limiting the foregoing, we and any person, firm, or corporation designated by us shall have the exclusive, perpetual, right throughout the Territory to manufacture, sell, distribute and advertise Phonograph Records and other reproductions embodying the Masters under any trademarks, trade names or labels, and to lease, license, convey and otherwise exploit and use the Masters by any method (whether now known or unknown) and in any media (whether now known or unknown) and to perform publicly Phonograph Records and other reproductions embodying the Masters, all upon such terms as we may approve, or we may refrain from doing any or all of the foregoing. You hereby irrevocably appoint us your attorney in fact solely for the purpose of executing transfers of ownership and other documents in your name, if necessary.[16]

(b)   Notwithstanding the provisions of Paragraph 5.a. above (nor limiting the same), you agree that to the extent, if any, that you may be deemed an "author" of any Work, you hereby grant, assign and transfer to us all right, title and interest in and to such Work throughout the

---

[13] The very subjective "commercially satisfactory" delivery standard makes it easy for the record company to reject your recordings. You should try for a merely "technically satisfactory" standard, but you probably won't get it.

[14] All the more reason to fight for the more objective "technically satisfactory" delivery standard. You don't want to lose your remaining advance or (God forbid) have to pay the record company back out of your own pocket.

[15] If you record at home, make sure that the record company agrees to accept your home studio as a "recording studio" for the purposes of this agreement.

[16] This paragraph establishes the record company as the "author" of the masters for copyright purposes.

Territory including, but not limited to the ownership of the Work and all rights of the owner of copyright specified in 17 U.S.C. 106. You hereby grant to us a power of attorney, irrevocable and coupled with an interest, to execute for you and in your name those documents and instruments necessary to effectuate the intents and purposes of this Paragraph 5.b. and to accomplish, evidence and perfect the rights granted to us pursuant to this Paragraph 5 (including, but not limited to documents to apply for and obtain all registrations of copyrights in and to any such Work, and documents to assign such copyrights to us).

6.   **Name and Likeness.** We shall have the perpetual right throughout the Territory to use and publish, and to permit others to use and publish, the name (including any professional name by which Artist is or may become known), likeness and biographical material concerning Artist and the name (including any professional name by which the person involved is or may become known) of the individual producer(s) and all others rendering services in connection with the Masters, for advertising and purposes of trade in connection with the promotion and sale of records made hereunder, or we may refrain from the foregoing.[17] Our rights with respect to Artist's name, likeness and biographical material pursuant to the immediately preceding sentence shall be exclusive during the Term of this Contract and non-exclusive thereafter.

7.   **Advances.** Provided you are not then in material breach of this Contract, we shall make available to you for the recording of the Albums hereunder the Recording Funds as set forth on Schedule A1. Such Recording Funds shall constitute advances recoupable from royalties (excluding mechanical royalties) earned by you hereunder:

(a)   (i)   In connection with each album listed below (excluding the First Album), the Recording Fund shall be computed as follows: the Recording Fund shall equal sixty-six and two thirds (66 2/3%) percent of the royalties accrued to your royalty account (with allowance for reasonable reserves not to exceed, solely for this purpose, thirty percent [30%]) with respect to net sales through normal retail channels in the United States of the "Previous Album" (as the term "Previous Album" is hereinafter defined) as of the "Qualifying Date" (as the term "Qualifying Date" is hereinafter defined), but not less than the minimum amount nor more than the maximum amount set forth on Schedule A1 attached hereto and incorporated herein. The "Previous Album" shall be the album of the Recording Commitment delivered by you to us immediately prior to the delivery of the album for which the Recording Fund is being made, and the "Qualifying Date" shall be the date twelve (12) months after the release in the United States of the "Previous Album". No Recording Fund shall be due in connection with any "greatest hits" or "best of"-type album which we may release and any such "greatest hits" album, "best of"-type album or any other re-packaged album shall not be considered a Previous Album for the purposes of any Recording Fund.[18]

(ii)   We shall pay you the balance of the applicable Recording Fund, less all Recording Costs paid or incurred by us, within ten (10) days of the delivery of the applicable Album to us in accordance with the terms hereof; provided, however, that we shall have the right to withhold such portion of such monies as may be necessary in our good faith judgment to cover unpaid recording costs for which we may be liable for up to thirty (30) days after delivery of such album.

(b)   One hundred percent (100%) of all monies paid by us or our licensees for tour support, independent promotion, independent marketing or independent publicity for records

---

[17] Always get approval over photos, bios, etc.

[18] You should ask for an advance with respect to "Greatest Hits" records, especially if they ask you for new tracks.

derived from any of the Masters hereunder shall constitute advances and shall be charged against and recouped from royalties due you hereunder.[19]

8.   **Royalties.**

Subject to the provisions of Exhibit "B" attached hereto (which is hereby incorporated herein by reference) and conditional upon your full performance of all the material terms hereof, we shall pay you on Net Sales of Phonograph Records embodying Masters a royalty computed by multiplying the Suggested Retail List Price ("SRLP") less the deductions hereafter provided by the applicable royalty rate set forth on Schedule A2 attached hereto and incorporated herein.

9.   **Royalty Payments and Accountings.**

(a)   We shall send to you statements for royalties payable on or before September 30th for the semiannual period ending the preceding June 30th and on or before March 31st for the semiannual period ending the preceding December 31st, together with payment of royalties, if any, earned by you hereunder during the semiannual period for which the statement is rendered, less all advances and charges under this Contract. We shall have the right to retain, as a reserve against charges, credits, or returns, such portion of payable royalties as shall be reasonable in our best business judgment.[20] You shall reimburse us on demand for any overpayments, and we may also deduct the amount thereof from any monies payable to you hereunder. Royalties paid by us on Phonograph Records subsequently returned shall be deemed overpayments.

(b)   No royalties shall be payable to you on sales of Phonograph Records by any of our licensees until payment on those sales has been received by us in the United States (or credited to our account against an advance previously received). Sales by a licensee shall be deemed to have occurred in the semiannual accounting period during which that licensee shall have rendered to us accounting statements and payments for those sales.

(c)   You shall be deemed to have consented to all royalty statements and all other accountings rendered by us hereunder and each royalty statement and other accounting shall be conclusive, final, and binding, shall constitute an account stated, and shall not be subject to any objection for any reason whatsoever unless you give us notice stating the specific basis for that objection within one (1) year after the date rendered. You may not maintain an action, suit, or proceeding of any nature against us in respect of any royalty statement or other accounting rendered by us hereunder (or in respect of the accounting period to which it relates) unless you commence that action, suit, or proceeding against us in a court of competent jurisdiction within one (1) year after the date rendered.[21]

(d)   We shall maintain books and records concerning the sale of Phonograph Records hereunder. You or an independent certified public accountant on your behalf may, at your own expense, examine and make extracts of those books and records (but may not examine any of our books or records relating to the manufacture of Phonograph Records hereunder) solely for the purpose of verifying the accuracy of royalty statements and other accountings rendered by us hereunder, only during our normal business hours and only upon reasonable written notice. Our books

---

[19] As we discussed in Chapter Four, some record companies will agree to make independent promo and publicity costs only fifty percent (50%) recoupable.

[20] Ask for a provision that limits reserves to a fixed percentage (in no event more than 35% is a reasonable place to start) and requires the company to liquidate the reserves over four consecutive accounting periods.

[21] This time period should be at least two years, if not three.

and records relating to a particular royalty statement or other accounting may be examined only within one (1) year[22] after the date rendered. We shall have no obligation to permit you to examine our books or other accounting more than once per year nor more than once with respect to a particular royalty statement hereunder. Such examination shall be conditioned upon the accountant's agreement to us that he will not voluntarily disclose any findings to any person other than you, or your attorney or other advisors and that he is not being compensated on a contingent fee basis. Further upon the conclusion of such audit, you shall immediately submit to us a copy of the audit report prepared by such accountant. The rights hereinabove granted to you shall constitute your sole and exclusive rights to examine our books and records.

(e)   All monies paid to you or (i) on your behalf or (ii) to or on behalf of any person, firm or corporation representing you, other than royalties payable pursuant to this Contract, shall be recoupable from any monies (other than mechanical royalties and Recording Funds [unless provided for herein]) payable by us under this Contract.

(f)   We shall have the right to deduct from any amounts payable to you hereunder that portion thereof as may be required to be deducted under any statute, regulation, treaty or other law, or under any union or guild agreement, and you shall promptly execute and deliver to us any forms or other documents as may be required in connection therewith.

(g)   Each payment made by us to you under this Contract, other than union scale payments, shall be made by a single check payable to you.

10.   **Musical Composition Licenses.**

(a)   You hereby grant to us and our designees the irrevocable nonexclusive right to reproduce each Controlled Composition on Phonograph Records and to distribute those Phonograph Records in the United States and Canada.

(b)   Mechanical Royalties shall be payable for each Controlled Compositions on the percentage of Net Sales of Phonograph Records for which royalties are payable pursuant to paragraph 8 above, and at the following rates:

(i)   On Phonograph Records sold in the United States, the rate for each Controlled Composition embodied thereon shall be the United States Mechanical Rate. The "United States Mechanical Rate" shall mean an amount equal to seventy-five percent (75%)[23] of the minimum statutory royalty rate (without regard to playing time) provided for in the United States Copyright Act which is applicable to the reproduction of Musical Compositions as of the date of delivery[24] to us of the first (1st) Master hereunder embodying the Controlled Composition in question, or, if earlier, as of the date upon which that first (1st) Master was required to be delivered hereunder.

(ii)   On Phonograph Records sold in Canada, the rate for each Controlled Composition embodied thereon shall be the Canadian Mechanical Rate. The "Canadian Mechanical Rate" shall mean an amount equal to seventyfive percent (75%) of the Canadian Rate. As used herein the Canadian Rate shall mean:

---

[22] Again, this is too short. It should be at least 2 or 3 years.

[23] As discussed in Chapter Four, this is customary, but you'd like to get 100% if possible. Good luck.

[24] It's best to have the mechanical rate calculated as late as possible (such as the date of release) because the statutory rate tends to increase every other year.

(1) If the copyright law of Canada provides for a minimum compulsory rate, the minimum compulsory mechanical license rate (without regard to playing time) applicable to the use of musical works under the copyright law of Canada as of the date of delivery of the first Master embodying such selection or, if earlier, as of the date upon which that first Master was required to be delivered hereunder;

(2) If the copyright law of Canada does not provide for a minimum compulsory rate, but the majority of the major record companies (including our Canadian licensee) and the majority of the major music publishers in Canada (collectively the "Canadian Record Industry") have agreed to a mechanical license rate, the rate equal to the minimum license rate (without regard to playing time) agreed to as of the date of delivery of the first Master embodying such selection or, if earlier, as of the date upon which that first Master was required to be delivered hereunder;

(3) Notwithstanding the foregoing to the contrary, if the copyright law of Canada does not provide for a minimum compulsory license rate, and the Canadian Record Industry has not agreed to a rate, the rate applicable under this paragraph 10 (b) (ii) will be six cents ($.06) (Canadian) per selection.

(c) Notwithstanding the foregoing:

(i) The mechanical royalty rate for a Controlled Composition, contained on a MidPriced Record, Budget Record, LongPlay Single, or EP shall be three-fourths (3/4ths) of the United States Mechanical Rate[25] or the Canadian Mechanical Rate, as applicable; no copyright royalty shall be payable in respect of Controlled Compositions which are arrangements of Selections in the pubic domain, except to the extent allowable under the applicable ASCAP or BMI formula for new or additional material, and then only if you provide us with an appropriate letter from the applicable society; and no mechanical royalties shall be payable on any Phonograph Records for which no royalties are payable pursuant to the provisions of Exhibit B attached hereto or with respect to any Musical Composition which is sixty (60) seconds or less in duration. Notwithstanding anything to the contrary contained herein, we shall not be obligated to pay more than one (1) mechanical copyright royalty with respect to the use of any particular Composition on a particular record hereunder.

(ii) The maximum aggregate mechanical royalty rate for all Selections, including Controlled Compositions, contained on a Phonograph Record for sales in the United States and Canada shall, regardless of the number of Selections contained thereon, be the product of (A) the United States Mechanical Rate (or Canadian Mechanical Rate, as applicable) and (B) ten (10)[26] for an LP (containing one (1) or more discs, tape, Digital Record or New Medium equivalent), four (4)[27] for an EP, two (2) for a Single and two (2) for a LongPlay Single. With respect to multiple LPs, the maximum aggregate mechanical royalty rate payable by us with respect thereto, regardless of the number of selections embodied therein or the playing time thereof, shall be the Maximum Aggregate Multiple LP Rate. As used herein, the "Maximum Aggregate Multiple LP Rate" for a particular multiple LP shall be the maximum aggregate mechanical royalty rate which would be applicable to a single disc LP delivered on the date such multiple LP was manufactured multiplied by a fraction, the numerator of which is the suggested retail list price of such multiple LP in disc form and the denominator of

---

[25] This means that your mechanical rate on these records is 75% of 75% of the minimum statutory rate. It's tough to get around this on mid-priced and budget records, but you may be able to avoid the additional reduction on EPs and long play singles.

[26] Try for 11.

[27] Try for 5.

which is our then prevailing suggested retail list price for single disc albums. If the aggregate mechanical royalty rate applicable to all of the Selections embodied on any Phonograph Record hereunder shall exceed the applicable maximum aggregate royalty rate set forth above for that Phonograph Record, then the aggregate mechanical royalty rate for the Controlled Compositions, if any, contained thereon shall be reduced by an amount equal to such excess. If the aggregate mechanical royalty rate applicable to all of the Selections embodied on that Phonograph record shall, even as reduced in accordance with the immediately preceding sentence, still exceed the applicable maximum aggregate mechanical royalty rate for that Phonograph Record then you shall, upon our demand, pay us an amount equal to the additional mechanical royalties payable as a result of that excess and we may, in addition to all of our other rights or remedies, deduct that amount from any monies payable by us hereunder.[28]

(d) We shall account and pay mechanical royalties on Controlled Compositions in accordance with the provisions of subparagraphs (a), (c), (d), (f) and (g) of paragraph 9 above, except we shall have the right to retain reasonable reserves[29] and we shall send you statements for those mechanical royalties on or before May 31st for the quarterannual period ending the preceding March 31st, on or before August 31st for the quarterannual period ending the preceding June 30th, on or before November 30th for the quarterannual period ending the preceding September 30th, and on or before February 28th for the quarter-annual period ending the preceding December 31st.

(e) You shall cause the issuance to us and our designees of mechanical licenses to reproduce on Phonograph Records Selections that are not Controlled Compositions and to distribute those Phonograph Records in the United States and Canada. Those mechanical licenses shall be at rates and on terms no less favorable to us and our designees than those contained in the standard mechanical license issued by The Harry Fox Agency, Inc. or any successor with respect to Phonograph Records distributed in the United States and by CMRRA or any successor with respect to Phonograph Records distributed in Canada; provided, however, in no event shall those rates exceed one hundred percent (100%) of the applicable minimum statutory rates. You shall also, upon our request, cause the issuance to us and our designees of mechanical licenses to reproduce Selections on Phonograph Records hereunder and to distribute those Phonograph Records outside the United States and Canada on terms no less favorable to us and our designees than those generally applicable to Phonograph Record manufacturers in each country in question. The obligation to account and pay publishing monies (including without limitation mechanical royalties) on sales of Phonograph Records and other exploitation of Masters outside of the United States and/or by our licensees shall be that of our affiliates or licensees, as the case may be.

(f) If the copyright in any Controlled Composition is owned or controlled by a person, firm or corporation other than you, you shall cause that person, firm or corporation to grant to us and our designees the same rights as you are required to grant to us and our designees pursuant to this paragraph.

(g) Any assignment, license or other agreement made with respect to Controlled Compositions shall be subject to the terms hereof.

(h) You grant to us and our designees the irrevocable, nonexclusive right to print and reproduce, at our election, the title and lyrics to each Selection embodied in a Master on

---

[28] This means that you get killed if you have lots of covers on your record, unless you get the publishers of the covers to comply with the constraints of this clause. You probably won't be able to.

[29] Try to get reserve limitations here as well.

the packaging of Phonograph Records embodying Masters throughout the Territory in perpetuity, without payment to you or any other person, firm or corporation of any monies or other consideration in connection therewith. If we are required to pay monies to any person, firm or corporation for the printing or reproduction of the title or lyrics of any Selection recorded in a Master on the packaging of Phonograph Records embodying Masters, then you shall, upon our demand, pay to us an amount equal to those monies paid by us in connection therewith and we may, in addition to all of our other rights or remedies, deduct that amount from any monies payable by us hereunder.

(i)   You hereby grant to us and our designees the irrevocable right to reproduce each Controlled Composition in Videos (as that term is hereafter defined), to reproduce such Videos, distribute them in any manner (including, without limitation, publicly and for profit), to manufacture and distribute Home A/V Devices and other copies of them, and to exploit them otherwise, by any method and in any form known now or in the future, throughout the world, and authorize others to do so. Neither we, or any of our licensees, will be required to make any payment in connection with those uses even if we (or our licensees) receive any payment in connection with any use of the Videos embodying the Controlled Compositions as aforesaid. In the event that you shall fail to cause any such music publishing company to issue any such license to us to use any Controlled Composition is Videos as aforesaid, and if we shall thereupon pay any fee to such music publishing company in order to obtain any such license, then we may deduct the amount of such license fee from any monies otherwise payable to you hereunder.

11.   **Exclusivity; Rerecording Restrictions.**

(a)   During the term of this Contract:

(i)   You shall not enter into any agreement or make any commitment that would interfere with your performance of any of the terms and provisions hereof.[30]

(ii)   You shall not perform for the purpose of making Phonograph Records in the Territory by or for any person other than us.

(iii)   You shall not authorize or knowingly permit the use of Artist's name (including Artist's current professional name or any professional name hereafter used by Artist), photograph, likeness or other identification, voice or other sound effects, or performance, for or in connection with the production, sale, advertising or exploitation of Phonograph Records in the Territory by or for any person other than us.

(iv)   In the event Artist makes any sound recordings for motion pictures, television, radio or any medium, or if Artist performs as a member of the cast in making sound recordings for a live theatrical presentation, you agree that you will do so only pursuant to a written contract prohibiting the use of such recordings, directly or indirectly, for Phonograph Record purposes.[31]

(b)   You agree that you shall not perform in any manner whatsoever any selection or portion thereof recorded and/or delivered hereunder during the Term, whether or not

---

[30] This is where you need to ask for the sideman and producer exclusions we covered in Chapter Four. Otherwise, you cannot legally play, sing or render production services on recordings released by any other company without your record company's permission.

[31] If you have clout, you may be able to carve out a once a year exclusion to do soundtrack work for movies and TV, but this is a toughie.

released by us, for the purposes of making records for distribution or sale in the Territory by or for any person other than us, at any time prior to the later of the following dates (such later date, with respect to any such selection, is hereinafter sometimes referred to as the "Restriction Date"): (i) five (5) years after the date of delivery to us of the last Master embodying such selection and (ii) two (2) years after the expiration or termination of the Term of this Contract or any subsequent agreement between us and any person relating to Artist's recording services.[32]

(c)   You shall not at any time manufacture, distribute or sell, or authorize or permit the manufacture, distribution, or sale in the Territory by any person other than us of Phonograph Records embodying (i) any performance rendered in any manner by Artist during the Term, or (ii) any performance rendered in any manner by Artist after the Term of a Selection recorded and/or delivered hereunder if such performance is rendered prior to the Restriction Date applicable thereto.

(d)   We may take such action as we deem necessary, in your name and/or in our own name, to enforce or protect our rights under this Contract, including, without limitation, taking action against any person who sells or imports records embodying Masters in the Territory in violation of our exclusive rights hereunder or who otherwise uses the performances, name, photograph, likeness, other identification, voice and/or sound effects of Artist in violation of our rights under this Contract. Artist shall cooperate fully with us in any controversy or litigation that may arise with a third party relating to our rights under this Contract.

12.   **Warranties and Representations.**

You represent, warrant and agree that:

(a)   You are free to enter into and perform this Contract, and you are not under any restrictions or obligations that will impair your full performance hereof of your obligations hereunder or impair our full enjoyment of our rights hereunder. Without limitation of the foregoing, you specifically warrant and represent that no selection recorded or to be recorded by you hereunder is or will be subject to any rerecording restriction under any previous recording contract to which you may have been a party, and that neither you nor any other person rendering services in connection with Masters is or will be a party to any contract which would in any way impair the rights granted to us hereunder. Artist is eighteen years old or older.[33]

(b)   Each Master shall be free of all liens and encumbrances, and there will be no claims, demands or actions pending or threatened with respect thereto.[34]

(c)   Neither any name(s) utilized by you, the Masters, any of the selections embodied therein, any other matters or materials supplied by you hereunder, nor any exploitation or use of any of the foregoing, shall violate or infringe upon any civil, personal or proprietary rights of any person, including, without limitation, trademarks, trade names, copyrights and rights of privacy and publicity.[35]

---

[32] This is the re-recording restriction that is almost impossible to knock out of any deal. At the very least, try to make it applicable only to songs embodied in recordings that are commercially released by the record company.

[33] Contracts entered into by minors are easily revocable (unless the agreements have been affirmed and ratified by a court of competent jurisdiction).

[34] Clear those samples.

[35] Make sure no one else is using your name, and takes steps to secure trademark and service mark rights, as we discussed in Chapter Seven. Also, make sure you have the right to use any copyrightable materials embodied in the packaging or artwork of your record.

(d)   The selections embodied in Masters shall be available for mechanical licensing to us in accordance with paragraph 10 above.

(e)   Other than as specifically set forth in this Contract, we shall be subject to no costs, fees, advances, charges or royalties for or in connection with the recording, sale, use or exploitation of the Masters.

(f)   Our acceptance and/or utilization of Masters or other matters or materials hereunder shall not constitute a waiver of any of your representations, warranties or agreements in respect thereof.

(g)   You agree to use your best efforts to record and produce commercially acceptable Masters hereunder.[36]

(h)   Artist (nor any individual member of Artist if Artist is a group) shall not render any services to or authorize or permit the Artist's name and likeness or any biographical material concerning the Artist to be used in any manner by any person, firm or corporation in the advertising, promoting or marketing of blank magnetic recording tape or any other product or device intended primarily for home use, whether now known or hereafter developed, which may be used for the fixation of sound alone or sound together with visual images.[37]

13.   **Indemnification.** You agree to indemnify and hold us and our parents, affiliates, subsidiaries, divisions, licensees, successors and assigns and our officers, directors and employees and such other entities harmless from and against any liability, damage, cost or expense (including costs and attorneys' fees) occasioned by or arising out of any claim, demand or action which is inconsistent with any agreement, representation, grant or warranty made or assumed by you hereunder which is reduced to final nonappealable judgment or settled with your written consent, which consent shall not be unreasonably withheld.[38] You agree to pay us on demand any amounts for which you may be responsible under the foregoing indemnity and, without limiting any of our other rights or remedies, upon the making or filing of any claim demand or action subject hereto, we shall be entitled to withhold sums payable under this Contract, in an amount reasonably related to the potential liability, plus costs and reasonable attorneys' fees.[39] If you reasonably fail to consent to a proposed settlement, we shall nonetheless have the right to enter into such proposed settlement, but, in such event, you shall not be liable for the amount of the settlement, but shall be liable for expenses (including costs and attorneys' fees) which we incurred up to and including the date as of which the claim is settled. Alternatively, if you fail to consent to a proposed settlement and we elect not to enter into such settlement agreement in accordance with the immediately preceding sentence or your failure to so consent is unreasonable, you shall, at our written request, thereafter directly bear all costs of defense and shall promptly reimburse us for all expenses incurred by us (including costs and attorneys' fees) up to and including the date as of which you failed to consent to such proposed settlement, and if you fail to promptly undertake such future costs and reimburse us for such accumulated expenses, we may settle such claim in our sole discretion and your indemnification shall apply to such settlement.

---

[36] This means you are in breach if they can prove you are trying to make "uncommercial recordings" for some reason. See: *Metal Machine Music* by Lou Reed.

[37] Record companies are still paranoid about home taping.

[38] This is totally standard stuff. For instance, if the record company gets sued because you didn't clear a sample, they will simply look to you to cover their legal fees and pay their damages, if any, as long as the claim is reduced to judgment or settled with your consent.

[39] You should ask for the right to post a bond, the purpose of which is to give the record company some security, thereby allowing them to release any monies that they would otherwise withhold pursuant to this paragraph.

14.   **Videos.**

(a)   In the event that we ask you to perform for the purpose of being filmed (on any medium now known or unknown) for promotional, commercial and other purposes in connection with the exploitation of Masters (hereinafter referred to as a "Video") you agree that you will so perform. We shall have all of the same rights with respect to each Video as are otherwise applicable hereto with respect to the Masters made hereunder, including, without limitation, the right to use and publish your name and likenesses in each Video for advertising and purposes of trade and the sole ownership of all rights in each Video in the Territory. Videos shall not apply in fulfillment of your Recording Commitment.

(b)   With respect to each Video: (i) the selection(s) to be embodied therein shall be designated by us; (ii) the Video shall be shot on such dates and locations to be mutually determined by us and you; and (iii) the individual producer and director of each Video and the concept or script of each Video shall be approved by both you and us.[40]

(c)   We shall engage the producer, director and other production personnel for each Video. We shall pay one hundred (100%) percent of the production costs of each Video in an amount not in excess of a budget to be established in advance by us (the "Production Budget"). The costs incurred by us in connection with the production of each Video up to the Production Budget shall be recoupable by us from fifty (50%) percent of all royalties payable to you which are derived from the sale of the Masters hereunder and one hundred (100%) percent of all costs incurred by us in connection with the production of each Video shall be recoupable by us from any and all royalties payable to you from the exploitation of Videos hereunder.[41] You shall be responsible for and shall promptly pay the production costs for each Video which are in excess of the Production Budget to the extent such excess costs are not paid by the producer and/or director of such Video. In the event that we shall pay any production costs for which you are responsible pursuant to the foregoing (which we are in no way obligated to do), you shall promptly reimburse us for such excess upon demand and, without limiting our other rights and remedies, we may deduct an amount equal to such excess from any monies otherwise payable to you hereunder.

(d)   Artist's compensation for performing in such Videos (as opposed to your compensation with respect to the exploitation of such Videos which is provided in paragraph 14(e) hereinbelow) shall be limited to any minimum amounts required to be paid for such performances pursuant to any collective bargaining agreements pertaining thereto (and such amounts shall be treated as an advance to you against all and any payments payable by us to you hereunder); provided, however, that Artist hereby waives any rights to receive such compensation to the extent such right may be waived. You agree to sign and comply with any union forms and agreements as shall be necessary and prescribed by such union with regard to the making of such Videos or otherwise necessary or desirable in connection with our rights with respect thereto.

(e)   We shall have the right to use and allow others to use each Video for advertising and promotional purposes with no payment to you. We shall also have the right to use and allow others to use the videos for commercial purposes. As used in this subparagraph "commercial purposes" shall mean any use for which we receive monetary consideration in excess of an incidental fee as a reasonable amount as reimbursement for our administrative costs and the actual costs incurred by us for tape, stock and duplication of the Videos and shipping. Compensation derived from

---

[40] Artists almost never have full creative control over videos.

[41] This is fairly standard. Some record companies try to apply 100% of your record royalties against video costs.

such commercial exploitation and due you hereunder shall be credited to your account as provided in Exhibit "B".

15.   **Unique Services.** You expressly acknowledge that your services hereunder are of a special, unique, intellectual, and extraordinary character which gives them peculiar value, and that in the event of a breach by you of any term hereof, we will be caused irreparable injury which cannot adequately be compensated by money damages. Accordingly, we shall be entitled to seek injunctive relief, in addition to any other rights or remedies that we may have, to enforce the terms of this Contract.[42]

16.   **Certain Remedies.**

(a)   The running of the Term and our obligations hereunder shall be automatically suspended if for any reason whatsoever you shall refuse, neglect, fail, or be unable to fulfill any of your obligations hereunder, or if as a result of an Act of God, accident, fire, labor controversy, riot, civil commotion, act of public enemy, law, enactment, rule, order, or act of any government or governmental instrumentality, failure of technical facilities, failure or delay of transportation facilities, illness or incapacity of you, or others, or other cause of a similar or dissimilar nature not reasonably within our control, we are hampered in the recording, manufacture, distribution, or sale of Phonograph Records or our normal business operations become commercially impractical. A suspension shall be for the duration of any such event or contingency, and, unless we notify you to the contrary in writing, the Contract Period during which that event or contingency shall have commenced shall be automatically extended by a number of days equal to the total number of days of the suspension, or such fewer number of days of which we may advise you in writing. No suspension shall in any manner suspend or otherwise impair our rights under this Contract.[43]

(b)   If you shall refuse, neglect, fail, or be unable to fulfill any of your obligations hereunder, including, without limitation, your obligation to record for and deliver to us Masters within the time periods set forth in paragraph 3 above or within the Recording Fund set forth in Schedule A1, we may, without limiting our other rights or remedies, terminate the Term upon written notice to you, in which event we shall have no obligations or liabilities to you under this Contract, except for our obligations, if any, with respect to Masters recorded prior to that termination. If we so terminate the Term you shall pay us, on demand, an amount equal to any unrecouped advances hereunder, other than any portion thereof specifically attributable to and paid in respect of an LP delivered by you to us in partial fulfillment of your Recording Commitment.

(c)   If we refuse to permit you to fulfill your minimum Recording Commitment for any Contract Period, other than as a result of an event or contingency referred to in subdivision (a) above, we shall have no obligations or liabilities to you in connection therewith unless within forty-five (45) days after our refusal you shall notify us of your desire to fulfill your minimum Recording Commitment for that Contract Period and within thirty (30) days after our receipt of that notice we shall fail to advise you in writing that we shall permit you to fulfill your minimum Recording Commitment for that Contract Period. If we shall fail to so advise you in writing that we shall permit you to fulfill your minimum Recording Commitment for that Contract Period, the Term shall expire as of the end of that thirty (30) day period and we shall have no obligations or liabilities to you whatsoever in connection with our failure to permit you to fulfill your Recording

---

[42] This is also standard. The purpose of this clause is to give the record company the right to enjoin you (i.e., stop you) from recording for another label in the event that you attempt to do so.

[43] This is a standard "force majeure" provision that allows the record company to suspend its obligations in the event of a major calamity that prevents the record company from operating. You should ask for a provision that limits any such suspension to a maximum of twelve months unless the entire record industry is affected by such force majeure event.

Commitment for that Contract Period. We shall, however, pay you promptly after the expiration of that thirty (30) day period, as an advance recoupable from royalties hereunder, an amount equal to the minimum union scale payments which would have been required to have been paid to the Artist for each LP for your minimum Recording Commitment for that Contract Period that we did not permit you to record. For the purposes of the foregoing, an LP shall be deemed to be comprised of eight (8) Masters.[44]

(d) If you are, as of the date of this Contract, a California resident, or become a California resident during the term of this Contract, paragraph 16 (e) below shall be effective. If you are or become a California resident during the term of this Contract, you shall give us prompt written notice thereof.

(e) (i) We agree to make annual payments of compensation ("Annual Payments") to each of the "Applicable Members" (as hereinafter defined) during each of the first seven (7) "Fiscal Years" (as hereinafter defined) of such amounts as are set forth in sections (1),(2) and (3) below. Each of the Applicable Members hereby agrees to accept all such Annual Payments. As used in this paragraph, "Fiscal Year" shall mean each consecutive twelve (12) month period during which this Contract is in effect, commencing with the date of commencement of the term of this Contract. At least thirty (30) days before the end of each Fiscal Year, you shall notify us in writing if each Applicable Member has not received compensation equal to the Annual Payment for such Fiscal Year and the amount of the deficiency, and we will pay you the amount of the deficiency:

(1) First Fiscal Year: Nine Thousand Dollars ($9,000.00);

(2) Second Fiscal Year: Twelve Thousand Dollars ($12,000);

(3) Third through Seventh Fiscal Years: Fifteen Thousand Dollars ($15,000) for each Fiscal Year.

(ii) You hereby warrant and represent that all payments made to you under this Contract during each Fiscal Year will be distributed equally among those members in whose names such payment is made (and for such purpose, any payment in the name of "Lawn Chocolate" shall be equally apportioned among all members of Artist). Each such apportioned share of a payment is referred to as the "Apportioned Share". Each member of Artist hereby acknowledges that each Appropriate Share to which he is entitled pursuant to the foregoing is shall be deemed received by him for the purposes of California Civil Code Section 3423.

(ii) If in any Fiscal Year the aggregate amount of the compensation (other than mechanical royalties) paid to the Applicable Members or allocated to the Applicable Members as an Appropriate Share under this Contract exceeds the Annual Payments due to the Applicable Members, such excess compensation shall apply to reduce the Annual Payments due to the Applicable Members for any subsequent Fiscal Years.

(iii) Subject to the preceding paragraph, each Annual Payment shall be due on or before the last business day of the Fiscal Year to which it applies; provided that if this Contract expires or terminates prior to the end of a particular Fiscal Year, the applicable Annual Payment to each Applicable Member shall be reduced proportionately, or shall be such greater amount, if any, as is required pursuant to California Civil Code Section 3423. Any failure by us to make an Annual Payment will not constitute a material breach of this Contract.

---

[44] This allows the record company to terminate the contract at their election. Ask to have this removed, or, in the alternative, ask them to insert a more meaningful "pay or play" provision along the lines of the provision I covered in Chapter Four.

(iv)   We shall have the right to pay any Applicable Member or any other member of Artist at any time any additional amounts which may be required to be paid as a condition to our petitioning for an injunction pursuant to Section 526 of the California Code of Civil Procedure and California Civil Code Section 3423 (5th) of the California Civil Code ("Additional Payments"). Each member of Artist hereby agrees to accept any and all such Additional Payments. The Appropriate Share of all compensation (other than mechanical royalties) paid to Artist hereunder which is not applied to the Annual Payments theretofore due the Applicable Members will be credited toward satisfying the obligation to make Additional Payments as a prerequisite to seeking injunctive relief hereunder. If we actually make any Additional Payments and thereafter elect not to seek such injunction, such additional payments shall constitute advances hereunder.

(v)   Each Annual Payment and Additional Payment, if any, will constitute an Advance and will be applied in reduction of any and all monies (other than mechanical royalties) due or becoming due you under this Contract. Notwithstanding anything to the contrary contained herein, whenever in this Contract we have the right to deduct excess expenditures (including, without limitation, excess Recording Costs, mechanical royalties and special packaging costs) from any and all monies otherwise due or becoming due you under this Contract, our such right shall not extend to deducting such excess expenditure from any Annual Payments or Additional Payments.

(vi)   As used in this Contract, the term "Applicable Members" shall mean John Doe and Fred Johnson.[45]

17.   **Producer and Other Royalties.** You shall be solely responsible for and shall pay all royalties and other compensation which may be payable to any producers of the Masters or to any others rendering services in connection with the recording of the Masters.[46]

18.   **Definitions.** The terms used herein shall be deemed to have the meaning set out in Exhibit "A" attached hereto and incorporated herein by reference.

19.   **Assignment.** We shall have the right, at our election, to assign any of our rights hereunder, in whole or in part, to any subsidiary, affiliated, controlling or other related company and to any person firm or corporation owning or acquiring a substantial portion of our stock or assets, and any rights so assigned may also be assigned by the assignee. You hereby agree that we shall be released from any liability hereunder to the extent of such assignment of rights. You shall not have the right to assign any of your rights hereunder.

20.   **Notices.** All notices to be given to you hereunder and all statements and payments to be sent to you hereunder shall be addressed to you at the address set forth on page 1 hereof or at such other address as you shall designate in writing from time to time. All notices to be give to us hereunder shall be addressed to us at the address set forth on page 1 hereof or at such other address as we shall designate in writing from time to time. All notices shall be in writing, by registered or certified mail, return receipt requested, or served by to the attention of an officer of ours if to us. Except as otherwise provided herein, notices shall be deemed given when personally delivered,

---

[45] Paragraph 16 (e) is included in response to a California Civil Code provision which is designed to guarantee a certain amount of minimum compensation to persons signed to personal services contracts (such as exclusive recording agreements). If California law applies to a contract, it would be impossible for a record company to enjoin an artist from recording for another label without including a provision such as this. Of course, a record company is still entitled to sue you (and possibly your new record company) for damages suffered as a result of your breach of the contract whether or not this provision is in your contract.

[46] You should ask the record company to accept letters of direction so that you don't have to deal with the fuss of paying producers directly.

mailed as aforesaid, except that notices of change of address shall be effective only after actual receipt. A copy of all notices to us shall be sent to Jethro Bodine, Esq. 1234 Burton Way, Beverly Hills, CA 90211.

21.   **Leaving Member Provisions.**

(a)   The term "Artist" as used in this Contract refers individually and collectively to the members of the group currently known as "Lawn Chocolate" and (whether presently or hereafter signatories to or otherwise bound by the terms of this Contract) hereinafter referred to as the "Group". A breach of any form of this Contract or a disaffirmance or attempted disaffirmance of this Contract on the ground of minority by or with respect to any member of the Group shall, at our election, be a breach by or with respect to the entire Group.

(b)   Individuals in addition to those presently members of the Group may become members of the Group only with our prior written approval. Additional members shall be bound by the terms of this Contract relating to the Artist and Artist shall cause any additional member to execute and deliver to us such documents as we may deem necessary or desirable to evidence that individual's agreement to be so bound. You shall not, without our prior written consent, record any Master Recordings embodying the performances of any additional member prior to your delivery to us of those documents, and if you do so, those Master Recordings, if we so elect, shall not apply towards the fulfillment of your Recording Commitment.

(c)   A "Leaving Member" shall mean an individual member of the Group who ceases to record as a member of the Group, and to engage in other professional activities of the Group. If any individual member of the Group shall become a Leaving Member, you shall promptly give us written notice thereof by certified or registered mail, return receipt requested. You shall designate a replacement member for that Leaving Member and we shall have the right to approve of the replacement member. The replacement member shall be bound by the terms of this Contract relating to the Artist and you shall cause a replacement member to execute and to deliver to us such documents as we may deem necessary or desirable to evidence that replacement member's agreement to be so bound. You shall not, without our prior written consent, record any Master Recordings embodying the performances of a replacement member prior to your delivery to us of those documents, and if you do so, those Master Recordings, if we so elect, shall not apply towards the fulfillment of your Recording Commitment.

(d)   (i)   We shall have the irrevocable option for the exclusive recording services of any Leaving Member. We may exercise our option by written notice to you no later than sixty (60) days after the date upon which we shall have received a written notice required to be sent by you and referred to in subparagraph (c) above. If we shall so exercise our option with respect to any Leaving Member, you shall be deemed to have executed an exclusive recording contract with us for such leaving member (a "Leaving Member Contract") pursuant to which that Leaving Member shall render his or her exclusive recording services to us on the same terms contained in this Contract, except as otherwise hereinafter provided:

(1)   The term of a Leaving Member Contract shall consist of an Initial Period commencing as of the date of our written notice to that Leaving Member pursuant to the preceding provisions of this subparagraph (d) and shall continue until the later of (1) the date twelve (12) months after the date of commencement of that Initial Period and (2) the date one hundred and eighty (180) days, or such fewer number of days of which we may notify the Leaving Member in writing, after the Leaving Member's delivery to us of the last Master recordings required to be delivered to us during the Initial Period. We shall have the same number of options, each to extend the Term of the Leaving Member Contract for a Renewal Period, as equal to the number of separate renewal options remaining under this Contract pursuant to paragraph 2 above as of the

date that individual became a Leaving Member, but in no event shall we have fewer than two (2) renewal options. Each Renewal Period under the Leaving Member Contract shall run consecutively and shall commence upon the expiration of the immediately preceding Contract Period thereunder and shall continue until the later of (1) the date eighteen (18) months after the date of commencement of that Renewal Period and (2) the date one hundred and eighty (180) days, or such fewer number of days of which we may notify the Leaving Member in writing, after the Leaving Member's delivery to us of the last Master Recordings required to be delivered thereunder to us during that Renewal Period. Each option shall be automatically exercised unless we notify you by written notice of our election to do so at any time prior to the commencement of the Renewal Period for which it is exercised.

(2)   During the Initial Period and each Renewal Period of the Leaving Member Contract, the Leaving Member shall record and deliver to us, at such times as we shall designate or approve, at a minimum, six (6) Master Recordings embodying that Leaving Member's performances, plus, at our election, additional Master Recordings embodying that Leaving Member's performances, but in no event shall the Leaving Member be required to record for or deliver to us in excess of twenty-four Master Recordings during the Initial Period or during any Renewal Period of the Leaving Member Contract.

(3)   The Recording Funds set forth in Schedule A1 shall not apply to the Master Recordings recorded by a Leaving Member under a Leaving Member Contract. We shall pay the Recording Costs of the Master Recordings recorded at recording sessions conducted in accordance with the terms of the Leaving Member Contract in an amount not in excess of the Recording Budget therefor approved by us in writing.

(4)   With respect to Master Recordings embodying the performances of a Leaving Member recorded pursuant to a Leaving Member Contract, the royalty rates pursuant to Schedule A2 shall be seventy (70%) percent of the rate otherwise provided therein.

(5)   An amount equal to all unrecouped advances or charges against royalties pursuant to this Contract as of the date of the commencement of a Leaving Member Contract shall constitute an advance recoupable from royalties payable by us under that Leaving Member Contract.

(ii)   At our request, any Leaving Member shall execute and deliver to us any and all documents as we may deem necessary or desirable to evidence the foregoing.

(iii)   If we shall enter into a contract with a Leaving Member, that Leaving Member shall, upon our request, record and deliver to us at such times as we shall indicate no fewer than four (4) so-called "Demo Recordings", each embodying that Leaving Member's performance as the sole featured artist of a single Musical Composition previously unrecorded by that Leaving Member and approved by us and each Demo Recording shall be recorded in its entirety in a recording studio. We shall pay the costs in accordance with the terms hereof in an amount not in excess of a Recording Budget therefor approved in connection with the recording of the Demo Recordings any such costs paid by us shall be recoupable from royalties payable by us under the Leaving Member Contract. Notwithstanding anything to the contrary contained herein, we may, at our election, terminate our Leaving Member Contract with a Leaving Member, upon sending such Leaving Member written notice of our election to do so within sixty (60) days after our receipt of the completed Demo Recordings, and thereby be relieved of any obligations or liabilities under that Leaving Member Contract. We shall own the Demo Recordings and all reproductions and derivatives thereof to the same extent that we own the Masters; provided we shall not release such Demos as Masters.

(e)   Notwithstanding any of the foregoing, if any member of the Group shall be a Leaving Member or if the Group shall completely disband, we may, without limiting our other rights and remedies, terminate this Contract by written notice to you and shall thereby be relieved of any obligations or liabilities hereunder, except our obligations with respect to Masters recorded prior to that termination. In the event we elect to so terminate this Contract, subparagraph (d) above shall be applicable to each member of the Group as if each member were a Leaving Member.

(f)   If a Key Member shall become a Leaving Member and we do not terminate this Contract, then with respect to each LP delivered under this Contract subsequent to the date on which that Key Member became a Leaving Member, the advances set forth in Schedule A1 shall be reduced by twenty-five (25%) percent and the royalty rates set forth in Schedule A2 shall be reduced by fifteen (15%) percent. As used herein the term "Key Member" shall mean a member of the Group whose contribution to the Group, in the recording studio or at live performances or otherwise, is, in our opinion, material.

(g)   If any member of the Group shall become a Leaving Member, that member shall not have the right thereafter during the Term to use any name utilized by the Group or any name similar thereto. Without limiting the generality of the foregoing, that member shall not, in connection with any of his or her professional activities, use the phrase "formerly a member of Lawn Chocolate" or any similar expression.

(h)   We may send notices to a Leaving Member to your address above, or at such other address of which that Leaving Member shall have advised us in writing.[47]

22   **Miscellaneous.**

(a)   This Contract set forth your and our entire understanding relating to its subject matter. No modification, amendment, waiver, termination or discharge of this Contract or of any of its terms shall be binding upon either of us unless confirmed by a document signed by you and by a duly authorized officer of ours. No waiver by you or us of any term of this Contract or of any default hereunder shall affect your or our respective rights thereafter to enforce that term or to exercise any right or remedy in the event of any other default, whether or not similar.

(b)   We shall not be deemed to be in breach of any of our obligations hereunder unless and until you shall have given us specific written notice by certified or registered mail, return receipt requested, describing in detail the breach and we shall have failed to cure that breach within thirty (30) days after our receipt of that written notice.[48]

(c)   Except where otherwise expressly provided elsewhere in this Contract, your approvals or consents shall be given by written notice of such approval or disapproval or of consent or nonconsent within five (5) business days after such notice is received and in the event of disapproval or nonconsent, such notice shall contain the specific reasons therefor. Failure to give notice as aforesaid shall be deemed to be your consent or approval, as the case may be, with respect to the matter submitted.

---

[47] I covered leaving member provisions in great detail in Chapter Four. The leaving member provision in this contract is fairly typical of those found in most major label recording agreements, which is to say it leaves everybody in worse shape (including remaining members) when a member leaves the band or is fired.

[48] Try to make this mutual.

(d)   Nothing herein contained shall constitute a partnership or a joint venture between you and us. Except as otherwise expressly provided herein you are performing your obligations hereunder as an independent contractor. Neither party hereto shall hold itself out contrary to the terms of this subdivision, and neither you nor we shall become liable for any representation, act or omission of the other contrary to the provisions hereof.

(e)   This Contract shall not be deemed to give any right or remedy to any third party whatsoever unless we specifically grant that right or remedy in writing to that third party.

(f)   The provision of any applicable collective bargaining agreement between us and any labor union or guild which are required by the terms of that agreement to be included in this Contract shall be deemed incorporated herein as if those provisions were expressly set forth in this Contract.

(g)   In the event of any action, suit or proceeding arising from or based upon this Contract brought by either party hereto against the other, the prevailing party shall be entitled to recover from the other its attorney's fees in connection therewith in addition to the costs of that action, suit or proceeding.

(h)   Except as otherwise expressly provided herein all rights and remedies herein or otherwise shall be cumulative and none of them shall be in limitation of any other right or remedy.

(i)   This Contract has been entered into in the State of California, and its validity, construction, interpretation and legal effect shall be governed by the laws of the State of California applicable to contracts entered into and performed entirely with the State of California. Any claim, dispute or disagreement in respect of this Contract may be brought only in the courts of the State of California, in Los Angeles, or the federal courts within the State of California, in Los Angeles, which courts shall have exclusive jurisdiction thereof, and you and/or Artist hereby waive any claim that such courts do not have jurisdiction or are an inconvenient forum.

(j)   The paragraph headings herein are solely for the purpose of convenience and shall be disregarded completely in the interpretation of this Contract or any of its terms. This Contract shall not become effective until signed by you and countersigned by a duly authorized officer of ours. If the foregoing correctly reflects your agreement with us, please so indicate by signing below.

Very truly yours,

Thrifty Scot Records, Inc.

By:_____

AGREED AND ACCEPTED:

_____

John Doe
SS#

_____

Fred Johnson
SS#

Individually and collectively pka "Lawn Chocolate"

EXHIBIT "A"

DEFINITIONS[49]

The following words shall, where the context allows, have the following meanings whether such words shall appear in lower case or with the first letter of each word capitalized (the foregoing shall apply to all other defined terms used in the Contract):

(a) "Budget Record" shall mean a Phonograph Record which bears an SRLP in any particular configuration in the country in question which is sixtysix and twothirds (66-2/3%) percent or less of the SRLP of the majority of our (or our affiliates or licensees) then-current newly-released top-price records in such configuration;

(b) "Contract Period" shall mean the Initial Period or any Option Period of the Term (as they may be suspended or extended);

(c) "Controlled Composition" shall mean a Musical Composition or other Selection, written or composed by Artist, you, or any producer of the Masters or which is owned or controlled, in whole or in part, directly or indirectly, by you, any of the producers of the Masters or any person firm or corporation in which you, or any producer of the Masters have a direct or an indirect interest other than as a shareholder in a public corporation;

(d) "delivery to us" or words of similar connotation used in connection with Master Recordings or Masters shall mean delivery to our record production manager at our offices in Anytown, California of fullymixed, leadered, sequenced and equalized two-track stereo 15 ips master tapes (assembled on one [1] or, if necessary, on two [2] master reels) or 1610 Digital Master in proper form for the production of the parts necessary to manufacture Phonograph Records therefrom and delivery to us at said offices of all multitrack master tapes (including, but not limited to, any twentyfour (24) track master tapes), all consents, approvals, copy and publishing information, credits, first use mechanical licenses and other material and documents reasonably required by us to release Phonograph Records embodying those Master Recordings or Master and to manufacture album covers or other packaging therefor;

(e) The words "Digital Record" shall mean a record the signals of which are encoded and decoded by so-called "digital" technology whether now known or hereafter devised as opposed to so-called "analog" technology, and shall include without limitation Compact Discs, Digital Audio Tape records and Digital Compact Cassettes.

(f) "EP" or "MiniLP" shall mean a 12inch 331/3 rpm or 45 rpm disc Phonograph Record, or its tape,

---

[49] These are fairly standard definitions. They tend not to be terribly negotiable in any event.

Digital Record or New Medium equivalent, embodying no fewer than four (4) Musical Compositions and no more than six (6) Musical Compositions;

(g) "LongPlay Single" shall mean a 12inch 331/3 rpm or 45 rpm disc Phonograph Record, or its tape, Digital Record or New Medium equivalent, embodying no more than three (3) Musical Compositions;

(h) "LP" and "album" shall mean a 12inch 331/3 rpm longplaying disc Phonograph Record of no fewer than fortyfive (45) and no more than fifty-five (55) minutes in duration, or its tape, Digital Record or New Medium equivalent, and, where the context requires, Masters sufficient to constitute the same.

(i) "Master Recording" shall mean every form of recording (whether now known or unknown), embodying sound alone, or sound accompanied by visual images, which may be used in the recording, production or manufacture of Phonograph Records;

(j) "Master" shall mean a Master Recording embodying the performances of the Artist recorded hereunder;

(k) "MidPriced Record" shall mean a Phonograph Record bearing an SRLP in any particular configuration in the country in question in excess of sixtysix and twothirds (66 2/3%) percent of the SRLP of the majority of our (or our licensees or affiliates, as applicable) then-current, newly-released top-price records in such configuration but not more than the greater of (i) eighty (80%) percent of the SRLP of our (or our affiliates or licensees, as applicable) then current newly-released top-price records in such configuration, or (ii) Two Dollars ($2.00) (or the local currency equivalent thereof) less than the SRLP of the majority of our (or our licensees or affiliates, as applicable), then current newly-released records in such configuration;

(l) "Multiple LP" shall mean a single package containing two (2) or more LPs, or their tape, Digital Record or New Medium equivalent, which is sold as a single unit, and where the context requires, Master Recording sufficient to constitute a single package containing two (2) or more LPs, or their tape, Digital Record or New Medium equivalent, which is sold as a single unit;

(m) "Musical Composition" and "Composition" shall mean a single musical composition and, for the purposes of computing mechanical royalties hereunder, shall include a medley;

(n) "Net Royalty", "Net FlatFee" or "Net Receipts" shall mean the royalty, flatfee, or receipt as the case may be, received by us from a person, firm or corporation from the exploitation by that person, firm or corporation of rights in those Masters, less all "outofpocket" costs paid or incurred by us in connection with the exploitation of those rights and the collection of those monies (it being understood that such costs shall not include our overhead), less all taxes actually paid and adjustments and less all royalties or other sums payable by us to any person, firm or corporation in connection with the exploitation of those rights, except for royalties or other sums payable to producers of those Masters, which shall be borne solely by you;

(o) "Net Sales" shall mean, in the case of sales of records by us and our licensees, eighty-five (85%) percent of the aggregate number of LPs sold[50] for which we have been paid or credited and seventy-seven (77%) percent of the aggregate number of Singles sold for which we have been paid or credited, in each applicable royalty category, after deducting returns, reserves against anticipated returns, rebates and credits on records returned in each royalty category.

(p) "Net Sales through Normal Retail Distribution Channels" shall refer to Net Sales of Phonograph

---

[50] This record company pays royalties on less than 100% of net sales in lieu of taking a standard free goods deduction.

Records hereunder through us or our principal distributor in the country in question for resale through record or other retail stores for which a royalty is payable hereunder (and, without limiting the generality of the foregoing, shall exclude sales or distributions referred to in paragraph A of Exhibit "B");

(q) "New Medium Record" means a record in any medium which is not in general commercial distribution in the United States as of the date hereof (and shall specifically include so-called "DAT", "DCC" and Sony "Mini-discs")

(r) "Phonograph Record" and "Record" shall mean every form of reproduction (whether now known or unknown), embodying sound alone, or sound accompanied by visual images, distributed primarily for home use, school use, juke box use, and use in means of transportation, including, without limitation, discs of any speed or size, reeltoreel tapes, cartridges, cassettes, or other prerecorded tapes;

(s) "Recording Costs" shall mean and include all union scale payments made to the Artist, all payments made to any other individuals rendering services in connection with the recording of the Masters, all other payments which are made pursuant to any applicable law or regulation or the provisions of any collective bargaining agreement between us and any union or guild (including, without limitation, payroll taxes and payments to union pension and welfare funds), all amounts paid or incurred for studio or hall rentals, tapes, engineering, editing, remixing costs, instrument rentals and cartage, all mastering costs, transportation and accommodations, immigration clearances, trademark and service mark searches and clearances, any socalled "per diems" for any individuals (including the Artist) rendering services in connection with recording of the Masters, together with all other amounts paid or incurred in connection with the recording of the Masters which are customarily recognized as recording costs in the recording industry.

(t) "Selection" shall mean a Musical Composition, poem, dramatic work, comedy routine, or other verbal expression;

(u) "Single" shall mean either (i) 7inch disc Phonograph Record (ii) a so-called cassette single, (iii) Digital Record single or New Medium equivalent.

(v) "Suggested Retail List Price" and "SRLP" shall, except as otherwise herein provided, mean: (I) On Phonograph Records (other than Digital Records) sold in the United States, whenever we or our licensees are able to and do specify a retail price at which records are to be sold to members of the public, such retail price as may be specified by us, exclusive of any sales taxes which may be included, if any, in such price; (ii) On Phonograph Records sold outside of the United States by or through our licensees or affiliates (except as otherwise herein provided), an amount equal to one hundred thirty percent (130%) of our licensees' or affiliates', as applicable, published price to dealers of each such Phonograph Record (or if no such published price exists, then an amount equal to one hundred thirty percent (130%) of the actual price charged to dealers for the majority of such Phonograph Records by our licensees or affiliates, as applicable) less value added tax or any other applicable sales tax or similar taxes and/or levies and/or duties which form a recognizable distinct element in the price and which are recovered as part of the selling price to dealers from the inception of production thereof up to and including the ultimate sale thereof to such dealer; (iii) Notwithstanding the foregoing to the contrary, on sales of Digital Records (or other New Medium Records) in the United States, the SRLP shall mean with respect to a particular Digital Record or New Medium Record, in the case of sales by our manufacturer an amount equal to one hundred thirty percent (130%) of the manufacturer's box-lot price to dealers or our manufacturer's box-lot price to independent distributors and military exchanges on sales to those classes of customers.

A.   Notwithstanding anything contained in Paragraph 8 of the Contract:

1. On Phonograph Records sold outside normal retail distribution channels through a direct mail or mail order distribution method (including, without limitation, through socalled "record clubs"), through retail stores in connection with special radio or television advertisements (sometimes referred to as "key outlet marketing"), or through any combination of the foregoing, the royalty rate shall be onehalf (1/2) of the otherwise applicable royalty rate; provided, however, on those Phonograph Records manufactured and sold by a licensee of ours, your royalty shall be an amount equal to fifty (50%) percent of the Net Royalty from the sale of those Phonograph Records.

2. On Phonograph Records sold for use as premiums or in connection with the sale, advertising, or promotion of any other product or service (it being understood that no such Phonograph Record embodying solely Masters shall be sold by us in the United States without your prior written consent), the royalty rate shall be onehalf (1/2) of the otherwise applicable royalty rate and the SRLP of those Phonograph Records shall be deemed to be an amount equal to the monies actually received by us from the sale of those Phonograph Records, unless manufactured and sold by a licensee of ours, in which event the SRLP shall be deemed to be the price used by that licensee in accounting to us.

3. On MidPrice Records the royalty rate shall be threefourths (3/4) of the otherwise applicable royalty rate, and on Budget Records the royalty rate shall be onehalf (1/2) of the otherwise applicable royalty rate.

4. On Phonograph Records sold to the United States Government, its subdivisions, departments or agencies (including Phonograph Records sold for resale through military facilities) or to educational institutions or libraries, the royalty rate shall be onehalf (1/2) of the otherwise applicable royalty rate.

5. On LongPlay Singles and on EPs the royalty rate shall be two thirds (2/3) of the otherwise applicable royalty rate for LPs.

6. On Multiple LPs, the royalty rate shall be the lesser of: (A) the otherwise applicable royalty rate and (B) the otherwise applicable royalty rate multiplied by a fraction, the numerator of which is the SRLP of the Multiple LP and the denominator of which is the product of the SRLP of a topline Conventional singledisc LP and the number of discs contained in the Multiple LP.

7. On Digital Records (other than New Medium Records), the royalty rate shall be eighty (80%) percent of the otherwise applicable royalty rate.[51]

8. On Masters licensed by us to nonaffiliated licensees on a flatfee basis for their manufacture and sale of Phonograph Records or for any other uses, your royalty shall be an amount equal to fifty percent (50%) of the Net FlatFee from the sale of those Phonograph Records or from those other uses of the Masters.

9. With respect to records sold via television and/or radio advertisements through mail order, telephone order or special retail outlets (such as "KTel" type packages), by our licensees, the

---

[51] This is a pretty crummy CD rate. Shoot for 100%, settle on 87 1/2 with escalations as certain sales plateaus are met.

[52] Try to limit this to the accounting period during which the campaign takes place, at the very least.

[53] These are standard packaging deductions.

royalty shall be one-half (1/2) of the net receipts received by us from our licensees less any royalties payable to producers or other royalty participants with respect to such sales. Notwithstanding the foregoing, in the event that we shall sell records directly (and not through licensees) via television and/or radio advertisements through mail or phone order in the United States, then such sales, for purposes of this paragraph, shall be deemed sales through normal retail channels and, accordingly, you shall be paid royalties with respect thereto in accordance with paragraph 8 of the Contract but only with respect to eightyfive (85%) percent of such net sales.

10. In the event that we shall sell or license third parties to sell "records" via telephone, satellite, cable or other direct transmission to the consumer over wire or through the air, such sales shall be deemed sales of such "records" through normal retail channels for all purposes and, accordingly, you shall be paid royalties with respect thereto at the rates set forth in Schedule A2 and in the manner set forth in paragraph 8, as applicable, but with respect to any such sales in the United States royalties shall only be paid with respect to eightyfive (85%) percent of such sales. For purposes of calculating royalties payable in connection with such sales, the SRLP of such "records" shall be deemed to be the thencurrent SRLP of tape copies of such records, and the same packaging deduction shall be made for such sales in accordance with paragraph B.4. of this exhibit as is applicable to tape copies of such records.

11. On Masters licensed by us to nonaffiliated licensees on a royalty basis for their manufacture and sale of Phonograph Records in the United States, your royalty shall be an amount equal to onehalf (1/2) of the Net Royalty from the sale of those Phonograph Records.

12. On Masters promoted or advertised by means of paid television or radio advertising in the Territory outside of the United States, your royalty shall be one half (1/2) of the otherwise applicable royalty.[52]

13. Notwithstanding any provision to the contrary contained herein, the royalty rate for each country of the Territory in respect of net sales through normal retail channels of copies of any record in any New Medium shall be the otherwise applicable royalty rate, but the SRLP of a record in any New Medium shall be deemed to be the SRLP of a Conventional LP in the analog cassette configuration embodying the same Masters as are embodied in that New Medium record applicable to the first net sale of such record through normal retail channels in the applicable country. Except as provided to the contrary in this paragraph A.13., the royalty payable hereunder in respect of Net Sales of any record in any New Medium shall be prorated, reduced, computed and paid in accordance with the provisions of this Contract.

B.   Notwithstanding anything contained herein or in the Contract:

1. No royalties shall be payable on Phonograph Records furnished as free or bonus Phonograph Records to members, applicants, or other participants in any record club or other direct mail distribution method; on Phonograph Records distributed for promotional purposes to radio stations, television stations or networks, record reviewers, or other customary recipients of promotional Phonograph Records; on socalled "promotional sampler" Phonograph Records; on Phonograph Records sold as scrap or as "cutouts"; on records licensed or distributed for airline, background or other transportation use; or on Phonograph Records (whether or not intended for sale by the recipient) distributed as a sales inducement or otherwise and invoiced on a "no charge" basis to independent distributors, subdistributors, dealers and others ("Sales Inducement Records").[53]

---

[52] Try to limit this to the accounting period during which the campaign takes place, at the very least.

[53] You should try to impose a limit on the number of "Sales Inducement Records" distributed, especially since you are only getting paid on 85% of sales to begin with.

2. Royalties on Phonograph Records (whether or not intended for sale by the recipient) sold at a discount to distributors, subdistributors, dealers, or others, whether or not affiliated with us (except for Phonograph Records sold at less than fifty [50%] percent of their regular wholesale price, for which no royalties are payable hereunder) shall be reduced in the same proportion as the regular wholesale price of those Phonograph Records is reduced on those sales.

3. For purposes of computing royalties, there shall be deducted from the SRLP (or other applicable price, if any, upon which royalties are calculated) of Phonograph Records hereunder an amount equal to any excise, sales, value added, or comparable or similar taxes actually included in the price.

4. For purposes of computing royalties, there shall be deducted from the SRLP (or other applicable price, if any, upon which royalties are calculated) of Phonograph Records hereunder an amount equal to ten percent (10%) thereof for Singles (other than so-called cassette singles) packaged in color or other special printed sleeves, and for LPs, EPs, MiniLPs and LongPlay Singles in disc form packaged in our standard singlefold jackets without any special elements (such as, but not limited to, plastic, cardboard, or printed inner sleeves, inserts, or attachments); fifteen percent (15%) thereof for all other LPs, EPs, MiniLPs or LongPlay Singles in disc form (other than in a gate fold sleeve), and for all other Phonograph Records in disc form; twenty percent (20%) thereof for all Phonograph Records in tape, cartridge, cassette (including so-called cassette singles) or reel to reel form which are packaged in standard Norelco type boxes only (whether embodying sound alone or sound accompanied by visual images), and for Home AudioVisual Devices in disc form, and twentyfive (25%) percent for Digital Records, for all phonograph records in tape form packaged in or with anything other than standard Norelco type boxes for all LPs, EPs or Long Play Singles packaged in a gate fold sleeve and for all other recorded devices other than vinyl discs.[53]

5. Royalties shall be computed and paid upon Net Sales for which payment has been received; provided, however, that if any licensee distributing Phonograph Records hereunder through record clubs or other methods of mail order distribution shall compute and pay royalties to us on those Phonograph Records on less than one hundred (100%) percent of Net Sales, your royalties hereunder on those Phonograph Records shall be computed and paid on the same percentage of sales as that licensee shall utilize in computing and paying to us royalties on those Phonograph Records.

6. Phonograph Records distributed in the United States by any of our affiliated branch wholesalers shall be deemed sold for the purposes of this Contract only if sold by that affiliated branch wholesaler to one of its independent third party customers.

7. The royalty payable to you hereunder on a Phonograph Record or other device embodying Masters together with other master recordings shall be computed by multiplying the otherwise applicable royalty rate by a fraction, the numerator of which shall be the number of Selections contained on the Masters which are embodied on that Phonograph Record or other device and the denominator of which shall be the total number of royalty bearing Selections embodied on that Phonograph Record or other device.

8. The royalty payable to you hereunder and the Recording Costs chargeable to you hereunder on a Master recorded by you jointly with any other artist or musician to whom we are obligated to pay a royalty in respect of that Master (it being understood that we shall not, without your prior consent, cause you to record any such joint recording) shall be computed by multiplying the otherwise applicable royalty rate and Recording Costs by a fraction, the numerator of which shall be one

---

[54] These are standard packaging deductions.

(1) and the denominator of which shall be the sum of one (1) and the total number of other artists or musicians whose performances are embodied on that Master.

C.   Notwithstanding anything to the contrary contained herein with respect to records sold in any country of the Territory in which governmental or other authorities place limits on the royalty rates permissible for remittances to the United States in respect of records sold therein, the royalty rate payable to you hereunder in respect of sales of records in each such territory shall equal the lesser of (A) the otherwiseapplicable royalty rate payable in respect of records sold therein, and (B) the effective royalty rate permitted by such governmental or other authority for remittances to the United States, less (C) the sum of (1) a royalty equivalent to four (4%) percent of the retail list price (or other applicable base against which the applicable royalty percentage rate is applied pursuant to the terms hereof), and (2) such monies as we or our licensees shall be required to pay to all applicable union funds in respect of said sales.

D.   We may at any time elect to utilize a different method of computing royalties from that specified above so long as such method or methods are applicable to substantially all persons similarly engaged by us, and provided that no such method reduces the net monies due you. In the event that we shall no longer designate an SRLP for records hereunder in any particular configuration (e.g. vinyl disc albums, cassette tape albums, 7inch single records, 12inch single records, compact discs, MiniLPs) and price category (e.g. fullprice, midprice and budget records) in the United States, then for the purpose of computing royalties hereunder with respect to sales of records in such configuration and price category through normal retail channels in the United States, the SRLP of such records in such configuration and price category shall be deemed to be a dollar amount computed by multiplying our price to subdistributors (before consideration of any discount resulting from the distribution of Free Goods) for such records in such configuration and price category by a fraction, the numerator of which is the SRLP for the majority of our records in such configuration and price category as of the date when we cease to designate an SRLP for records in such configuration and price category, and the denominator of which is our price (or our distributor's price) to subdistributors for the majority of our records in such configuration and price category as of the date when we cease to designate an SRLP for records in such configuration and price category (before consideration of any discount resulting from the distribution of Free Goods).

E.   We shall pay you a royalty with respect to the exploitation for commercial purposes of Videos as follows:

1. With respect to all incomeproducing exploitation of Videos for "commercial purposes" (as defined in paragraph 14(e)) by us or our licensees other than the uses specified in paragraph E(2) hereinbelow, a royalty equal to fifty (50%) percent of the Adjusted Gross Video Receipts. "Adjusted Gross Video Receipts" means one hundred (100%) percent of monies actually received by us (or credited to our account) in the United States from the such exploitation of Videos in the Territory less the following deductions in the following order: (A) twenty-five (25%) percent thereof as a distribution fee; (B) all outofpocket distribution expenses actually paid or incurred by us other than our general overhead expenses; (C) any and all payments required to be made to third parties, including without limitation, to unions or guilds or to publishers of non-Controlled Compositions (but expressly excluding any "Royalty Participant" as that term is hereinafter defined) in connection with the production and/or exploitation of Videos; (D) all sales, gross receipts, foreign withholding, excise, use, value added, personal, property or similar taxes paid or incurred by us with respect to the production or exploitation of Videos.

2. In the event that we manufacture and distribute in the United States audiovisual devices intended primarily for home consumer use ("Home A/V Devices") embodying one (1) or more Videos, alone or together with one (1) or more audio-only recordings, then we shall pay to you a royalty with respect to net sales of such Home A/V Devices (subject to the proration provisions hereinbelow) equal to ten (10%) percent of our Video Royalty Base Price (as hereinafter defined) in

lieu of any other sum with respect to such exploitation. Such royalties shall at all times be subject to retroactive adjustment for returns, refunds, credits, settlements, allowances, rebates, discounts and other similar adjustments. As used herein the "Video Royalty Base Price" means the wholesale price to subdistributors of such Home A/V Devices less an amount equal to ten percent (10%) thereof.

     3. In the event we couple Videos with videos which are not Videos hereunder, the amounts otherwise payable to you hereunder with respect to such coupled Videos shall be multiplied by a fraction, the numerator of which is the number of Videos involved and the denominator of which is the aggregate number of videos (including Videos) involved.

     4. The royalties payable in accordance with this paragraph E shall be inclusive of all royalties that may be payable to the producers of the Masters embodied on each Video, the publishers of any Musical Compositions embodied on the Video, any unions or guilds who are entitled to a royalty or any other payment in connection with the production and/or exploitation of the Videos and any directors or other third parties who are entitled to a royalty in connection with the exploitation of thereof (collectively, "Royalty Participants"). In the event that we make any such payments to Royalty Participants, we shall have the right to deduct such payments from royalties otherwise payable to you in connection with Videos.

SCHEDULE A1

Recording Fund

Album	Minimum	Maximum
First Album	$150,000	N/A
Second Album	$200,000	$400,000
Third Album	$250,000	$500,000
Fourth Album	$300,000	$600,000
Fifth Album	$350,000	$700,000
Sixth Album	$400,000	$800,000
Seventh Album	$450,000	$900,000
Eighth Album	$500,000	$1,000,000

SCHEDULE A2

Royalty Rates

Payable on USNRC Net Sales:
     Twelve percent (12%) percent on LPs.[55]
     Nine percent (9%) percent on Singles.
Payable on Ex-US:
     Eighty-five percent (85%) of US rate: Canada
     Seventy-five percent (75%) of US rate: EEC, Japan, Australia
     Sixty percent (60%) of US rate: Rest of World

---

[55] Twelve percent isn't really an awful royalty rate for your first album, but the rate should increase (by at least one or one-half percent) as certain sales levels are met. You should also be able to get a higher starting royalty rate for each album under the deal. For example, you might ask for a 13% royalty for album two, a 13 1/2% royalty for album three, and so on.

SAMPLE RECORDING BUDGET

PROPOSED RECORDING BUDGET[1]

LAWN CHOCOLATE
C/O Thrifty Scot Management, Inc.
1234 Main Street
New York, NY 10000
Phone (555) 555-6232

ARTIST: Lawn Chocolate
PRODUCER: Brian McPherson[2]
STARTING DATE: July 1, 1998

ENGINEER: Roger The Engineer
STUDIO: Thrifty Scot Sound
TODAY'S DATE: May 22, 1998

PRE-PRODUCTION

Rehearsal Space	7 days @ $200	$1,400.00
Studio		$0.00
Rentals 8-track mixer & misc.		$850.00
Tape		$0.00
Subtotal: Pre-Production		$2,250.00

TRACKING & OVERDUBS

Studio	31 days @ $600.00	$18,600.00
Tape	2-Inch: 12 reels @ $145.00	$1,740.00
DATS	10 @ $10.00	$100.00
Cass	25 @ $2.50	$62.50
Outboard Rental	31 days @ $300	$9,300.00
Equipment Rental		$1,500.00
Cartage		$500.00
Subtotal: Tracking & Overdubs		$31,802.50

MIXING

Studio	17 days @ $1,750.00	$29,750.00
Tape	1/2 inch: 10 reels @ $70.00	$700.00
DATS:	10 @ $10.00	$100.00
Cass:	25 @ $2.50	$62.50
Outboard Rental:	NA[3]	
Subtotal: Mixing		$30,612.50

---

[1] Remember that all major labels require a written recording budget before they let you go into the studio. It might look something like this.

[2] What I really want to do is produce.

[3] Mixing studios are pretty expensive. If you're paying $1,750 a day, the studio better have nearly every conceivable piece of outboard gear. This studio apparently does, hence no allocation for outboard gear at this stage.

TALENT (AFM Rates)[4]
Fred Johnson[5]

AFM[6]			
Scale[7]	15 sides @	$285.47	$4,282.05
Pension[8]	10% of scale	$28.55	$428.21
AFTRA[9]			
Scale	40 sides @ $132.50		$5,300.00
Pension	11% of scale		$583.00

John Doe

AFM		
Scale	15 Sides @ $285.47	$4,282.05
Pension	10% of scale $28.55	$428.21

Other Musicians

Drums	$4,000.00
Bass	$3,000.00
Subtotal: Talent	$22,303.52

TRAVEL & LIVING EXPENSES

Air Transport		$2,000.00
Car Rental	55 days @ $17.00	$935.00
Apartment	55 days	$3,000.00
Per Diem	55 days @ $25.00 each	$2,750.00
Subtotal: T&L		$8,685.00

MISCELLANEOUS

General miscellaneous	$1,000.00

ENGINEER FEES

Roger the Engineer	31 days @ $250.00	$7,750.00

MASTERING $3,500.00

PRODUCER ADVANCE

Brian McPherson	$30,000.00

TOTAL BUDGET $137,903.52

---

[4] Most major labels are signatories to agreements with the two major US music unions, the American Federation of Musicians (AFM) and the American Federation of Television and Radio Artists (AFTRA). If you sign to a major label, they will probably require all musicians in your band to join the AFM. Vocalists will be asked to join AFTRA. Those who sing and play need to join both unions. The record label's agreements with the unions require the labels to pay a minimum amount to recording artists during recording sessions. Most recording agreements deduct the scale payments from your recording fund.

[5] I should mention that it costs money to join the unions. If you can't get the record company to pay the fees for you, you will have to foot the bill.

[6] The AFM Phonograph Record Labor Agreement establishes scale payments for leaders, instrumentalists, contractors, arrangers, copyists and orchestrators working on a union recording session.

[7] Artists entitled to a royalty of at least 3% under a recording agreement are called "royalty artists." Royalty artists receive minimum union scale per track, no matter how long it takes to cut the track.

[8] 10% of scale payments must be paid into the union pension fund on your behalf.

[9] AFTRA represents singers, actors, announcers, narrators and sound effects artists working in the TV, radio and record industries. Since Fred is a singer and a musician, he is a member of AFTRA and the AFM. John doesn't sing, so he needn't worry about AFTRA.

SAMPLE INDIE PROFIT-SPLIT LICENSING AGREEMENT

SWERVE RECORDS
1234 Main Street
Anytown, CA 90000

January 1, 1998

John Doe and Fred Smith
PKA Lawn Chocolate
1111 San Viejo Boulevard
Los Angeles, CA 90000

Re: Lawn Chocolate -w- Swerve Records - Exclusive Master License Agreement ("Agreement")

Dear John and Fred:

The following, when signed by you and us shall constitute our Agreement until a more formal agreement can be executed:

1 - **TERRITORY**: The World.

2 - **PRODUCT**: Newly recorded master recordings ("Masters") sufficient to constitute one (1) full-length album ("Album").

3 - **ADVANCE**: Ten Thousand Dollars ($10,000.00) payable at the following times and in the following manner: One Thousand Seven Hundred Dollars ($1,700.00) on February 1, 1998; One Thousand Six Hundred-Fifty Dollars ($1,650.00) on March 1, 1998; One Thousand Six Hundred-Fifty Dollars ($1,650.00) on April 1, 1998; and $5,000 (minus any recording costs paid directly by Swerve) payable on delivery of the Album with accompanying artwork. All advances to you or on your behalf hereunder (including any recording costs paid by us to you or to a third party on your behalf) are recoupable from any future monies and royalties payable to you hereunder.

4 - **TERM**: Swerve shall have the exclusive territory wide right to exploit the Album and the Masters embodied therein in any and all media for a period ending the later of: seven (7) years following initial U.S. release of the Album or the end of the semi-annual accounting period during which recoupment of advances paid to you hereunder occurs. Swerve shall have a non-exclusive six (6) month sell off period following the end of the term.

5 - **ROYALTIES/MECHANICAL ROYALTIES/ACCOUNTINGS**: Payable per the standard Swerve royalty provisions, a copy of which is attached hereto.

6 - **STANDARD TERMS/MORE FORMAL AGREEMENT**: It is contemplated that you and we shall enter into a long form agreement incorporating the foregoing terms plus such additional terms (to be negotiated in good faith) as are customarily contained in artist recording agreements in the United States music industry, including, without limitation, recording restrictions and conditions, notice provisions, etc. Unless and until such more formal agreement is executed, this Agreement, which is deemed to incorporate such additional terms and provisions, shall constitute a binding Agreement between you and us which may only be amended by a written instrument executed by all of the parties hereto.

If the foregoing is not consistent with your understanding and agreement, then please contact us immediately as we are proceeding in reliance thereof; otherwise, please sign in the respective spaces provided below for your names.

Very truly yours,

SWERVE RECORDS

By:_____
    An Authorized Signatory

AGREED AND ACCEPTED:

ARTIST

By: _____
    John Doe
    Soc. Sec. #_____

By: _____
    Fred Smith
    Soc. Sec. #_____

SWERVE RECORDS - STANDARD ROYALTY PROVISIONS

I. ROYALTIES (inclusive of all payments to Artist, third parties, publishers, songwriters and the producers of the masters delivered hereunder): [1]

    (a) On Records sold by Swerve through Pull Back & Stop Records ("Distributor"): Swerve shall pay to Artist an all-in (i.e., inclusive of producer, mechanical and artist royalties) royalty in the amount of sixty percent (60%)[2] of Swerve's "net profits" in connection with the sale of the Record ("Artist's Share"), after deduction from the Artist's Share of any advances or recording costs paid to Artist or to a third party on Artist's behalf hereunder. As used herein, the term "net profit" shall mean all gross income actually paid to Swerve by Distributor from the sale of such record, minus all legitimate costs and expenses incurred by Swerve in connection with the sale and promotion of such Record ("Expenses"). Expenses include but are not limited to: manufacturing costs, artwork preparation costs, advertising costs, independent promotion costs, independent publicity costs, mastering costs, recording costs, free goods, postage, shipping and video production.[3]

---

[1] In this type of deal, "all-in" takes on new meaning. As you can see, the profit split is inclusive of record royalties *and* mechanical royalties.

[2] Swerve is nice — they pay 60% of net profits instead of the standard 50%.

[3] If you enter into a deal like this having already spent your own money on recording costs, make sue that any such recording costs are deemed "Expenses" under the deal, but only to the extent that you don't receive an advance sufficient to cover those costs. Otherwise, you end up paying for all the recording costs out of your share of the net profits, and that kind of runs counter to the idea of a true profit split.

(b) On Records sold by our licensees: Swerve shall pay to Artist an all-in (i.e., inclusive of producer, mechanical and artist royalties) royalty in the amount of fifty percent (50%) of Swerve's "net profits" in connection with the sale of the Record ("Artist's Share"), after deduction from the Artist's Share of any advances paid to Artist hereunder. For the purposes of this paragraph 1 (b), "net profits" shall mean any advances or royalties received by Swerve (or credited to Swerve's account in reduction of a previous advance) from the licensee with respect to such Record, minus any legitimate costs or expenses (including, but not limited to, legal fees and costs of collection) incurred by Swerve with respect to the negotiation and execution of such agreement.

(c) On Masters licensed for non-record use (whether such license is secured by Swerve or Artist): Swerve shall pay to Artist an all-in (i.e., inclusive of producer, mechanical and artist royalties) royalty in the amount of fifty percent (50%) of Swerve's "net profits" in connection with the license of any Master for a non-record use (e.g., master use licenses for motion pictures and advertisements) ("Artist's Share"), after deduction from the Artist's Share of any advances paid to Artist hereunder. For the purposes of this paragraph 1 (c), "net profits" shall mean any advances, fees or royalties received by Swerve (or credited to Swerve's account in reduction of a previous advance) with respect to such license, minus any legitimate costs or expenses (including, but not limited to, legal fees and costs of collection) incurred by Swerve with respect to the negotiation and execution of such license.

(d) Notwithstanding anything to the contrary contained herein, no royalties shall be paid to Artist unless and until Swerve, in the aggregate, shows a net profit with respect to the sale of Artist's Records hereunder and until all advances and/or recording costs paid to Artist or to a third party on Artist's behalf are recouped from Artist's Share of net profits (the foregoing shall not apply to recording costs paid by Swerve and recouped by Swerve prior to the showing of a net profit).

2. MUSICAL COMPOSITIONS. Artist hereby waives its right to receive mechanical royalties in connection with the exploitation of Masters and Records hereunder, and Artist hereby grants to Swerve a license for the use of the musical compositions written and/or controlled by Artist and embodied on the Masters free of charge with respect to all exploitations of the Masters pursuant to this Agreement, including, but not limited to, the mechanical reproduction of such musical compositions on audio-only records, audio-visual recordings and CD-ROMS.

SAMPLE DEMO AGREEMENT

Thrifty Scot Records, Inc.
1234 Main Street
Anytown, CA 90000

Dated: June 1, 1998

John Doe and Fred Smith, collectively pka
"Lawn Chocolate"
c/o Art Cheatum, Esq.
Dewey, Cheatum & Howe
11111 San Viejo Boulevard
Los Angeles, California 90000

Dear John and Fred:

Thrifty Scot Records, Inc. (hereinafter referred to as "Company" or "we") hereby request you to produce and record for us four (4) demonstration recordings (each such demonstration recording being individually referred to herein as a "Demo" and all such demonstration recordings being referred to herein as the "Demos'") embodying your performances, and you hereby agree to produce and record the Demos in accordance with the following provisions:

1.   You shall produce and record the Demos, and deliver them to us, within thirty (30) days after the date of this agreement.

2.   You shall engage the individual producer and all musicians, recording studios, or other personnel or facilities for the recording sessions for the Demos.

3.   You shall pay and be solely responsible for all recording costs (as the term "recording costs" is defined below) for the Demos. You shall deliver to us copies of substantiating invoices, receipts, vouchers, and similar satisfactory documentary evidence of such recording costs at the same time you deliver the Demos to us. Promptly after execution hereof we shall pay to you the sum of Five Thousand Dollars ($5,000.00) in full consideration of all rights granted, services rendered and materials delivered hereunder.

4.   You shall deliver to us a two-track stereo tape and all multi-track master tapes for each Demo. All original session tapes and any derivatives or reproductions thereof shall also be delivered to us or maintained at a recording studio or other location designated or approved by us, in our name and under our control.

5.   (a) All Demos, and your performances embodied thereon, are and shall be entirely our property, in perpetuity, throughout the universe, during and from their creation. You agree that, upon our request, you and all other persons rendering services in connection with the Demo will execute and deliver to us a written assignment (in a form satisfactory to us) of all sound copyright rights (including renewal and extension rights) that you or such persons may have.

(b) Notwithstanding anything to the contrary contained in this Agreement, we shall not commercially exploit the Demos without your prior written consent, which you may withhold for any reason.

6.   (a) We shall notify you in writing at your address first set forth above within ninety (90) days[1] after your delivery to us of the Demos whether or not we desire to enter into a recording contract with you for your recording services and neither you nor any third party shall offer your recording services to any person other than us or play the Demos[2] for any person other than us during such ninety (90) day period.

        (b) If we notify you within such ninety (90) day period that we desire to enter into a recording contract with you, then you and we shall promptly begin good faith negotiations regarding the material terms and provisions of such recording contract and during such negotiations neither you nor any third party shall offer your recording services to any person other than us or play the Demos for (or deliver them to) any person other than us. If you and we are unable to agree on the material terms of a recording contract after such good faith negotiations, then you shall have the right to offer your recording services to third parties and to enter into a recording contract ("Third Party Recording Contract") with any such third party ("Third Party Record Company") but only if the terms and provisions of the Third Party Recording Contract are more favorable to you[3] than the terms offered to you by us. Notwithstanding the foregoing, in no event shall you or any third party have the right to offer your recording services to any person other than us or to play the Demos for any person other than us prior to sixty (60)[4] days after the commencement of negotiations regarding the terms of a recording contract between you and us.

        (c) If we shall fail to notify you within the ninety (90) day period referred to in subparagraph 6(a) above that we desire to enter into a recording contract with you (or if we notify you that we do not desire to enter into such an agreement with you), then you shall have the right to offer your recording services to third parties for the purpose of entering into a Third Party Recording Contract and (subject to paragraph 8 below) to use the Demos for the purpose of attempting to induce any Third Party Record Company to enter into a Third Party Recording Contract.

7.   If you and we enter into a recording contract, we shall have the right to recoup any and all sums paid by us pursuant paragraph 3 hereof (and any other costs incurred by us in connection with the Demos) from any and all royalties (excluding mechanical royalties) payable to you thereunder.

8.   If you enter into a Third Party Recording Contract, you shall cause such contract to provide for the Third Party Record Company to reimburse us for all sums paid by us pursuant to paragraph 3 hereunder from the first monies payable to you under the Third Party Recording Contract.[5] Promptly after we have received such reimbursement, we shall assign to you or your designee all of our right, title and interest in and to the Demos.[6]

9.   You represent, warrant and agree that:

        (a)   You are free to enter into and perform this agreement and you are and will be free to enter into and perform a recording contract in respect of your recording services if you and we agree to enter into same.

---

[1] Try to reduce this to thirty days (or even less). The record company should know within a few days whether the demos are compelling enough to sign the band, and you don't want to be left hanging.

[2] Kind of hard to police, don't you think?

[3] This means better money, royalties, etc.

[4] This time period should also be reduced. You will know whether a deal can be made after a few phone calls between your attorney and the record company business affairs people.

[5] You can try to eliminate this, but it's not totally unfair.

[6] Ask for the right to purchase the Demos even if you don't enter into a Third Party recording Contract. You may want to put them out yourself.

(b)   Each Demo shall be free of all liens and encumbrances, and there will be no claims, demands or actions pending or threatened with respect thereto.

(c)   Other than as specifically set forth in this Agreement, we shall be subject to no costs, fees, advances or other charges for or in connection with the recording of the Demos. Without limiting the foregoing, except for the payment provided in paragraph 3 hereof, you shall be solely responsible for and shall pay, to any producer of the Demos, to any and all other persons participating in the production of the Demos, and to any other third parties, any and all compensation that may be payable to them by reason of the production of the Demos hereunder. Notwithstanding the foregoing, if we elect to pay any costs in connection with the Demos that are over and above that amount described in paragraph 3 above, which we are under no obligation to do, then all such costs shall be subject to the provisions of paragraphs 7 and 8 above.

10.   Definitions: (a) "person" means a person, firm or corporation: (b) "Demo" means a fully-mixed, edited, equalized and leadered two-track stereophonic original studio (as opposed to "live") 15 i.p.s. quarter Inch tape recording, theretofore unreleased, that embodies a performance featuring only you, that has been recorded by you in a recording studio, and that has a playing time of not less than two and one-half (2 1/2) minutes; (c) "selection" or "composition" means a single musical composition, including a medley, and all components thereof: (d) "recording costs" shall refer to all direct costs incurred in the production of the Demos, including, without limitation, the sums paid to you, the individual producer(s), musicians, vocalists, conductors, arrangers, orchestrators, copyists; all costs incurred in connection with the rental and cartage of instruments, music and equipment; transportation costs, hotel and living expenses incurred in connection with the preparation for your attendance and the attendance of all other artists. The individual producer(s), musicians and other essential personnel at recording sessions; the cost of any studio or rehearsal hall rental; payments to sound engineers; all costs incurred for tape, editing, mixing and other similar functions; and all other costs and expenses incurred hereunder that are now or hereafter recognized as recording costs in the phonograph record industry.

11.   This Agreement shall be effective as of the date first set forth above. Nothing contained herein shall constitute a partnership between or a joint venture by the parties hereto, or constitute either party the agent or employee of the other. This Agreement shall be governed by the laws of the State of California applicable to contracts made and to be wholly performed in the State of California.

Very truly yours,

Thrifty Scot Records, Inc.

By:_____

AGREED AND ACCEPTED:

_____

John Doe

_____

Fred Smith

Individually and collectively pka "Lawn Chocolate"

SAMPLE PRODUCER AGREEMENT WITH LETTER OF DIRECTION

BIFF LOMAN
c/o Art Cheatum, Esq.
Dewey, Cheatum & Howe
11111 San Viejo Boulevard
Los Angeles, California 90000

Dated as of 1 April, 1998

Fred Dobbs
c/o Jethro Bodine, Esq.
1234 Burton Way
Beverly Hills, CA 90211

Dear Fred:

The following, when fully executed, will constitute the agreement between Fred Dobbs (hereinafter referred to as "Producer" or "you") on the one hand, and Biff Loman (hereinafter referred to as "Artist" or "I" or "me") on the other hand, with respect to my engagement of your producing, engineering and mixing services with respect to master recordings embodying my performances ("Masters").[1]

I.   PRODUCING ENGAGEMENT

01   I hereby engage you to record, produce, mix and deliver to Thrifty Scot Records, Inc. ("Company") Masters embodying my featured performances. The Masters are intended to be embodied on the first long playing record album (the "LP") required to be recorded by Artist pursuant to the recording agreement ("Record Contract") by and between Artist and Company dated May 1, 1997, as amended.

02   The Producer's services will be rendered in connection with the recording of no less than sixteen (16) Masters (the "Product Commitment").

03   The term of this agreement shall commence upon the full execution hereof and shall continue until such time as you shall have completed your services hereunder. Your prompt, exclusive and continuous rendition of services according to the agreed upon schedule of recording and mixing (which schedule is attached hereto and is incorporated by this reference as Exhibit A)[2] is of the essence of this agreement.[3]

---

[1] Well lookee here! Ol' Biff has gone solo and got hisself a record deal!

[2] Don't look for this schedule — it doesn't exist.

[3] This last bit of language was inserted at Biff's request, because he was worried that Fred wouldn't finish his prior gig in time to start this project. Accordingly, Biff wanted to be able to fire Fred if he was even a day late starting on the project

2.   **RECORDING PROCEDURE**

01   The Producer will follow the procedure set forth below in connection with Masters made under this agreement:

(a) The Producer shall notify the appropriate Local of the American Federation of Musicians in advance of each recording session.

(b) The Producer shall timely supply Artist with all of the information it reasonably requires in order: (1) to make payments due in connection with such Masters; (2) to comply with any other material obligations I or Artist may have in connection with the making of such Masters; and (3) to prepare to release records derived from such Masters. Without limiting the generality of clause (2) of the preceding sentence, the Producer shall furnish Artist with all information it requires (including sample clearances with respect to samples furnished by Producer or included at Producer's request) to comply with its material obligations under its union agreements, including, without limitation, the following:[4]

(i)   If a session is held to record new tracks intended to be mixed with existing tracks (and if such information is requested by the American Federation of Musicians), the dates and places of the prior sessions at which such existing tracks were made, and the AFM Phonograph Recording Contract (Form "B").

(ii)   Each change of title of any composition listed in an AFM Phonograph Recording Contract (Form "B").

(iii)   A listing of all the musical selections contained in recordings made under this agreement.

(iv)   Complete written Musician Contracts (AFM Form B-44), W-4 Forms, AFTRA Reports for recording sessions and INS Form I-9 (immigration clearances) in connection with Masters hereunder.

(v)   All union contract forms and report forms for recording sessions hereunder, all bills pertaining to such recording sessions, and all payroll forms (including, but not limited to, all 19, W4 and other withholding tax forms) pertaining to such recording sessions shall be submitted by you to Company within forty-eight (48) hours after each recording session in accordance with the rules and regulations of all unions having jurisdiction over the recording thereof, so that Company shall be able to make all payroll payments without penalty for late payment. In the event that Company or I shall incur any penalties for late payments solely by reason of your failure to comply with the material terms and provisions of the immediately preceding sentence for reasons under your control, you shall, upon my or Company's demand, promptly pay me or Company an amount equal to such penalties from any monies payable by me to you hereunder.

---

[4] We haven't talked too much about unions in this book, but you should know that most major labels are signatories to agreements with the major music unions, the American federation of Musicians (AFM) and the American Federation of Television and Radio Artists (AFTRA). Since Thrifty Scot is a signatory to agreements with both of these unions, any recording sessions conducted under Thrifty Scot's recording license must comply with union requirements. This means that only union members are supposed to play and sing on the recordings and that all union member musicians and vocalist must be paid according to union scale. Since the producer is getting paid a bunch of money to conduct recording sessions, he is charged with the responsibility of getting all of the appropriate union paperwork together.

(c) The Producer will deliver to me fully mixed, edited, and equalized Masters, commercially[5] and technically satisfactory to Company and me for Company's manufacture and release for sale of records, as well as all original and duplicate Masters of the material recorded, together with all reasonably necessary licenses (excluding mechanical licenses) and appropriate permissions. Each Master will be clearly marked to identify the Artist as the recording artist, and to show the title(s) of the Composition(s) and recording date(s). Each such mix shall be subject to the approval of Company and me.[6] The musical compositions to be recorded by me hereunder shall be designated by me, after consultation with you. All individuals rendering services in connection with the recording of the Masters shall be subject to my approval. Company shall have the right and opportunity to have Company's representatives attend each such recording session.

(d) No recording sessions shall be commenced hereunder nor shall any commitments be made or costs incurred in connection therewith unless and until a proposed recording budget for the Masters to be recorded at such sessions has been submitted by you[7] in writing and approved in writing by me and Company. Neither Company nor I shall be responsible for any payments to any individuals rendering services in connection with the recording of the Masters which exceed union scale unless such excess and the proposed recipient thereof are specified in said budget and approved by me and Company. In the event the recording costs of any Masters shall exceed the approved budget therefor for reasons solely within your control, you shall, upon my or Company's demand, promptly reimburse me or Company for all such excess costs, or I may, at my election, deduct an amount equal to such excess costs from any and all royalties payable to you.

3. **RECORDING COSTS**

01 As between Producer and Artist, Artist will pay all talent costs (including, without limitation, all costs of instrumental, vocal and other personnel and arrangements and copying specifically approved by me in respect of the recording of such Masters).

02 The term "Recording Costs" shall have the same meaning herein as accorded the term in the Record Contract.[8]

4. **ADVANCES**

01 As compensation for your production services hereunder, you shall receive an all-in, recoupable, non-returnable fee of twenty-five thousand dollars ($25,000.00) ("Advance"). One-half (1/2) of such amount shall be paid on commencement of pre-production and the balance shall be paid on delivery of the Masters in fully finished form to Company's satisfaction and full execution of this agreement.

---

[5] The producer's attorney should check to see if this is the delivery standard that applies to Biff under Biff's recording agreement. If not, he should try to get "commercially" taken out. On the other hand, Biff is paying Fred a lot of money to make his recordings sound radio ready, so he's not about to take this out.

[6] This language is well and good, but Fred isn't going to remix any masters without an additional advance.

[7] The producer is supposed to put together the budget for the project (along with the artist's manager and A&R person)

[8] Fred's attorney should ask for a copy of the definitions in Biff's recording agreement.

5. <u>RIGHTS IN RECORDINGS</u>

01   Each Master made under this agreement, from the inception of recording, will be considered a "work made for hire" for Company; if any such Master is determined not to be a "work made for hire," all rights in it which are attributable to Producer's participation in its authorship will be deemed transferred to Company by this agreement. All Masters made under this agreement, from the inception of recording, and all matrices and records manufactured from them, together with the performances embodied on them, shall be Company's sole property, free from any claims whatsoever by you or any other person; and Company shall have the exclusive right to copyright the Master in its name as the owner and author of them and to secure any and all renewals and extensions of such copyright throughout the world. You will execute and deliver to Company such instruments of transfer and other documents regarding their rights in the Masters as I or it may reasonably request to carry out the purposes of this agreement, and I may sign such documents in your name and make appropriate disposition of them in the event that you fail to do so within five (5) days of my written request. Upon your written request, I will provide you with copies of any such documents executed on your behalf. Without limiting the generality of the foregoing, Company, Artist and any person authorized by Artist shall have the unlimited and exclusive rights to manufacture records by any method now or hereafter known, derived from the Masters made under this agreement, and to sell, transfer or otherwise deal in the same under any trademarks, trade names and labels, or to refrain from such manufacture, sale and dealing, throughout the universe.[9]

6. <u>NAMES AND LIKENESSES</u>

01   (a)   Subject to your prior approval in each instance (which such approval shall not be unreasonably withheld) Company, Artist and any licensee of ours each shall have the right and may grant to others the right to reproduce, print, publish, or disseminate in any medium your name, portraits, pictures and likeness, as well as biographical material concerning you, as news or information, for the purposes of trade, or for advertising purposes in connection with the sale and promotion of phonograph records.

(b)   I will accord you a credit on the liner notes and outside packaging of all records embodying Masters and in all 1/2 page or larger advertisements in national trade publications (including Billboard Magazine page one "strip" ads) in the following form: "Produced by Fred Dobbs." No inadvertent failure by me or Company to accord you such credit shall be deemed a breach of this agreement, provided that upon your written notice to me or Company of any such failure, Company and I shall use best efforts to prospectively cure such failure.[10]

7. <u>ROYALTIES</u>[11]

01   (a) Conditioned upon your full and faithful performance of all of the material terms and provisions hereof, you shall be paid in respect of the sale by Company, or the Company's licensees, of phonograph records embodying the Masters recorded hereunder and in respect of any other exploitation by Company, or the Company's licensees, of such Masters, the following royalties upon the terms hereinafter set forth:

---

[9] Absent this language, an argument can be made that the producer shares in the copyright of the masters because he helped create them. This language establishes that the masters are works made for hire and that the copyright does not belong to the producer. This is standard stuff and not subject to negotiation.

[10] Credit is important to a producer because a prominent credit on a particularly good and/or successful record is the best advertising a producer can get.

[11] We discussed producer royalties in sickening detail back in Chapter Five. This is a pretty standard deal.

(b) In respect of net sales of phonograph records embodying solely the LP through normal retail distribution channels in the United States (such sales are hereinafter referred to as "U.S. LP Retail Sales"), you shall receive a basic royalty at the rate of three percent (3%) ("Your Basic LP Rate") of the suggested retail list price ("SRLP") from time to time of such records.

(c) Your royalty rate for sales of records embodying the Masters which are not U.S. LP Retail Sales shall bear the same ratio to Your Basic LP Rate as Artist's royalty rate under the Record Contract in respect of such sales bears to Artist's basic royalty rate in respect of U.S. LP Retail Sales (without regard to any escalations with respect thereto), as of the date hereof (herein referred to as "Artist's Base Rate").

(d) Except as provided hereinabove, your royalty for sales of records embodying the Masters shall otherwise be reduced, computed or otherwise determined in the same manner and on the same terms and conditions as is Artist's royalty in respect of such sales (with escalations only as provided in paragraph 7.01 (e) below). As used herein, the term "computed" shall include all reductions in royalties or royalty base price provided for in the Record Contract, including, but not limited to, any reductions thereunder for "free goods" and packaging or container charges, but shall expressly not include any escalation other than as provided for in paragraph 7.01 (e) hereof.

(e) Your Basic LP Rate pursuant to clause 7.01 (b) shall apply to the first five hundred thousand (500,000) units of U.S. LP Retail Sales of the LP consisting entirely of the Masters. Notwithstanding the foregoing, Your Basic LP Rate shall be increased in the same proportion and in the same manner as the royalty credited to Artist by Company is increased on U.S. LP Retail Sales of the LP consisting entirely of the Masters in excess of five hundred thousand (500,000) units and on U.S. LP Retail Sales of the LP consisting entirely of the Masters in excess of One Million (1,000,000) units. By way of example only, the escalation of Your Basic LP Rate shall be determined by multiplying Artist's sales based royalty escalation (for example, 1%) by a fraction, the numerator of which shall be Your Basic LP Rate and the denominator of which is Artist's Base Rate.

(f) Notwithstanding any of the foregoing, no royalty shall be payable to you hereunder unless and until all Recording Costs incurred with respect to the master recordings embodied on the LP (including the Masters) have been recouped by the Company from "Net Royalties" earned in respect of the master recordings (including the Masters) embodied in the LP. As used herein, the term "Net Royalties" shall mean, with respect to the Masters and any particular use thereof, the royalty payable to Artist pursuant to the Record Contract less the royalty payable to you and any royalty payable to other producers or mixers rendering services in connection with the master recordings embodied in the LP (including the Masters). After recoupment of such Recording Costs in accordance with the preceding sentence, Artist shall thereafter credit to your account for payment, at the next regular accounting date hereunder, all royalties, if any, earned by you hereunder retroactive to the first such record sold embodying the Masters, subject to recoupment from such royalties of the Advance and all other advances paid to you hereunder.

(g) With respect to records where Artist is entitled to a percentage of Company's net receipts in connection with the exploitation of a Master produced hereunder, you shall be entitled to that portion of Artist's net receipts determined by multiplying Artist's share of such receipts by a fraction, the numerator of which shall be Your Basic LP Rate with respect to such Masters and the denominator of which is Artist's Base Rate, provided that with respect to so-called videos, your share of such net receipts shall be fifty percent (50%) of the sum computed pursuant to the preceding formula. [12]

---

[12] The theory on the reduced video royalty is that the recording is only half of the video (with the visual image comprising the other half).

(h) Without limiting the generality of the foregoing, the royalty payable to you hereunder with respect to any phonograph record embodying the Masters hereunder, together with any other master recordings, shall be computed by multiplying the otherwise applicable royalty rate by a fraction, the numerator of which shall be the total number of Masters embodied on such record, and the denominator of which shall be the total number of selections which are embodied on such record.[13]

(i) In the event any of the Masters are produced by you, jointly or separately, with another record producer or mixer, Artist shall have the right to give such producer or mixer appropriate credit on such master in which such additional services were rendered, provided that you are credited as producer prior to the credit of such other producer or mixer and that your credit shall be no less prominent than any credit given to another producer.

(j) Notwithstanding anything to the contrary contained herein, you shall not earn any monies in respect of any exploitation of the Masters for which Artist is not entitled to receive or does not earn a royalty.

8. ROYALTY ACCOUNTINGS

01 Artist shall use best efforts to cause Company to pay Producer on Artist's behalf the royalties payable to Producer hereunder and to render statements and payments directly to Producer at the same times as Company renders payments and statements to Artist per a letter of direction. In the event Company refuses to send statements directly to you, Artist shall send statements as to royalties payable hereunder to you within thirty (30) days after Artist's receipt of such statements from Company. Statements shall be accompanied by a payment of accrued royalties, if any, earned by you hereunder during the applicable period, less all advances and charges under this agreement.

02 You understand that in rendering statements to you, Artist will be relying on statements and accountings rendered to Artist by Company. Accordingly, and notwithstanding anything to the contrary contained herein, statements rendered to Producer by Artist shall be deemed accurate, and you shall have no right to object thereto, insofar as such statements accurately reflect Company's accountings to Artist. All royalty statements rendered to you by Artist or Company shall be conclusively binding upon you and not subject to any objection by you for any reason unless specific objection in writing, stating the basis thereof, is given to Artist within two (2) years from the date such statement is rendered ("Time Frame"). Failure to make specific objection within the Time Frame shall be deemed approval of such statement. You will not have the right to sue Artist or Company in connection with any royalty accounting, or to sue Artist or Company for royalties on records sold during the period a royalty accounting covers, unless you commence the suit in a court of competent jurisdiction within three (3) months after Artist's receipt of the aforesaid specific written objection.

03 You shall not have the right to audit the books or records of the Company. However, you or an attorney, certified public accountant or professional financial planner, may, at your sole expense, upon written notice to Artist, examine and make copies of royalty statements sent to Artist by Company in connection with the sale of phonograph records hereunder, but solely with respect to those portions of such statements specifically pertaining to royalties payable to you hereunder. Such audit shall be conducted in a manner so as not to disrupt Artist's other functions and shall be completed promptly. Artist shall have no obligation to permit you to examine any such particular royalty statements more than once. Artist's books relating to any particular royalty statement

---

[13] Assuming Biff's record has ten tracks, five of which are produced by Fred, Fred's 3% royalty is effectively reduced to 1.5% (in terms of the entire album).

may be examined as aforesaid only during normal business hours, upon thirty (30) days notice and within the Time Frame. These rights granted to you shall constitute your sole and exclusive rights to examine Artist's books and records.[14]

04   No royalties shall be payable to you in respect of sales of records by any of Company's licensees until payment therefor has been received by Artist or credited to Artist's account against advances previously received by Artist. Sales by any such licensees shall be deemed to have occurred in the semiannual accounting period during which such licensees shall have rendered to Company accounting statements for such sales.

05   All monies paid to you or on your behalf or to or on behalf of any firm, person, or corporation representing you, other than royalties payable under this agreement, shall constitute advances recoupable from any royalties payable under this agreement.

06   Artist shall have the right to deduct from any amounts payable to you hereunder such portion thereof as may be required to be deducted under the applicable provisions of the California Revenue and Taxation Code or under any other applicable statute, regulation, treaty or other law, or under any applicable union or guild agreement, and you shall promptly execute and deliver to Artist such forms and other documents as may be required in connection therewith.

9.   LICENSES FOR MUSICAL COMPOSITIONS

01   You warrant that no musical composition wholly or partially written by Producer, or owned or controlled directly or indirectly by Producer or any party associated or affiliated with Producer ("Controlled Composition") is embodied in a Master.[15]

10.   WARRANTIES; REPRESENTATIONS; RESTRICTIONS; INDEMNITIES

01   You warrant and represent:[16]

(a)   You have the right and power to enter into and fully perform the material terms of this agreement.

(b)   Neither Company nor Artist shall be required to make any payments of any nature for, or in connection with, the rendition of your services or the acquisition, exercise or exploitation of rights by Artist pursuant to this agreement except as specifically provided in this agreement.

(c)   During the term of this agreement you shall become and remain a member in good standing of any appropriate labor union or unions with which Artist or Company may at any time have an agreement lawfully requiring such union membership.

(d) The Masters shall be recorded in accordance with the rules and regulations of all labor unions having jurisdiction over the recording thereof.

02   You will at all times indemnify and hold Artist, Company and any licensee of

---

[14] Fred's attorney should ask for a provision that makes it clear that Fred is entitled to his pro-rata share of any audit recovery (to the extent the recovery is comprised of unpaid royalties from masters Fred produced, of course).

[15] Some producers are writers as well. I guess Fred isn't.

[16] Blah blah blah . . .

Company harmless from and against any and all losses, claims, damages, liabilities, costs and expenses, including legal expenses and reasonable counsel fees, arising out of any breach by you of any warranty or representation made by you in this agreement, which claims are reduced to a final, non-appealable judgment or settled with your consent, which consent you shall not unreasonably withhold, provided that your consent shall be deemed given in all cases where the monies paid to settle such claim are less than ten thousand dollars ($10,000.00). Pending the resolution of any claim in respect of which Company or Artist is entitled to be indemnified, Company or Artist shall be entitled to withhold monies which would otherwise be payable to you in an amount reasonably related to your potential liability to Company or Artist under this paragraph. You shall have the right to post a bond in an amount and with a bonding company reasonably satisfactory to Artist and Company, and in the event you shall post such a bond, Artist or Company shall release such monies held hereunder in connection with the claim, action or proceeding in respect of which such bond shall be posted. Artist or Company shall release any monies withheld as aforesaid if a lawsuit directly related to such claim is not commenced within twelve (12) months of Artist's or Company's withholding thereof.

03   You have obtained or will obtain all necessary sample clearances with respect to the material furnished solely by you and you will obtain written agreements, reasonably satisfactory to Artist and Company as to form and content, from the appropriate parties in the form and content prescribed by Artist, and the same shall be obtained at no cost or expense to Artist or on terms approved by Artist in writing. Producer agrees to provide copies of sample clearance documentation to Artist for the purpose of determining compliance with the terms of this paragraph. In connection with the foregoing, Producer agrees to indemnify and hold Artist and Company harmless from and against any and all losses, damages, liabilities, costs, fines, expenses and penalties (including reasonable attorneys' fees) resulting from any claims, proceedings or action arising out of or in connection with the use of any samples furnished solely by Producer and embodied in the Masters, which claims are reduced to a final judgment or settled with your consent, which consent you shall not unreasonably withhold, provided that your consent shall be deemed given in all cases where the monies paid to settle such claim are less than ten thousand dollars ($10,000.00).[17]

04   Neither Company, Artist nor Producer shall be deemed in breach of this agreement unless and until the non-breaching party(ies) shall give the allegedly breaching party(ies) specific written notice by certified or registered mail, return receipt requested setting forth the nature of such breach and the allegedly breaching party(ies) shall have failed to cure such breach within thirty (30) days following the allegedly breaching party's receipt of such written notice.

11.   **DEFINITIONS**

Except as expressly provided in the contrary herein, all terms used herein shall have the same meaning as used in the Record Contract.[18]

12.   **AGREEMENTS, APPROVAL & CONSENTS**

01   As to all matters treated herein to be determined by mutual agreement, or as to which any approval or consent is required, such agreement, approval or consent shall not be unreasonably withheld.

---

[17] Samples are messy. Fred's attorney wants to make sure that Fred is only responsible for clearing samples which are his idea, while Biff's attorney would like to hold Fred responsible for at least logging all samples, no matter who had the idea. In practice, it's getting tougher and tougher to make producers responsible for samples (due to the incredible liability and licensing problems), but if a producer is known to be a heavy sampler, try to insist that he shoulders some of the workload. By workload I mean clearing and paying for the samples before it's too late.

[18] Once again, ask for a copy of the definitions from Biff's deal.

02   Your agreement, approval or consent, whenever required, shall be deemed to have been given unless you notify me otherwise within five (5) days following the date of my written request to you therefor.

13.   **NOTICES AND PAYMENTS**

01   All notices required to be given to me shall be sent to me at my address first mentioned herein, and all royalties, royalty statements and payments and any and all notices to you shall be sent to you c/o Jethro Bodine, Esq., 1234 Burton Way, Beverly Hills, CA 90211, or such other address as each party respectively may hereafter designate by notice in writing to the other. All notices sent under this agreement shall be in writing and, except for royalty statements, shall be sent by personal delivery, registered or certified mail (return receipt requested) or telegraph (prepaid) and the day of mailing (or transmission in the case of telegraphs) of any such notice shall be deemed the date of the giving thereof (except notices of change of address, the date of which shall be the date of receipt by the receiving party).

14.   **MISCELLANEOUS**

01   This agreement contains the entire understanding of the parties relating to its subject matter. No change or termination of this agreement will be binding unless it is made by an instrument signed by the party to be charged. A waiver by either party of any provision of this agreement in any instance shall not be deemed to waive it for the future. All remedies, rights, undertakings, and obligations contained in this agreement shall be cumulative and none of them shall be in limitation of any other remedy, right, undertaking, or obligation of either party.

02   Those provisions of any applicable collective bargaining agreement between Company and any labor organization which are required, by the terms of such agreement, to be included in this agreement shall be deemed incorporated herein.

03   I may assign my rights under this agreement in whole or in part to any person or entity, provided that party shall assume all obligations hereunder and I shall remain secondarily liable. You shall have the right to assign this agreement to a "loan out" corporation wholly owned by you.[19]

04   This agreement has been entered into in the State of California, and the validity, interpretation and legal effect of this agreement shall be governed by the laws of the State of California applicable to contracts entered into and performed entirely within such State. The California courts (state and federal) only will have jurisdiction of any controversies regarding this agreement and the parties hereto consent to the jurisdiction of said courts. Any process in any action, suit or proceeding arising out of or relating to this agreement may, among other methods, be served upon you by delivering it or mailing it in accordance with Article†13 above. Any such process may, among other methods, be served upon Artist or any other person who approves, ratifies, or assents to this agreement to induce me to enter into it, by delivering the process or mailing it to the Artist or the other person concerned in the manner prescribed in Article†13. Any such delivery or mail service shall be deemed to have the same force and effect as personal service in California.

05   In entering into this agreement and in providing services pursuant hereto, you shall have the status of independent contractor and nothing herein contained shall contemplate or constitute you or the Producer as my agent or employee.

---

[19] Producers and artists sometimes form shell corporations to avoid personal liability (see Chapter Eight). Many producers contract with artists through their corporation.

06   This agreement shall not become effective until executed by all proposed parties hereto.

If the foregoing is consistent with your understanding of the agreement between Producer and Artist, please so indicate by signing below

AGREED TO AND ACCEPTED BY:

PRODUCER   ARTIST

By:_____   By: _____
   Fred Dobbs   BIFF LOMAN
   SS#_____

LETTER OF DIRECTION

April 1, 1998

THRIFTY SCOT RECORDS, INC.
1234 Main Street
Anytown, CA 90000

Gentlemen:

1.   I have engaged Fred Dobbs (the "Producer") to produce recordings constituting one (1) album (the "Recordings") to be made pursuant to the agreement between you and me dated May 1, 1997 (the "Agreement").

2.   Although the Agreement requires me to pay for the services of Producer, I hereby request and authorize you to make payments for his services on our behalf, as follows:

(a) An advance of Twelve Thousand Five-Hundred Dollars ($12,500.00) following the later of the commencement of recording or receipt of this letter and a further advance of Twelve Thousand Five-Hundred Dollars ($12,500.00) upon the delivery to you of all of the Recordings in accordance with the Agreement (to the extent that there are monies remaining in the Recording Fund for such Recordings) together with all necessary licenses and applicable approvals and consents. Those advances will be recoupable by you from all monies becoming payable to the Producer for his services under paragraph 2(b) below or otherwise. Each such advance will also be applied against the recording budget applicable to the Recordings under the Agreement.

(b) (1) A royalty (the "Producing Royalty") on net sales of phonograph records derived from the Recordings, computed and paid in the same manner as the royalty payable to me under the Agreement, at the same times, and subject to the same conditions, but at a basic LP rate of Three percent (3%) instead of the basic LP rate fixed in the Agreement, prorated by a fraction, the numerator of which is the number of Recordings produced by Producer which are contained on the record concerned, and the denominator of which is the total number of recordings (including the Recordings produced by Producer) contained on said record with proportionate reductions on all sales for which reduced royalties are payable under the Agreement. Notwithstanding the foregoing, the Producing Royalty shall apply to the first five hundred thousand (500,000) units of U.S. LP Retail Sales of the LP consisting entirely of the Recordings. Notwithstanding the foregoing, the Producing Royalty shall be increased in the same proportion and in the same manner as the royalty credited to me by you is increased on U.S. LP Retail Sales of the LP consisting entirely of the Recordings in excess of Five Hundred Thousand (500,000) units and on U.S. LP Retail Sales of the LP consisting entirely of the Recordings in excess of One Million (1,000,000) units. By way of example only, the escalation of the Producing Royalty shall be determined by multiplying our sales based royalty escalation (for example, 1%) by a fraction, the numerator of which shall be the base Producing Royalty and the denominator of which is our Base Rate. Producer's royalty shall not be escalated for any other reason. The amount of the Producing Royalty will be deducted from all royalties payable or becoming payable to me under the Agreement (excluding mechanical royalties).

---

[20] From both the artist's and the producer's point of view, it is crucial that the record company accept the letter of direction. Otherwise, the producer cannot be assured that he will be paid, and this might scare him away from an otherwise interesting project.

(b) The Producing Royalty will not be payable until you have recouped all recording costs attributable to the Recordings under the Agreement. After such recoupment, the Producing Royalty will be computed retroactively and paid on all such records from the first record sold. Such recoupment will be computed at our net royalty rate as reduced to reflect the deduction of the Producing Royalty. Notwithstanding the foregoing, the Producing Royalty shall not be payable unless and until all advances to Producer have been recouped from the Producing Royalty earned hereunder.

3.   All monies becoming payable under this authorization will be remitted to Producer at the following address or otherwise as Producer directs you in writing:

Fred Dobbs
c/o Jethro Bodine, Esq.
1234 Burton Way
Beverly Hills, CA 90211

and will be accompanied by statements with respect to those payments. I understand that royalty payment instructions of this nature are usually placed in effect with respect to the accounting period in which you receive them if they are delivered to you within the first three (3) months of that period, and with respect to the next accounting period if delivered after that time, although administrative factors may result in variations from that procedure.[21]

4.   Your compliance with this authorization will constitute an accommodation to me alone; the Producer is not a beneficiary of it. All payments to Producer under this authorization will constitute payment to me and you will have no liability by reason of any erroneous payment or failure to comply with this authorization. I will indemnify and hold you harmless against any claims asserted against you and any damages, losses or expenses you incur by reason of any such payment or otherwise in connection herewith.

Very truly yours,

By:_____
Biff Loman

---

[21] In other words, get those letters of direction in as soon as possible, or run the risk of missing an accounting period. This can be a problem for the artist if he ends up owing the producer royalties at this stage.

SAMPLE EXCLUSIVE SONGWRITER AND CO-PUBLISHING AGREEMENT[1]

THRIFTY SCOT SONGS, LLC
1234 Main Street
Anytown, CA 90000

Dated as of: October 1, 1998

John Doe and Fred Johnson, p/k/a "Lawn Chocolate"
c/o Dewey, Cheatum & Howe
11111 San Viejo Blvd.
Los Angeles, CA 90000
Attn: Art Cheatum, Esq.

Re: Exclusive Songwriter and Co-Publishing Agreement

Gentlemen:

The following, when signed by you and by us, will constitute the terms of the exclusive songwriter and co-publishing agreement between you and us.

1.   SERVICES.

We hereby engage you, individually and collectively, to render your exclusive services as songwriters and composers. You hereby accept such engagement and agree to render such services exclusively for us during the Term (as hereinafter defined) of this agreement upon the terms and conditions set forth herein.[2]

2.   TERM.

(a)   The term of this agreement (the "Term") shall consist of the Initial Period, together with such Option Periods, if any, for which we may exercise our option pursuant to paragraph 2 (b) hereof. The Initial Period of this agreement shall commence on the date hereof and shall expire on the date which is the later of one (1) year from the date hereof, or thirty (30) days following our receipt of a copy of the final mix of the Qualifying LP (as hereinafter defined) delivered in fulfillment of your Minimum Delivery Commitment (as hereinafter defined) for the First Option Period and as accepted for release by a Major Label (as hereinafter defined), together with written notice from the Major Label specifying the scheduled release date for such Qualifying LP as established by the Major Label.

---

[1] This sample agreement is fairly representative of the average songwriter/co-publishing deal offered to a new band signed to a major label. The terms of this particular deal tend to favor Thrifty Scot.

[2] In other words, neither Fred nor John may write or compose for any other publisher during the Term of the agreement without the permission of Thrifty Scot. This is standard, but you should ask for an exclusion that allows you to compose songs for motion pictures from time to time, because the producers of most major motion pictures will pretty much require you to give their publishing designee 50-100% of the copyright to the song in question. You will not be able to do this under a deal like this without the permission of your co-publisher.

(b)   You hereby grant to us three (3) separate, consecutive and irrevocable options[3] to extend the Term of this agreement for additional Option Periods (the "First Option Period," "Second Option Period," etc.). The Initial Period and each Option Period are sometimes referred to generally as a "Contract Period." The Option Periods shall run consecutively beginning at the expiration of the immediately preceding Contract Period and shall continue in accordance with the same provisions of this agreement that are applicable to the Initial Period (except as otherwise provided herein). We may exercise each such option by sending you a notice by not later than the expiration date of the Contract Period which is then in effect (the "then Current Contract Period"). If we exercise an option, the Option Period concerned will begin immediately after the end of the then Current Contract Period and, except as specified in the following sentence, will continue until thirty (30) days following our receipt of a copy of the final mix of the Qualifying LP delivered in fulfillment of your Minimum Delivery Commitment for the succeeding Option Period as accepted for release by a Major Label, together with written notice from the Major Label specifying the scheduled release date for such Qualifying LP as established by the Major Label, but not earlier than one (1) year after commencement of the Option Period concerned. If we exercise our option for the Third Option Period, the Third Option Period will end thirty (30) days after we have received written notice from you accurately reflecting that you have fulfilled your Minimum Delivery Commitment for the Third Option Period, but not earlier than one (1) year after commencement of the Option Period concerned.[4]

3.   **GRANT OF RIGHTS.**

(a)   You hereby irrevocably transfer, assign, convey and grant to us, our successors and assigns, in perpetuity,[5] all of the following:

(i) The entire right, title and interest throughout the universe, including, without limitation, the copyright, the right to secure copyright registration and any and all rights of renewal and extension of copyright, in and to any musical compositions and other musical material, including the title, words and music thereof, which are created by you during the Term hereof (to the extent of your fractional interest therein)[6] (the "New Compositions");

(ii) The entire right, title and interest throughout the universe, including, without limitation, the copyright, the right to secure copyright registration and any and all rights of renewal and extension of copyright, in and to those musical compositions and other musical material, including the title, words and music thereof, which are created by you prior to the Term (to the

---

[3] As with nearly any deal, fewer options are better for you. Most new artist publishing deals provide for an initial period and give the co-publisher anywhere from two to four options.

[4] This is essentially an album to album agreement. If you have clout, you may want to require the publisher to contractually commit to picking up the first option, much as you would go for "two firm" in a recording agreement. You should ask for a provision which ends the Term no later than the release date of the final Qualifying LP under the deal.

[5] Thrifty Scot will co-own and exclusively administer your Compositions forever, or at least for as long as copyright law allows. Obviously, you should try to get your copyrights back at some point. If you do not have the clout to get reversion of all of your copyrights at some post-Term date (the number of years is negotiable), try to get reversion of Compositions that you delivered but which were not commercially exploited during the Term. See Chapter 6 for more details on the important subject of reversions.

[6] In other words, if Fred and Joe have co-written a song with another writer, only their share of such song needs to be assigned under this deal.

extent of your fractional interest therein) (The "Existing Compositions")[7] which are set forth in Exhibit "B" attached hereto; and

(iii) The entire right, title and interest throughout the universe, including, without limitation, the copyright, the right to secure copyright registration and any and all rights of renewal and extension of copyright, in and to any musical compositions and other musical material, including the title, words and music thereof, which are acquired by you or by any Affiliated Person at any time during the Term (to the extent of your fractional interest therein) (the "Acquired Compositions").

All of the foregoing are sometimes individually and collectively referred to herein as the "Compositions." At our request, you agree to execute a short form copyright assignment with respect to each Composition in the form attached hereto as Exhibit "A".[8]

(b)   You hereby acknowledge that we have initially acquired hereunder one hundred percent (100%) of the entire right, title and interest throughout the Territory in and to the Compositions. We hereby assign to your publishing designee, Lawn Chocolate Songs ("Your Designee"), an undivided fifty percent (50%) of the copyright in and to the Compositions, subject to all of our rights hereunder. Without limiting the generality of the foregoing, Your Designee shall not grant or assign any of its right, title or interest in and to the Compositions to any person, firm or corporation other than us.

(c)   If you collaborate with any other person in the creation of a musical composition, no less than a fraction of the entire Territory-wide right, title and interest in and to that musical composition shall be subject to this agreement as a Composition, the numerator of which fraction is one (1) and the denominator of which is the total number of writers credited with co-writing that musical composition. You shall use reasonable efforts to cause that collaborator to execute a separate agreement with us in a form acceptable to us covering the co-written musical composition subject hereto in part as a Composition.[9]

---

[7] If you have a substantial catalogue of songs, you may not want to throw them into your deal as "Existing Compositions" unless you feel you are getting an advance which adequately reflects the value of the songs. Lawn Chocolate is a new band with a small catalogue, so this isn't a major issue in this deal. One other note: You want to make sure any "Existing Songs" count towards your Minimum Delivery Commitment for the Initial Period if any of those songs make it onto the first Qualifying LP released under the deal.

[8] Lawn Chocolate Songs (LCS) initially owned 100% of the copyright in and to each Composition. Under this deal, LCS assigned these rights to Thrifty Scot (which then re-assigned 50% back to LCS since this is a co-publishing agreement in addition to an exclusive songwriter agreement). Note that under some co-publishing deals, the writer's publishing designee assigns only 50% of the copyright in and to each subject composition, thereby eliminating the need to re-assign the 50% back to the writer's publishing designee. The result is the same either way. While most publishers and co-publishers acquire copyrights in this manner (that is, via assignment from the initial copyright owner), it is important to note that some deals provide that musical compositions written during the term of a contract are "works made for hire." As we discussed in Chapters 2 and 6, this is bad for the songwriter, because works made for hire are never owned by the true author, so there is no transfer to terminate. Conversely, when copyrights are transferred (as they are under this deal and under most co-publishing deals), copyright law allows the original owner to terminate the transfer and reclaim ownership 35 years hence.

[9] In other words, if John writes a song with his friend Zeke, this deal obligates John to deliver 50% of the copyright in and to that song to Thrifty Scot. Additionally, John must use "reasonable efforts" to get Zeke to sign an agreement "acceptable" to Thrifty Scot covering Zeke's piece of the song. This

(d)   You acknowledge and agree that we shall have and are hereby granted the sole and exclusive right throughout the Territory, in our sole discretion, to subpublish, administer and exploit one (1) or more of the Compositions in any manner or media now known or unknown, to license any and all reproductions and other exploitations of one (1) or more Compositions in any and all manner-or media now known or unknown and to execute in our own name any and all licenses and agreements regarding the reproduction and exploitation of one (1) or more of the Compositions, including, but not limited to, licenses for the mechanical reproduction, public performance, dramatization, synchronization and/or subpublication of one (1) or more of the Compositions. Without limiting the generality of the foregoing, we and our successors and assignees, shall have, at our election, the sole and exclusive right throughout the universe to do any and all of the following:[10]

(i)   To receive and collect any and all monies and other income for and in advance of any and all reproductions and other exploitations of any one (1) or more of the Compositions in any and all manner or media now known or unknown whenever earned (including, without limitation, income earned prior to the start of the Term);

(ii)   To perform the Compositions publicly for profit by means of public and private performance, radio broadcasting, television, or any other means, whether now known or which may hereafter come into existence. Small performing rights in the Compositions, to the extent permitted by law, shall be assigned to and licensed by ASCAP, SESAC or BMI, as applicable (the "Organization"). Said Organization shall be and hereby is authorized to collect and receive all monies earned from the public performance of the Compositions and to pay directly to us the entire amount allocated by said Organization as the publisher's share of public performance fees for the Compositions. If, by operation of law, the Organization shall cease to be entitled to license certain public performance rights and/or to collect fees derived therefrom, then we shall have the sole and exclusive right, on behalf of you, and any other writers and any co-publishers, to license any such rights and to collect income derived therefrom, or to assign such rights to any person, firm, corporation or society having the legal right to issue any such license and collect fees therefrom on our behalf;

(iii)   To secure copyright registration and protection for the Compositions in our name or otherwise as we may desire, and to have and to hold said copyrights, renewals, extensions and all rights of whatsoever nature thereunder existing, for and during the full term of all of said copyrights and of all renewals and extensions thereof;

(iv)   To substitute a new title or titles for any Composition, to make any arrangement, adaptation, translation, dramatization or transposition of any or all of the

---

puts John in a tough spot: What if he made only a small contribution to the song and he and Zeke agree that he is entitled to 10% share of the song? If John delivers less than 50% of the song, he is in breach of the agreement. While it is unlikely that any major publisher would bust John's chops in this particular scenario, John and Fred would be better off with language that requires them to deliver only their fractional interest in and to any co-written song (whether that interest is 1% or 99%).

[10] This is a significant paragraph in that it gives the publisher the right to issue all kinds of licenses and to otherwise exploit the Compositions in any manner. This is standard ñ after all, this is what you are paying the publisher to do. However, this paragraph doesn't place any restrictions on how the publisher can exploit or alter your songs, nor does it obligate the publisher to comply with the terms of your controlled composition clause. Most songwriters like to have some degree of control over how their songs are exploited. Now is a good time to go back and review the marketing restrictions I covered in Chapter 6.

Compositions, in whole or in part, and in connection with any other musical, literary or dramatic material, and to add new lyrics to the music of any of the Compositions or new music to the lyrics of any of the Compositions, all as we deem necessary or desirable in our best business judgment.[11] If we engage the services of any person(s) to arrange or adapt Compositions, or to set new lyrics or translations or music to the Compositions or to otherwise revise or rewrite same and we agree to pay such person or persons a royalty, all royalties which would otherwise be payable to you hereunder will be reduced by the amount payable to such other person(s) but in no event to exceed fifty (50%) percent in respect of the musical compositions so revised or rewritten.[12]

(v)   To print, publish and sell sheet music, orchestrations, arrangements and other editions of the compositions, including the right to include any or all of the Compositions in song folios or lyric magazines, with or without music.

(vi)   To exploit in perpetuity in any manner or media any and all other rights now or hereafter existing in all Compositions under any common law rights and all copyrights and renewals, extensions and revisions thereof.[13]

4.   NAME AND LIKENESS.

You hereby grant to us the perpetual right to use and publish and to permit others to use and publish, throughout the world and universe, your name (including any professional name heretofore or hereafter adopted by you), your photograph or other likenesses, and biographical material, in connection with the reproduction and other exploitation of the Compositions in any manner or media now known or unknown, in connection with the institutional advertising of Thrifty Scot Songs and its licensees and in connection with our music publishing business and products,[14] or we may refrain from all of the foregoing. Our rights with regard to your name, likenesses and biographical materials shall be exclusive during the Term and nonexclusive thereafter. During the Term, you shall not authorize or permit the use or reproduction of your name, likeness or biographical material for or in connection with any musical composition (whether or not a Composition) other than by or for us. You hereby grant to us the exclusive right during the Term to refer to you as our "Exclusive Songwriter and Composer."

5.   EXCLUSIVE WRITING AND COMPOSING SERVICES.

During the Term, you shall not create any musical composition or other musical material for any person, firm or corporation other than us, shall not deliver in any form or convey any interest in any musical composition or other musical material to any person, firm or corporation other than us and shall not authorize or permit any person, firm or corporation other than us to use or reproduce your name, likeness or biographical materials in any manner or media in connection with any musical composition or other musical material. You will deliver to us a cassette tape copy

---

[11] You should try to get the right to approve any changes in the title, lyrics, music or basic structure of any composition under any kind of publishing deal. Otherwise, Thrifty Scot can make any changes it wants to the Compositions.

[12] This part of the paragraph allows the publisher to give away as much as half of your royalty when someone else messes with your songs. Obviously, you want the right to veto this.

[13] This is a "catch all" provision which reiterates that Thrifty Scot can do whatever it wants to with the Compositions.

[14] You should limit the use of your name and likeness to the promotion of your songs and the institutional advertising of the publisher.

and typed lyric sheet of each New Composition immediately upon the completion thereof.[15] We, in our sole discretion, shall reasonably make studio facilities available for you so that you, subject to our supervision and control, may make demonstration recordings of the Compositions. If you make any demonstration recordings, you shall deliver to us a 15 i.p.s master tape thereof. You shall not incur any liability for which we may be responsible in connection with any demonstration recording session without having first obtained our written approval as to the nature, extent and limit of such liability. Fifty (50%) percent of any costs incurred by us in producing such demonstration recordings shall constitute an advance against royalties payable to you hereunder. We shall own any and all such demonstration recordings.[16]

6.   **MINIMUM DELIVERY COMMITMENT.**

You shall deliver each New Composition to us immediately following its creation. During each Contract Period, you will deliver to us one (1) newly-recorded, LP-length studio recording released by a Major Label (as such term is hereinafter defined) featuring your performances together as the group "Lawn Chocolate" (the "Group") and containing New Compositions comprising at least seventy percent (70%) percent of the musical compositions embodied in such album (a "Qualifying LP"). The term "Major Label" shall refer to any label owned by Sony, WMG, EMI, PolyGram, BMG, UMG, any label which is exclusively distributed by any of the foregoing companies, or any record company acceptable to us in our sole discretion. The foregoing obligation is referred to herein as your "Minimum Delivery Commitment" for the applicable Contract Period.[17] It is expressly understood that "greatest hits," "best of," "live," and "re-mix" LPs cannot constitute "Qualifying LPs," and that if more than one LP-length record is included in a single package, such package shall nonetheless count only as one LP. For the sake of clarification, we will not pay you any advance for an album which is not a Qualifying LP, nor shall that album satisfy your Minimum Delivery Commitment for the applicable Contract Period.[18]

7.   **ROYALTIES AND ACCOUNTING.**

(a)   Provided that you are not in breach of any of your material obligations hereunder, we shall credit your royalty account with the so-called "writer's share" of royalties with respect to monies received by us from our exploitation of Compositions in accordance with

---

[15] While publishers would really like you to do this, this provision is more important with respect to true songwriters that write primarily for other performers. However, this is a material obligation. Now, I would NEVER encourage any of my clients to commit fraud, but it seems to me that if you satisfy your Minimum Delivery Commitment, why should the publisher get any other songs if you don't get an advance for them? I guess if you somehow forget to submit new songs to your publisher, they'll never know about them, and what they don't know . . . .

[16] Make sure the publisher cannot commercially exploit or otherwise distribute these demos without your prior written consent.

[17] Note that the Minimum Delivery Commitment for a true songwriter (as opposed to a performer/songwriter) is usually a specific number of songs instead of a percentage of songs on the writer's album, since many songwriters do nothing but write for other performers.

[18] Let's say John and Fred deliver their second album under this deal and it contains recordings of ten songs, four of which are covers. Bad news — since only 60% of the songs are Compositions, this album doesn't really "count," although Thrifty Scot still owns the 6 songs the band did write. How could this calamity have been averted? Stop using outside material or have your attorney reduce the minimum percentage (although 70% seems pretty reasonable to me).

Schedule "A" attached hereto, all such royalties to be based on Gross Income (as defined in paragraph 13 (f), below).[19]

      (b)   In addition to your songwriter royalties, and provided that you are not in breach of any of your material obligations hereunder, we shall credit to your royalty account royalties in an amount equal to the fifty percent (50%) of Net Income (as such term is defined in paragraph 13 (g), below).[20]

      (c)   We will account to you (and make payment where appropriate) within 90 days following the end of the semi-annual accounting periods ending June 30th and December 31st of each year. However, if the amount due for a specific statement is less than $50.00, payment (but not the rendering of a statement) may be deferred until the aggregate amount due to you exceeds $50.00. We shall use the exchange rates used by third parties in accounting to us in accounting to you hereunder.

      (d)   All royalty statements rendered by us to you shall be binding upon you and not subject to any objection whatsoever unless specific objection is made, in writing, stating the basis thereof, to us within one (1) year[21] from the date rendered. No action, suit or proceedings of any nature in respect of any royalty statement or other accounting may be brought against us unless such action, suit or proceeding is commenced against us in a court of competent jurisdiction within one (1) year after the date rendered. You shall have the right, upon the giving of at least thirty (30) days prior written notice to us and not more frequently than once in any consecutive twelve (12) month period, to appoint a duly qualified certified public accountant not then engaged in another audit of our books and records to inspect our books and records, insofar as the same concerns you, at your expense, at reasonable times during normal business hours, for the purpose of verifying the accuracy of any royalty statement rendered to you hereunder. Our books and records relating to activities during any accounting period may only be examined as aforesaid during the one (1) year[22] period following the date we render the statement for said accounting period and we shall have no obligation to permit the examination of such books relating to any particular statement more than once. The rights conferred to you by this paragraph shall constitute your sole right to examine our books.

      (e)   No royalties shall be accountable or payable to you in connection with the use or exploitation of the Compositions by us or any of our licensees until the period in which an accounting payment in connection therewith has been received by us in the United States. In the event that we shall not receive payment in United States dollars in the United States from any foreign licensee, we may deposit to your credit (and at your expense) in such foreign currency, in a depository selected by us, any payments so received as royalties applicable to this contract which are

---

[19] This is a standard way of computing royalties under a co-publishing agreement. The key here is how "Gross Income" and "Net Income" are defined, so take a look at paragraph 13.

[20] Let's look at some hypothetical numbers to see what John and Fred end up with under this deal. Assuming that the Compositions generate $1,000 in mechanical royalties outside of the U.S. and $1,000 in the U.S. during a particular accounting period, and assuming that Thrifty Scot's subpublishers retain 25% of the ex-U.S. royalties as their fee, Gross Income would equal $1,750. Half of this ($875) would be credited to John and Freds' account as writer royalties. The remaining $875 (minus any other properly deductible fees and costs) is deemed Net Income. Net Income is split 50/50 between Thrifty Scot and Lawn Chocolate Songs. How can this deal be better for John and Fred? They should try to eliminate or reduce the percentages retained by Thrifty Scot's foreign subpublishers. At the very least, they should try to change this deal so that the subpublisher fees are deducted from the publisher's share of income only.

[21] Should be more like 2 or 3 years.

[22] Ditto.

then payable to you, we shall notify you thereof promptly and such deposit shall constitute our full compliance with our obligation to pay such royalties to you.[23]

8. **ADVANCES.** [24]

Provided that you are not in breach of any of your material obligations hereunder we shall pay to you the following advances recoupable from all royalties payable hereunder:

(a)   For the Qualifying LP Released in the Initial Period: $150,000, payable $100,000 promptly following the execution of this agreement, and $50,000 promptly following our receipt of notice of the initial United States release by a Major Label of the first Qualifying LP.

(b)   For Qualifying LPs Released in Option Periods: An amount equal to two-thirds (2/3) of the U.S. mechanical royalties[25] credited to your account hereunder from sales of the immediately preceding Qualifying LP during the last twelve (12) months of the immediately preceding Contract Period, subject to the following minimums and maximums:

Option Period	Minimum	Maximum
First Option Period	$175,000	$350,000
Second Option Period	$200,000	$400,000
Third Option Period	$225,000	$450,000

Advances for Option Periods shall be payable as follows: twenty percent (20%) promptly following our exercise of our option for the Contract Period concerned; and (ii) eighty percent (80%) promptly following our receipt of written notice accurately reflecting the initial United States release by a Major Label of the subject optional Qualifying LP.

(c)   (i) The advances provided in this paragraph apply only to Qualifying LPs. To the extent that any Qualifying LP is comprised of musical compositions which are not Compositions controlled by us hereunder, we shall pay to you, in lieu of the applicable advance, an advance equal to the product of (A) the otherwise applicable advance, and (B) a fraction, the numerator of which is the percentage of New Compositions on the album subject to exclusive exploitation hereunder, and the denominator of which is one hundred (100). In no event shall such fraction exceed one (1).[26]

---

[23] This is standard.

[24] I've seen publishing deals with NO advances (avoid those) and deals with seven figure advances. What can you expect? Ask your attorney.

[25] You should try to have your performance royalties and ex-U.S. mechanical royalties (including your share of "pipeline" royalties, i.e., your share of Gross Income credited to the account of Thrifty Scot's affiliated subpublishers outside the U.S. but for which Thrifty Scot has not yet been accounted to) thrown into this calculation as well, for obvious reasons.

[26] Let's recap: In order to count as a "Qualifying Album," 70% of the songs must be written or controlled by John and Fred. Let's assume that John and Fred wrote 75% of the songs on their second album. Assuming that only the minimum advance ($175,000) is payable, John and Fred will only receive 75% of $175,000, or $131,250. While pro-ration is customary and fair, John and Fred's attorney might have asked that pro-ration of the advance occur only if less than 90% of the songs on a Qualifying Album are Compositions.

(ii)   The advances provided in this paragraph apply only to Compositions on which at least seventy-five percent (75%) of the minimum U.S. statutory mechanical royalty is collectible. If you compromised or at any time compromise such rate in your agreement with any record company (e.g., you negotiated a lower rate, or an aggregate "cap" on mechanical royalties payable by the record company, or allow the record company any offset right against mechanical royalties payable on so-called "controlled compositions"), or if we cannot collect at least such seventy-five percent (75%) rate, on all sales of records, for any other reason, then advances and any royalties otherwise payable hereunder shall be reduced by the shortfall in earnings collected by us.[27]

9.   **POWER OF ATTORNEY.**

You irrevocably authorize and appoint us as your true and lawful attorney (with full power of substitution and delegation) in your name, and in your place and stead, or in our name, to take such action, and to make, sign, execute, acknowledge and deliver any and all instruments or documents which we, from time to time, may deem desirable or necessary to vest in us, our successors, assigns and licensees, any of the rights or interests granted by you hereunder pertaining to the Compositions, including but not limited to, a short form copyright assignment in the form attached hereto as Exhibit "A" and the letter attached hereto as Exhibit "C". Our appointment hereunder shall be deemed to be a power coupled with an interest.[28]

10.   **WARRANTIES, REPRESENTATIONS, INDEMNITIES AND AGREEMENTS.** [29]

(a)   You warrant, represent, covenant and agree as follows:

(i)   You have the full right, power and authority to enter into and perform this agreement and to grant to and vest in us all rights granted to us in this agreement, free and clear of any and all claims, demands, obligations or other encumbrances;

---

[27] Nearly every co-publishing agreement contains a provision like this. By now you should know that every record deal contains a "controlled composition clause" which typically limits aggregate mechanical royalties payable per album to ten times the minimum statutory rate (and more typically, 75% of this rate) in effect when an album is delivered. Most record deals also allow the record company to apply mechanical royalties against recording cost overages and the like. Publishing companies don't like this, so most major publishers include language similar to this in their deals. Let's look at an example to see what damage this provision can do under certain circumstances: Let's say the next Lawn Chocolate album contains 15 songs, all written by John and Fred. That's great, but the band's record deal only provides for payment on 10 songs at 75% of the minimum statutory rate. Under this provision, you have promised your publisher that it will receive no less than 75% of the minimum statutory rate royalty on every Composition on your album, even if you are only entitled to receive royalties on 10 songs. So even though you thought you were doing well by shunning outside songs, your publisher is screwing you, because the five song mechanical royalty shortfall can be deducted from royalties and advances otherwise payable to you. Solution: If you can't eliminate this clause, furnish the publisher with your controlled composition clause and make them acknowledge it and abide by its terms. Beyond this they should abide by the controlled composition language embodied in any record deal you enter into in the future, as long as the terms are customary and reasonable.

[28] This provision should be altered slightly so as to give you 5 or 6 days to sign any such documents yourself before the publisher signs them for you.

[29] This is the part of the deal where John and Fred pledge that they are not signed to another deal that would preclude them form signing this one and that none of their songs infringe the rights of any other person or entity.

(ii)   All of the Compositions and all other results and proceeds of your services hereunder, and each and every part thereof, are and shall be new and original and capable of copyright protection throughout the world;

(iii)   No Composition shall, in whole or in part, be an imitation or copy of, or infringe upon, any other material, or violate or infringe upon any common law or statutory rights of any person, firm or corporation, including, without limitation contractual rights, copyrights and rights of privacy;[30]

(iv)   Each Composition and part thereof shall be deemed created and subject hereto no later than when the Composition or part of a Composition initially is or could be the subject matter of copyright and in which copyright protection subsists or could subsist in accordance with the copyright laws of the United States or, if earlier, in accordance with the copyright laws of any other country throughout the world;

(v)   The Compositions shall be free and clear of any claims, demands or other encumbrances by any person, firm or corporation;

(vi)   You have neither sold, assigned, leased, licensed or in any other way disposed of or encumbered any Composition or any interest therein, in whole or in part, or any other rights granted to us hereunder, nor shall you sell, assign, lease, license or in any other way dispose of or encumber any of the Compositions, in whole or in part, or any of our rights under this agreement, except under the terms and conditions hereof;

(vii)   You are affiliated with or a member of Broadcast Music Incorporated ("BMI") and shall remain affiliated with or a member of BMI during the Term;[31] and

(viii)   You and Your Designee warrant and represent that neither you nor Your Designee have received prior to the date of this agreement and shall not receive after the date of this agreement any monies from any person, firm or corporation other than us which is recoupable in whole or part from any monies earned on any reproductions or other exploitations of the Composition occurring at any time before, during or after the date of this agreement.

(b)   You hereby indemnify and hold us, and our parent, subsidiary and affiliated companies and its and their respective officers, employees and agents, harmless from any and all loss, damage, liability, claims and demands, (including reasonable attorneys' fees and court costs) arising out of or connected with any claims by a third party which are inconsistent with any of the representations, warranties or agreements made by you in this agreement,[32] and you agree to reimburse us, on demand, for any payment made by us, at any time after the date hereof (including after the date this agreement terminates), with respect to any liability or claim to which the foregoing indemnity applies. Pending the determination of any such claim, we may withhold payment of royalties or any other monies hereunder in an amount reasonably related to the potential liability in connection therewith, until any such claim has been fully settled, determined and paid and we have been reimbursed our actual out-of-pocket costs and expenses, including the reasonable legal fees incurred in

---

[30] This means that John and Fred promise not to deliver Compositions which infringe other copyrightable songs, etc.

[31] Or ASCAP or SESAC — Lawn Chocolate Songs just happened to choose BMI.

[32] This indemnity should be limited to claims which are settled with John and Freds' consent or which are reduced to a final, non-appealable judgment by a court of competent jurisdiction.

connection therewith.[33] You shall have the right to participate in the defense of any such claim at your own cost and expense but you agree that any such claim may be compromised or settled by us without your consent.

11.   UNIQUE SERVICES.

You acknowledge that the services to be rendered hereunder by you are of a special, unique, unusual, extraordinary and intellectual character which gives them a peculiar value, the loss of which cannot be reasonably or adequately compensated in damages in an action at law, and that a breach by you of any of the material provisions of this agreement will cause us great and irreparable injury and damage. We shall be entitled to seek the remedies of injunction and other equitable relief to prevent a material breach of this contract or any provision hereof, which relief shall be in addition to any other remedies, for damages or otherwise, which may be available to us.

12.   ACTIONS; CURE OF BREACHES.

(a)   We may take such action as we deem necessary in your name or in our own name, against any person to protect all rights and interests acquired by us hereunder. You will, at our request, cooperate fully with us in any controversy which may arise or litigation which may be brought concerning our rights and interests obtained hereunder. We shall have the right, in our absolute discretion, to employ attorneys and to institute or defend any action or proceeding and to take any other proper steps to protect our right, title and interest in and to each of the Compositions and every portion thereof and in that connection, to settle, compromise or in any other manner dispose of any matter, claim, action or proceeding and to satisfy any judgment that may be rendered, in any manner as we in our sole discretion may determine; provided, however, that we shall consult with you in respect of the settlement of any claim or action.[34] Any legal action brought by us against any alleged infringer of any of the Compositions shall be initiated and prosecuted by us, and if there is any recovery made by us as a result thereof, after deduction of the expense of litigation, including but not limited to reasonable attorneys fees and court costs, such recovery shall be deemed Gross Income hereunder.

(b)   Failure by you or us to perform any of your or our respective obligations hereunder (other than your obligation to render exclusive services and timely satisfy your Minimum Delivery Commitment) shall not be deemed a breach of this agreement unless the other party gives notice and the notified party fails to cure within 30 days (15 days in the case of failure to pay monies actually due and not in dispute) after receiving notice; provided, that if the alleged breach is of such a nature that it cannot be completely cured within 30 days, the notified party will not be deemed to be in breach if the notified party commences the curing of the alleged breach within such thirty-day period and proceeds to complete the curing thereof with due diligence within a reasonable time thereafter. However, either party shall have the right to seek injunctive relief to prevent a threatened breach of this agreement by the other party.

---

[33] If someone makes a claim which results in the withholding of monies otherwise payable to you, these monies should be released to you if a law suit has not been filed within six months or one year of the claim. This protects you against spurious claims. Additionally, you should ask for a provision which requires your co-publisher to release any withheld royalties if and to the extent that you provide your co-publisher with a satisfactory surety bond. Finally, you should ask that any withheld monies be kept in an interest bearing account (for your benefit).

[34] You should have the right to participate in any such action with an attorney of your choosing (but at your own expense).

13. **DEFINITIONS.**

As used in this agreement, the following terms shall have the meanings set forth below:

(a) The term "person" means and refers to any individual, corporation, partnership, association or representatives of the foregoing.

(b) The word "you" is used in this agreement to refer individually to you and collectively to you and any Affiliated Person.

(c) The term "album" shall refer to a collection of recordings of not fewer than ten (10) musical compositions.

(d) "Affiliated Person" means any individual, corporation, partnership or other organized group of persons that (i) is owned or controlled by you, directly or indirectly, (ii) that owns or controls you, directly or indirectly, or (iii) is under common ownership or control with you, directly or indirectly.

(e) "Territory" means the universe.

(f) "Gross Income" means all monies earned and actually received by us in the United States, as compensation for the use of any Compositions. You acknowledge that outside of the United States the Compositions may be subpublished by our licensees; that such licensees may retain up to twenty-five percent (25%) of all mechanical income received at source (fifty percent (50%) with respect to Cover Recordings); fifty percent (50%) of public performance income; and twenty-five percent (25%) of all other income; and that the balance of such income that is remitted to us shall constitute "Gross Income" hereunder.

(g) "Net Income" means Gross Income less the songwriter royalties payable to you pursuant to Schedule "A" and any amounts we are permitted to deduct from such Gross Income pursuant to the terms of this agreement, including, without limitation, any amounts paid to partial owners of Compositions or other publishers, if any, the costs incurred in connection with the registration of copyrights, fees or costs connected with the preparation and distribution of lead sheets of the Compositions, fees paid to or charged by a third party trustee or collecting agent for the licensing of the Compositions, all expenses (including reasonable counsel fees) incurred by us in connection with any claim or suit brought by or against us concerning the Compositions, demo costs, and all other actually documented, out of-pocket expenses related solely and directly to the Compositions and their exploitation hereunder. Expenses constituting salaries of employees, rent and overhead will not be deducted.

(h) "Cover Recording" means each recording of a Composition on any configuration of phonograph record, other than (i) the initial recording of a Composition; or (ii) a recording recorded and/or produced by you.

---

[35] As we discussed earlier, the percentage of fees payable to subpublishers which can be deducted "off the top" of Gross Income should be reduced or eliminated.

14.   **NOTICES/CONSENTS/STATEMENTS.**

All notices which are required or desired to be given hereunder shall be in writing and may be served upon the other party personally or by registered or certified mail return receipt requested, or by telegram, followed by a copy by regular First Class mail addressed to that party at its address specified in this agreement or such other address and/or addresses as the respective parties may from time to time designate by notice given in conformity with the above. The date of deposit of any such notice in the post office or telegraph office, postage or charges prepaid, shall be deemed the date of service thereof. All statements and payments may be sent by regular First Class mail. You shall send an additional copy of each notice served upon us to Queen, Fergus, Jones, Palermo & Beginner, LLP, 1234 Lover's Lane, Millennium City, CA 98765, Attention: Lil Beginner, Esq.

15.   **ENTIRE AGREEMENT.**

This agreement supersedes all prior negotiations, understandings and agreements between the parties hereto with respect to the subject matter hereof. Each of the parties acknowledges and agrees that neither party has made any representations or promises in connection with this agreement nor the subject matter hereof not contained herein.

16.   **MISCELLANEOUS.**

(a)   This agreement may not be canceled, altered, modified, amended or waived, in whole or in part, in any way, except by an instrument in writing signed by the parties hereto. The waiver by us of any breach of this agreement in any one or more instances, shall in no way be construed as a waiver of any subsequent breach (whether or not of a similar nature) of this agreement by you. No termination of this agreement for any reason whatsoever shall affect in any way any other agreement between us. The headings of any paragraph of this agreement are for convenience only, and shall not be deemed to limit or in any way affect the scope, meaning or intent of this agreement or any part thereof.

(b)   We shall have the right to assign this agreement to any party owning or acquiring a substantial portion of our stock or assets or to any subsidiary, parent or affiliated company, or pursuant to any reorganization or amalgamation or otherwise. We shall also have the right to license any of our rights hereunder as may, in our sole judgment, be desirable or necessary. You shall not have the right to assign any of your rights hereunder. This agreement shall inure to the benefit of and be binding upon each of the parties hereto and their respective successors, permitted assigns, heirs, executors, administrators and legal and personal representatives.

(c)   If any action, suit or proceeding arising from or based upon this agreement is commenced by either party hereto against the other, the prevailing party shall be entitled to recover from the other party its attorneys' fees in connection therewith in addition to the other costs of that action, suit or proceeding;

(d)   The waiver of the applicability of any provision of this agreement or of any default hereunder in a specific instance shall not affect the waiving party's rights thereafter to enforce such provision or to exercise any right or remedy in the event of any other default, whether or not similar.

(e)   This agreement shall be subject to the laws of the State of California applicable to contracts made and to be wholly performed therein. All claims, disputes or disagreements which may arise out of the interpretation, performance or breach of this agreement shall be submitted exclusively to the jurisdiction of the state courts of the State of California or the Federal District courts located in Los Angeles; provided, however, if we are sued or joined in any other court or forum (including an arbitration proceeding) in respect of any matter which may give rise to a claim by us hereunder; you consent to the jurisdiction of such court or forum over any such claim which may be asserted by us. Any process in any action or proceeding commenced in the courts of the State of California arising out of any such claim, dispute or disagreement, may among other methods, be served upon you by delivering or mailing the same, via registered or certified mail, addressed to you at the address given in this agreement or such other address as you may from time to time designate.

17.   **LEADING MEMBERS.** [36]

(a)   A change in the Group name and/or any change in Group membership shall not affect the validity of this agreement. As used herein, the term "Leaving Member" shall mean any member of the Group who ceases to perform and work together with the Group, or any and all Group members in the event that the Group completely disbands. In the case of the former, any of you who continue as members of the Group shall be deemed a Remaining Member. In the event that there is a Leaving Member, you shall promptly notify us in writing (the "Leaving Member Notice") and the following provisions shall apply:

(i)   (a)   If the Leaving Member is replaced by a new member, the new member will be deemed substituted as a party to this agreement in the place of the leaving member and you will cause the new member to execute and deliver to us such instruments as we, in our judgment, may require to accomplish that substitution.[37]   Thereafter, you will have no further obligation to furnish the songwriting services of the Leaving Member under this agreement, but you (and the Leaving Member individually) will continue to be bound by the other provisions of this agreement including, without limitation, paragraph 17(a)(iii) below.

(b)   We will have the right to terminate the Term of this agreement with respect to any Remaining Member of the Group by notice given to you at any time before the expiration of ninety (90) days after our receipt of your Leaving Member Notice.[38] In the event of such termination, all of the Remaining Members will be deemed Leaving Members as of the date of such termination notice, and paragraph 17 (a)(iii) will apply to all of them, collectively or individually as we elect.

(ii)   Each advance becoming payable under this agreement after the Leaving Member ceases to perform as a member of the Group will be reduced in that proportion

---

[36] Publishers want to protect their investment just like record companies do, so they put leaving member provisions in their agreements. Nearly all of the comments I made with respect to leaving member provisions in recording agreements apply to leaving member provisions found in publishing agreements.

[37] See my comments in footnote 43, below.

[38] The publishing company wants the right to do this because the Leaving Member may well be the primary or most gifted songwriter, and the publisher wants to be able to end the deal with the other songwriters.

which the number of Leaving Members bears to the size of the Group as constituted before their departure, whether or not the Leaving Member is replaced by another performer.[39]

          (iii)   You grant to us an option to engage the exclusive songwriting services of each Leaving Member ("Leaving Member Option"). The Leaving Member Option may be exercised by us by notice to the Leaving Member at any time before the expiration of ninety (90) days after the date of: (i) our receipt of your Leaving Member Notice under paragraph 17(a), or (ii) our termination notice pursuant to paragraph 17 (a)(i)(b), as the case may be. If we exercise that Option, the Leaving Member concerned will be deemed to have executed our standard form of songwriter agreement in use at the date of this agreement,[40] containing the following provisions: (1) the Term will commence on the date of our exercise of such Leaving Member Option and may be extended by us, at our election exercisable in the manner provided in paragraph 2(b) of this agreement, for the same number of additional periods as the number of option periods, if any, remaining pursuant to paragraph 2(b) at the time of our exercise of the Leaving Member Option;[41] (2) the Minimum Delivery Commitment for each Option Period of such Term will be the same as that granted to us in paragraph 6 of this agreement; and (3) if your royalty account under this agreement is in an unrecouped position at the date of our exercise of the Leaving Member Option, a part of the amount of that unrecouped balance, determined in inverse proportion to the reductions prescribed in paragraph 17(a)(ii), will constitute an advance recoupable from those royalties.[42]

        (b)   In addition to the foregoing, if an additional member joins the Group at any time during the Term hereof, you shall give us prompt notice thereof and cause such additional member to become a signatory hereto and to execute this agreement.[43] If you fail to deliver to us a signed copy of such agreement within ten (10) days after our notice, we shall have the right to terminate the

---

[39] Let's say John leaves the Group and Thrifty Scot exercises its Leaving Member Option. Pursuant to this paragraph, the advance payable to him under the new deal would be one-half of the advance payable to the Group as originally constituted. Publishers try to justify this reduction by pointing out that they are getting one less songwriter for their money (although the Leaving Member songwriter and any retained Remaining Member songwriters are still obligated to fulfill the Minimum Delivery Commitment in their new deals) and that leaving members are essentially new artists in the eyes of the public. This is true in many cases, but there are always exceptions like Sting and George Michael. Obviously, you want any advances under Leaving Member deals to be reduced as little as possible. If there is one writer in the Group who tends to write most of the Group's songs (similar to a "key member" in a record deal) it is sometimes possible to get away with a small reduction or no reduction at all.

[40] This is really vague and fishy. Some publishers like to "punish" Leaving Member songwriters by making them sign shitty new deals. In this instance, what was a songwriter/co-publishing agreement becomes a straight songwriter deal (i.e., Thrifty Scot will own 100% of the copyright instead of 50%). The terms of the new agreement should be no less favorable than the terms of this agreement, except with respect to reduction of advances as provided for in paragraph 17 (a) (ii). At the very least, make sure the publisher furnishes a copy of the "standard songwriter agreement" before you sign off on this deal.

[41] This isn't too bad — some publishers will add language like "but no less than three option periods in any event."

[42] This means that a Leaving Member will be responsible only for a portion of the band's unrecouped balance. This is better than being on the hook for the whole thing.

[43] This provision doesn't necessarily need to be in the "leaving member" part of this agreement, in that it applies to new members regardless of whether there are leaving members. However, the terms of this paragraph are pretty strict, and it is difficult to force a new member to do something he doesn't want to do. Moreover, the new member might already have a publishing deal. You should try to water this provision down (by pledging to use "reasonable efforts" to cause the new member to sign on to your publishing deal and eliminating the "penalty" provision), or, better yet, eliminate it entirely.

Term of this agreement with respect to the other member(s) of the Group by notice given to you at any time within ninety (90) days after that ten (10) day period. In the event of such termination, all of the members of the Group will be deemed Leaving Members as of the date of such termination notice, and paragraph 17(a)(iii) will apply to each of them, collectively or individually as we elect.[44]

If the foregoing is in accordance with your understanding of the agreement between you and us in respect of the subject matter hereof, please so indicate by signing in the space provided below.

Very truly yours,

THRIFTY SCOT SONGS, LLC

By:_____
   Colin MacFrugal
   Senior Vice President
   Legal and Business Affairs

ACCEPTED AND AGREED TO:

_____   _____

FRED JOHNSON   JOHN DOE

p/k/a "Lawn Chocolate"

LAWN CHOCOLATE SONGS

By:_____
   An Authorized Signatory

---

[44] As I noted in footnote 43, this is pretty harsh.

SCHEDULE "A"

SONGWRITER ROYALTIES

1. Writer's share of public performance income: if collected directly by us and not through a performing rights organization: 50% of Gross Income, which shall be paid to you without regard to recoupment of advances.[45]

2. Original Mechanical Royalty Income: 50% of Gross Income

3. Cover Recording Mechanical Royalty Income: 40% of Gross Income[46]

4. Synchronization Income: 50% of Gross Income

5. Foreign Income: 50% of Gross Income

6. Other Income (including, without limitation, print income): 50% of Gross Income

All royalties set forth above shall be prorated with respect to any musical composition which is subject hereto only in part as a Composition.

---

[45] This is paid without regard to recoupment of advances because you normally receive your writer's share of public performance income directly from your performing rights organization, even if you are hopelessly unrecouped.

[46] As I noted in Chapter Six, publishers always try to retain a larger chunk of income generated by covers (and synch licenses too, although they were not successful on that count under this deal). Limit this to covers/synch licenses secured directly by the publisher.

EXHIBIT "A"

COPYRIGHT ASSIGNMENT

KNOW ALL MEN BY THESE PRESENTS:

FOR AND IN CONSIDERATION of the sum of One ($1.00) Dollar and other good and valuable consideration, receipt of which is hereby acknowledged, the undersigned do hereby sell, assign, transfer and set over unto the THRIFTY SCOT SONGS, LLC its successors and assigns and to its successors and assigns, all right, title and interest in and to the copyrights in the following musical compositions which were written by the following indicated persons:

Title	Writer	Share	Copyright Office Registration No.

and all of the right, title and interest of the undersigned, vested and contingent, in and to the full term of copyright therein and thereto. Each of Thrifty Scot Songs, LLC and Lawn Chocolate Songs shall own an undivided fifty (50%) percent interest in and to such compositions.

IN WITNESS WHEREOF, the undersigned has hereunto set his hand and seal this ___ day of ___, 199_.

_____

_____

EXHIBIT "B"

"EXISTING COMPOSITIONS"

1 – "Just Like Biff Loman's Blues"
2 – "Tube Top"
3 – "Magpie"
4 – "Revolux"
5 – "Corduroy"
6 – "Burst Into Flames"
7 – "Roxy"
8 – "Tropicalia"

EXHIBIT "C"[47]

Date: October 1, 1998

Publisher Relations Department
Broadcast Music, Inc.
320 West 57th Street
New York, New York 10019

Gentlemen:

This is to advise BMI that we have entered into an agreement with another BMI publisher for the administration of our catalog, and that BMI's records should be marked to reflect the agreement as follows:

1.   Name of BMI publisher acting as our administrator: THRIFTY SCOT SONGS, LLC

2.   Effective date of agreement:

_____ Immediately, including all royalties now payable or which hereafter become payable, regard less of when performances took place.

CHECK ONE

_____ Effective with performances on and after _____ 199_. (Must be as of the beginning of a calendar quarter, i.e., January 1, April 1, July 1 or October 1.)

3.   Checks for all our BMI royalties, both domestic and foreign, should be made payable to the administrator and should be sent together with the statements and all other correspondence to the administrator at its address on BMI's records.

We understand that BMI cannot mark its records at this time so as to indicate the termination date of the administration agreement and that, therefore, the above information will continue to be reflected on BMI's records until such time as we or the administrator notifies BMI that the administration agreement is about to terminate.

Very truly yours,

_____

JOHN DOE

_____

FRED JOHNSON

collectively d.b.a. Lawn Chocolate/Lawn Chocolate Songs

_____

[47] This letter lets the appropriate performing rights organization (BMI in this case) know that Thrifty Scot will be entitled to collect the publisher's share of public performance royalties until further notice. There is a letter similar this attached to every publishing agreement.

SAMPLE MECHANICAL LICENSE[1]

COPYRIGHT LICENSE AGREEMENT ON BEHALF OF: Thrifty Scot Records, Inc.
1234 Main Street
Anytown, CA 90000

With respect to the release of

    Artist: LAWN CHOCOLATE
    Selection Number: TS666
    Album Title: THIS IS LAWN CHOCOLATE
    Release Date: 6/15/99

AGREEMENT made and entered into between

PUBLISHER: PERCENTAGE CONTROLLED:
                                               100.00%[2]

Lawn Chocolate Songs
c/o Dewey, Cheatum & Howe
11111 San Viejo Blvd.
Los Angeles, CA 90000
Attention: Art Cheatum, Esq.

(hereinafter called the "Licensor") and Thrifty Scot Records, Inc. (hereinafter called the "Licensee").

1.   Licensor warrants and represents that it is the owner of a valid United States copyright in the following musical composition:

    Title: Just Like Biff Loman's Blues[3]
    Writer(s): John Doe/Fred Smith
    Timing: 4:12

(hereinafter called the "Composition"), and has the right, free from any claim by any other party, to grant the license herein provided.

2.   Licensor grants to Licensee the non-exclusive right, privilege and license, irrevocably during the terms of the copyright and all renewals and extensions thereof, to use the Composition, to make and/or use arrangements thereof, and to use the title thereof, in the manufacture and sale of parts of instruments serving to reproduce the Composition, including sound recordings in all forms, whether

---

[1] As an accommodation to artists and publishers, record companies will often send mechanical licenses to the publisher (even though it is the publisherís responsibility to do so). This is fine, as long as the terms mirror those found in the applicable recording agreement. This sample is based on a mechanical license drafted from a record company perspective.

[2] It seems our heroes somehow managed to maintain complete ownership of their publishing. Accordingly, their publishing designee (Lawn Chocolate Songs) is the Licensor of mechanical reproduction rights. If Fred and John each owned and administered their 50% share of this song separately, each publishing company would have to issue a separate license to the record company for 50%.

[3] Some record companies prefer to include only one song per license, while others list all controlled compositions on one license.

now or hereafter devised or discovered (all hereinafter called "Records") throughout the United States, its territories and possessions (the "Territory").[4]

3. (a) Licensee shall pay copyright royalties to Licensor at the following rate on the basis of net Records manufactured and sold[5] by Licensee in the territory during the term of said copyright and all renewals and extensions thereof (excluding records distributed for promotional purposes of "Free", whether or not intended for resale):

Base Royalty Rate for Share Listed Above: $0.0484[6]

Rate pursuant to paragraph 10 of the agreement between Thrifty Scot Records, Inc. and Lawn Chocolate dated January 1, 1999. AFG: 50%[7]

(b) In respect of mid-price Records, budget Records, long-play singles and EPs, the rate shall be 75% of the specified rate herein.[8]

4. Licensee shall render to Licensor quarterly statements and payments therefor, of all royalties payable hereunder, within 45 days after March 31, June 30, September 30 and December 31, for each quarter for which any such royalties accrue pursuant to the terms hereof. Licensee shall have the right to retain a reasonable reserve[9] against subsequent charges, credits or returns. All royalty statements and all other accounts rendered by Licensee to Licensor shall be binding upon Licensor and not subject to any objection by Licensor for any reason unless specific objection in writing, stating the basis thereof, is given to Licensee within one year[10] from the date rendered.

5. No royalties shall be payable under the agreement with respect to: (a) Records exported to countries where copyright royalties are payable in connection with their importation or sale, or (b) devices (such as masters, mothers, and stampers) exported for use in the manufacture and sale of Records.

6. The license herein shall include the right to embody the Composition on promotional videos and to distribute and perform these videos throughout the world and to authorize others to do so for the purposes of promoting sales of Records embodying the Composition, without payment, so long as such use is promotional in nature.[11]

---

[4] This is the actual grant of rights paragraph. Note that the license is for the U.S. only. The record company needs to get a separate license for Canada.

[5] Notice that this license pays mechanical royalties only on records sold (save for 50% of album free goods). This is standard for a mechanical rights licenses issued pursuant to a controlled composition clause.

[6] Lawn Chocolate Songs will be paid almost five cents per song on the album. How did I figure this out? The current statutory rate is 7.1 cents per song. The band's record deal pays a reduced rate (75%) on a maximum of ten songs per album. 75% of 7.1 is 5.325 cents. Since there are eleven songs on the album, the mechanical royalty payable for each song is 4.84 cents (53.25 divided by eleven). All of this assumes that there are no non-controlled songs on the album.

[7] "AFG: 50%" means that mechanical royalties will be paid on 50% of album free goods.

[8] This means that the mechanical royalty rate is equal to 75% of 75% for these kinds of sales.

[9] The same contract provisions that govern record royalty reserve policies should govern mechanical royalty reserve policies.

[10] This isn't much time.

[11] Whether or not you get mechanical royalties on videos is negotiated in the recording agreement.

7.	Licensor indemnifies, and shall hold Licensee harmless from all loss, damage or expense (including legal expenses and attorney's fees) (a) arising out of or connected with any claim by a third party which is inconsistent with any of Licensor's warranties herein, or (b) by reason of any adjudication invalidating the copyright in the Composition.

8.	This agreement is assignable by either party, and shall be binding upon the heirs, legal representatives, successors and assigns of the parties hereto. Such an assignment shall not relieve Licensor of its obligations pursuant to paragraph 7 above. The execution of the agreement by Licensee shall constitute and is accepted by Licensor as full compliance with all obligations of Licensee to Licensor, statutory and otherwise, arising from or connected with Licensee's use of the Composition as provided herein.

LICENSOR: Lawn Chocolate Songs

By: _____
Federal Tax I.D. Number or
Social Security Number:

LICENSEE: Thrifty Scot Records, Inc.

By: _____

SAMPLE PARTNERSHIP AGREEMENT[1]

This Partnership Agreement ("Agreement") is made and entered into as of this 1st day of January, 1999, by and among JOHN DOE, FRED JOHNSON and BOB SMITH, currently collectively professionally known as "LAWN CHOCOLATE" (hereinafter referred to collectively as the "Partners" and individually as "Partner").

WITNESSETH:

WHEREAS, the Partners have heretofore conducted business as LAWN CHOCOLATE together under an oral partnership agreement (the "Prior Partnership").

WHEREAS, the Partners desire to enter into this written Agreement concerning the business of the Partners, which Agreement shall supersede and cancel all prior understandings and agreements, oral or written, concerning such business, including the Prior Partnership.

NOW, THEREFORE, in consideration of the mutual promises contained herein, the parties hereto agree as follows:

ARTICLE I
FORMATION OF GENERAL PARTNERSHIP

1.1 **Type Of Business**. The parties hereto hereby form a general partnership ("Partnership"), upon the terms herein set forth. The Partnership shall engage in the business of utilizing and commercially exploiting the collective talents of the Partners as the musical group professionally known as "Lawn Chocolate" (the "Group") in all media of public entertainment throughout the world, including phonograph recordings, motion pictures, television, radio, advertising, literary and dramatic endeavors, merchandising, publications, and all other related activities ("Partnership Business"). Notwithstanding the foregoing, the Partnership Business shall not include any music publishing or songwriting activities of any of the Partners (or any of their affiliated or related entities), and the Partners anticipate entering into separate agreements with respect to such activities.[2]

---

[1] This is a fairly thorough partnership agreement that gives each partner equal voting rights and equal shares of partnership profits and losses.

[2] Many bands find it beneficial to exclude songwriting and publishing matters from the scope of the general band agreement. This makes sense for a number of reasons. For instance, if all of the band's songs are written by one or two members, keeping the publishing out of the general band partnership keeps the publishing income away from the non-writing members. Another reason to exclude publishing from a general band partnership: song copyrights can be very valuable. If someone successfully sues the partnership, those valuable copyrights (and the royalties flowing from them) are at risk. If you elect to exclude publishing matters from your partnership agreement, make sure your attorney draws up a separate agreement that specifies which writers own what shares of the songs written by the band. Under this sample agreement, record royalties, live performance income and merchandising income are the major income sources involved. Note that some bands also exclude live performance income and activities from their partnership agreement. As discussed in Chapter 8, these bands typically form separate touring entities (usually corporations) as a hedge against personal liability. Finally, some bands also choose to exclude so-called "outside activities" (such as producing records by other artists, acting, painting, whatever) from the scope of the band agreement.

1.2 **Name Of Partnership.** The name of the Partnership shall be "THE LAWN CHOCO-LATE PARTNERSHIP" and the Partnership shall operate and conduct business under such name.[3]

1.3 **Place Of Business.** The principal place of business of the Partnership shall be at such place or places within or without the State of California as the Partners may, from time to time, determine.

1.4 **Term Of Partnership.** The Partnership shall commence as of January 1, 1999, and shall continue until dissolved in accordance with this Agreement.

ARTICLE 2
PARTNERSHIP CAPITAL

2.1 **Initial Capital.** Each Partner shall contribute to the Partnership his or her exclusive services as a member of the Group as reasonably necessary to conduct Partnership Business during the term hereof in all activities throughout the field of entertainment, and as required by any agreement heretofore or hereafter entered into by the Group or the Partnership, and all results and proceeds of such services as a member of the Group, as further provided by Section 1.1 above.[4] Notwithstanding the foregoing, no Partner shall be required to contribute to the Partnership any songwriting services or the results and proceeds of songwriting services or any music publishing activities. The initial capital of the Partnership shall consist of all assets and obligations of the Prior Partnership, including the following:

(a) All right, title, and interest in and to the name "Lawn Chocolate" (the "Group Name");[5]

(b) All trademarks, service marks, and goodwill of the Prior Partnership;

(c) All equipment and other assets owned by the Prior Partnership; and

(d) The recording agreement entered into as of June 1, 1998 by and between John Doe, Bob Smith and Fred Johnson on the one hand, and Thrifty Scot Records, Inc., on the other (the "Recording Agreement").

(e) Notwithstanding the foregoing, the Partners hereby agree that all of the instruments, musical, sound and video equipment presently owned by each Partner and used in connection with the activities of the Partnership shall continue to belong to such Partner according to such Partner's present ownership interest therein, but during the term of the Partnership, in the event that such Partner shall remain a Partner, the Partnership shall be entitled to the full use thereof, free of charge, except for insurance and repairs. All other instruments, musical, sound and/or video equipment hereafter acquired in connection with the Partnership activities, shall be paid for from the Partnership

---

[3] You can give your partnership any name you want, but most bands name the partnership after the band and file a "doing business as" notice in the county where they conduct their business.

[4] Some bands require each partner to contribute a certain amount of cash to the partnership at inception, but the members of Lawn Chocolate are simply contributing their services and other assets.

[5] As we have discussed, the band name is a very important asset. This provision establishes that the Group Name belongs to the Partnership and that the use of the name is governed by the terms of the Partnership Agreement.

monies and shall be deemed assets of the Partnership. Notwithstanding anything to the contrary contained herein, upon the Termination (as hereinafter defined) of any Partner due to expulsion or withdrawal from the Partnership, such Terminated Partner (as hereinafter defined) shall have the right to acquire from the Partnership, all right, title and interest in and to such equipment owned by the Partnership as utilized exclusively by such Partner (for example, guitars, pianos, amplifiers, etc.) prior to such Partner's Termination for a sum equal to the fair market value of such equipment.[6]

2.2 Capital Accounts.[7]

(a) An individual capital account shall be maintained for each Partner. Initially, a Partner's capital account shall equal the amount of such Partner's capital account in the Prior Partnership, as adjusted for such Partner's share of income, expense, gain and loss incurred by the Prior Partnership through the effective date of this Agreement. The Partners hereby agree that for purposes of valuing the Partners' capital accounts, the assets specified in paragraphs 2.1(a) and (b) hereof shall be deemed to have zero value.[8]

(b) Each Partner's capital account shall be increased by (i) the amount of cash contributed to the Partnership by such Partner, (ii) the fair market value of property contributed to the Partnership by such Partner net of any liabilities securing such contributed property that the Partnership assumes or takes subject to, and (iii) the portion of any Partnership net income or gain allocated to such Partner. Each Partner's capital account shall be decreased by (i) the amount of cash distributed by the Partnership to such Partner, (ii) the fair market value of property distributed by the Partnership to such Partner net of any liabilities securing any such distributed property that such Partner assumes or takes subject to, and (iii) the portion of any Partnership net loss allocated to such Partner.

2.3 Additional Contributions to Capital.
No Partner shall be required to make additional contributions to the capital of the Partnership. Any voluntary contributions to the capital of the Partnership must be authorized by Partnership Vote (as hereinafter defined).

2.4 Withdrawal of Capital.
No Partner shall withdraw any portion of the capital of the Partnership without approval by Partnership Vote, and any withdrawal of capital by a Partner shall reduce such Partner's capital account by the amount of such withdrawal.

2.5 Loans To Partnership.
No Partner shall loan or advance money to the Partnership without approval by Partnership Vote. Any loan by a Partner to the partnership shall be separately recorded in the Partnership books as a loan to the Partnership, shall bear interest at a rate determined by Partnership Vote and shall be evidenced by a promissory note delivered to the lending Partner and executed in the name of the Partnership by one or more of the non-lending Partners.

---

[6] I picked this provision out of an agreement drafted by a former colleague, and it allows a Terminated Partner to leave with things like guitars and other pieces of equipment that musicians tend to get attached to. This would not include equipment like computers, trucks or PA systems.

[7] WARNING: We're getting into accountant territory here, so just remember that I'm an attorney, not an accountant.

[8] This is important, because it is very difficult to calculate the value of a name or a trademark. For instance, it's safe to say that the mark "The Beatles" is extremely valuable, and that the mark "Lawn Chocolate" is much less so. Assigning a fixed value to such rights (whether the value is $1.00 or $1,000,000) makes it easier to manage the Partnership when it comes to leaving members, etc.

2.6 Deficit Capital Accounts. If any Partner's capital account has a deficit balance following the liquidation of such Partner's interest in the Partnership, then such Partner or such Partner's estate shall restore the amount of such deficit to the Partnership within the later of (a) the close of the Partnership's taxable year in which such liquidation occurs, or (b) ninety (90) days after the date of the liquidation.

ARTICLE 3
ACCOUNTINGS, BOOKS AND RECORDS

3.1 Method of Accounting. The accounting books of the Partnership shall be kept on (i) the cash receipts and disbursements method of accounting or (ii) the accrual method of accounting in accordance with generally accepted accounting principles and practices[9] as all the Partners shall agree.

3.2 Fiscal Year. The fiscal year of the Partnership shall be the calendar year.

3.3 Accountings. As soon as reasonably practicable, but no later than ninety (90) days after the close of each fiscal year, a full and accurate accounting shall be made of the affairs of the Partnership as of the close of such fiscal year. As part of such accounting, the Partnership shall furnish to each Partner a copy of a balance sheet of the Partnership as of the last day of such fiscal year, a statement of income or loss of the Partnership for such fiscal year, a statement of allocations pursuant to this Agreement for such fiscal year, and a statement of tax allocations for such fiscal year pursuant to the Internal Revenue Code, as amended (the "Code").[10]

3.4 Books of Account. Complete and accurate books of all transactions of the Partnership shall be maintained at the principal place of business of the Partnership until such time as the Partnership elects to engage an accountant for the Partnership (hereinafter, the accountant for the Partnership shall be referred to as the "Accountant"), who shall be designated from time to time by Partnership Vote. Each Partner shall, at all reasonable times, have access to the Partnership's books and may inspect and copy such books, provided that any such inspection is made in good faith.

3.5 Bank Accounts. The Partnership shall maintain checking and/or savings accounts at such bank or banks as determined by Partnership Vote. All funds shall be deposited in the name of the Partnership, and may be withdrawn only upon the signature of such person or persons designated in writing by Partnership Vote.

ARTICLE 4
PROFITS, LOSSES AND DISTRIBUTIONS

4.1 Allocation of Profits and Losses. Net Profits and Net Losses (as such terms are defined in paragraph 4.2 below) of the Partnership shall be allocated equally among the Partners.[11]

---

[9] Ask your accountant what these are.

[10] Remember that a partnership doesn't pay taxes. Instead, your accountant will file an informational tax return for the Partnership that allocates profits and losses to individual Partners. Each Partner then files an individual tax return based on his or her share of profits or losses from the Partnership.

[11] Pay attention — this is the section of the Partnership agreement that divvies up the profits and losses of the Partnership. As I mentioned at the start of the Agreement, the three Partners in Lawn Chocolate have elected to share equally in the profits and losses of the Partnership. Keep in mind however that you can come up with any kind of split you want as long as you specify it in the agreement or agree to subject the allocation to a Partnership Vote.

4.2 **"Net Profits" and "Net Losses."** "Net Profits" and "Net Losses" shall be defined as the net profits and net losses of the Partnership, derived from any source whatsoever, for each fiscal year of the Partnership as finally determined for federal income tax purposes under the method of accounting provided by Article 3.1 hereof.

4.3 **Distributions.** Promptly following the rendering of financial statements for each fiscal year of the Partnership, and after consulting with the Accountant, the Partnership shall distribute to the Partners in the proportion set forth in paragraph 4.1 any cash not reasonably necessary for the operation of the Partnership business.[12] Such distributions shall occur no less frequently than on a semi-annual basis. Said amount shall be determined by the unanimous approval of the Partners. The Partnership shall make additional distributions to the Partners from the capital of the Partnership at such other times and in amounts to be determined by Partnership Vote. Any such distributions shall, however, be in proportion to the Partner's shares of the Partnership's Net Profits as provided pursuant to paragraph 4.1. Notwithstanding the foregoing, and subject to the provisions of Article 7 hereof, no Partner shall be entitled to receive cash or other property, compensation or remuneration in connection with or on account of performances or other services performed by the Partnership with respect to which said Partner shall fail or refuse to render his or her services.[13]

ARTICLE 5
DUTIES OF PARTNERS

5.1 Each Partner hereby agrees that the Partnership shall be entitled during the term hereof to his or her personal services to record and deliver such master recordings as may be required pursuant to the Recording Agreement, and that such Partner shall further perform on behalf of the Partnership all personal services which the Partnership shall request and direct in connection therewith, unless the Partners shall otherwise agree pursuant to a Partnership Vote. For purposes hereof, such services of such Partner shall include without limitation any and all personal appearances in musical concerts and any other entertainment event of any kind, nature or description, motion pictures, filmed and live television, all fields of recording, including, without limitation, the recording of commercial phonograph records, tapes and audio-visual recordings, or other reproductions by any method existing presently or in the future, merchandising, commercials, commercial tie-ups, endorsements, and any other activities customarily deemed within the entertainment field as well as any and all related or incidental activities in connection with the advertising, exploitation or advancement of the aforesaid areas of endeavor or the results and proceeds of any of the aforesaid services and such other activities as the requisite Partners may agree to conduct pursuant to a Partnership Vote, but shall specifically exclude the Partners' songwriting services (or the results and proceeds of the Partners' songwriting services) and music publishing activities. Each such Partner further represents and warrants that such Partner has neither made nor will make any contractual or other commitment which would hinder or interfere to any degree with the nature of or his or her full and complete performance of the aforesaid services, except with the consent of the Partners pursuant to a Partnership Vote.

---

[12] "Any cash not reasonably necessary for the operation of Partnership business" is the cash left over after paying agency, management and accounting and legal fees, as well as any foreseeable costs of running the Partnership (office overhead, anticipated rehearsal and equipment costs, etc.).

[13] In other words, if you don't play, you don't get paid. Some bands make exceptions to this rule in cases where a Partner is disabled due to circumstances beyond that Partner's control.

5.2 Subject to Article 7 hereof, the failure of any Partner to render any personal services required hereunder for any reason other than death, disability, expulsion or withdrawal shall constitute a material breach of this Agreement by said Partner, and shall render said Partner liable to the remaining Partners and the Partnership to the full extent of any damages suffered as a result thereof.[14] Each Partner further acknowledges and agrees that his or her services to be rendered hereunder are special, unique, unusual, extraordinary and of an intellectual character giving them a peculiar value, the loss of which cannot be adequately compensated in damages in an action at law, and that in the event of a breach of this Agreement by the failure of that Partner to render services as provided hereunder, the remaining Partners and/or the Partnership shall (in addition to any other available remedies) be entitled to seek the equitable remedies of preliminary and permanent injunction, specific performance and any other equitable relief.

5.3 INTENTIONALLY DELETED[15]

5.4 Each Partner hereby grants to the Partnership the worldwide right in perpetuity to use and to authorize third parties to use and display his or her name (both legal and professional), voice and likeness and biographical materials concerning him or her as same may be identified or associated with the Group. Said right of the Partnership shall be nonexclusive. Each such Partner further agrees that such Partner shall not transfer or attempt to transfer any right, privilege, title or interest in or to any such right, nor grant such right to, authorize, or willfully permit any person, firm or corporation to infringe upon any such right hereby granted to the Partnership, and each such Partner hereby authorizes the Partnership, in his or her name or otherwise, to institute any legal proceeding or proceedings to prevent such infringement.[16]

ARTICLE 6
MANAGEMENT

6.1 **Partnership Vote**.

(a) Except as otherwise specified herein, the management and conduct of the general Partnership Business and all decisions with respect thereto shall be decided by majority vote of the Partners (such majority vote is referred to in this Agreement as a "Partnership Vote"). For purposes of this Agreement, each Partner shall have one (1) vote. Without limiting the generality of the fore-

---

[14] This is important. Let's say the Partnership signs a contract to headline the giant Woodstock 2000 concert, and let's say Fred decides he doesn't want to play the gig because "he doesn't feel like it." The band cancels the gig and the promoters of the concert sue the Partnership. Assuming the promoters win a judgment of $100,000 against the Partnership, all Partners would be responsible for paying the judgment. However, this provision makes Fred solely liable among the Partners, and the Partners can seek recovery from Fred of the $100,000 judgment.

[15] You may be asking yourself, "Why the hell do lawyers include paragraphs that say 'intentionally deleted?'" It's like this: In most agreements there are provisions that refer to other provisions of the agreement. However, sometimes certain paragraphs aren't appropriate for certain agreements. Since deleting such a paragraph will result in the re-numbering of all the paragraph numbers, savvy attorneys simply put in the "intentionally deleted" language to retain correct paragraph numbering (and save time and money).

[16] This provision gives the Partnership the right to authorize third parties to use the name, likeness, etc. of the Partners in connection with Partnership Business. As I am sure you are aware, the use of name and likeness is important in nearly all aspects of the music and entertainment business, from merchandising and record sales to advertising for concerts, etc.

going and except as otherwise specified herein, no Partner shall have the authority to act on behalf of the Partnership in any capacity except with the approval of a majority of the Partners' votes.[17]

(b) Notwithstanding the foregoing, a unanimous vote of the Partners shall be required in the following matters:[18]

(i) Borrowing money in the Partnership's name;

(ii) Loaning Partnership funds;

(iii) Transferring, mortgaging, pledging, assigning, hypothecating, or otherwise granting, disposing of, or encumbering any Partnership assets, including goodwill;

(iv) Entering into any agreement that would place a Partner in conflict with, or in breach of, any provision of this Agreement, the Recording Agreement or of any other agreement entered into by the Partnership concerning the Partnership Business (collectively, the "Approved Agreements");

(v) Confessing a judgment against the Partnership;

(vi) Making, executing, delivering or guaranteeing any commercial paper on behalf of the Partnership;

(vii) Compromising or releasing of debt owing to the Partnership;

(viii) Submitting a Partnership claim or liability to arbitration;

(ix) Expelling or admitting a new partner to the Partnership;

(x) Spending money on behalf of the Partnership in excess of Five Hundred Dollars ($500.00) with respect to any single transaction or incurring any obligation on behalf of the Partnership with payment obligations greater than $500;

(xi) Executing any recording, management, agency or merchandising agreement; or

(xii) Amending this Agreement.

6.2 **Managing Partner.** Pursuant to Partnership Vote, the Partners may, from time to time, designate a managing partner with such powers and duties and subject to removal upon such terms and conditions determined by Partnership Vote. The Partnership's right of consent or approval under

---

[17] This is yet another key provision in that it specifies how the Partners vote on business matters. While this particular agreement gives each Partner one vote and requires a majority vote, some bands elect to give certain members more than one vote. In such a case, the Partnership Agreement should state that a majority vote shall be determined by the number of relevant votes and not by the number of Partners.

[18] The band has decided to require a unanimous vote when it comes to less mundane matters such as these.

any Approved Agreement may be exercised by the managing partner or any other person designated by Partnership Vote. Unless and until otherwise agreed as set forth herein, the managing partner shall be Fred Johnson.[19]

6.3 **Deadlock.** If the Partners become deadlocked on an issue that requires a unanimous or majority vote of the Partners, then such issue shall not be decided until a unanimous or majority vote (as the case may be) of the Partners is obtained.[20]

6.4 **Personal Liability.** Any Partner who enters into any contract or incurs any obligation on behalf of, or on the credit of, the Partnership in violation of the provisions of this Agreement shall indemnify the other Partners for any and all losses or expenses incurred pursuant to such contract or obligation.[21]

6.5 **Meetings.** Upon reasonable notice, and pursuant to Partnership Vote, the Partners may, from time to time, elect to call a meeting of the Partners at any reasonable time at the Partnership's principal place of business. In such event, any and all expenses incurred by the Partners in attending such meeting shall be borne solely by each said Partner unless the Partnership agrees otherwise pursuant to a Partnership Vote.

ARTICLE 7
TERMINATION OR ADMISSION OF A PARTNER

7.1 **Death of a Partner.** Upon the death of a Partner, the legal representative of the deceased Partner shall be obligated to sell to the Partnership, and the Partnership shall be obligated to purchase, the deceased Partner's interest in the Partnership. The acquisition of such deceased Partner's interest in the Partnership shall be accomplished in accordance with the terms of this Agreement and shall become effective as of the date of death of such deceased Partner.[22]

7.2 **Expulsion of a Partner.** Any Partner may be involuntarily expelled from the Partnership with or without cause ("Expelled Partner"), by the affirmative act of a majority of the Partners.[23] Expulsion from the Partnership shall be effective thirty (30) days after delivery to said

---

[19] This comes in handy when a decision needs to be made quickly and it is impossible or difficult to arrange for a Partnership Vote. For instance, the record company may need approval to put a recording in a TV ad, or may need approval on some artwork. This provision gives Fred the right to give or withhold such approval without a Partnership Vote (but only with respect to circumstances where an Approved Agreement calls for the band's consent on a given matter). While I have found that it is a good idea to appoint a Managing Partner, you should choose him or her wisely.

[20] Some bands allow their manager or attorney to cast a tie-breaking vote in certain situations.

[21] Once again, while the Partnership is liable for the acts or omissions of Partners acting within the scope of the partnership agreement, this doesn't mean that you can't add a provision (like this one) that aims to protect the partners and the partnership from the stupid or negligent acts of other partners.

[22] This provision forces the spouse or heir of a Partner to sell a deceased Partner's interest in the Partnership to the remaining Partners. This makes sense, since it is unlikely that the spouse or heir of the deceased will possess the unique skills necessary to contribute to the Partnership Business.

[23] In other words, any two Partners can kick the other Partner out of the band for any reason at all. This is obviously a crucial part of any band agreement, and you want to give serious thought as to whether to include this procedure. For instance, some bands allow expulsion only if the Partner to be expelled is disabled by his or her own behavior (e.g., drug or alcohol abuse). This is a tough issue, but it's really important.

Expelled Partner of written notice of expulsion by the Partnership. The expulsion of any Partner shall not dissolve the Partnership (but rather the remaining Partners agree to continue the Partnership) or in itself constitute a breach of this Agreement.

7.3 **Withdrawal of a Partner.** Any Partner may voluntarily withdraw from the Partnership, provided that (1) notwithstanding such withdrawal that Partner shall remain obligated to exclusively perform his or her personal services for the Partnership (as required by Article 5.1 hereof to the extent the nonperformance of his or her said services (in the sole judgment of the Partnership) would constitute or cause, directly or indirectly, the breach of any agreement between the Partnership and any third party (including the Approved Agreements), or otherwise subject the Partnership to any damages, costs, expenses, liabilities or other obligations (whether actual or contingent), and (2) provided further that such withdrawal shall not modify or limit in any respect the rights of the Partnership or of the remaining Partners with respect to any breach of this Agreement or any agreement between the Partnership and any third party otherwise committed by the Withdrawing Partner (as hereinafter defined).[24] The withdrawal of any Partner shall not dissolve the Partnership or in itself constitute a breach of this Agreement. Withdrawal from the Partnership shall be effective thirty (30) days after the delivery to all Partners of written notice of withdrawal signed by the Withdrawing Partner. The term "Withdrawing Partner" shall be defined as any Partner who voluntarily withdraws from the Partnership hereunder.

7.4 **Disability of a Partner.** A Partner may be expelled from the Partnership by reason of a Disability. For purposes of this Agreement, a Partner shall be deemed to be "Disabled" or subject to a "Disability" if he or she is substantially unable to render all of the services performed by him or her immediately prior to such purported disability for a continuous period of six (6) months.[25] A Partner's Disability shall be deemed to commence upon the last day of the foregoing period of six (6) continuous months. The Partnership shall not be dissolved upon the Disability of any Partner, but rather the remaining Partners agree to continue the Partnership.

7.5 **Purchase and Sale of Partnership Interest.**[26] Upon the withdrawal, expulsion, Disability or death (hereinafter collectively referred to as the "Termination") of any Partner in accordance with this Article 7 (hereinafter, any such Withdrawing Partner, Expelled Partner, Disabled Partner, or deceased Partner shall be referred to as a "Terminated Partner"), such Terminated Partner, or such Terminated Partner's estate, shall, in accordance with Article 8, sell to the Partnership, and the Partnership shall purchase, for an amount calculated in accordance with Article 8, the Terminated Partner's interest in the Partnership; provided, however, that no such obligations shall exist if, upon such Termination, the Partnership elects by Partnership Vote, within thirty (30) days after such Termination, to liquidate and wind up the Partnership in accordance with this Agreement.

---

[24] This provision allows any Partner to quit as long as they stay around long enough to allow the band to fulfill its obligations. For instance, if Fred decides to quit in the middle of a tour, this provision obligates him to stay in the band for the rest of the tour if leaving the band would result in the breach of any contracts. Does this mean that Fred is a slave to the band? Of course not, but he would be liable to the Partnership for damages if he didn't finish the tour.

[25] You want to consider the definition of "disability" very carefully. For instance, should a partner be deemed disabled if he or she is suffering from an illness from which he or she may recover? Should drug addiction or alcoholism be considered disabilities? The definition of "disability" in this agreement is extremely broad.

[26] This provision (along with Article 8) "prenegotiates" the exit deal for any Partner — this is one of the primary reasons why bands enter into written band agreements. This way, there is little room for negotiation once a Partner dies, quits or is expelled.

7.6 Bankruptcy, Incompetence or Insolvency. For purposes of this Agreement, a judicial declaration of the incompetence, bankruptcy, or insolvency of a Partner shall automatically constitute a withdrawal of such Partner from the Partnership, to which withdrawal the provisions of paragraph 7.3 shall apply, effective as of the last day of the month during which any such event occurs.[27]

7.7 Restrictions on Transfer. No Partner shall transfer any or all of such Partner's interest in the Partnership, whether voluntarily or involuntarily (including by way of sale, assignment, gift, will, intestate succession, marital dissolution, or death of a spouse), to any person (including any other Partner) without the prior unanimous consent of the Partners. If a Partner attempts to transfer any or all of his interest in the Partnership to any transferee without such consent, then such purported transfer shall constitute a withdrawal of such Partner from the Partnership, to which the provisions of paragraph 7.5 shall apply, and such purported transferee shall not receive any interest in either the Partnership or any Partnership assets. The parties agree that the current spouse(s) and any prospective spouse(s) of all Partners shall execute a Spouse's Consent in the form of the Spouse's Consent attached hereto and incorporated herein as Exhibit "B."[28]

7.8 New Partners. New Partners may be admitted to the Partnership only upon the unanimous written consent of the Partners.[29] A new Partner shall be admitted upon the receipt by the Partnership of the new Partner's capital contribution (as described below), provided that the new Partner simultaneously executes an agreement and such other documents as may be reasonably requested by the Partners, under the terms of which such Partner agrees to be bound by all of the provisions hereof, as amended, as if a signatory hereto. Unless expressly agreed upon by the unanimous vote of the Partners, such new Partner shall be deemed a non-voting Partner and shall have no interest whatsoever in the Group Name apart from the limited right to be known as a member of the Group. Such new Partner's capital contribution, if any, and share of the Partnership's Net Profits and Net Losses shall be agreed upon by unanimous written consent of the Partners (except the new Partner).

ARTICLE 8
PURCHASE PRICE OF A PARTNERSHIP INTEREST

8.1 Partnership Obligation. The full purchase price required to be paid by the Partnership for a Terminated Partner's interest in the Partnership shall be an obligation payable solely from Partnership assets (both present and future) and not a personal obligation of the Partners, and shall consist solely of the amounts, and payable in the manner, specified in this Article 8.

8.2 Elimination of Capital Account. As of the effective date of the Termination of a Partner (hereinafter the effective date of a Termination shall be referred to as the "Valuation Date"), the Terminated Partner's individual capital account shall be adjusted to reflect the Terminated Partner's share of Net Profits or Net Losses of the Partnership from the beginning of the fiscal year in which such Termination occurs until the end of the month preceding the Valuation Date, taking into account for such purpose all Partnership expenses paid or accrued during such period. If, after such adjustment, there remains a credit balance in the Terminated Partner's capital account, then such credit balance shall be paid to the Terminated Partner (if a Terminated Partner is deceased, then any reference in this Agreement to either payments to or from, or statements submitted to, such

---

[27] You don't see this kind of provision isn't in every partnership agreement, but I guess the band wants to rid itself of any members with severe financial problems.

[28] See note 22, above.

[29] This is yet another key point to consider in a band agreement. Lawn Chocolate obviously decided it was a crucial and important issue since they made a unanimous vote necessary to add members.

Terminated Partner shall be interpreted as payments to or from, or statements submitted to, such Terminated Partner's estate) in accordance with paragraphs 8.2(a), (b), and (c) below.

(a) If the credit balance of a Terminated Partner's capital account is equal to or less than Ten Thousand Dollars ($10,000.00), and the Partnership possesses adequate readily available funds, then such credit balance, together with interest on such balance at the Prime Rate in effect on the Valuation Date, shall be paid by the Partnership to the Terminated Partner within ninety (90) days after the Valuation Date.

(b) To the extent the credit balance of a Terminated Partner's capital account exceeds Ten Thousand Dollars ($10,000.00), or in the event that the Partnership does not possess adequate readily available funds to make payment to a Terminated Partner as forth in paragraph 8.2(a) above, then such credit balance and/or excess, as applicable, shall be paid, together with interest on the unpaid balance at the Prime Rate in effect on the Valuation Date, in six (6) equal semi-annual installments, commencing six (6) months after the Valuation Date.[30] The foregoing obligation shall be evidenced by a promissory note executed by the Partnership. The amount of any such promissory note shall be reduced by the amount, if any, of the Terminated Partner's obligations to the Partnership under paragraphs 6.4, 8.5 and 9.3 hereof.

(c) Notwithstanding the provisions of paragraphs 8.2 (a) and (b) above, the Partnership shall (i) have the option upon the unanimous consent of the remaining Partners to pay, without penalty, the payments therein provided at a date earlier than required in such paragraphs, and (ii) use its best efforts to pay such payments at the earliest date possible consistent with the best business judgment of the Partnership exercised in good faith.[31]

(d) Notwithstanding the foregoing, in the event that there remains a debit balance in the Terminated Partner's capital account after the adjustment as set forth in this paragraph 8.2 above, then such debit balance shall be restored to the Partnership by the Terminated Partner in the same manner as provided in subparagraphs (a) through (c) of this paragraph 8.2, as if such debit balance were a credit balance.[32]

8.3 **Valuation of Capital Account.** For the purpose of valuing a Terminated Partner's capital account, no value shall be ascribed to any Approved Agreement to which the Partnership is a party or in which the Partnership shall acquire any rights and/or interests hereunder. Except as provided in the previous sentence, all of the assets of the Partnership (other than real property, securities, and other investments owned by the Partnership) shall be valued at the amounts carried on the books of the Partnership. All real property, securities, and other investments owned by the Partnership shall be valued at their fair market value as of the Valuation Date. Any real property owned by the Partnership shall be appraised by an appraiser selected by the remaining Partners, and such appraisal shall constitute a binding determination of the fair market value of the property; provided, however, that the Terminated Partner (or his or her representative, in the case of a deceased

---

[30] A provision like this allows the Partnership to satisfy its obligation to a Terminated Partner without depleting all available Partnership cash at once.

[31] This provision theoretically prevents the remaining Partners from delaying a payoff to a Terminated Partner unless there is a legitimate reason.

[32] In some instances, a Terminated Partner may actually owe the Partnership money. This provision requires the Terminated Partner to pay such monies back to the Partnership in the same manner that the Partnership would be obligated to pay the Terminated Partner if the Terminated Partner was owed money.

or disabled Partner) shall have the right, at his sole cost and expense, to select his own appraiser. If the two appraisers cannot agree upon a value for the property they shall mutually select a third appraiser (the "mediator") whose valuation shall constitute a binding determination of the fair market value of the property. The costs of any appraisal by an appraiser selected by the remaining Partners shall be borne by the Partnership except in the event of a voluntary withdrawal, in which event the withdrawing Partner shall pay such costs.[33] Except as otherwise provided in the previous sentence the costs of any appraisal by an appraiser selected by the Terminated Partner, including the costs of the mediator, shall be borne by the Terminated Partner or his estate, as applicable. Nothing contained in clause (i) of this paragraph 8.3 shall affect the Partnership's obligations as provided under paragraph 8.4 below.

8.4 **Payment of Future Partnership Income.** Notwithstanding anything contained herein to the contrary, within sixty (60) days after receipt by the Partnership of the following revenues, the Partnership shall pay to the Terminated Partner his or her allocable share of such revenues:[34]

(a) Net Record Royalties.

(i) Net Record Royalties (as defined in paragraph 8.4(a)(ii) below) received by the Partnership after the Valuation Date pursuant to the Recording Agreement on account of sales of records containing Masters (as hereinafter defined) that were recorded by the Partnership on or before the Valuation Date if (A) such Terminated Partner participated in the recording of such Masters and (B) the results and proceeds of such Terminated Partner's participation are embodied in such Masters (Masters that satisfy conditions (A) and (B) , above, are hereinafter referred to as "Pre-Valuation Masters") If such records embody both Pre-Valuation Masters and other Masters, then the Net Record Royalties attributable to such records and otherwise payable to the Terminated Partner shall be reduced by multiplying such Net Record Royalties by a fraction, the numerator of which is the number of Pre-Valuation Masters embodied on such record and the denominator of which is the total number of Masters embodied on such record. In calculating the Net Record Royalties payable pursuant to this paragraph 8.4(a), a Terminated Partner shall receive the benefit of any increases in Net Record Royalties that become effective (whether prospectively or retroactively) after the Valuation Date, regardless of whether the Masters with respect to which such increased Net Record Royalties are payable were recorded on or before the Valuation Date;

(ii) The term "Net Record Royalties" shall be defined as the difference between (A) royalties received by the Partnership after the Valuation Date pursuant to the Recording Agreement on account of sales of records in all formats embodying "Masters" (which term shall be defined any recording of sound, whether combined with a visual image, by any method or any substance or material, whether now or hereafter devised which is extended for the use in the recording

---

[33] This valuation stuff is more or less accountant territory. It is wise to ascribe no value to any existing agreements, since many fired band members have filed lawsuits against their former mates on the basis that a recording or publishing agreement is worth something. Of course, you know that the "worth" of such agreements extends as far as guaranteed cash advances.

[34] This is where you spell out how much and for how long a Terminated Partner is entitled to receive income from various sources.

production or manufacture of records recorded by the Partnership), and (B) all Partnership expenses attributable thereto.[35]

(b) Merchandise Income. Revenues received by the Partnership that are attributable to either (i) sales before the Valuation Date of merchandise embodying the Group Name or (ii) sales of merchandise embodying the name, likeness or representation of the Terminated Partner.[36] Notwithstanding anything to the contrary contained in this paragraph 8. 4 (b) (i) or (ii), in the event that the Terminated Partner shall be the creator or designer of the logo and/or the artwork embodied on any Partnership merchandise, such Terminated Partner shall be entitled to continue to receive his or her allocable share of such Partnership merchandise income.

(c) Other Income. Revenues received by the Partnership after the Valuation Date that are not specified in paragraphs 8.4(a) or 8.4(b) and that are attributable to, or derived from, any materials, projects, or items completed or created by the Partnership on or before the Valuation Date, less all Partnership expenses attributable thereto, if (i) the Terminated Partner participated in such project or the creation of such materials or items, and (ii) the results and proceeds of such Terminated Partner's participation are embodied in the projects, materials, or items from which such income is derived; provided, however, that the Terminated Partner shall not be entitled to receive any portion of income received by the Partnership after the Valuation Date attributable to a license or other grant of the right to use the Group Name unless, pursuant to such license or other grant, the Terminated Partner's name, photograph, or likeness are used in conjunction with the Group Name.[37]

8.5 **Overpayments.** Notwithstanding anything to the contrary contained herein, if, at any time after the Valuation Date, the actual income of the Partnership (as reflected on statements received by the Partnership, audits conducted on behalf of the Partnership, or otherwise) indicates that any Terminated Partner received, prior to the Valuation Date, an allocation of an advance or other income described in Article 4 that is disproportionately greater than such actual income, then such Terminated Partner shall promptly repay to the Partnership the amount of the excess advance or other income. In the event that a Terminated Partner fails to make any payment required, by this paragraph 8.5, then, without limiting any of the Partnership's other remedies, the Partnership shall have the right to deduct the amount of such payment from any and all monies otherwise payable to the Terminated Partner.

---

[35] This means that a Terminated Partner gets his full share of record royalties with respect to records that are sold pursuant to the Recording Agreement (and not under any future recording agreement), but only to the extent that those records contain masters embodying the performances of the Terminated Partner. These royalties are net of Partnership expenses, such as management, accounting and legal fees, etc. This is actually kind of generous. Some bands like to reduce royalties payable to Partners that are kicked out for certain reasons (e.g., they play bad, are drug addicts, can't get along with anyone, etc.) and this is the part of the agreement where any such reduction should be addressed. Another common provision provides that Partners who leave a Partnership of their own free will do not receive their full share of record royalties if they don't participate in the inevitable tour and promotional activities in support of a record. Again, it's up to you.

[36] In other words, if Fred gets kicked out of the band during a tour, this provision provides that he doesn't get any money from sales of merchandise after he gets kicked out unless said merchandise features his name or likeness. This seems a bit harsh, especially if it applies to a founding member of a band who has toiled to build up goodwill for years and is kicked out of the band for no good reason. On the other hand, this provision is consistent with the valuation given to the Group Name in this agreement (i.e., ZERO).

[37] This is a "catch all" provision for random income.

8.6 **Complete Termination of Partner's Interest.** The payment of the amounts set forth in this Article 8 shall constitute a complete buy-out, settlement, and liquidation of any and all right, title, and interest that a Terminated Partner may have in, to, or against the Partnership or the Partners. Without limiting the generality of the foregoing, except as specifically provided in this Article 8, no Terminated Partner shall have any interest in income received by the Partnership after the Valuation Date.

ARTICLE 9
PROVISIONS REGARDING TERMINATION

9.1 **Statements and Inspection of Records.** In connection with ongoing payments that may be required to be made to a Terminated Partner pursuant to Article 8, the Accountant shall furnish to the Terminated Partner or his or her legal representative, as applicable, annual statements regarding any such payments made during the prior twelve (12) month period, and the basis of such payments. Each such statement shall be binding upon the Terminated Partner or his estate, as applicable, unless (a) an objection is made in writing stating the basis therefor and notice of such objection is delivered to the Partnership within two (2) years after the date of such statement, and (b) if the Partnership denies the validity of such objection, then suit is instituted within two (2) years after the date notice of such objection is delivered to the Partnership. During said two (2) year period, upon reasonable advance notice and at reasonable times, the Terminated Partner or his or her legal representative, as applicable, shall have the right to inspect the portion of the Partnership's books and records that relate to monies payable to such Terminated Partner hereunder.[38]

9.2 **Third Party Books and Records.** It is agreed and understood that in rendering the statements and making the payments required by Articles 8 and 9, the Partnership shall rely on statements it receives from third parties. Accordingly, the Partnership shall have no liability to any Terminated Partner if such payments or statements are accurately based on the information supplied to the Partnership by such third parties. The Partnership shall make available to the Terminated Partner copies of the portions of such third party statements that relate to monies derived from assets produced or acquired by the Partnership on or before the Valuation Date.[39]

9.3 **Damages.** Notwithstanding anything to the contrary contained in this Agreement, (a) in the event a Partner is expelled by the Partnership for a breach of a material provision of this Agreement, including the withdrawal of a Partner earlier than permitted under paragraph 7.3, then such Partner shall be liable for any damages suffered by the Partnership from such material breach, and (b) such Terminated Partner shall be liable for payment to the Partnership for such, Terminated Partner's allocable share of any claim, action, liability, damage, cost, or expense arising out of, or in connection with, any Pre-Valuation Masters, or any materials, projects, or transactions acquired, produced, consummated, or completed by the Partnership on or before the Valuation Date ("Pre-Valuation Liabilities"). Such Terminated Partner's allocable share of Pre-Valuation Liabilities shall be based on such Terminated Partner's allocable share of Net Profits and Net Losses at the time such Pre-Valuation Liabilities were incurred. Without limiting any of the Partnership's other rights or remedies, any such damages or Pre-Valuation Liabilities shall be (i) deducted from the amount of any monies that the Partnership is required to pay to the Terminated Partner under this Agreement, or (ii) added to the amount of any monies that the Terminated Partner is required to pay to the Partnership under this Agreement.[40]

---

[38] This is a standard audit provision that can be found in most agreements that deal with ongoing royalties or profit participation. It is especially important in an agreement such as this because of the acrimony that can develop between former band mates and business partners.

[39] Ditto.

[40] This clause makes it clear that a Terminated Partner is on the hook for any breach of the Partnership Agreement that occurred prior to termination and that any damages that result from such breach can be deducted from any monies otherwise payable to the Terminated Partner.

9.4 Assignment of Former Partner's Rights. Except as expressly provided in paragraph 2.1(e) and Article 8, a Terminated Partner shall not have any rights, claims, or interest in or to (a) any Masters recorded either before or after the Valuation Date under or pursuant to the Recording Agreement or otherwise; (b) any other tangible or intangible assets of the Partnership, including the Group Name and any goodwill, whether created or acquired before or after the Valuation Date; or (c) any proceeds derived from or arising out of the foregoing. Accordingly, and without limiting the generality of the foregoing, effective immediately upon the Valuation Date, the Partnership shall become the assignee of all such Terminated Partner's right, title, and interest in and to all tangible and intangible assets of the Partnership, including all Masters, the Group Name and any goodwill and all proceeds thereof and the Terminated Partner or his estate, as applicable, agrees to execute any and all documents necessary to effectuate such assignment. Notwithstanding the foregoing, in the event that the Terminated Partner or his estate, as applicable, shall not execute such assignments within five (5) days after receipt of written notice from the Partnership, each Partner hereby irrevocably appoints the Partnership as his attorney- in- fact for the purpose of executing in the Terminated Partner's name and on his behalf any such assignments. Such power-of -attorney is hereby irrevocable and coupled with an interest.[41]

9.5 The Group Name.[42]

(a) From and after the Valuation Date, neither the Terminated Partner nor representatives thereof shall avail themselves of or use the Group Name or any substantially similar name or designation in any medium or manner; provided, however, that, notwithstanding anything to the contrary in this Agreement, except as otherwise provided in the Recording Agreement, any Terminated Partner shall have the right to refer to himself or herself as being formerly a member of the Group;[43] provided, however, that no Terminated Partner shall refer to himself or herself as being formerly a member of the Group in any manner that would confuse or mislead a reasonable person into believing that such Terminated Partner is a member of the Group at the time of, or at any time after, such reference. From and after the Valuation Date, the Partnership shall have the continuing and unrestricted right in and to the use of the Group Name and all substantially similar designations in any medium or commercial manner.[44]

(b) Notwithstanding anything to the contrary in this Agreement, if the Partnership dissolves and winds up or otherwise ceases to operate, then all rights in and to the Group Name, including the right to use the Group Name as a professional recording and/or performing group, shall vest jointly in the Partners who are Partners at the time the Partnership ceases to operate. The Group Name shall thereafter be administered by unanimous vote of such Partners. If such Partners

---

[41] This reiterates that a Terminated Partner leaves the Partnership without rights to the name or any other assets (tangible or otherwise), except for any equipment he or she may choose to purchase.

[42] As I mentioned in Chapter 8, every band must reach an agreement with respect to the ownership and use of the Group Name.

[43] Alternatively, your band may decide that no Terminated Partner can use the Group Name in any manner — it's entirely up to you.

[44] This is important, because rock history is littered with stories of former (and usually minor) members of bands passing off their solo records as records by their former band via clever use of fine print or stickering.

are unable to decide by unanimous vote regarding a particular use of the Group Name, then no such Partner shall have the right to such particular use of the Group Name.[45]

9.6 Name and Likeness of Former Partner.

(a) From and after the Valuation Date, the Partnership shall have the continuing and unrestricted nonexclusive right to use the name, photograph, likeness, voice and biographical materials of the Terminated Partner on or in connection with, inter alia, the following:

(i) All records and tapes manufactured from Masters embodying, in whole or in part, the performances of the Terminated Partner;

(ii) All musical compositions written in whole or in part by the Terminated Partner and recorded or partially recorded (whether or not released) by the Partnership; and

(iii) The exploitation of all projects or items, including merchandising items, which the Terminated Partner created or designed, or in which he participated prior to the Valuation Date, subject to the terms as set forth herein.

(b) In no event shall the Termination of a Partner in any way affect or detract from any grant made by the Partnership before the Valuation Date of rights in and to the results and proceeds of the services of such Terminated Partner, or the rights to use such Terminated Partner's name, likeness, photograph, voice, or biographical materials.[46]

9.7 Assumption of Partnership Obligations. Upon any purchase of a Partnership interest pursuant to this Agreement, the Partnership shall assume all Partnership obligations incurred after the Valuation Date, and shall protect and indemnify the Terminated Partner from liability for any such obligations. The preceding sentence shall not relieve a Terminated Partner of such Terminated Partner's share of Pre-Valuation Liabilities.[47]

9.8 Publication of Notice. Upon the purchase of a Partnership interest pursuant to this Agreement, the Partnership shall, at its own expense, and as soon as reasonably practicable, cause to be prepared, published, filed, and served all such notices as may be required by law to protect a Terminated Partner against liabilities incurred by the Partnership after the Valuation Date.

---

[45] Let's say the band breaks up and the Partnership dissolves as a result. Years go by, solo careers flounder, and both Fred and John decide to front new versions of "Lawn Chocolate" without their old chums. In order to do this, all three former Partners would have to consent to the use of the Group Name by the two "new" bands. Since most band splits tends to be acrimonious, a provision such as this will likely mean that no former member will have the right to use the Group Name (unless the Partners who want to use the name are willing to pay off the other Partners). For alternate ways to deal with the name issue, see Part Two of Chapter 8.

[46] It would be very expensive to go back and remove the name and likeness of a Terminated Partner from every record, t-shirt, poster, songbook, etc. This provision makes it clear that the Partnership shall have the right to use such name and likeness on any products made pursuant to any agreements made prior to the Valuation Date.

[47] For example, let's say Fred is a Terminated Partner and that the Partnership completes the purchase of Fred's partnership interest on December 31, 1998, which also happens to be the Valuation Date. If the band takes angel dust and attacks the Backstreet Boys with knives and chains on January 15, 1999, Fred should not be found liable in any criminal or civil action.

9.9 **Nondisclosure.** The Partners specifically agree that neither they nor their agents or representatives shall at any time after the execution hereof knowingly provide to any third party any information concerning this Agreement, other than as shall be necessary in connection with the exercise of rights granted herein or as required by law. Promptly following the withdrawal, disability or expulsion of a Terminated Partner, the Partnership and such Terminated Partner shall issue a joint press release regarding such withdrawal, disability or expulsion, which press release shall be approved by Partnership Vote and by the Terminated Partner. If, however, the parties shall be unable to agree upon the form and content of such a press release, then no press release shall be issued. Neither the Partnership nor any Partner shall disseminate any information or make any statements that would reflect in a negative manner on the Terminated Partner, and the Terminated Partner shall not disseminate any information or make any statements that would reflect in a negative manner on the Partnership or any Partners.[48]

ARTICLE 10
DISSOLUTION AND TERMINATION OF PARTNERSHIP

10.1 The Partnership shall be dissolved and terminated upon the happening of any of the following events:

(a) The adjudicated bankruptcy (or assignment for the benefit of creditors) of the Partnership;

(b) Upon the happening of any event which makes it unlawful for the business of the Partnership to be carried on, or for the Partners to carry on the Partnership;

(c) Upon the decree of a court of competent jurisdiction;

(d) Upon the agreement of all the Partners;

10.2 Notwithstanding the dissolution or termination of the Partnership, the Partnership may continue to perform all acts necessary or appropriate in order fully to discharge and perform all obligations of the Partnership under all executory contracts and may, in connection therewith, exercise all rights, powers and authority, including the purchasing of goods and services.

10.3 Except as otherwise provided herein, upon dissolution and termination of the Partnership, the assets of the Partnership shall be distributed equally amongst the Partners in accordance with the Partners' respective then existing capital account balances. Non-cash assets shall be valued and distributed to Partners in a manner determined by Partnership Vote. In the event that the Partnership cannot agree on a method of distributing non-cash assets, the non-cash assets shall be liquidated and the proceeds shall be distributed equally amongst the Partners in accordance with the Partners' respective then existing positive capital account balances.

ARTICLE 11
OUTSIDE ACTIVITIES

Each Partner shall devote his or her best efforts as required to the operation of the Partnership and the advancement of Partnership Business and any other business of the Partnership. The Partnership

---

[48] Once again, any time a band breaks up or loses a member, there are bound to be hard feelings. And who wants mud slung at them in the press? This provision attempts to limit this by prohibiting either side from issuing statements or giving interviews that would reflect poorly on each other.

and each Partner expressly acknowledge and agree that any Partner may engage in any activity or make any investment for his, her or its own benefit or advantage without the consent of the other Partners, so long as such activity does not interfere in any manner whatsoever with or compete with the Partnership Business or any other business of the Partnership (as agreed by the Partners pursuant to a Partnership Vote) or with the complete and conscientious discharge by such Partner of his or her duties to the Partnership. It is further agreed that any of the foregoing activities as may be engaged in by any Partner shall be deemed individual activities outside the scope of this Agreement, and that Partner shall be entitled to retain any and all proceeds therefrom.[49]

ARTICLE 12
MISCELLANEOUS

12.1 **Notices.** All notices, requests, demands and other communications required or permitted to be given hereunder shall be in writing and shall be deemed to have been duly given if given personally, by prepaid telegram, or mailed first class mail, postage prepaid, by registered or certified mail, as follows:

TO JOHN DOE: 1234 Silver Lake Blvd., Los Angeles, CA 90026
TO BOB SMITH: 1234 Silver Lake Blvd., Los Angeles, CA 90026
TO FRED JOHNSON: 1234 Silver Lake Blvd., Los Angeles, CA 90026

Any mailed notice given as aforesaid shall be deemed received on the third business day following the deposit of the same in the United States mail. Any notice given by any other manner shall be deemed received when actually received by the party to whom addressed. Any party may change the address to which notices are to be sent hereunder, by giving notice of such change of address to the other party or parties in the manner herein specified.

12.2 **Governing Law.** This Agreement shall be governed by and construed in accordance with the laws of the State of California applicable to contracts made and to be performed in California, including, without limitation, the Uniform Partnership Act of California.

12.3 **Survival of Rights.** Subject to the terms and provisions hereof, this Agreement shall inure to the benefit of and be binding upon the parties hereto, and their respective successors, legal representatives and assigns of said parties.

12.4 **Entire Agreement.** This Agreement contains the entire agreement of the parties relating to the subject matter hereof. Any prior agreements, promises, understandings, representations or warranties relating to the subject matter hereof are of no force or effect.

12.5 **Severability.** In the event that any provision of this Agreement (or any part thereof) is, or is for any reason adjudged to be, void, unlawful, unenforceable or invalid, then disregarding such, provision or provisions (or any void, unlawful, unenforceable or invalid part thereof), the remaining provisions of this Agreement shall subsist and remain valid and be carried into full force and effect.

12.6 **Interpretation.** Article headings in this Agreement are for convenience and are not a part of the agreement of the parties and shall not be used in the construction thereof. Whenever in

---

[49] This allows the Partners to do things that don't fall under the category of Partnership Business as long as such activities don't interfere with a Partner's duties. What are "outside activities?" Producing other artists, playing or singing on other artist's records, solo records, etc.

this Agreement the context requires, references to the singular shall be deemed to include the plural and the plural the singular, and the masculine or the feminine the neuter, the neuter the masculine or the feminine, as the case may be, the masculine the feminine and the feminine the masculine.

12.7 **Waiver.** The waiver by any party hereto of any breach or violation of any provision of this Agreement shall not operate or be construed as a waiver of a subsequent breach or violation hereof.

12.8 **Remedies.** The remedies herein provided shall be deemed cumulative and the exercise of one shall not preclude the exercise of any other remedy, nor shall any specification of remedies herein exclude any rights or remedies at law or in equity which may be available hereto to the parties, including any rights to damages or injunctive relief

12.9 **Attorneys' Fees.** In the event that any action, suit or proceeding in connection with or arising out of this Agreement is instituted by one or more of the parties hereto against any other party or parties, the prevailing party or parties shall be entitled to recover reasonable attorneys' fees and court costs incurred in any such action, suit or proceeding.

12.10 **Counterparts.** This Agreement may be executed in several counterparts, each of which shall be deemed to be an original and which together shall constitute one and the same instrument.

ARTICLE 13
AMENDMENT OF AGREEMENT

This Agreement may be terminated, supplemented, modified or amended only by the written consent of all Partners pursuant to a Partnership Vote. Notwithstanding the foregoing, however, any provision hereof which requires the unanimous approval or consent of the Partners may only be amended by the unanimous approval or consent of the Partners.

ARTICLE 14
PREPARATION OF AGREEMENT

This Agreement was prepared on behalf of all parties hereto by the law firm of Dewey, Cheatum and Howe of 11111 San Viejo Blvd., Los Angeles, California 90000, and all parties hereto have heretofore voluntarily consented to the preparation of this Agreement on behalf of all parties by Dewey, Cheatum and Howe. Each Partner has been advised and understands that each such Partner has the right to be represented by separate and independent counsel in connection with this Agreement, and each such Partner has had the full and ample opportunity to secure such separate and independent representation. In the event each such Partner was not represented by independent counsel, such Partner acknowledges and agrees that his, her or its failure to be represented by independent legal counsel was determined solely by himself or herself and not by Dewey, Cheatum and Howe or any partner or associate thereof, in whole or in part.[50]

---

[50] In Chapter 8, I talked about the conflict of interest that occurs when the band's attorney drafts a partnership agreement on behalf of all band members. Recognizing this conflict, Art Cheatum wisely included this provision which reminds the Partners that this conflict exists and (theoretically) shields Art from a lawsuit based on such a conflict.

IN WITNESS WHEREOF, the Partners have executed this Agreement as of the date and year first above written.

By:_____
  Fred Johnson

By:_____
  John Doe

By:_____
  Bob Smith

EXHIBIT "B"

SPOUSE'S CONSENT

I acknowledge that I have read the foregoing Partnership agreement dated as of January 1, 1999 (the "Agreement") and that I know and fully understand its contents and have consulted with independent counsel with respect to same. I am aware that by its provisions, my spouse agrees to transfer all his or her right, title and interest in and to the Partnership including any community interest I may have in the Partnership, on the occurrence of certain events. I hereby consent to the transfer, approve of the provisions of the Agreement, and agree that my interest in the Partnership, if any, is subject to the provisions of the Agreement, and that I will take no action at any time to hinder operation of the Agreement.

By:_____

Date:_____

SAMPLE SIDEMAN AGREEMENT

John Doe and Fred Smith, collectively pka
"Lawn Chocolate"
c/o Art Cheatum, Esq.
Dewey, Cheatum & Howe
11111 San Viejo Boulevard
Los Angeles, California 90000

January 1, 1997

Biff Loman
6666 Seneca Way
Wawatosa, VA 23211

Dear Biff:

The following, when signed by each of us, shall confirm our understanding and agreement with regard to your rendering services to us in the entertainment field, including, without limitation, your rendering your services as musician and vocalist in connection with the creation of master recordings which will constitute the next Lawn Chocolate LP to be delivered to Thrifty Scot Records (the "Album").[1]

1.   We hereby employ you to render your exclusive services as a musician and vocalist and you hereby accept such employment and agree to appear and perform at times and places we shall designate, including, without limitation, recording sessions and rehearsal sessions. You agree to perform to our satisfaction all of the services required of you hereunder.[2]

2.   The term of this contract shall commence as of the date hereof and shall end the later of December 31, 1997 or completion of all work on the Album.

3.   Conditioned upon your full and faithful performance of all the terms and provisions hereof, we shall pay you the following as full and complete consideration for your services hereunder:

(a)   A salary of twenty-five thousand dollars ($25,000.00), payable in equal biweekly installments during the term hereof. During any tour or series of live engagements, you shall receive separate compensation.[3] Your salary for the purposes of recording the Album is inclusive of per diems and union scale. Per diems and salary payments shall be subject to paragraph 4 hereof and the withholding requirements set forth in paragraph 14 hereof. For the avoidance of doubt, you shall not be entitled to any other compensation (i.e., royalties) with respect to the Album

---

[1] This is a twelve-month sideman agreement that pays the sideman (Loman) a flat fee in exchange for his services as a musician and vocalist.

[2] Biff's task is pretty clear: he does what he is told.

[3] Note that while this agreement alludes to touring, the main focus is on Biff's services as a musician for the recording of Lawn Chocolate's anxiously awaited next album.

or masters recorded in connection with the Album.[4] For the sake of clarification, nothing contained herein shall foreclose you from receiving writer or publishing royalties if you are deemed the author of any composition embodied in the Album.[5]

       (b)   If you shall render services during the term hereof in connection with television appearances by us or in connection with audio-visual recordings embodying our featured performances, you shall be paid for such services at the applicable minimum union scale for such appearances but only if such payments are made by the appropriate producer or record company. You shall not be entitled to receive compensation for any such services to the extent that we are not entitled to receive compensation for the same services.

       (c)   You shall not render your services as a musician for any person other than us during the term hereof if such services would materially interfere with your duty to render services to us with respect to recording sessions hereunder.[6] During the term hereof, you shall remain ready, willing and able to perform with respect to masters recorded hereunder on a socalled "first call" basis. In connection therewith, you shall use best efforts to notify us of any proposed session work other than work contemplated hereunder, and you shall use best efforts to coordinate your schedule with us in respect thereof. We shall use reasonable efforts to notify you of any recording sessions for which we require your presence. Notwithstanding the foregoing, we shall not unreasonably object to or refuse to allow you to perform services as a session musician or a producer with third parties provided you give us reasonable advance notice and provided the same does not conflict with live performances which have been booked and which you have previously been made aware of.

       4.   We shall have the right, but not the obligation, to deduct from any amounts payable to you hereunder such portion thereof as may be required to be deducted under the applicable provisions of California revenue and taxation Code or under any other applicable statute, regulation, treaty or other law, or under any applicable union or guild agreement, and you shall promptly execute and deliver to us such forms and other documents as may be required in connection therewith.[7]

       5.   As between Thrifty Scot Records ("Thrifty Scot") and you and from the inception of the masters recorded in connection with the Album, Thrifty Scot shall own the entire worldwide right, title and interest in and to the same and the performances embodied thereon. Accordingly, Thrifty Scot shall have the sole and exclusive right in perpetuity and throughout the world to exploit and use the masters embodied in the Album upon such terms and in such manner as Thrifty Scot elects, in its sole discretion or to refrain therefrom and to lease, license, assign or otherwise convey to others the right to do so. In connection therewith, Thrifty Scot and its designees shall have the perpetual worldwide right to permit others to use your name, likeness and biographical material in connection therewith.

       6.   You acknowledge that your services hereunder are of a unique, innovative and personal nature and that it is reasonably foreseeable that your failure to perform at the times

---

[4] In exchange for the $25,000.00, Biff waives his right to royalties on the album.

[5] On the other hand, if Biff writes or co-writes any songs on the record, he will be entitled to receive publishing income.

[6] Although he is entitled to take on other work, Lawn Chocolate wants Biff to be on call for recording at any time during the term.

[7] This paragraph makes it clear that Biff has no claim in and to the copyrights to the master recordings he performs on. Additionally, Thrifty Scot can use Biff's name and likeness in connection with the Album.

and places required of you hereunder would cause us irreparable harm and damages (e.g., the delay and difficulty in finding and working in a suitable replacement). Accordingly we shall be entitled to damages and/or injunctive relief and such other remedies as we may deem appropriate. Neither party hereto shall be deemed in default of its obligations hereunder if performance thereof is delayed or becomes impossible or impractical by reason of any cause beyond such party's control such as war, fire, earthquake, strike, sickness rendering performance impossible, accident, civil commotion, epidemic, or act of government.

7.   You hereby warrant, represent, and agree that:

(a)   You are not under any disability, restriction, or prohibition, whether contractual or otherwise, with respect to your right to execute this contract, to grant the rights granted hereunder, or to perform each and every term and provision required to be performed by you hereunder.

(b)   During the term of this agreement you shall become and remain a member in good standing of any appropriate labor union or unions representing persons performing services of the type and character that you may be required to perform under this agreement.

8.   (a)   We reserve the right, at our election, to terminate the term of this contract, with proper cause, by sending written notice to you at any time, in which event we shall immediately be relieved of any further obligations to utilize your services hereunder or to pay you compensation in connection therewith. As used herein, the term "proper cause" shall mean your failure, refusal, neglect or inability or render services hereunder as, when and in the manner required to be performed by you hereunder, except for a so called "force majeure" event which affects a substantial portion of the recording industry.[8]

(b)   Notwithstanding any of the foregoing, you shall also have the right to terminate the term of this contract by sending written notice to us. Upon our receipt of such notice, we shall have the right, but not the obligation, to require you to continue to perform all of your obligations hereunder until completion of the Album.[9] In the event you shall fail to send us such written notice and to fully perform all of your obligations hereunder during the remainder of the recording and mixing sessions for the Album, or such portion thereof as we may designate, we shall be immediately relieved of any further obligations to pay you monies otherwise payable to you hereunder.

9.   We shall have the right, at our election, to assign any of our rights or obligations hereunder, in whole or in part, to any firm or corporation furnishing our services as an entertainer (i.e., a so-called "loan-out" company) and, to the extent of such assignment, we shall thereafter be relieved of our obligations hereunder. You shall not have the right to assign any of your rights or obligations hereunder.

10.   All notices to be given to you hereunder and all statements and payments to be sent to you hereunder shall be addressed to you at the address set forth on page 1 hereof or at such other address as you shall designate in writing from time to time. All notices to be given to us hereunder shall be addressed to us at the address set forth on page 1 hereof or at such other address as we shall designate in writing from time to time. All notices shall either be served by personal delivery (provided that a written receipt shall be obtained indicating that such delivery was

---

[8] Hmmm. Lawn Chocolate can pretty much fire Biff if they don't like the way he is playing on a particular day.

[9] Biff can quit, but the band has made sure they won't be left hanging in the middle of recording.

made), certified mail (return receipt requested), or telegraph, all charges prepaid. Except as otherwise provided herein, such notices shall be deemed given when personally delivered, mailed or delivered to a telegraph office, all charges prepaid, except that notices of change of address shall be effective after the actual receipt thereof.

11.   Upon the expiration or termination of the term of this agreement, or at such earlier time as we may request, you shall deliver to us any instrument, equipment, or other property belonging to us in as good condition as when received by you, reasonable wear and tear excepted, and you shall reimburse us on demand for any damage to any such property to the extent such damage is caused by you.

12.   You acknowledge and agree that you have no interest whatsoever in and to the name "Lawn Chocolate" or in any name similar thereto and you agree that you shall not at any time after the expiration or termination of this agreement use in any manner such name or any name similar thereto.[10]

13.   (a)   This contract sets forth the entire understanding of the parties hereto relating to the subject matter hereof. No modification, amendment, waiver, termination or discharge of this contract or of any of the terms or provisions hereof shall be binding upon either of us unless confirmed by a written instrument signed by you and by us. No waiver by either party hereto of any term or provision of this contract or of any default hereunder shall affect your or our respective rights thereafter to enforce such term or provision or to exercise any right or remedy in the event of any other default, whether or not similar.

(b)   We shall not be deemed to be in breach of any of our obligations hereunder unless and until you shall have given us specific written notice by certified or registered mail, return receipt requested, of the nature of such breach and we shall have failed to cure said breach within thirty (30) days after our receipt of such written notice.

(c)   Nothing herein contained shall constitute a partnership or a joint venture between you and us. Neither party hereto shall hold itself out contrary to the terms of this paragraph, and neither you nor we shall become liable for any representation, act, or omission of the other contrary to the provisions hereof.

(d)   In the event of any action, suit, or proceeding arising from or based upon this contract brought by either party hereto against the other, the prevailing party shall be entitled to recover from the other its reasonable attorneys' fees in connection therewith in addition to the costs of such action, suit, or proceeding.

(e)   This contract has been entered into in the State of California, and its validity, construction, interpretation and legal effect shall be governed by the laws of the State of California applicable to contracts entered into and performed entirely within the State of California.

14.   You hereby acknowledge and agree that your services are being provided hereunder as an employee; accordingly, and pursuant to your request, we shall withhold, report and pay so-called withholding taxes with respect to the compensation payable hereunder. So-called "withholding taxes" shall include, without limitation, federal and state income taxes, federal social security tax, and California insurance tax.

---

[10] These guys are smart to make this clear.

If the foregoing correctly reflects you understanding and agreement with me, please so indicate by signing in the space provided below.

Very truly yours,

_____

John Doe

_____

Fred Johnson

p/k/a Lawn Chocolate

AGREED TO AND ACCEPTED:

_____

Biff Loman

Social Security #123-45-6789

SAMPLE DEAL PROPOSAL FOR TOUR/RETAIL MERCHANDISING AGREEMENT[1]

THRIFTY SCOT MERCHANDISING, LLC
1234 Main Street
Anytown, CA 90000

Dated as of: October 1, 1998

VIA FACSIMILE AND U.S. MAIL

Art Cheatum, Esq.
Dewey, Cheatum & Howe
11111 San Viejo Blvd.
Los Angeles, CA 90000

Re: Lawn Chocolate/Exclusive Tour and Retail Merchandising Agreement

Dear Art:

It was great catching up with you in New York last week. Further to our conversations, what follows is our proposal for the merchandising rights for Lawn Chocolate's next two (2) album cycles:

RIGHTS: The rights to be acquired are the exclusive worldwide tour, retail, licensing and mail order rights for Lawn Chocolate.[2]

TERRITORY: The Universe.[3]

---

[1] OK, this isn't really an agreement, it's just a preliminary proposal for one. I thought you should see how these deals start. Now is a good time to go back and review Chapter Seven. Why do a merchandise deal? You may need the money — you can't expect to live on the advances from your record deal forever, and if doing a merch deal means you can put off selling your publishing until it makes sense, then a merch deal is a good option. Beyond the obvious financial considerations, manufacturing and selling merch is a pain in the ass, so a merch deal relieves you of this task in exchange for an advance and a share of the profits. One other general note: the touring business is down by 10-20% over the last few years ('97-'98), and the tour merch business has slowed down as well, especially for baby bands, so don't expect a fat offer (or any offer at all) unless you are doing brisk business.

[2] The deal proposed in this letter would pretty much cover every kind of merchandise through every conceivable sales channel throughout the world. Some artists try to segregate territories, and some like to do tour only or retail only deals. Others like to exclude mail order rights, if only for sales through their fan clubs. It's up to you and the merch company, but remember the general rule of thumb: the more rights you give up, the better deal (in terms of advances, royalties, etc.) you should get, and vice versa. Of course, merch companies are likely to be more flexible on these deal points if you are selling a lot of records and/or concert tickets. Otherwise, you will probably find your options limited.

[3] If the merch company offering you a deal does not have a strong international operation (and most legitimate merch companies do, to be honest), you may want to take a shot at a North America only or U.S. only deal.

TERM: The initial term of the agreement will be for a complete album cycle through which recoupment occurs. In no event shall the initial term be less than 18 months in any event. Thrifty Scot shall have an option for an additional album cycle. The option term shall extend from the start of the second album cycle through recoupment of all advances. In no event shall the option term be less than 18 months in any event.

ADVANCES: Initial Term

$25,000, payable as follows:
$10,000 on execution of the contract
$15,000 on tour gross of $50,000

Option Term

$30,000, payable as follows:
$10,000 on option exercise
$20,000 on tour gross of $60,000

---

[4] As I noted in Chapter Seven, an album cycle typically spans the period of time between the first show of a major tour until the last show prior to the release of the next album. Merch deal terms are structured this way because the length of a tour can vary depending on a number of factors and merch companies need to know that they have exclusive rights for entire tours.

[5] In other words, this deal does not necessarily end when the album cycle does. In fact, the term could conceivably exceed two album cycles and continue indefinitely as long as the band's royalty account is unrecouped. This is another way merch companies have locked up artists in the increasingly competitive tour merchandising business. Accordingly, the attorney should ask for some kind of "drop dead" time limit so that the deal doesn't go on forever. Alternatively, some merch companies will agree to let the artist terminate the agreement after one or two album cycles by paying back any unrecouped advances.

[6] This further protects the merch company in the event that an album cycle is unusually short for any reason.

[7] Time was when merch deals covered single tours or one album cycle. While superstars can still get such deal terms, newer and less established artists like Lawn Chocolate are faced with deals that give the merch company at least one option period. Of course, you should always try to avoid giving options if possible. But even if a merch company is willing to give you a "one off" deal, they will very likely ask for the right to match any offer made by a competing merch company for the merch rights to your next album cycle. While this is not as good as unrestricted free agency, you'd rather give your merch company a matching right than an option, because this will allow you to get a deal that pays you fair market value.

[8] While my advice with respect to advances is usually "Get as much as you can," I would advise you to exercise caution when it comes to merch deals. Why? Because advances can be returnable in some merch deals under certain circumstances. Also, you just learned that the term of a merch deal typically does not end until you are recouped. On the other hand, life is short, the music business is cruel and heartbreaking and you can always file bankruptcy, so fleece the bastards for every penny you can and worry later! Seriously, though: you may need a larger advance to fund your tour or to buy out the guitarist you just fired. Just try to be reasonable — not all merch companies are "nice" or "understanding" when you tell them you are unable to pay back your unrecouped advances.

[9] Calling all of this money an "advance" is a little misleading. The first $10,000 is clearly an advance. However, the $15,000 payment isn't triggered until the merch company collects $50,000 in tour merch revenue. At a 30% royalty, $15,000 of this money belongs to you. After deducting the $10,000 you received on signing, the merch company owes you $5,000. So the $15,000 advance is really only a $10,000 advance. Are you following me?

[10] Ask for a provision that increases option period advances based on the average sales of your last tour.

ROYALTIES - TOUR:

U.S.	30%[11] of gross sales[12] to increase to 32% upon recoupment
Canada/U.K.	29% of gross sales
EEC (Ex. U.K.)	26% of gross sales
Japan/Australia	
New Zealand	28% of gross sales
ROW	70% of net profits[13]
Tour Book	
Special Items[14]	65% of net profits

ROYALTIES – RETAIL:

U.S.	12% of net receipts[15]
Canada/U.K.	11% of net receipts
ROW	10% of net receipts

LICENSING:[16]

U.S.	70/30 of net receipts
ROW	65/35 of net receipts

MAIL ORDER:

All territories	12% of net receipts

PERFORMANCE GUARANTEE:

Lawn Chocolate will guarantee that during the during each album cycle within 18 months from the first tour date, Lawn Chocolate will perform before no less than 75,000 paid headline attendees.[17]

---

[11] This is a fairly respectable royalty rate for a new artist, and note that the rate escalates upon recoupment. A 30% royalty means that the artist will receive approximately $9 for every T-shirt sold at $30.00.

[12] Of course, the definition of "gross sales" is key. It usually means actual cash receipts minus taxes and hall fees (if any).

[13] The royalty for sales in minor territories is based on profits instead of gross sales because the risk of loss is higher for the company. Thus, they don't have to pay you royalties for these sales unless they make a profit (even if gross sales are huge).

[14] Same rationale as above. Programs and specialty items like leather jackets are really expensive to make, so the merch company wants to make sure it covers start up costs before it has to pay you any royalties.

[15] Thrifty Scot defines net receipts as their receipts from selling goods to retailers at a wholesale price (which is usually much lower than the retail price, since retailers need a lot of room to mark up the cost of the goods due to their overhead and advertising costs) minus "customary" deductions such as insurance, import duties, freight costs, taxes, etc. The general range for U.S. retail royalties is 9-16%.

[16] If the merch company licenses its rights to other companies, you get a fairly large share of the money it receives, since the merch company is acting as a middle man and is not responsible for manufacturing or selling the goods.

[17] While this requirement may seem innocuous, the implication here is that the band will have to pay back a portion of any advance if it does not meet the performance guarantee. Obviously, you want the performance guarantee to be as low as possible. I explore this critical topic more thoroughly in Chapter 7.

We can talk about other key deal points[18] if the foregoing meets with your client's approval. Please review the foregoing and let me know your thoughts as soon as possible.

Best.

Sincerely,

Colin McFrugal
Sr. Director of Business Affairs

CC: Seamus McTaggart
Ian McCheaply
Mick MacMcson

---

[18] Other key deal points include: creative matters, approvals, solo artist rights, accounting issues, leaving member issues, sell-off rights, cross-collateralizing retail and tour royalties, etc.

SAMPLE MOTION PICTURE SYNCHRONIZATION AND PERFORMANCE LICENSE

Date: JULY 1, 1998

Licensor: MUSIC PUBLISHING COMPANY, INC.
                   1234 Main Street
                   Los Angeles, California 90000

Licensee: THRIFTY SCOT FILMS, LLC
                   4321 Silver Lake Blvd.
                   Los Angeles, California 90026

Film: "The Brian McPherson Story"

Composition: "Tigers in My Own Garden (Exit Someone)"

Composer: P. McElwen

Percentage of composition owned or controlled by Licensor: 100%

Publisher Credit
For Cue Sheet: PREFAB SONGS INC./MUSIC PUBLISHING COMPANY, INC.
                        ADMIN BY MUSIC PUBLISHING COMPANY, INC.

Type and
Duration of Use: BACKGROUND VOCAL   1:55

Territory: THE UNIVERSE

      1.   Subject to the payment to Licensor of the fees required by paragraph 3, and to the delivery to Licensor of a cue sheet for the Film on Licensee's customary form, Licensor hereby

---

[1] This is the publisher that administers the rights to the musical composition in question.

[2] This is the company set up to produce the movie — I'll refer to it as the producer throughout this sample.

[3] Coming to a video store near you! You'll laugh — you'll cry — you'll kiss $2.50 goodbye!

[4] Some musical compositions are owned and/or administered by more than one publisher. In this example, the composition is co-published by the Licensor and the composer's publishing company, Prefab Songs, Inc. However, by virtue of the Licensor's copublishing agreement with Prefab Songs, the Licensor has the exclusive right to administer 100% of all rights in and to the composition.

[5] As I noted in Chapter Nine, the type and duration of use is a key consideration in any sync license. Generally, the longer and more prominent the use, the higher the fee.

[6] The publisher has the right to limit the territories in which the license is valid. Also note that the publishing rights to some musical compositions are owned or controlled by different publishers in different territories. If this is the case, a separate sync license must be obtained in each territory. In this example, the Licensor warrants and represents that it controls the rights for the universe, so only one license is necessary.

grants to Licensee, its successors and assigns the following non-exclusive,[7] irrevocable and (subject to paragraph 5, below) perpetual[8] rights with respect to that portion of the Composition indicated above as owned or controlled by Licensor:

(a) to record the Composition in synchronism or timed relation with the Film in any manner, medium, form or language, to make copies of such recordings, and to exploit the same in each country of the Territory in accordance with the terms, conditions and limitations contained in this license;

(b) to utilize the Composition as so recorded in advertisements, trailers, teasers, "film clips" to be shown on "talk shows" and other promotions for the Film[9] and, subject to obtaining mechanical licenses therefor (which Licensor agrees to issue at then-customary royalty rates), to include the Composition in soundtrack albums and other soundtrack recordings;[10]

(c) to publicly perform[11] and to authorize others to perform the Composition as so recorded in the exhibition of the Film (by direct projection, by television, or by any other means now or hereafter known) throughout the Territory to audiences in motion picture theatres and other public places of entertainment where motion pictures are customarily exhibited, and (subject to the provisions of paragraph 2, below) on all forms of television (including, without limitation, broadcast, satellite, and cable transmission); and

(d) subject to the payment of the fee(s) prescribed in sub-paragraph 3(c), below, to include the composition as so recorded in home video devices of all types and configurations (whether now or hereafter known)[12] and to manufacture, advertise, distribute and sell and/or rent the same throughout the Territory.

---

[7] Note that this is a non-exclusive license. In some cases, a movie producer will ask that a certain song nit be licensed for another movie for a certain period of time following release of the movie, and depending on the fee, this is sometimes done.

[8] The duration of the rights granted is another major point of negotiation. Most producers accept nothing less than perpetuity, because they do not want to have to keep renewing the license every few years.

[9] These rights are typically the subject of much negotiation. Publishers generally want more money for each extra type of use requested by the producer. In some cases, the publisher is unwilling to allow a song to be used in advertisements, trailers, etc. In the event that a publisher allows a song to be used in ads and/or trailers for the movie, the next question is whether the song will be used "in context" or not. By in context, I mean that the ad or trailer depicts the song exactly as it used in the movie. Out of context ad and trailer rights invariably cost more than in context rights. Let's look at an example: if you saw the TV ad for the recent movie *Wag the Dog*, I am sure you noticed that the song "Walking On the Sun" by Smashmouth was featured prominently. Since the song played over a melange of scenes from the movie, this was clearly an out of context use. Out of context trailer rights for hit songs usually cost a pretty penny.

[10] The "then-customary royalty rates" language seems a bit ambiguous to me. Does this mean customary in terms of the average record deal? As we know, this means a reduced rate (usually 75% of statutory) license. You should know that it is usually much easier to get a 100% statutory rate mechanical license when it comes to movie soundtrack albums.

[11] As I mentioned in Chapter Nine, the performing rights organizations do not issue public performance licenses or collect licensing revenue for US theatrical performances of songs, so these rights are usually granted in the context of the sync license.

[12] This language allows the producer to release the movie in any and all so-called "home video" formats, including those not yet invented. Publishers typically ask for and get additional licensing fees for home video rights. Some publishers insist on per-unit payments (kind of like a record royalty), but most producers resist this and instead agree to pay a one time flat fee for a "home video buyout." This license includes such a buyout in subparagraph 3(c).

2.   (a) Performance of the Composition in the Film by means of television (other than performance in theatres and other public places described in paragraph 1 (c), above), including but not limited to broadcast (so-called "free" broadcast television, whether network, syndicated, or local) cable (so-called "basic" or "CATV", "subscription" or "pay" cable, "pay-per-view", closed-circuit hotel television, and otherwise) and satellite transmission (whether received directly or through a cable system, and whether or not the transmission is clear or scrambled subject to decoding) (any person, firm or corporation by whom or through whom the signal is conveyed to the consumer being referred to below as a "Broadcaster") shall be permitted so long as the Broadcaster possesses a valid small performing rights license secured -

        (i) - by the Broadcaster from a performing rights society authorized to license the performance of the Composition in the Film in the country in which performance occurs; or

        (ii) - by a United States Broadcaster directly from Licensor; or

        (iii) - by Licensee directly from Licensor in respect of the United States.

        (b)   (i) If at any time performances of the types described in paragraph 2(a), above, are not administered by a performing rights society in the United States, or any United States Broadcaster or Licensee (or any successor or assignee of Licensee) (Licensee, such Broadcaster, or such successor or assignee being referred to below interchangeably as an "Entity") wishes to enter into a direct performing rights license with Licensor (whether of the "blanket" or "per-program" variety) such Entity shall be contractually required to so notify Licensor in writing in advance of such Entity's first presentation of the Film not undertaken pursuant to a performing, rights society "blanket license" and Licensor and such Entity shall negotiate in good faith for a period of 90 days thereafter with a view toward establishing an appropriate fee for such performance, and if they are unable to agree on an appropriate fee within such ninety-day period, they shall submit the matter to arbitration in Los Angeles, California in accordance with the then-applicable Rules for Commercial Arbitration of the American Arbitration Association, all costs of such arbitration (including Licensor's reasonable outside counsel fees) to be borne by such Entity.

        (ii) Each such Entity which accepts in writing the provisions of this paragraph 2(b) shall be permitted to perform the Composition as recorded in the Film during the pendency of such negotiations (and, if applicable, such arbitration). Any such Entity which does not deliver to Licensor such written acceptance prior to such Entity's first such performance shall not be permitted to avail itself of the provisions of this paragraph 2(b).

(c) The theatrical or television performance of the Composition as recorded in the Film in any country outside of the United States shall be subject to clearance by the applicable performing rights society authorized to license performing rights in the Composition in such country, in accordance with such society's customary practice and subject to payment to such society of such society's customary fees for such performance.

    3.   The fees[13] to be paid for the rights granted hereunder shall be as follows:

---

[13] This publisher segregates the total fee payable into three chunks for the different rights granted. Other licenses might simply provide "$3,000.00 for all rights granted hereunder."

(a) A synchronization fee, payable upon execution of this license,[14] in the amount of $1,000.00.

(b) A fee for U.S. theatrical performance, payable upon execution of this license, in the amount of $1,000.00.

(c) A video fee, payable upon execution of this license, in the amount of $1,000.00.

4.   (a) This license does not authorize or permit any use of the composition not expressly set forth herein, all rights not expressly granted herein being reserved to the Licensor. Specifically, and without limiting the generality of the preceding sentence, Licensee shall not have the right to alter the fundamental character of the music of the Composition, utilize the Composition if the Film is released with an "NC-17" rating, utilize a parody lyric with such music (except with the prior written consent of Licensor, which consent may be withheld in Licensor's sole discretion), utilize the title or subtitle of the Composition as the title of the Film, or utilize the story of the Composition;[15] and

(b) This license does not authorize the use of any "sound-alike" recordings in which an artist (solo or group) performs the Composition in such a way as to imitate an earlier recorded performance of the Composition by a different artist.

(c) Furthermore, in the event that less than 100% of the composition is indicated above as being owned or controlled by Licensor, it shall be Licensee's sole responsibility to obtain a license(s) from the co-publisher(s) of the Composition covering their interest(s).

5.   The rights granted hereby shall endure for the worldwide period of all copyrights in and to the Composition that Licensor may now own or control, and any and all renewals or extensions thereof which Licensor may hereafter acquire but, in the latter instance Licensee shall not be required to pay any additional fees or compensation beyond those prescribed above.

6.   (a) Licensor warrants and represents that it has the legal right and power to grant this license, and makes no other warranty or representation. Licensor agrees to indemnify Licensee and hold Licensee harmless from and against any and all loss, cost, damage or expense (including court costs and reasonable outside attorneys' fees) due to a breach of such warranty and representation resulting in a final, nonappealable adverse judgment or a settlement entered into with Licensor's prior written consent (such consent not to be unreasonably withheld).

(b) In each instance in which a claim, action or proceeding is commenced against Licensee (or its successors or assigns) in respect of which indemnity is to be claimed pursuant to the preceding paragraph, Licensor shall be given prompt written notice thereof, and Licensor shall have the right to participate in the defense thereof by counsel of Licensor's choice, at Licensor's sole cost and expense. To the extent required by Licensor's errors-and-omissions carrier, the carrier shall be permitted to control such defense or, in the alternative, Licensee (or its successor or assignee) may

---

[14] While this license provides that the fees shall be payable on execution of the license, most producers prefer to hold off making payment until the film is released. This is common practice, because sometimes songs don't make it to the final cut of the movie, and it's really hard to get money back once you pay it.

[15] These are similar to marketing restrictions you might find in a recording or publishing agreement.

retain such control but in such event the foregoing indemnity shall be limited to the fees paid or to be paid hereunder.[16]

7.   This license shall be binding upon, and shall inure to the benefit of, the parties and their respective successors and/or assigns, provided, that no assignment by Licensee or any successor to or assignee of Licensee shall be effective unless the assignee shall execute and deliver to Licensor an agreement to be bound by this license and to perform Licensee's further obligations hereunder.

8.   This license has been entered into in, and shall be interpreted in accordance with the laws of, the State of California, and any action or proceeding concerning the interpretation and/or enforcement of this license shall be heard only in the State or Federal Courts situated in Los Angeles County, and both parties hereby submit themselves to the jurisdiction of such courts for such purposes. In any action between the parties to enforce any of the terms of this Agreement, the prevailing party shall, in addition to any other award of damage or remedy, be entitled to court costs and reasonable attorneys' fees.

IN WITNESS WHEREOF, the parties have executed the foregoing license as of the day and year set forth above.

Licensor: MUSIC PUBLISHING COMPANY, INC.

By: _____
        Fred Smith
        President

Licensee: THRIFTY SCOT FILMS, LLC

By: _____
        Angus McBean
        Vice President

---

[16] Note that while the publisher indemnifies the producer, the indemnity is limited to the fee paid to the publisher. For example, let's say another publishing company (Lawn Chocolate Music, natch.) claims to own the song which is the subject of this license. Lawn Chocolate Music will likely sue Thrifty Scot Films (among others), because Thrifty Scot didn't get a license from Lawn Chocolate Music. In turn, Thrifty Scot turns will turn around and sue Music Publishing Company, because MPC warranted that it had the rights to issue the license. However, no matter what happens, Thrifty Scot will only be able to look to MPC for a maximum of $3,000, even if Lawn Chocolate Music successfully sues Thrifty Scot for much more than that. While this seems pretty f***ed up, it is standard procedure.

SAMPLE MASTER USE LICENSE[1]

This agreement is entered into on March 11, 1998, effective as of January 1, 1998 between Thrifty Scot Records, Inc.[2] 1234 Main Street, Anytown, CA 90000 ("Licensor") and Big Movie Productions, Inc., 666 Exploito Way, Culver Oaks, CA 66666 ("Licensee").

1.   Licensee is distributing the motion picture currently entitled "The Brian McPherson Story" (which together with all trailers, advertisements and promotional films therefor, as well as excerpts and clips therefrom, shall hereinafter be collectively referred to as the "Picture"):

2.   Licensee wishes to utilize that certain recording ("Master") embodying the composition "Just Like Biff Loman's Blues" (the "Composition") as performed by the recording artists collectively and professionally known as "Lawn Chocolate" ("Artist").

3.   The territory covered by this license is the Universe ("Territory").

4.   The term of this license shall be for perpetuity.

5.   The type and number of uses of the Master is one background vocal usage for one minute and fifty-two seconds (1:52) total duration.

6.   Licensor grants to Licensee, its successors and assigns:

(a) the non-exclusive right to record, re-record, dub and synchronize the Master in, and in connection with, the Picture,[3] and to exhibit, distribute, exploit, market and publicly perform the Picture throughout the Territory, in any and all media,[4] by any and all means, whether now known or hereafter devised; and

(b) the non-exclusive and irrevocable right, license, privilege and authority to cause or authorize the fixing of the Composition in and as part of the Picture on videocassettes, videodiscs (including laserdiscs, DVDs, and DIVXs), videotapes and similar compact audio-visual devices whether now known or hereafter devised ("Videograms"), including, without limitation, the rights to:

(i) sell, lease, license or otherwise make such Videograms available to the public as a device intended primarily for "home use" (as such term is commonly understood in the entertainment industry); and

(ii) use such Videograms for any and all purposes.[5]

---

[1] You will note a strong similarity between this license and the sync license. Accordingly, many of the comments I made with respect to the sync license apply here as well. Remember that the sync license covers the use of a song while the master license covers the use of a recording.

[2] Since Thrifty Scot owns he copyright in and to the master in question (per the band s recording agreement with Thrifty Scot), it is Thrifty Scot's right to issue the license and collect the proceeds therefrom.

[3] Note that this includes the right to use the Master in ads, trailers, promotions, etc. because of the way "Picture" is defined in paragraph 1 of the license.

[4] This includes all forms of TV, theatrical release, etc.

[5] This is a fairly comprehensive "home video buyout" provision.

7.   For the use of the Master in the Picture as set forth above in paragraph 6, provided the Master is included in the final, edited version of the Picture as generally released, Licensee shall pay to the Licensor the sum of Ten Thousand Dollars ($10,000), payable upon the later of complete execution of the License or initial U.S. release of the Picture. No further amounts shall be payable by Licensee to Licensor in connection with the use of the Master in the Picture.

8.   Licensor agrees that, subject to good faith negotiations with respect to record royalties (which shall in any event be calculated and reduced worldwide on the same basis as Licensee's royalty rate is calculated and reduced worldwide), the Master may be included on a soundtrack album derived from the Picture.[6]

9.   Licensee shall prepare and deliver to Licensor a cue sheet for the Picture, indicating the use and time sequences of the Master upon execution of this license agreement.

10.   Licensor represents and warrants that it owns or controls one hundred percent (100%) of the copyright, including renewals, in and to the Master, throughout the Territory; that it owns or controls all other rights necessary to enter into and to fully perform this agreement, and that neither the consent of the Artist(s) nor any other party (with the sole exception of the copyright proprietor(s) of the underlying musical Composition) is required in connection with the licensed use. In the event of the breach, or alleged breach, in whole or in part, of any warranty, representation, covenant or agreement made by Licensor herein, Licensor shall indemnify, defend and hold harmless Licensee, its assigns, successors, affiliates and licensees, and the officers, directors, shareholders, representatives and employees of each of the foregoing, from and against any and all damages, claims, liabilities, judgments, losses, costs and expenses incurred by Licensee as a result of or in connection with the breach of any such warranty, but only to the extent of the consideration paid by Licensee to Licensor.

11.   In the event of any breach of any provision of this agreement by Licensee, Licensor's sole remedy will be an action by law for damages, if any, and in no event will Licensor be entitled or seek to enjoin, interfere or inhibit the distribution, exhibition or exploitation of the Picture.[7]

12.   Licensee is proceeding in reliance on the terms of this agreement as such terms are specified above; Licensee shall have no obligation hereunder in the event that the Master is not included in the Picture as generally released.[8]

13.   All questions with respect to the subject matter of this agreement shall be determined in accordance with the laws of the State of California applicable to contracts entered into and to be fully performed within the State of California. All claims, disputes or disagreements which may arise out of the interpretation, performance or breach of this agreement shall be submitted exclusively to the jurisdiction of the state courts of the State of California or the federal district courts located in Los Angeles, California. In any such action commenced in any of the above-referenced courts, both parties agree to accept personal service, both within and outside of the State of

---

[6] This paragraph is a little sketchy on details, and if I represented the record company I would suggest either leaving it out or making it a bit more explicit as to record royalties, advances, recoupment, etc.

[7] This is an important provision for the movie producer. Without this provision, the Licensor could attempt to enjoin or halt the distribution and release of the Picture if the Producer breaches a provision of the license.

[8] In other words, if the producer decides not to use the Master in the Picture, it doesn't have to pay the licensing fee.

California, of any summons, order to show cause, writ, judgment, decree or other process. Upon the delivery of any such instrument, both parties shall become subject to the personal jurisdiction of the California courts as though they were served within the State of California.

14.   This instrument constitutes the entire agreement of the parties hereto relating to the subject matter hereof, and any prior agreements, understandings, representations and commitments concerning such subject matter, whether oral or written, are hereby superseded and terminated in their entirety and are of no further force or effect. There are no contemporaneous oral agreements between the parties hereto relating to the subject matter hereof, and Licensor has not executed this agreement in reliance upon any representation or promise other than those specified herein. This agreement can be modified or terminated only by a written instrument executed by both Licensor and Licensee.

IN WITNESS WHEREOF, the parties have caused the foregoing to be executed as of the day and year first above written.

BIG MOVIE PRODUCTIONS, INC.

By:_____
    An Authorized Signatory

THE FOREGOING IS AGREED TO AND ACCEPTED BY:

THRIFTY SCOT RECORDS, INC.

By:_____
    An Authorized Signatory

Federal Identification Number: 95-0000000

SAMPLE MOTION PICTURE SOUNDTRACK AND SOUNDTRACK ALBUM RECORDING AGREEMENT[1]

Agreement made as of the 1st day of August, 1998, between Scotvision, Inc. ("SI") and Fred Johnson and John Doe p/k/a "Lawn Chocolate" (jointly and severally called "Artist") with respect to a master recording which shall be individually produced by Brian McPherson ("Producer") and shall embody the performances by Artist of the musical composition entitled "The Girlfriend Plan"[2] (the "Composition") (said master recording embodying Artist's performance shall hereinafter be called the "Master") for the motion picture currently entitled "A Fist Full of Haggis" (the "Picture").

1.   SI hereby engages Artist[3] to record, produce and deliver the Master, individually produced by Producer and embodying Artist's performance thereon, to SI. Artist shall select the recording studio and third parties to render services at the recording session(s) involved, subject to the terms hereof. Artist shall be solely and fully responsible for paying or causing to be paid all recording costs incurred in connection with the Master. As used herein, the term "recording costs" means all direct costs incurred in the production of the Master which are now or hereafter recognized as recording costs in the motion picture and recording industries, including without limitation, payments to persons rendering services in connection with the recording of the Master, to any union or guild trustee or fund based on services at recording sessions, payroll taxes, studio or rehearsal hall rental, payments to sound engineers, and for tape, editing, mixing and other similar functions, costs for rental and cartage of instruments, musical equipment and transportation thereof; payments to payroll services; and, travel and living expenses in respect of any individuals rendering services in connection with the recording and production of the Master. Artist shall discharge all of the obligations of an employer, whether imposed by law, by applicable union rules and regulations or otherwise with respect to all persons who are employed/engaged to render services in connection with the recording/production of the Master (including, without limitation, the obligations of an employer under the U.S. Immigration Reform and Control Act of 1986). Artist shall not engage any persons other than Artist to serve as the "lead" or "featured" performing artist of the Master nor shall Artist engage any persons other than Producer to serve as the Master's producer, without SI's express prior written authorization.[4] Under no circumstances shall the services of any third parties under any exclusive service contracts and/or any minors be engaged with respect to the Master, without the express prior written consent of SI. No costs or expenses shall be incurred in the name of SI with respect to the Master without the express prior written consent of SI.

2.   As full consideration for the services of Artist and Producer and all rights herein acquired by SI:

---

[1] This is essentially a single song recording agreement between a movie producer and the artist in which the artist records a master for the film producer as a work for hire. Since the movie producer owns the master, it may do anything it wants with the master (e.g., put it in the movie, the soundtrack album, refrain from doing one or both, license the master to others, etc.), subject to the restrictions in this agreement.

[2] Note that the producer of the movie and the artist have already agreed on which song will be recorded. This is fairly common in movie soundtrack/soundtrack album deals.

[3] Note that the movie producer is engaging the artist directly. In order to do this, the artist must get permission from its record company, since the record company likely has the exclusive right to the artist's recording services. Accordingly, the producer has included a short waiver of exclusivity provision at the end of the agreement that the artist's record company needs to sign off on. Note that some record companies negotiate directly with the movie producers.

[4] The movie producer wants to make sure he is getting a top quality Lawn Chocolate recording (as if there is any other kind).

(a) SI agrees to pay Artist the sum of $30,000 (which includes applicable minimum union scale for all services rendered by Artist and Producer in connection with the Master and all sums necessary for the recording of the Master[5]) less any required withholding payable as follows:

(i) $15,000 (less any required withholding) upon the later of: signature of a Letter of Confirmation in the form attached hereto as Exhibit "A" or commencement of services hereunder; and

(ii) $15,000 (less any required withholding) upon the later of: delivery to SI of the Master, delivery to SI of copies of this agreement signed by Producer and Artist's record company, Thrifty Scot Records, Inc. ("Company"), and completion of services hereunder.

(b) If the Master is included in phonorecords distributed under the "Distribution Agreement" (as defined in subparagraph 13.(f) below), Artist and Producer shall be entitled to a "Phonorecord Royalty" in connection therewith as follows:

(i) A royalty of 12% of the suggested retail list price of long playing albums, and 10% of the suggested retail list price of standard singles, if any, less packaging charges and applicable taxes, pro-rated as provided in the immediately succeeding sentence and subject to clauses (ii) and (iii) hereinbelow. The Phonorecord Royalty, if any, payable to Artist pursuant to this subparagraph 2.(b) shall be pro-rated by the total number of recordings contained on the phonorecord involved, (which for this purpose shall be deemed to equal twelve (12) such recordings with respect to any long playing album).[6]

(ii) All aspects of said Phonorecord Royalty shall be subject to the contractual provisions set forth in the Distribution Agreement regarding definition, computation, reduction and payment of phonorecord royalties (excluding any royalty escalation provisions) including, without limitation:[7]

(1) reduction for long-play singles sales, sales outside the United States, for mail order and record club sales, for tape device sales by tape licensees, for budget label sales, for mid-priced sales and for premium sales;

(2) computation/reduction of royalties for compact disc sales, for sales of other new configurations and for flat fee/flat royalty licenses of the Master for use in and as part of phonorecords;

(3) definition of royalty base price, exclusions and discounts for so-called "free goods" and discount sales;

---

[5] The $30,000 fee is an "all-in" recording fund, which means that the artist must pay all recording costs (including producer advances, studio rental, enginers, etc.) out of the fund. The artist can keep anything left over.

[6] The upshot of all this is that the artist will receive a 1% royalty per album.

[7] The movie producer makes a separate deal with a record company to put out the soundtrack album. These deals usually pay the producer an advance (which the producer uses to acquire music for the soundtrack of the movie and the soundtrack album) and a royalty. The royalty payable to the movie producer is typically higher than that which would be paid to an artist, because the producer must pay all of the artists out of its royalty. In any event, the movie producer needs to make sure that the royalty payable to any artist contributing to the soundtrack album is paid in the same or no more favorable manner as the royalty payable to the movie producer.

(4) deductions for packaging and applicable taxes;

(5) percentage of sales on which paid, and reserves against returns; and

(6) computation of royalties should the Distributor elect to change the method by which it computes royalties to some other basis (e.g., from a retail to a wholesale basis).

(iii) SI shall be entitled to deduct and retain from said Phonorecord Royalty an amount equal to the following:

50% of the sums described in 2(a)(i) and 2(a)(ii) above[8] plus "conversion costs"[9] (as defined in subparagraph 13(c) below) of the Master.

(c) SI will use reasonable efforts to cause the Distributor to account directly to Artist[10] for its Phonorecord Royalty after all advances paid by the Distributor in connection with the soundtrack phonorecords for the Picture have been recouped by the Distributor. Unless and until the Distributor so accounts to Artist, SI will account to Artist for its Phonorecord Royalty under 2.(b) above within thirty (30) days following SI's receipt of its royalty statements from the Distributor under the Distribution Agreement, and in accounting to Artist SI shall be entitled to rely on the Distributor's royalty statements to SI. Each accounting to Artist shall be accompanied by a royalty statement pertaining thereto. Artist shall be deemed to have consented to each royalty accounting to Artist hereunder, and each such accounting shall become final and binding upon Artist unless Artist renders specific written objection, stating the basis thereof, no later than one (1) year following the date of SI's rendition of such accounting to Artist and if SI gives Artist written notice that it denies the validity of the objection, unless suit is instituted thereon no later than six (6) months following the date of SI's rendition of such written notice to Artist. Artist shall have the right, at Artist's expense, to audit SI's books and records which have not then been rendered incontestable, but no more often than once per twelve (12) month period, relating to the sale of phonorecords embodying the Master, during normal business hours and on reasonable notice. Artist has no independent right to audit the Distributor's books and records relating to Artist's Phonorecord Royalty under 2.(b). If SI elects to audit the Distributor's books and records relating to phonorecords containing the Master distributed under the Distribution Agreement (which SI shall have no obligation to do), Artist shall receive its pro-rata share of any "net" recovery therefrom (the "net" recovery being the gross recovery remaining after deduction of the costs of such audit as well as any other costs incurred in securing the gross recovery). In the event any overpayment is made to Artist in accountings for its Phonorecord Royalty (e.g. by reason of an accounting error or by paying royalties on phonorecords returned later) Artist shall reimburse SI or SI's designee, for such overpayment, but only to the extent such overpayment is not deducted from future accountings to Artist under this 2.(c) for its Phonorecord Royalty.

---

[8] In most record deals, 100% of recording costs and advances are recoupable from the record royalties payable to the artist. In this case, the master will be used in the movie and on an album, so the theory is that a portion of the advance should be deemed a nonrecoupable flat fee for the use of the master in the movie. Here, that portion is 50%. Accordingly, the artist needs to recoup $15,000 (plus conversion costs) before it will be paid record royalties.

[9] Conversion costs are the costs incurred by the movie producer in converting a recording created for use in a movie to a recording suitable for use on a record. This may include equalizing, mastering, mixing, editing, "sweetening," etc.

[10] This language is a little soft — the artist should make sure that it gets accounted to directly from the record company, not the movie producer. Most record companies agree to do this in their deals with movie producers. If you allow the movie producer to account to you, it will likely take longer to get your money (if you get your money).

3.　　(a) If the Master is contained in the Picture as first generally released, Artist shall receive appropriate recording artist credit, and Producer shall receive appropriate master recording producer credit, on all positive prints of the Picture, in the end titles, located among, and in the same size as the corresponding, respective "lead" recording artist credits and master recording producer credits accorded with respect to the other master recordings embodying songs contained in the Picture.[11] All other aspects of such screen credit to Artist shall be determined by SI in its sole discretion. SI agrees to use reasonable efforts to cure prospectively any material failure to accord screen credit to Artist and/or Producer as provided in this subparagraph 3.(a) on any prints of the Picture as may be made subsequent to SI's receipt of written notice from Artist specifying the details of such material failure. SI will advise its subdistributors as to SI's screen credit obligations hereunder, but in no event shall SI be responsible for the failure of any third party to comply with the credit provisions hereof.

(b) If the Master is contained in the Picture's soundtrack album or in the album inspired by the Picture (the "Album"): if on the back cover (or the equivalent for non-traditional vinyl disc configurations), master recording artist credit is accorded to "lead" recording artists featured on other master recordings contained in the Album, then Artist shall also be accorded recording artist credit on the back cover, in the same size as such recording artist credits to such other recording artists and, if on the back cover (or the equivalent for non-traditional vinyl disc configurations), individual Master recording producer credit (as distinguished, for the avoidance of doubt, from credit to so-called "album producers" and/or "executive album producers", etc.) is accorded the master recording producers of other master recordings contained in the Album, then Producer shall also be accorded master recording producer credit on the back cover, in the same size as such master recording producer credits to such other master recording producers. In addition, with respect to 7" and/or 12" singles phonorecords containing the Master and released under the Distribution Agreement by the Distributor, SI shall instruct the Distributor to accord recording artist credit to Artist and master recording credit to Producer in such size, style, placement, etc. as the Distributor shall determine in its sole discretion. It is understood that if the Distributor fails or refuses to accord credit in accordance with any or all of the provisions of this subparagraph 3.(b), SI shall not be liable therefor and it shall not be a breach hereof; however, SI shall use its reasonable efforts to cause the Distributor to prospectively cure any such failure to accord credit on future pressings of the phonorecord(s) involved for the U.S. market, so long as it is understood that if the Distributor fails or refuses to so do, it shall not be a breach hereof. No casual or inadvertent failure to comply with any of the credit provisions of this paragraph shall constitute a breach of this Agreement.

4.　　Artist shall be solely responsible for and shall pay any and all royalties or other sums which may be payable to secure any necessary consent(s) from any person, firm or corporation whose consent may be required in respect of Artist's and/or Producer's rendering services hereunder, the rights to be acquired hereunder by SI, and any exploitation of such rights by SI and SI's successors, assigns and licensees. Producer and Artist shall have only a right to seek damages, and no right to seek injunctive relief, rescission of rights or any other equitable relief for any breach of this Agreement. In addition, Artist and Producer shall secure the written confirmation of the back-up vocalists/musicians engaged by Artist and/or Producer in connection with the recording of the Master so that, in the event of any dispute regarding the Master, said persons shall not have the right to injunctive relief or rescission of rights in connection with the Picture, the Master and/or any exploitation, promotion, advertising and/or publicizing thereof. Artist shall be solely responsible for and shall pay any and all royalties or other sums which may be payable to secure any necessary consent(s) from any person, firm or corporation whose consent may be required in respect of Artist's rendering services hereunder and the rights to be acquired hereunder by SI.

---

[11] You want to make sure that you receive appropriate screen credit.

5.   Effective as of the date hereof, Artist agrees not to rerecord the Composition for anyone other than SI for a period extending to five (5) years after the first general release of the Picture in the U.S.[12]

6.   (a) From inception SI will own the Master (including without limitation, all performances embodied therein) and all rights therein, other than rights to the Composition,[13] on an exclusive basis throughout the universe in perpetuity, including, without limitation, all rights of copyright therein and thereto, and may freely utilize all, or any portion of same, solely in and in connection with the Picture and Album,[14] in any and all media now or hereafter known, on such terms and conditions as SI, in its sole discretion, may deem appropriate, and SI may license or designate others to exercise any or all of its rights; or SI may refrain from any or all of the foregoing. Without limiting the foregoing, Producer and Artist specifically acknowledge and agree that the results and proceeds of Company's, Producer's and Artist's services hereunder shall be "works made for hire" for the purpose of the U.S. Copyright Act of 1976 and for all other copyright laws throughout the world. SI and its assigns, successors and licensees shall have the right to edit or delete from the Master in any manner they deem appropriate for purposes of including all or portions of such Master in the Picture's soundtrack and/or for purposes of including such Master on phonorecords.[15] Producer and Artist waive any and all so-called "moral rights". SI shall also have the right, throughout the universe, in perpetuity to use Artist's name, and Producer's name and the approved likeness and approved biographical material (other than mere references to Producer's and Artist's professional credits which shall not require any approval) solely in connection with the Picture and the Master and any or all promotion, advertising and exploitation thereof, (excluding use for endorsements of any product or service other than the Picture, Album, or Single Records derived therefrom unless Artist and/or Producer otherwise consents), or to refrain therefrom (except as otherwise provided in Paragraph 3. herein). Artist agrees to furnish SI with at least 3 approved likenesses of Artist and Producer and with an approved biography of Artist and Producer within five (5) business days following Artist's receipt of SI's request therefor. If Artist fails to so do, SI shall be free to use any likeness or biographical material of Artist without having to secure the approval of any person, firm or corporation with respect thereto. Producer and Artist shall have only a right to seek damages, and no right to seek injunctive relief or rescission of rights for any breach of this Agreement other than a breach consisting of the commercial release by SI or Distributor of the Master on a phonorecord other than the Album without Artist's consent.

      (b) Notwithstanding anything to the contrary contained herein, Artist shall have the right to use the Master in one "Artist Solo LP".[16] The foregoing is subject to the restriction that neither the title of the Composition nor the title of the Picture shall be used as the title or subtitle of the Artist Solo LP, and no elements of the Picture (e.g., artwork, etc.) and no reference to the title of the

---

[12] The movie producer doesn't want the artist to record another version of the song, because it dilutes the value of the soundtrack album.

[13] The producer will have to obtain a sync license from the song's publisher, as these rights are not included in this agreement.

[14] Although the Master is a work made for hire owned by the movie producer, this sentence limits the producer's rights to use the master to the Picture and the Album. Absent this language, the producer could do whatever it wanted with the master.

[15] It's fairly customary to allow the producer the right to edit the master for the movie, because rarely is a master used in its entirety. However, the artist should ask for the right to approve any editing or other alteration of the master when it comes to the soundtrack album.

[16] Any time you give up ownership of the master, you want to make sure that a) the producer does not have the unfettered right to use the master outside of the movie and the soundtrack album, and b) that you will have the right to use the master on at least one of your own records at some point and at no cost. The latter is achieved with this provision.

Picture shall be used by Artist, Artist's record company designee or their licensees in connection with the Artist Solo LP and/or any advertising/promotion/exploitation thereof. Artist's right to use the Master in and as part of the Artist Solo LP shall be exercisable no sooner than six (6) motnhs following the initial release of the Picture in the U.S.[17] Credit to Artist and/or Producer with respect to any use of the Master under this subparagraph 6.(b) shall be a matter to be determined solely among Artist, Producer and Artist's record company designee and in no event shall SI have any liability, obligation and/or responsibility to Artist, Producer and/or Artist's record company designee with respect thereto. Neither Producer, Artist nor Artist's record company designee shall be obligated to pay any sums to SI and/or Distributor with respect to the use of the Master in and as part of the Artist Solo LP, but Artist and/or Artist's record company designee shall be responsible for, and shall pay, all other third party obligations in connection with the exploitation of the Master in and as part of the Artist Solo LP, including without limitation, payments to Artist, to Producer, to union and guild trustees, and to publisher(s) of the Composition. SI shall have no obligation to pay Producer, Artist, Artist's record company designee, or any other person, firm or corporation any sums under this Agreement or otherwise in connection with the exploitation of the Master in and as part of the Artist Solo LP (which such exploitation will be in a manner only as provided in this paragraph) and Artist and Company will indemnify SI and hold SI harmless against any claims or demands by any person, firm or corporation for any monies in connection with the use of the Master in and as part of the Artist Solo LP and any advertising/promotion/exploitation thereof. If the Master is included in the Artist Solo LP, the sound recording copyright notice shall read as dictated by SI and the Distributor. No use of the Master, other than as provided in this paragraph, shall be made by or on behalf of Company, Artist and/or Producer without the express prior written consent of SI and the Distributor.

7.   Subject to paragraph 16 below, in the event SI and/or the Distributor wishes to prepare or cause to be prepared any promotional music video(s) containing the Master and to feature in whole or in part Artist's on-camera performance(s) of the Composition (it being understood that neither SI nor the Distributor shall be under any obligation to prepare or cause to be prepared any such music video[s]) the following shall apply: [18]

(a) Artist shall render on-camera performance(s) of the Composition. Such on-camera performance(s) shall be rendered at no additional cost to the producer of the music video(s) it being understood that the consideration payable to Artist hereunder includes any and all applicable minimum union scale for such services. The foregoing shall be subject to Artist's reasonable availability if SI and/or the Distributor request Artist to render such services subsequent to the first general release of the Picture.

(b) Any such music video(s) prepared hereunder by or for SI shall be used solely for promotion, publicizing and advertising, in any and all media now or hereafter known, of the Picture, the Picture's soundtrack and/or the musical material contained therein, as SI may determine in its sole discretion, including without limitation, in and as part of promotion/advertising and/or publicity for the Picture contained in the videogram version of any motion picture(s) other than the Picture. In the case of any music video(s) prepared by or for the Distributor, such music video(s) may be used in any and all media now or hereafter known, provided such use(s) is/are for promotional purposes only. It is understood that the compensation payable to Artist hereunder includes remuneration in full to Artist on behalf of itself and Company for use(s) of the Master/Composition/music video(s) under this paragraph 7.(b).

---

[17] This six month time period is commonly referred to as a "hold back" period.

[18] Music videos are typically made for only one or two soundtrack album cuts.

8.   (a) Producer and Artist warrant, represent and agree that:

(i) Neither Artist nor Producer is under any disability, restriction or prohibition, whether contractual or otherwise, with respect to Producer's and Artist's right to execute this Agreement, to grant the rights herein granted and to perform each and every term and provision hereof. Neither Artist nor Producer is subject to or party to any agreement that would derogate from the rights to be acquired by SI hereunder.

(ii) The results and proceeds of Producer's and/or Artist's services hereunder will not violate or infringe upon any common law, statutory or other right of any person, firm or corporation, including, without limitation, contractual rights, copyrights and rights of privacy.

(iii) The Master is not and shall not be subject to any liens or encumbrances, and neither Producer nor Artist have made or shall make any commitments which would derogate or tend to derogate in any way form the rights to be acquired hereunder by SI and its successors, designees, assigns and/or licensees and/or from SI's/their enjoyment of such rights.

(b) It is understood that Artist is engaged hereunder on an independent contractor basis. Artist represents and warrants that Artist is the employer of all persons rendering services in connection with the recording and production of the Master, including without limitation, Producer and that Artist will discharge all of the obligations of an employer, whether imposed by law (including, without limitation, taxes, unemployment and disability insurance, compensation insurance and social security), by applicable union rules and regulations, or otherwise. Artist further acknowledges that the foregoing representations and warranties will be relied upon by SI for the purpose of determining whether or not it is necessary to make withholdings for U.S. Federal/State taxes from monies being paid to Artist hereunder, and Artist agrees that if withholdings are not made from said payments, and if thereafter it is determined that such withholdings were legally required, Artist will indemnify SI against all loss, costs, damages and expenses relating thereto.

(c) Producer and Artist hereby indemnify, save and hold SI and its agents, directors, officers, successors, licensees and assigns (collectively "indemnified parties") harmless from and against any and all damages, liabilities, costs, losses and expenses (including reasonable attorneys' fees) arising out of or connected with any claim, demand or action which is inconsistent with any of the warranties, representations or covenants made by Producer and/or Artist in this Agreement. SI agrees to give Artist notice of any action to which the foregoing indemnity applies, and Company may participate in the defense of same, at Artist's expense, through counsel of Artist's choosing; however, the final control or disposition of same (by settlement, compromise or otherwise) shall remain with SI. [19]

9.   Artist represents and warrants that Producer and all other persons rendering services in connection with the recording/production of the Master are, or will become, a member in good standing of any union or guild having jurisdiction of the services to be performed by Artist hereunder. Wherever there may be conflict between any provision of this Agreement and such union or guild agreement, the provisions of the former shall be curtailed to the minimum extent necessary to conform to the latter. All compensation payable pursuant to this Agreement shall include minimum scale compensation required by any such union or guild agreement. The Master shall be produced as

---

[19] This clause should be revised so that all parties agree to indemnify each other.

a motion picture recording under applicable union and guild agreements. SI shall be responsible for any reuse, new use and special trust fund payments in connection with the Album.[20]

10.   Producer and Artist acknowledge that Producer's and Artist's performance and the services of Artist hereunder, and the rights granted to SI herein, are of a special, unique, extraordinary and intellectual character which gives them peculiar value, the loss of which cannot be reasonably or adequately compensated in damages in an action at law, and that a breach by Producer and/or Artist of this Agreement will cause SI irreparable injury. SI shall be entitled to seek injunctive and/or other equitable relief to prevent a breach of this Agreement by Producer and/or Artist, which relief shall be in addition to any other rights or remedies which SI may have, whether for damages or otherwise.

11.   Any failure by SI to utilize the Master or other services of Producer and/or Artist, in whole or in part, shall not be deemed a breach of this Agreement by SI, and in any such event neither Producer nor Artist shall be entitled to any damages by reason thereof; provided however, that if Producer and Artist shall fully and faithfully perform and observe the material terms and conditions of this Agreement, such failure shall not relieve SI of its obligation to pay the compensation herein provided, subject, however, to any other provisions of this Agreement relieving SI of its obligation to pay such compensation. Nothing herein contained shall be construed to obligate SI to incorporate the Master or any parts thereof in the Picture, in phonorecords, or in any other work(s); and nothing herein contained shall be construed to prevent SI from interpolating in the Picture, phonorecords, and music videos, other master recordings, compositions and musical material either produced by a person or persons other than Producer and/or embodying the performances of a person or persons other than Artist.[21]

12.   All notices which either party is required or desires to give to the other shall be in writing and shall be effective when delivered personally; when deposited, postage prepaid, in the U.S. mail (certified or registered mail, return receipt requested, in all cases other than royalty statements); or when deposited, toll prepaid, at any telegraph office in the United States. Addresses for notices shall be as follows, or such other addresses as either party may designate by notice given as aforesaid:

        To Artist: Art Cheatum, Esq.
                        Dewey, Cheatum & Howe
                        11111 San Viejo Blvd.
                        Los Angeles, CA 90000

        To SI: Scotvision, Inc.
                        1234 Oak Street
                        Suite 400
                        Los Angeles, CA 90000

---

[20] The producer and Distributor are signatories to union agreements, so Fred and John must represent that they are members of the appropriate musical unions. As for reuse and new use fees, these are the fees payable to the union whenever a recording embodying performances by union members is used in a medium other than the one it was created for (e.g., a master recorded for a movie is used on a record, and vice versa). Reuse and new use fees vary and depend on the number of union musicians that play on a recording. The bottom line: don't let the producer or record company stick you with them.

[21] In other words, as long as the Artist delivers the Master in accordance with the agreement, SI is obligated to pay the $30,000. However, it is under no obligation to use the master in the movie or on the album.

13.   Definitions of terms used in this Agreement:

(a) "deliver" or "delivery" means: physical delivery of a two-track stereo tape of the Master (and any and all versions thereof SI may require) completed, fully edited and mixed (both a record mix and a film mix) and all 24-track session tapes, derivatives and any reproductions thereof. SI shall have the right to approve the final film mix and the final record mix of the Master.[22] The Master shall be subject to SI's approval as satisfactory for use in and as part of the manufacture and sale of phonorecords and for use in the Picture. Delivery shall not be deemed complete until SI has been furnished all label copy information and consents from all third parties to enable SI to embody the Master in the Picture and in and as part of phonorecords.

(b) Intentionally deleted.

(c) "conversion costs" means: the costs of converting the Master from a recording made for the Picture to a recording suitable for use in "phonorecords" (as defined in 13.(d) below), including, without limitation, re-recording costs, reuse fees, and costs of editing, re-editing, mixing, re-mixing, mastering, equalizing, reference dubs, sweetening, etc.

(d) "phonorecord" means: any device, at any speed, on any material, now or hereafter known, utilized for the reproduction of sound only.

(e) "Distributor" refers to Arthroscope Records, Inc. and its licensees.

(f) "Distribution Agreement" means: the agreement between SI and the Distributor, as the same may be modified, extended, renewed and substituted.

14.   If because of any act of God; accident; strike or labor dispute; riot or civil commotion; act of public enemy; rule, act or order of government or governmental instrumentality; failure of technical facilities; failure or delay of transportation facilities; or any other cause not reasonably within SI's control, SI is materially hampered in the performance of its obligations to Artist hereunder, then without limiting the rights of SI, SI shall have the option by giving Artist notice, to suspend SI's obligations hereunder for the duration of any such contingency.

15.   This Agreement shall also inure to the benefit of SI, and its respective successors, assigns, licensees, and associated, affiliated and subsidiary companies. Producer and Artist agree that SI and any subsequent assign may freely assign this Agreement and grant or license any and all rights, privileges and benefits hereunder, in whole or in part, to any person, firm or corporation. This Agreement is personal to Producer and Artist and may not be assigned by Producer and/or Artist. This Agreement is the entire agreement of the parties, and all negotiations and understandings are merged herein. This Agreement may not be modified except by an instrument, in writing, executed by both parties. Only the final, signed Agreement is admissible as the written agreement between the parties. If this Agreement has been revised during the course of negotiation, such revisions and prior drafts incorporating such revisions or original language may not be used, and shall not be admissible, as evidence for any purpose in any litigation that may arise between the parties. This Agreement shall be deemed to have been drafted by all the parties hereto, since all parties were assisted by their counsel in reviewing and agreeing thereto, and no ambiguity shall be resolved against any party by virtue of its participation in the drafting of this Agreement. A waiver of any breach by either party in any one instance shall not constitute a waiver of any subsequent breach, whether or not similar. Nothing

---

[22] This is important, because SI doesn't have to pay the last half of the fee until actual "delivery" occurs.

herein contained shall constitute a partnership between, or joint venture by, either party hereto, or constitute either party the agent of the other. This Agreement is not intended for the benefit of any third party. In the event of any conflict between any provision of this Agreement and any present or future statute, law, ordinance or regulation, the latter shall prevail, but in such event, the provision of this Agreement affected shall be curtailed and limited only to the extent necessary to bring it within legal requirements. Without limiting the foregoing, if any compensation or other monies payable hereunder shall be in excess of the amount permitted by any such statute, law, ordinance or regulation, payment of the maximum amount allowed thereby shall constitute full compliance by SI with the payment requirements of this Agreement. All compensation or other monies payable hereunder shall be subject to all required tax and other governmental withholdings. This Agreement shall be governed by the laws of the State of California applicable to contracts to be wholly negotiated and performed therein. Any claim, dispute or disagreement with respect to this Agreement shall be submitted to the courts of the State of California or if appropriate, the Federal courts within the State of California, which courts shall have the exclusive jurisdiction thereof.

16.   Notwithstanding the provisions of paragraphs 6 and 7 above to the contrary, SI shall not authorize the Distributor to, and the Distributor shall not, commercially release Single Records which include reproductions of the Master without first obtaining Artist's and Company's written approval; and unless Artist and Company[23] grant SI such written approval to authorize the release of such Single Records, Company shall not be required to cause Artist to render Artist's on-camera performances of the Composition for purposes of preparing a promotional music video pursuant to paragraph 7 above.

ACCEPTED AND AGREED TO:

SCOTVISION, INC.

By:_____
Its: _____

ARTIST

By:_____
    John Doe

By:_____
    Fred Johnson

---

[23] Whether or not the Master may be released as a single is another hotly contested point in this kind of deal, and it is not uncommon for a producer to pay the Artist or record company additional consideration for such a right.

PRODUCER

By:_____
    Brian McPherson

Insofar as its rights are concerned, the undersigned hereby consents to the execution of the forego-ing Agreement by Artist, to the terms and provisions thereof (in the case of subparagraph 8.(b) of the foregoing Agreement, the undersigned ratifies the provisions thereof and joins in all covenants, rep-resentations and warranties made by Company therein, as if the undersigned were a direct party thereto), to Artist's performance of all services to be performed by them thereunder and to the rights granted to and/or acquired by SI, therein. [24]

THRIFTY SCOT RECORDS, INC.

By:_____
Its:

EXHIBIT "A"

LETTER OF CONFIRMATION

The undersigned hereby confirm that the results and proceeds of all services rendered by the under-signed in connection with any and all versions of the master recording embodying the composition "The Girlfriend Plan", as embodied in or inspired by the motion picture "A Fist Full of Haggis", shall constitute a "work made for hire" created pursuant to an agreement dated as of August 1, 1998 between John Doe and Fred Johnson p/k/a/ "Lawn Chocolate" and Scotvision, Inc. ("SI") (the "Agreement") and that SI shall own all rights (under copyright and otherwise) in and to the results and proceeds of all such services rendered (excluding rights to the underlying musical composition), with the right to make such uses thereof and such changes thereto, subject to the terms of the Agreement, as Producer may determine, in its sole discretion, throughout the universe and forever.

Dated:_____   By:_____
                                    John Doe

                                  By:_____
                                    Fred Johnson

---

[24] This is where Artist's record company signs off and assents to Artist entering into the deal directly.

APPENDIX C

Addresses, Resources, Websites

A GUIDE TO MUSIC INDUSTRY RESOURCES AND ORGANIZATIONS

Here's a handy (but by no means exhaustive) list of resources to help you on your way to fame and fortune.

LEGAL RESOURCES

Thomson & Thomson
500 Victory Road
North Quincy, MA 02171 -3145
Toll Free: (800) 692-8833
Phone: (617) 479-1600
Fax: (617) 786-8273
Website: http://www.thomson-thomson.com
E-mail: support@thomson-thomson.com

The largest professional copyright and trademark search firm.

United States Copyright Office
Copyright Office
Publications Section, LM-455
101 Independence Ave. SE
Washington DC 20559-6000
Phone: (202) 707-3000
Pre-recorded information: (202) 707-9100
Website: http://www.lcweb.loc.gov/copyright

Forms and information about registering your copyrights.

United States Patent and Trademark Office
Assistant Commissioner for Trademarks
900 Crystal Drive
Arlington, VA 22202-3513
Phone: (703) 308-9000
Fax: (703) 703-308-7016
Website: http://www.uspto.gov

Information regarding trademarks and trademark registration.

GUILDS, UNIONS, ORGANIZATIONS AND TRADE ASSOCIATIONS

American Federation of Musicians (AFM)

AFM New York
Paramount Building
Suite 600
1501 Broadway
New York, NY 10036
Phone: (212) 869-1330
Toll free: (800) 762-3444

AFM Los Angeles
1777 Vine Street, Ste. 500
Hollywood, CA 90028
Phone: (213) 461-3841

Trade union that represents professional U.S. and Canadian musicians in collective bargaining and contract negotiations in all aspects of the entertainment industry.

American Federation of Television and Radio Artists (AFTRA)

AFTRA New York
260 Madison Ave. 7th Fl.
New York, NY 10016
Phone: (212) 532-0800

AFTRA Los Angeles
6922 Hollywood Blvd., 8th Floor
Los Angeles, CA 90028
Phone: (213) 634-8100

Trade union that represents performing artists in radio and television in collective bargaining and contract negotiations.

Association for Independent Music (formerly NAIRD)
PO Box 988
Whitesburg, KY 41858
Phone: (606) 633-0946 or (800) 607-6526
Fax: (606) 633-1160

114 Lark St.
Altamont, NY 12009-0465
Phone: (518) 861-7037
Fax: (518) 861-7038

Trade group representing independent record distributors and manufacturers.

California Lawyers for the Arts (CLA)

CLA Headquarters
Fort Mason Center
Building C, Room 255
San Francisco, CA 94123
Phone: (415) 775-7200

CLA Los Angeles
1549 11th Street
Ste. 200
Santa Monica, CA 90401
Phone: (310) 395-8893
http://www.sirius.com/~cla/

A nonprofit organization that assists artists with legal questions and offers an attorney referral service.

National Academy of Recording Arts & Sciences (NARAS)

NARAS Los Angeles
3402 Pico Blvd
Santa Monica, CA 90405
Phone: (310) 392-3777
Fax: (310) 392-2778

NARAS New York
157 W. 57 St.
Ste. 902
New York, NY 10019
Phone: (212) 245-5440
http://www.naras.org

NARAS provides scholarships, research grants, workshops, publications and a career handbook. Members select winners of the Grammy Awards.

Recording Industry Association of America (RIAA)
1020 19th St. NW
Ste. 200
Washington, DC 20036
Phone: (202) 775-0101
Fax: (202) 775-7253

Trade group whose member companies create, manufacture and/or distribute more than 90 percent of all legitimate sound recordings sold and produced in the United States. The RIAA also administers the Gold, Platinum, and Multi-Platinum Awards Program.

Songwriters Guild of America

SGA Los Angeles
6430 Sunset Boulevard
Hollywood, CA 90028
Phone: (213) 462-1108
Fax: (213) 462-5430

SGA Nashville
1222 16th Ave. South
Suite #25
Nashville TN 37212
Phone: (615) 329-1782
Fax: (615) 329-2623

SGA New York
1560 Broadway
Suite #1306
New York NY 10036
Phone (212) 768-7902
Fax: (212) 768-9048

Website: http://www.songwriters.org

The nation's oldest and largest songwriters' association. Provides standard form agreements, information and services to members.

PERFORMING RIGHTS ORGANIZATIONS AND ROYALTY TRIBUNALS

American Society of Composers, Authors and Publishers (ASCAP)

ASCAP New York
One Lincoln Plaza
New York, NY 10023
Phone: (212) 621-6000

ASCAP Los Angeles
7920 Sunset Boulevard, Ste. 300
Los Angeles, CA 90046
Phone: (213) 883-1000
Fax: (213) 883-1049

ASCAP Nashville
Two Music Square West
Nashville, TN 37203
Phone: (615) 742-5000
Fax: (615) 742-5020

Website: http://www.ascap.com
E-mail: info@ascap.com

A membership association of over 75,000 composers, songwriters, lyricists and music publishers that protects the rights of its members by licensing and paying royalties for the public performances of their copyrighted works.

Broadcast Music, Inc. (BMI)

BMI New York
320 West 57th Street
New York, NY 10019
Phone: (212) 586-2000

BMI Nashville
10 Music Square East
Nashville, TN 37203
Phone: (615) 401 -2000

BMI Los Angeles
8730 Sunset Blvd. 3rd Flr West
Los Angeles, CA 90069
Phone: (310) 659-9109

Website: http://www.bmi.com
E-mail: research@bmi.com

Distributes royalties to its 200,000 member songwriters, composers, and publishers, for the public performance and digital home copying of their works. In the future, will distribute potential new royalties for the use of members' works in cyberspace.

SESAC

SESAC Nashville
55 Music Square East
Nashville, TN 37203
Phone: (800) 826-9996/(615) 320-0055
Fax: (615) 321-6290

SESAC New York
421 West 54th Street
New York, NY 10019
Phone: (212) 586-3450
Fax: (212) 489-5699

Website: http://www.sesac.com
E-mail: info@sesac.com

European Performing Rights Society, which collects and distributes royalties for its members.

Society of Composers, Authors and Music Publishers of Canada (SOCAN)
41 Valley Brook Drive
Don Mills, Ontario
M3B 2S6
Canada
Phone: (416) 445-8700

Canada's performing rights organization.

Harry Fox Agency
711 Third Avenue
New York, NY 10017
Phone: (212) 370-5330
Fax: (212) 953-2384

Website: http://www.nmpa.org/hfa.html
E-mail: clientservice@harryfox.com

Handles mechanical and synchronization licensing of copyrighted musical compositions and the distribution of royalties based on those licenses.

National Music Publishers Association (NMPA)
711 Third Avenue
New York, NY 10017
Phone: (212) 370-5330
Fax: (212) 953-2471

Website: http://www.nmpa.org

Parent company of the Harry Fox Agency. The NMPA actively lobbies for the rights of songwriters and publishers. The NMPA recently represented U.S. music publishers in its negotiations with U.S. record companies on a new 10-year mechanical royalty agreement that will take effect on January 1, 1998.

INTERNET RESOURCES

United States Copyright Office Online Royalty Payment Information
http://lcweb.loc.gov/copyright/circs/circ74

This is a good place to start if you need to secure a compulsory mechanical license.

Musician's Assistance Site
http://www.musicianassist.com

Information for musicians regarding manufacturing and promoting independent records. Features extensive searchable databases.

Stanford University Copyright & Fair Use Page
http://fairuse.stanford.edu/

Comprehensive resource and analysis of fair use issues, including those relating to "sampling."

IUMA: Internet Underground Music Archive
http://www.iuma.com

The Internet's largest repository for music by unsigned acts, plus extensive industry information.

Lawgirl.com
http://www.lawgirl.com

An interactive legal resource with focus on music issues. Features copyright registration help, a legal question and answer board and a music law forum.

UBL: Ultimate Band List
http://www.ubl.com

A huge searchable index of information and contacts for bands, record labels, venues, trade publications and more.

DIRECTORIES AND TRADE PUBLICATIONS

The Album Network's Yellow Pages of Rock
120 North Victory Boulevard
3rd Floor
Burbank, CA 91502
Phone: (800) 222-4382
A handy volume chock full of addresses and phone numbers of record companies, publishers and the like.

Billboard Magazine
1515 Broadway
39th Floor
New York, NY 10036
Phone: (212) 764-7300

Website: http://www.billboard-online.com

The weekly bible of the music industry.

Hits Magazine
14958 Ventura Blvd.
Sherman Oaks, CA 91403
Phone: (818) 501-7900

A highly influential weekly radio and retail "tip sheet" and forum for industry gossip.

Pollstar Magazine
4333 North West Ave.
Fresno, CA 93705
Phone: (800) 344-7383

The bible of the touring business.

Index

Books About the Music Business from Hal Leonard

GET IT IN WRITING
The Musician's Guide to the Music Business
by Brian McPherson

Confused by today's music business? Did you ever wish that that some super-knowledgeable music attorney would sit you down and explain the whole thing to you? Well, that's what this book is all about. *Get It in Writing* is actually three books in one: 1) An overview of the entire music business and the players involved; 2) Interviews with top industry professionals; and 3) A huge collection of sample agreements with extensive commentary from the author. This indispensible book covers: recording contracts, demo deals, copyrights and trademarks, music publishing, performance rights, motion pictures & TV, artist management, producers, band partnerships, and plenty more. All of this info coupled with expert insider advice makes this book every musician's best tool for success in the music business.

00330239   (352 pages, 8-1/2" x 11")...............................$29.95

GOING PRO
Developing a Professional Career in the Music Industry
by Kenny Kerner

Everything musicians need to know to go pro, including information about personal managers, music attorneys, business managers and booking agents, record companies, A&R, publishing, songwriting, demo tapes and press kits, self-promotion, and much more.

00695322   (200+ pages, 6" x 9") $19.95

MAKING A LIVING IN YOUR LOCAL MUSIC MARKET - REVISED EDITION
Realizing Your Marketing Potential
by Dick Weissman

You can survive happily as a musician in your own local music market! The newly revised and expanded edition of this book will show you how. It includes detailed analysis of the latest regional music scenes that have developed; an extensive new section (written by Ron Sobel - vice president of ASCAP in Los Angeles) on opportunites for musicians and composers in developing and selling music in new mediums including the Internet, Greenhouse Channels, Theme Parks, and Desk Top Films; info on how music distribution and retailing is changing to meet the challenges of the 21st century; and many more essential tips. Also features a new appendix and a helpful Resources section after each chapter.

00330421   (304 pages, 6" x 9") $14.95

FILM AND TELEVISION COMPOSER'S RESOURCE GUIDE
by Mark Northam and Lisa Anne Miller

Many musicians are finding a new market for their music scoring for films and television. This comprehensive resource guide provides all the practical tools and information needed about how to organize and run a film and television music business. Section I contains helpful marketing materials, such as sample letters, brochures, postcards, resumes, and product packaging. Section II provides forms, documents and examples for the management, production, recording and delivery of music for projects. Section III features frequently used sample contracts and agreements, and Section IV lists other composer resources, such as a glossary of terms and abbreviations, info on performing rights organizations, attorneys and agents, listings of different markets to tap, internet resources, and much more. Essential for any musician interested in a career in film and television music.

00330420   (198 pages, 8-1/2" x 11").................................$34.95

ALL AREA ACCESS
Personal Management for Unsigned Musicians
by Marc Davison

Success in the music business isn't the result of a whimsical journey fueled by a few good tunes; it's a destination reached after a long and well-planned trip over a road filled with potholes, detours, and speed bumps. This book is your road map. It tells you what you need to know and to do, step by step, to market your act and your music. Topics include starting a band, booking gigs, press and the media, recording, copyright laws, merchandising, touring, finances, managers and agents, and record deals. Author Marc Davison draws on his twenty-five years of experience - from playing and touring with bands to booking and managing them - to give you *All Area Access* to musical success.

00330295 (348 pages, 8-1/2" x 11") $24.95